The *Titanic* - "Everything Was Against Us"

Simon Angel

ISBN 978-1475127935

Contents

Starboard view of the R.M.S "Titanic"

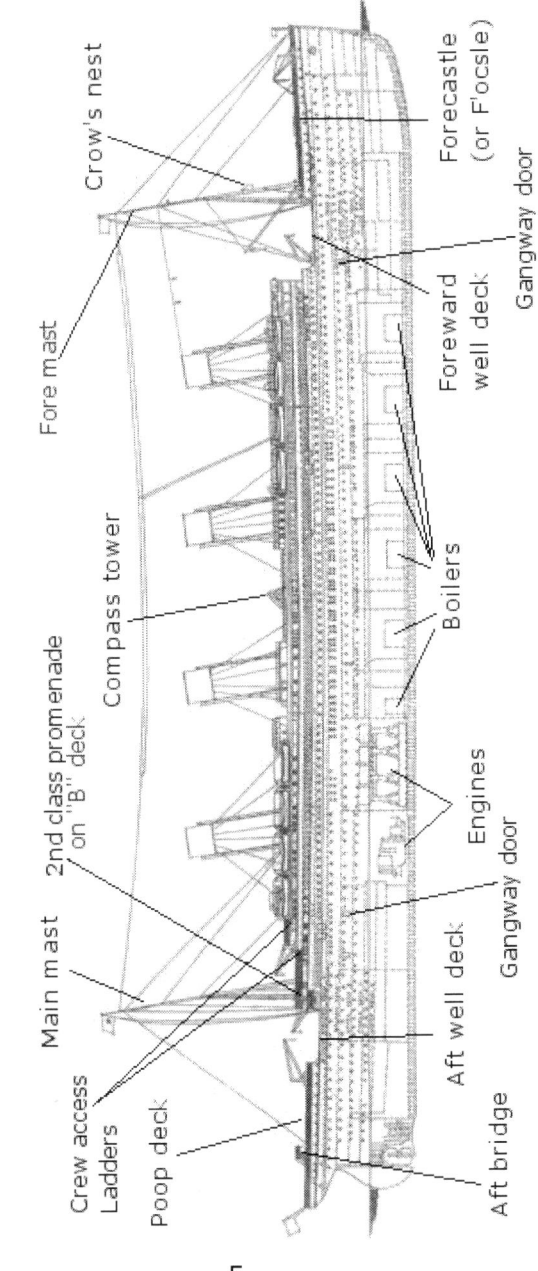

Crow's nest

Forecastle (or F'ocsle)

Gangway door

Fore mast

Foreward well deck

Compass tower

Boilers

2nd class promenade on "B" deck

Engines

Main mast

Gangway door

Crew access

Ladders

Aft well deck

Poop deck

Gangway door

Aft bridge

5

Boat Deck

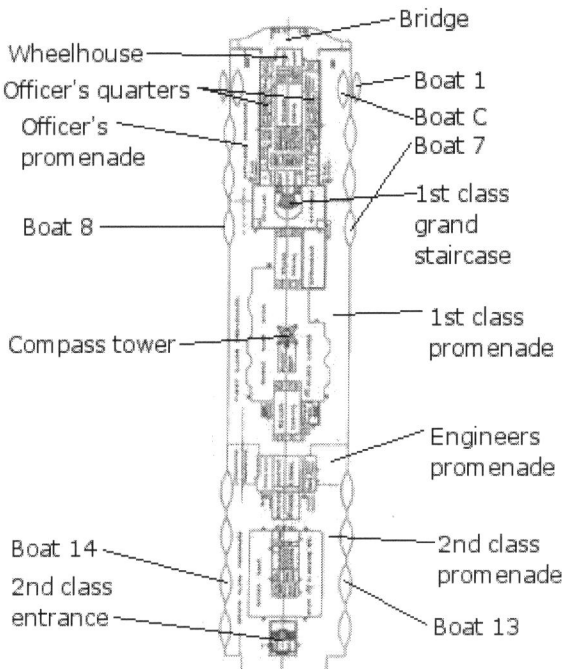

Bridge

Wheelhouse

Officer's quarters

Officer's promenade

Boat 1

Boat C

Boat 7

1st class grand staircase

Boat 8

1st class promenade

Compass tower

Engineers promenade

2nd class promenade

Boat 14

2nd class entrance

Boat 13

Port is to the left when facing the bow (the top of the diagram), starboard is to the right. Lifeboats have odd numbers on the starboard side, even on the port

E Deck

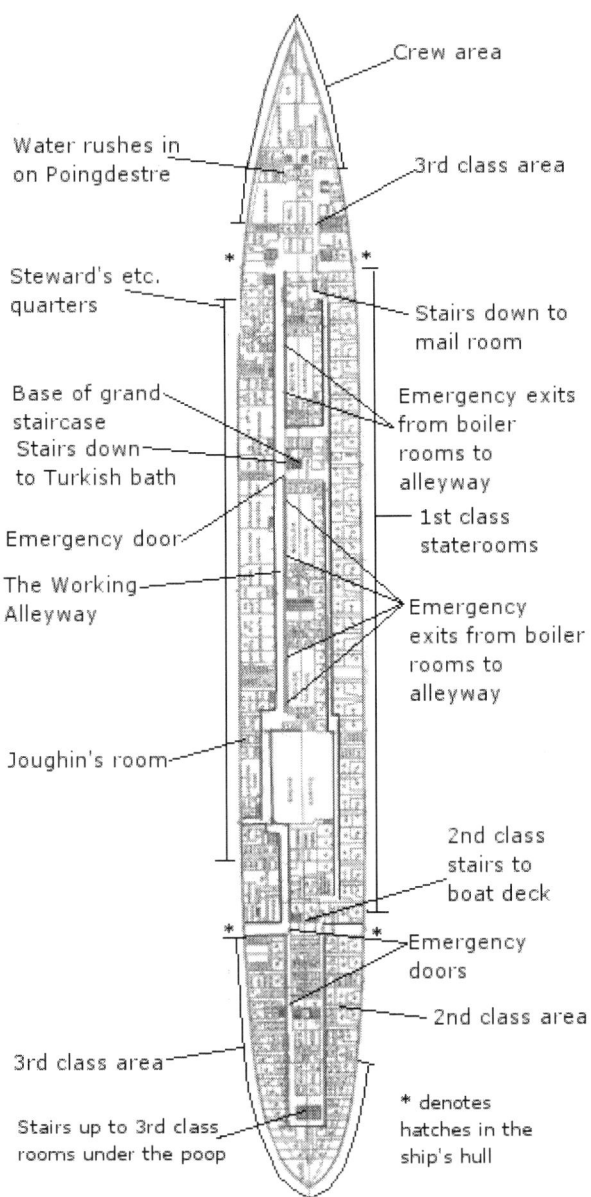

Crew area

Water rushes in on Poingdestre

3rd class area

Steward's etc. quarters

Stairs down to mail room

Base of grand staircase
Stairs down to Turkish bath

Emergency exits from boiler rooms to alleyway

1st class staterooms

Emergency door

The Working Alleyway

Emergency exits from boiler rooms to alleyway

Joughin's room

2nd class stairs to boat deck

Emergency doors

2nd class area

3rd class area

Stairs up to 3rd class rooms under the poop

* denotes hatches in the ship's hull

Tank Top

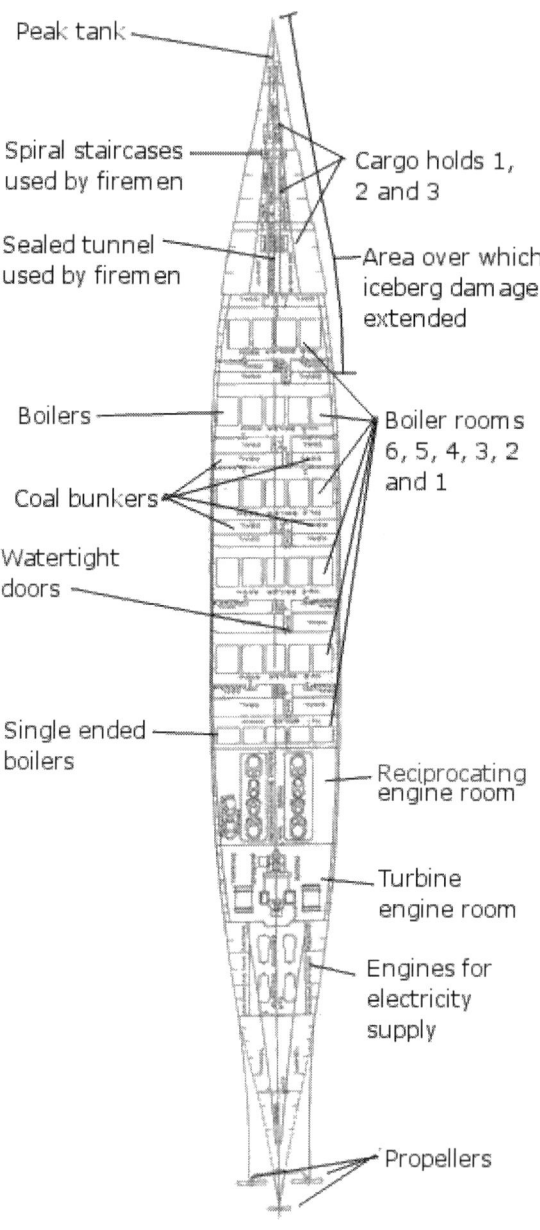

Peak tank

Spiral staircases
used by firemen

Cargo holds 1,
2 and 3

Sealed tunnel
used by firemen

Area over which
iceberg damage
extended

Boilers

Boiler rooms
6, 5, 4, 3, 2
and 1

Coal bunkers

Watertight
doors

Single ended
boilers

Reciprocating
engine room

Turbine
engine room

Engines for
electricity
supply

Propellers

8

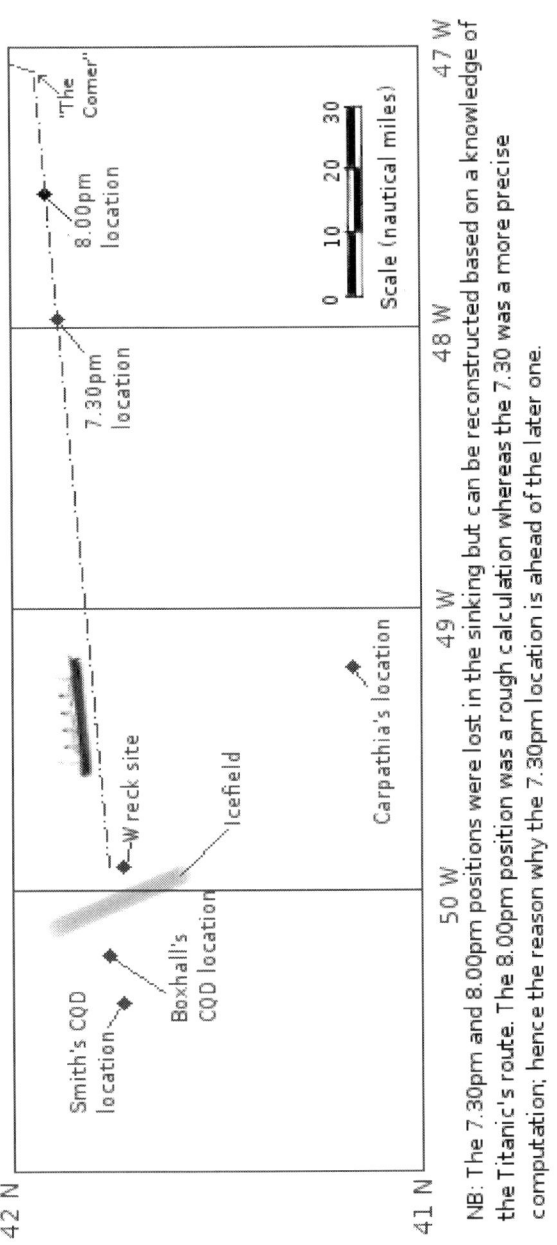

42 N

Smith's CQD
location

Boxhall's
CQD location

Wreck site

Icefield

Carpathia's location

7.30pm
location

8.00pm
location

"The
Corner"

Scale (nautical miles)

0   10   20   30

41 N

50 W   49 W   48 W   47 W

NB: The 7.30pm and 8.00pm positions were lost in the sinking but can be reconstructed based on a knowledge of
the Titanic's route. The 8.00pm position was a rough calculation whereas the 7.30 was a more precise
computation; hence the reason why the 7.30pm location is ahead of the later one.

Introduction

"Everything was against us."

So said Commander Charles Lightoller, the highest ranking surviving officer of the *Titanic* during his interrogation at the British Inquiry in 1912. Subjected to a barrage of questioning, and no doubt with the intention of protecting his employers, the White Star Line, he attempted to persuade the court that his ship was the subject of a confluence of events that were exceptionally rare; there was no moon to illuminate the iceberg and no breaking waves at the base which would, he argued, have provided an earlier warning of its proximity. The *Titanic* was little more than "a helpless victim of fate," as succinctly described by one writer. The simplistic reduction of the cause of the accident was soon exposed by the findings of the two courts of Inquiry (the other one being in America); the ship had been travelling too fast and into an area strewn with icebergs. A number of ice warning messages had already been transmitted to the *Titanic* but most of them were never seen by the bridge crew, and their fate remains a mystery. What is astonishing is the utter lack of accountability on the ship.

Lightoller's argument cannot completely explain or excuse the tragedy...unless one considers other possible influences. The presence of the Chairman of the Line, J.Bruce Ismay on board, perhaps?

No, "Fate" cannot account for these missed ice warnings. "Fate" cannot account for the lifeboats leaving with only approximately 2/3rds of their capacity. "Fate" cannot describe why comparatively few 3rd class passengers survived. "Fate" cannot describe why the *Titanic* was actually travelling faster that night than at any other time in her short life. One must brush aside such appeals to the conveniently inexplicable forces of "Fate" and "Destiny", and look to more mundane explanations - human error, the perennial source of mishaps in many an accident, before and after the *Titanic*.

Was the *Titanic* disaster avoidable? Obviously, the answer is yes. The somewhat lax practises of those who made the law and those who practised it learned the lessons, and regulations regarding lifeboat numbers, and the use of wireless telegraphy and distress rockets were revised. In retrospect, it astonishing that such appeals to "common sense" were not made sooner. Sadly, it took a catastrophe like the *Titanic* for the world to realise that its own complacent practises fell far short of what was required. If one operates a ship with a capacity of so many people, it makes sense to ensure that there is a seat in each lifeboat for each person on board, regardless of whether the law blindly permits a smaller number of boats. The huge loss of life was an obvious, much-needed jolt. Were it not for the large casualty figures, one could say that the world needed "a *Titanic*." It is depressing to think how much longer the maritime trade would have wilfully tolerated small boat numbers had not the White Star Line ship foundered in 1912.

So, what are the basic facts? Briefly recapitulated, they are as follows: travelling at 22.5 knots, or nearly 26 miles per hour, the White Star Line's newest ship, the *Titanic*, hit an iceberg four days out on her maiden voyage from Southampton to New York. Inadequate provision for lifesaving equipment decreed that at least half of the people would die in the icy waters, and not even that many were saved. After wallowing for 2 hours and forty minutes, the ship sank taking 1500 lives with her. A little under two hours later, a steamship run by the rival Cunard steamship company, the *Carpathia* and captained by Arthur Rostron, arrived and rescued the 20 boatloads of little more than 700 shivering, frightened souls.

The gross details of what transpired on the ship between departure from Southampton and the rescue by the *Carpathia* have been repeated in numerous other works. This book analyses both the gross and subtle details of the disaster, as well as highlighting the plethora of facts uncovered since 1912. Can anything new be said on the disaster?

The answer is yes.

This book is an honest attempt to analyse and reconcile nearly 100 years of fact and fable. Many who read it will no doubt have been seduced by the depiction of the romance and chivalry of the *Titanic*. It is so very easy to be mesmerised by the spectacle provided by multi-million dollar adaptations of the story and find kith with fictional characters. In 1912, and before the advent of female emancipation, there certainly was chivalry in abundance, as can be seen in the numerous tales of men escorting their ladies to safety...and then stepping back, or turning away with emotion. But the *Titanic* story is not romantic. It is, simply put, a shambolic tale of confusion, incompetence and neglect, but with no one apparently to blame. Even litigation after the disaster was not conclusive; the White Star line sought to limit its liability, and accusations of negligent navigation shuttled back and forth between various courts, appeals heard, evidence taken ... and the White Star Line settled out of court.

This author has tried to be fair to all sides, while offering suggestions to some of the more perplexing mysteries of the night the *Titanic* went down. This has inevitably spawned new theories, some of which will no doubt be controversial, but they are based on a laborious trawl through the inquiry transcripts, and personal accounts of the disaster which, when integrated, forms a holistic view of the disaster.

The structure of this book is an experiment rooted in a novel enterprise. Punctuating the main chapters are diversions from the narrative to explore certain aspects of the sinking - so called "*Titanic* Interludes." To relegate these subsidiary chapters into appendices would have reduced their value to little more than glorified footnotes. However, splicing the contents of these analyses into the chronology would have seriously impacted upon their worth as the necessary data and discussions would have become fragmented. By combining the details into self-contained chapters, the reader has the ability to assess the evidence, without their impact being diluted by being surrounded by trivia, or the minutiae of other incidents. It is to be hoped that readers who desire a simple retelling of the *Titanic* story can devour the main chapters without the need to wade into the detail afforded by the "Interludes."

While the author has endeavoured to be fair in presenting an accurate picture of the drama that that led to the calamitous sinking of April 15th, 1912, certain omissions of people's statements or testimony are inevitable. Some of these are simply because the subject matter is trivial or banal. For instance, the colourful antics of Baron Von Draschedt (a.k.a Alfred Nourney) in his lifeboat are not mentioned, where he fired his gun repeatedly leading to 3rd Officer Pitman to advise him to save his bullets. Similarly, the touching recollection of Walter Hawksford who described the actions of those in his boat as the *Titanic* slipped away: they raised their hats, bowed their heads and silence fell upon the boat for some minutes. There are similar, wonderfully descriptive evocations that create vivid mental images, but to focus on many of them would divert significantly from my narrative. On the other hand, certain stories that have been accepted as fact have the traits of inaccuracy, careless use of language, embellishment or simple lies. It is not convenient to simply ascribe dubious statements to the deleterious ravages of time on the human memory. Indeed, one need only compare the contemporary

13

stories with the later versions to realise that the early variants are more coherent and accurate. One should not rely heavily on newly acquired knowledge that materialised in decades following any event; the malleable human mind is prone to manipulation in unconscious or even deliberate ways.

Some of these deviations from the accepted norm have been noted in the main body of the text. Others in this massive list include; Dr Washington Dodge has Ismay leaving the ship in boat 15, forgets to mention his steward who pushed him into a boat and doesn't mention the near flattening of boat 13 as 15 descended on top of it; Lady Duff Gordon writing in her autobiography that "boat after boat" was launched from the port side before she and her party went to the other side (at most only one boat had gone from the port side at the time they crossed over to starboard; in fact there is no mention in 1912 accounts of them being on the port side at all); Mrs Thayer's fanciful observation of a nearby ship "from which rockets were being sent up"; Henry Harper's account mentions there being a thin hint of moon whereas in fact there was no moon; May Futrelle saying that male passengers were sequestered on "B" deck; Jack Thayer Jr's pamphlet published in 1940 having Ismay push his way into a boat on the deck below the bridge; Irene Harris mentioning that she passed through the bridge, and was told the time was 2.20, and the *Titanic* sank at 2.30 (given that she left in the last boat to be lowered on the port side, more time must have elapsed); Edith Brown's comments during television interviews that "Americans" had filled up the 1st class accommodation, forcing the Brown family to be relegated to 2nd class (there was plenty of room for them in 1st class); and so on.

A notable omission from our story is 2nd class passenger 7 year old Eva Hart. Her stories of her mother having a premonition and staying up all night and sleeping by day are not confirmed in letters that Mrs. Hart wrote; indeed, she is reported to have told her husband that "[the ship] will never reach the other side" yet she said in a letter to a friend in England and written on-board that her correspondence would remain on board and go back when the ship travelled back across the Atlantic. Her own letters even describe her as taking meals during the day. Similarly Eva's account of hearing "Nearer My God To Thee" in church months after the disaster where it rekindled memories of the sinking with emotional results is not borne out; in an interview in 1980 for a *Titanic* movie, she says, "I remember the ragtime music and that's all I can say for sure." Another item of questionable accuracy occurred in the 1970s and 1980s, when Eva stated that the *Titanic* sank intact 'right before

14

[her] eyes.' In 1982, Eva said that her mother had seen the ship split apart but that she had not yet. A year later she had changed her opinion and declared that the ship went down in two pieces. Coincidentally, Eva's friend, researcher Walter Lord had also changed his opinion about whether the ship was really intact at about this time.

The warning of "caveat lector" applies spectacularly well to the autobiography of Charles Lightoller. In his tome, he says that the junior wireless operator was reading a vital ice warning in bed (his wife later claimed that this "revelation" got Lightoller into trouble with the Marconi wireless company); boat 4 leaving before boat 6 (boat 4's launching was considerably delayed because no one could access it after it was lowered to the next deck down; the inference from Lightoller's book is that it was filled from the boat deck); shaking hands with the engineers on deck just before the end (at the inquiries, he said they were never seen); talking to senior wireless operator Phillips in the lifeboat; waving an unloaded pistol to entice stowaways to vacate emergency boat 2 (a boat he never even filled, let alone helped to lower); and his statement that he gauged how far the *Titanic* had sunk by watching the water creeping up the steps of a crew ladder from the boat deck down to "C" deck (as described, Lightoller "nipped off" between one boat being lowered and the next one being prepared; but this staircase did not become awash until the very end, when only two boats under davits remained on the ailing liner).

The problems of ascertaining whether a story has elements of doubt are obvious. When does one feel the need to arbitrarily dispense with a certain account because details do not tally with others? The answer is not obvious. Should accounts of the disaster be rejected when a significant number of "errors" are discovered? How can one ascertain what this rejection threshold is? And what of those elements of a story that have no corroboration? Does one accept these fragments blindly, especially if portions of the remainder of that survivor's account are dubious? This had led to the accusation that some researchers preferentially select certain aspects of an account that support their conclusions, contrary evidence being damned (this practise is known as "cherry picking").

Some discrepancies obviously cause huge hurdles in assessing the evidence and creating a cogent account of the unsinkable ship's last hours above water and the torment of those who survived, but it is the intent that the decisions made by this author in selecting survivor's accounts have been fair, which allow some meaningful conclusions to be drawn. But there is only so much that an analysis of people's

15

recollections can accomplish. Even if one ignores the possibility that witnesses lied or were so traumatised that their memories were rendered unreliable, there is only a finite amount that we can ever know. Readers of this book may be disappointed at the (sometimes) lack of concrete conclusions and the use of indeterminate words like "may," "perhaps," and "possibly." Given the paucity of evidence and the low survival rate, this is inevitable. For instance, from the engineering staff, the postal clerks, the band, the "ship's boys" and the pursers, little is known. None of them survived.

In short, this book will be realistic about the uncertainties in the evidence: where there is doubt, this author will say there is doubt, even if no reconciliation between the disparate strands of evidence is possible.

Without any hint of hubris or pomposity, this author does not purport to present this work as the concluding chapter of the *Titanic* story. Indeed, new forensic discoveries from the wreck itself, and newly unearthed letters from survivors may significantly revise portions of the story that are blurred or have been obscured by a lack of knowledge. It is this author's sincere hope that this work may aid in a better understanding of the end of the "Unsinkable" *Titanic*, and how the people intimately attached to the ship thought and acted.

The standard caveats exist; no work is ever error free and all mistakes are purely due to oversights made by the author. The author welcomes suggestions from readers for improvements or corrections and any such material will be receive an attribution in later editions.

Simon Angel
simonangel53@gmail.com

Chapter 1: The Bold Vision

The conception of the *Titanic* story customarily begins in 1907. Perturbed at the imminent introduction into service by steamship company Cunard of two gigantic ocean liners, the *Mauretania* and the *Lusitania* on the North Atlantic trade, Joseph Bruce Ismay, the Managing Director of the Oceanic Steam Navigation Company (thankfully known colloquially as the White Star Line, based on its house flag) and Lord Pirrie, who operated the shipyard that built their vessels, Harland and Wolff in Belfast, conceived a plan of introducing their own gargantuan breed of new superliners. Envisaged to be nearly a hundred feet longer and over 10,000 tons more massive than the new Cunarders, but sporting a similar four funnel configuration (though only the first three were used to vent smoke from the boilers, the last was used to provide ventilation for the engine rooms), they concocted plans over dinner. Providentially, the introduction of the new ships, with the rampant publicity associated with them, would also be of benefit to the International Mercantile Marine (I.M.M.), the conglomerate of shipping lines owned by the monopolist John Pierpont Morgan that had absorbed the White Star Line. Acting on a suggestion by Pirrie, Ismay was the president of this combine.

At some point, names derived from Greek mythology were designated for the new ships; *Olympic* and *Titanic*, in keeping with the White Star's tradition of ships ending with the '-ic' suffix[1].

The keel of the *Olympic* was laid on 16th December 1908, that of the *Titanic* on 31st March of the following year. The obvious choice to command these massive liners was Captain Edward John Smith, whose career with the White Star Line was a catalogue of near perfection and immense popularity with the fare paying public.

The bare hulk of the *Olympic*, painted light grey for, we are told, visibility reasons, was launched on October 20th, 1910. For the next 7 months her innards were transformed into a mix of both the functional and the palatial. On the day that the *Olympic* was handed over to the White Star Line after completing her sea trials, the *Titanic* was launched. As was the White Star custom, there was neither fanfare nor a bottle of champagne cracked open on the bow. Signal flags and rockets being sent aloft was the only intimation, other than the presence of Ismay and other luminaries, of launch. Since the ships were contracted to carry mail, they were allowed to be adorned with the prefix R.M.S (Royal Mail Steamship), as opposed to the "standard" S.S. (Screw, or propeller, ship). The ship had a dedicated area near the squash court for mail workers to sort and sift through the post, preparing it for ultimate dispatch at its destination.

As grand and as large as she was, there was little about the *Olympic* class vessels that were revolutionary. True, they may have had the first swimming pools on board an ocean liner, but she was a simple extrapolation of existing White Star Line design, with the caveat that her propulsion system included a turbine engine to complement the two reciprocating (piston) engines that drove her outer two propellers.

But there was one feature that the *Olympic* shared with all other ocean going passenger liners; her lifeboat accommodation was practically archaic. The *Titanic*'s - and *Olympic*'s - outdated lifeboat coverage can be traced back to an 1894 law; the amount of space required for vessels of 10,000 tons and more dictated a minimum of 16 boats under davits (cranes to lower boats to the sea).[2] The UK Government seemed to be content to allow a form of self-regulation to exist and had convinced itself that because of the low casualty rate in shipping, advances in technology (particularly wireless telegraphy) and so on, there was no need to update the lifeboat laws. Ships were grouped into classes depending on whether they were foreign, cargo ships, passenger liners etc., and not on the ability to carry people; where practicable, some vessels were able to increase their boat accommodation. But for some ships, where deck space was an issue, it became impracticable. Nevertheless an epiphany had emerged not long before the *Titanic* disaster in which a need for more boats was recognised. The new suggestions became mired in the tedium of "Advisory Committees," the much-loved minutes of officialdom and stability tests on lifeboat designs.

If ship owners wanted more boats, they were free to supply them, but there was no legal obligation to do so. The *Titanic* was over 4 times the size of the largest vessel under 1894 rules...but was still legally entitled to go to sea with space for only 962 people or 27% of her maximum complement of 3547 people. When the rules were drawn up, the largest ship afloat was the *Lucania*, a ship of 12,952 tons, and certified to carry 1857 people. By the standards of the most modern ship of the day, the rules had fallen far short, necessitating an alteration to the wording of the rules, for "ships of 10,000 tons and upwards." It is very difficult to understand a legal mind that flouts common sense: if you have 4000 people on board, then you should have space for 4000 people in the lifeboats. It is a simple argument, rooted in logic and to argue otherwise is unconscionable. But some persisted, and arguments have been proposed that lifeboats were seen as "ferries," to help other ships in trouble. But what if help was conceivably days away? What if the *Olympic* or *Titanic* had caught fire? With no other ship in the conceivable vicinity, the occupants of the lifeboats could have perished from exposure, drowning or malnutrition. But, for vessels belonging to the United Kingdom, between 1892 and 1901 66 westbound and 7 eastbound passengers perished; from 1902 to 1911, 8 died[3] on the westbound route, and only one eastbound. The total number of passengers carried in UK ships was "the majority" of a total of over 3¼ million fare paying travellers between 1892 to 1911, and "the majority" of 6 million people who traversed the Atlantic route from 1902 to 1911. It seemed to be difficult to imagine a ship foundering before help could arrive; boats for everyone would therefore not be needed. The notion of this idea does have some little merit to it as Captain Edward Smith, who would later command these new White Star super liners had said had said, "I will say that I cannot imagine any condition which could cause a ship to founder. Whatever happens there will be time enough before the vessel sinks to save the life of every person on board. I cannot conceive of any vital disaster happening to this vessel. Modern shipbuilding has gone beyond that." This was in 1907. Two years later, the White Star ship s.s. *Republic* collided with the s.s. *Florida* in fog. The *Republic* stayed afloat long enough for everyone on board to be ferried, by the use of lifeboats to the *Florida*; then another transshipping commenced, from the Florida and the Republic to another vessel that had heard the wireless call for help, the s.s. *Baltic*, another White Star Line vessel. Although only 5 people died in the collision, it may have cemented the "ferry" notion in people's minds...but the *Republic* had stayed afloat for a successful rescue operation. The successful use of wireless technology to summon help could also have placated Captain Smith when he gave his comment. But what if a ship did indeed founder before help arrived? The late author Walter Lord compiled statistics and found that, based on a random sampling of shipping data, this problem was not just limited to British law. Regulations for other nations did not specify a "boats for all" rule. Indeed, American Law was happy to accept the life saving appliance rule calculated by the Board of Trade, which was a monolithic UK Government body responsible for, amongst others, administering British shipping and had admitted the 1894 rules into law; at the British Inquiry into the *Titanic*'s loss, the boat provision for two German liners were admitted into evidence, and they showed that there was space for only 1/3rd of those on board. One gentleman who had pressed for reform

19

(and who ironically worked in the shipyard where the *Titanic* and *Olympic* were built) observed that providing space for all the souls on board would "have drawn attention" and been noted by other operators on the North Atlantic run. Better to keep quiet, it would seem. The design discussions for the *Olympic* and *Titanic* treated the lifeboat capacity as a niggle, one that occupied scant minutes in discussions that lasted many hours over furnishings and fittings. Before the *Olympic* had been launched, questions were raised in the UK Government about the number of boats that were to be carried, and whether a modification to the existing law was necessary; discussion within the Board of Trade was slow and long-winded, and one correspondent devised a new way of calculating the total boat capacity that would have provided space for everyone on the new liners' maiden voyage, but not their full complement of over 3500 people. However, there was a caveat: if a ship builder could convince the Board of Trade that the bulkheads were of satisfactory design and construction, the number of boats could actually be reduced. Anticipating a change in the law, the *Olympic* had been equipped with a type of davit (lifeboat crane) manufactured by the Swedish Welin company; this new davit could launch one boat, be cranked inwards, pick up another ("inboard") boat, launch this new one, and so on. Although touted as being a new design, they had been used on ships such as the *Balmoral Castle* and the *Kortnaer* in 1910. It was reported in specialist engineering journals in the summer of 1910 that the new White Star Line ships would feature these new davits and that, "Up till the present, any proposal embodying this arrangement has been checked by the fact that the Board of Trade has refused to recognize the inboard boat as fulfilling the clause in it's regulations, which requires a boat to be "under davits"... The sea going public unquestionably thoroughly appreciates the advantages presented by clear deck space, as well as unrestricted view, and as both these are rendered more easily possible by double-banking of the boats, shipowners will doubtless not ignore a decision, recently reached by the Board of Trade, on this point. In conformity with this decision, the Board's rules have been amended in such a way that, in certain cases, the inboard boat of two double-banked boats shall now count as forming part of the regulation complement, when fitted in an efficient manner." What was revolutionary about these davits was they could launch 4 boats apiece, meaning that the *Olympic*'s lifeboat capacity could be increased from 16 to 64, enough for everyone on board; indeed, plans exist to this day which show the boat deck of the *Olympic* class liners with 32 boats; at the British Inquiry into the loss of the *Titanic*, it was claimed that Harland and Wolff had drawn up a plan showing two boats per davit, while the Welin company had created a similar diagram showing three boats. Still, if the *Olympic* was to host 32,

48 or even 64 boats under these new davits, the boat deck could hardly function as an effective promenade for passengers with so much clutter. Functional economics, and not prescience, dictated these new davits. Still, when she set sail, the *Olympic* had but 16 boats under davits (14 of them regular boats, with two emergency boats, or "wooden cutters"), and 4 Englehardt "collapsible" boats whose canvas sides could be erected. Two of these were stowed on the roof of the officer's quarters, abreast of the first funnel[4]. Their location may give credence to the "cluttered decks" theory; after the *Titanic* sank, a deck littered with life saving implements was no longer viewed as a problem.

   The real innovation of the *Olympic* class vessels were the so-called watertight bulkheads; there were 15 of them, from bow to stern, creating 16 sealable watertight compartments. By activating a lever on the bridge, the interconnecting doors at the lowest level could be closed; alternately, they could be closed from within the compartment if the bridge control became inoperative, or they would close automatically if water entered the room and raised a float. Watertight doors in the crew and passenger quarters were closed by hand. The ultimate aim of the bulkheads was that the ship would become her own lifeboat and remain buoyant indefinitely, or until assistance arrived. But the designs of the bulkheads were only as good as the imagination of the designers: a ship ploughing broadside into the ship would open up, at most, two adjoining compartments, and thus, that is what the *Olympic* class vessels were designed to cope with. A head-on collision would be survivable too, as any three of the four forward compartments could be flooded without the ship foundering, thereby providing some redundancy in the "two compartment flooded" design[5]. Unfortunately, the reality of the watertight doors and compartments hid an unfortunate design flaw.

   To allow easy passageway for the crew and 1st class passengers, the bulkheads only extended as high as "E" deck for a fair portion of the ship's length; the forward and after bulkheads, encompassing "collision bulkheads" designed to crumple, and an enclosure surrounding the propellers to prevent ingress into the rest of the hull, proceeded much higher above the waterline. But still, the ship seemed superficially impervious to mishap; under the two compartment flooded rule, and with the bulkheads reaching "E" deck, the *Olympic* and her kin were safe. The inclusion of doors, bulkheads and the like led to one specialist periodical describing the ships as "practically unsinkable." But, as researcher George Behe has found, one pamphlet for the White Star Line omitted the "practically." It seems as if everyone believed the *Olympic* class

21

vessel's invincibility This was reinforced in September 1911, when the *Olympic*'s great tidal wash sucked a smaller vessel, the H.M.S. *Hawke* into her side, leaving a massive hole and two compartments open to the sea. The damage extended below the waterline and up to "D" deck, predominantly affected 3rd class cabins, but also impinged slightly into 2nd class space too; only the fact that occupants of this area were at lunch spared people's lives. The watertight doors were closed, and the *Olympic* remained afloat. Captain Smith, in command of the *Olympic* at the time, was convinced that the ships were indeed "unsinkable", as was Thomas Andrews (the ship's designer), Harold Sanderson (a director of the White Star Line), Phillip Franklin (Vice President of the I.M.M.)...and Bruce Ismay himself.

Many people, including those who stood on the decks of the dying ship in April 1912, believed the myth. It is not a case of the ship acquiring the "unsinkable" moniker post-disaster to exaggerate the irony[6]. With the widely held notion that the *Olympic* class ships were "unsinkable", thoughts of too few lifeboats were probably irrelevant to most people on board. This does not excuse the woeful lack of foresight to amend and update the 1894 rules. Or the inertia by ship builders and owners not to be proactive in supplying a full complement.

As pleased as he was with the *Olympic* following her maiden voyage in the summer of 1911, Ismay wanted some changes to the *Titanic*. "B" deck was the focus of most of the alterations; the 1st class promenade seemed excessive, given that the two decks immediately above also catered for the upper classes perambulations. It would be more lucrative to convert this little used space to passenger cabins to generate more revenue. These extra cabins included two so-called "parlour suites" with private promenades. Also on "B" deck, the 2nd class enclosed promenade was truncated, and the restaurant extended to the port side of the *Titanic*; on the starboard side came the addition of a Cafe Parisien. Other changes included an enlargement of the reception room on "D" deck; on the *Olympic* this room was particularly popular especially when the ship's band were playing and had become overcrowded at times. Other changes were more cosmetic...the front of the wheelhouse was altered to have a flat front, rather than a rounded one...the location of the wireless rooms and officers cabins were altered and more passenger cabins added...bulwarks near the bridge were now made of steel rather than wood...the bridge wing "cabs" (where the navigation sidelights and Morse lamps were to be found) now extended over the side of the ship, as was the docking bridge all the way aft on the poop deck. To anyone viewing pictures of the *Titanic* and the *Olympic*, the best way to differentiate between them was that the forward half of "A" deck on the *Titanic* had screens which housed glass windows that could be raised and lowered. The first mention of these screens is on Valentine's Day, 1912. They were fitted, we are told, because of passengers complaining of being hit by spray issuing from the bows. With the majority of "B" deck now converted to cabins on the *Titanic*, the only place that 1st class passengers could freely perambulate without the fear of being drenched was on "A" deck – with new screens included. The *Olympic* and her "B" deck would remain as they were, which may explain why she was not retrofitted with "A" deck screens during the massive post-disaster overhaul in 1912 to improve her design (other features that were on the *Titanic*, such as overhanding bridge wing "cabs" were added to the *Olympic* during the refit).

The *Titanic* was launched on May 31st, 1911 and was immediately taken to the fitting out area at Harland and Wolff; the engines and boilers were eased through cavernous openings in the upper decks, before the work of crafting her interiors began, from the sumptuous 1st class to the spartan 3rd class. It would take 10 months, punctuated only briefly by a diversion of workers to repair the *Olympic* after her collision with the *Hawke* (see above). Delayed a day by high winds, the *Titanic* passed her sea trials after a fairly cursory check of her propulsion and manoeuvring capabilities. Given a clean "bill of health" she passed through the Irish sea on April 2nd and was tied up to the wharf in Southampton later that night.

One of the first tasks in Southampton was to replenish the ship's bunkers with coal; a filthy task involving specially outfitted boats. The mere act of coaling covered the ship in a fine miasma of coal dust that took much effort to remove. There were a multitude of outstanding chores to attend to; the stores required loading, for one. But there were other matters that required attention; despite the *Titanic* taking 3 months longer to outfit than the *Olympic*, she was not completed when she arrived in Southampton. It seems a little unlikely that the inability to complete the ship was due to the *Hawke-Olympic* collision, whose repairs had taken just 40 days to perform, or from the replacement of one of the *Olympic*'s propeller blades which she had lost just mere weeks previously and which also diverted Harland and Wolff employees from the *Titanic*. If shipyard workers had been requisitioned for the repairs, this would have chiefly affected those responsible for the maintenance to the propulsion machinery, which had already been installed in the *Titanic* before the

Hawke incident. The small damage to the passenger areas inflicted by the *Hawke* would only have probably caused the diversion of a tiny crew to repair fittings to cabins and passageways etc. The *Titanic* was fully plated; efforts to replace the damaged hull areas would not impinge on the newer sister's outfitting.

In short, those craftsmen, artisans and others given the task of transforming the empty hulk to a floating palace, would not have been massively distracted by work needed to bring the *Olympic* back into service. Indeed, an initial date of March 20th of *Titanic*'s entrance into service had been touted as far back as September, and before then, January had been mooted, no doubt influenced by the *Olympic*'s outfitting time of 7 months. Perhaps one reason for the inability to complete the *Titanic* was simply because of the extra work needed? "B" deck required dozens of new cabins added, and this is the most likely reason for the delay. Even so, the change of date was announced on the same day that engineers in Belfast had the first opportunity to assess the damage to the *Olympic* following the *Hawke* collision[7].

The *Titanic*'s outward appearance was majestic, but the proud countenance hid a problem for the White Star Line. Their wonder ship was simply not ready to sail, and hordes of workmen laboured to resolve the issue. Many of the tasks seemed to be small (for instance, steward Walter Williams mentioned that the paint on some of the lockers was still wet), but there was still plenty to tackle.

Thomas Andrews wrote on April 2nd, "We are getting more shipshape by the hour, but there is still a great deal of work to be done." But 8 days later he was still concerned and told a fellow 1st class passenger as such, who recorded: "Another thing that is not generally known is that the *Titanic* was not ready to sail at the time she did. Mr. Andrews told me himself and said that the only reason they allowed her to go when they did was that the sailing date had already been fixed and they just simply had to start. While the ship was fitted up most sumptuously once could not help but notice that she was not prepared to sail." This same passenger had experience of the incompleteness: "There were none of the usual printed notices in the cabins. The frames for them were on the walls, but the notices themselves were not there." A trivial matter, certainly, and there were more than a few of them; the (then) 2nd Officer Blair's daughter recalled that carpet was still being laid. And on the trip down from Belfast, the clock at the centre of a fabulous carving on the forward 1st class "Grand Staircase" had a surrogate replacement: a mirror[8]. The three red and white warning signs at the stern advising passing ships of the triple- propeller screw configuration of the ship were installed at Southampton, as were sundry elements like the punch bag for the ship's gymnasium. Although the basic infrastructure of the ship was completed and sound, there still remained a lot to do, including stocking the ship with all the coal, food, drink, linen etc. required for the inaugural voyage.

Even after leaving Southampton, the ship was not finished. 2[Nd] class passenger Imanita Shelley noticed that her "new" cabin was half finished and she had problems with the heating system too. After much complaining, she was moved to a completed berth (and upgraded to 1st class); she later found out that the 3rd class's heating was faulty too. Shelley observed that the ladies "toilet room" still had some of their fixtures in crates.

The 1st Class cabins also had their issues. A passenger from "D" Deck complained that her cabin looked incomplete with the usual passenger framed notices missing. Another 1st Class passenger from "D" Deck reported that electricity in her (and two adjoining) staterooms was lost on Friday morning but was fixed later on - which she was thankful for as she would have needed her heater for the ever colder nights. A Canadian gentleman from "C" Deck reported that there was absolutely no hot water in his cabin and Miss Isham had a faulty steward call-button, which never worked. Mrs Snyder said that the window in their cabin did not seal properly and cold air permeated the room. And, to add to the catalogue of woe, stewardess Maud Slocombe found "liquor bottles and half eaten sandwiches in every bureau drawer" in her domain, the Turkish Bath. By Sunday, she claimed, the Bath were finally ready after she and her colleague, Bert Crosby, had cleared the rooms of detritus[9].

Even more ominously, 1st class passenger Daisy Minahan swore an affidavit at the later U.S. Inquiry in which she says, "A stewardess who had been saved told me that after the *Titanic* left Southampton that there were a number of carpenters working to put the doors of the air-tight compartments in working order. They had great difficulty in making them respond, and one of them remarked that they would be of little use in case of accident, because it took so long to make them work."

This is hearsay evidence; Assistant Electrician Albert Ervine wrote a letter to his mother on April 11th in which he described partaking in a full dress rehearsal of an emergency; the alarm bells all rang for 10 seconds, then about 50 doors slid down, closing each compartment. His number of "50" is an overestimate; there were less than a quarter this number of doors that "slid down." From a study of the testimony of the survivors of the disaster, it is likely that a drill involving the closing of the manually operated doors was not carried out. As we shall soon see, there is more than a hint that the hand-worked door near the Turkish baths would not close after the iceberg impact.

The observance on Easter between 5th and 8th April would no doubt have compressed the available time to get the *Titanic* ready even further when only a skeleton crew was left aboard. Little wonder then that the White Star Line had posted notices proclaiming "Sightseers need not apply!" In the summer of 1911, the *Olympic* had been opened up for inspection, but with the *Titanic* still unfinished, there was no time for public relations[10].

To compound the teething difficulties of the *Titanic* entering service and the myriad of unfinished work, Captain Smith had decided to enlist the services of an old colleague from the *Olympic*: Chief Officer Henry Wilde. Previously Chief, William Murdoch thus became the 1st Officer, and Charles Lightoller was temporarily demoted from 1st to 2nd. The original 2nd Officer, David Blair left the ship much to his regret. The rankings of the junior officers (3rd Officer Herbert Pitman, 4th Officer Joseph Boxhall, 5th Officer Harold Lowe and 6th Officer James Moody) remained unchanged. Why was the duty roster altered with such little notice? It is not known, but of the officers originally enlisted on the *Titanic*, only Smith and Murdoch had experience with the *Olympic* class of vessels and Smith may have needed another experienced hand. Wilde signed on the day before sailing.

Captain Smith certainly provides some puzzles to modern day researchers; it is said, and oft repeated, that the *Titanic*'s outbound maiden voyage was to be his last for the White Star Line prior to retirement, and he would return home as a passenger. Some researchers scoff at this; it was apparently not customary to change commanders half-way through a voyage. Modern day *Titanic* researcher David Gittins has unearthed some evidence that suggests that, based on newspaper information, Smith was to remain as captain until a bigger and finer vessel was built, but this was at least a few years away. Certainly, Smith had passed the age of 60, when it is believed that retirement was mandatory. He signed on the ship's inventory and listed his age as 59, but he was really 62. Perhaps the confusion over his "retirement" was partly instigated by his recent retirement from the Royal Navy Reserves, with whom he held the rank of Commander. Smith never mentioned retirement in the letters to his nephew, Frank Hancock, or to his wife, Eleanor. Then we have the story that, a little while before the maiden voyage, Captain Smith visited the father of stewardess Sarah Stap, himself a master mariner and told him that this would be his last crossing, and he would be returning as a passenger. While on the *Titanic*, Smith is alleged to have told 2nd class passenger Edith Brown and her parents that he was looking forward to having more time at the end of that voyage to take his dog for walks. The lack of advance publicity from anyone about the imminent retirement of this much loved mariner is remarkable. What is also remarkable is that Smith was not removed from command following the *Hawke* incident. Obviously, the White Star Line had absolute confidence in Smith. In retrospect, and the Stap/Brown stories notwithstanding, perhaps the irony of a "retiring captain" was just more grist to the mill of a public hungry for an irony-ridden voyage, to go with the inadequate lifeboat coverage, the "unsinkable" moniker and so on?

The *Titanic* had been subjected to dozens of inspections by the Board of Trade while in Belfast; a final inspection in Southampton was all that was required. Under the scrutiny of another Board representative, the electrically operated watertight doors were raised and lowered and certified as acceptable. Two lifeboats were lowered into the water, rowed around and then raised. One aspect that missed the microscopic analysis were the lifebelts. Although enough were on board for everyone, not everyone found them to be easily accessible when the order came to abandon ship a few days hence. Some complained later that lifebelts were not where they were supposed to be, or that they were absent from their cabins altogether. People working in the engine and boiler rooms found their own lifebelts could not be retrieved due to the fact that their quarters were already flooded when they were relieved of duty. As it turned out, spare belts were to be found in convenient lockers; nonetheless, enough people noted the lack of belts, particularly some of the few 3rd class survivors, that it could be viewed as another example of the unfinished state of the *Titanic*.

Finally, sailing day arrived. Wednesday, April 10th, 1912. 1st class passengers, either on foot or on the special boat train from Waterloo station arrived, as did 2nd and 3rd class, all ready for departure at noon. The steerage[11] and crew had a special ordeal to endure; an inspection by a doctor to ensure that physically and mentally, there was no reason why they could not sail. It was a small price to pay for the majority of the 3rd class; the dreams of wealth and success in the New World were alluring. And the White Star was anticipating, like the situation with their other ships, that the majority of the revenue generated by the *Titanic* would come from 3rd class emigrants. Still, the *Titanic*'s maiden voyage was not as big an event as some authors have described. There was no fancy send-off, no brass band, and certainly no speech. Like the launch, it seemed almost "low-key". And the *Titanic* herself was hardly full; she could have accommodated about 1300 more people. And the total number of about 2200 had itself been boosted by the passengers transferring from other ships[12]. Just mere days before the maiden voyage, a massive strike by workers at coal pits had finally come to an end. But the effect it had on the shipping industry was nothing less than crippling. Dozens of ships were tied up, impotent to operate. Their bunkers had been raided and coal transferred to ensure the *Titanic*'s maiden voyage, and their passengers reallocated space on board the new giant liner. But still, the *Titanic's* maiden voyage would still be massively undersubscribed. To counter this, the White Star Line would not be averse to a gentle massaging of the truth ... Mrs Hippach and her daughter charged the Line with making false representations. They wanted to take the new vessel only if the passenger list was large as this would, they thought, be a test of the public's confidence in the ship. When they booked passage at the Paris offices of the White Star Line, they were told that there was one stateroom left, and they avidly purchased tickets. Subsequently, they found that scores of other passengers had been duped.

The cargo and baggage were loaded aboard the latest addition to the White Star fleet, until all seemed ready for departure. Suddenly, there was a commotion on the quayside; several of the "black gang" (stokers, greasers etc.) had lingered too long over a last drink in a nearby pub before heading to the docks. A train approached the gang, and two members cut across the tracks to the *Titanic*. Four men (three brothers from the Slade family and a man named Penney) elected to wait till the train has passed. By the time they got to the *Titanic*, the gang plank had been pulled back, and despite their protestations and gesticulations, the four men were left behind; the officer at the hatchway was not too concerned as other men were already on board who could take the place of the four "deserters." Not realising their luck, the four melted into the throng at the dock as the *Titanic* was nudged from her slumber by 6 small tugs. The *Titanic* picked up speed, under her own power this time, but danger lurked ahead. Moored ahead was the liner s.s. *New York*, alongside another White Star ship, the s.s *Oceanic*. In a manner hauntingly similar to the suction experienced by the *Hawke* the previous September, the *New York*'s stern broke free and swung towards the *Titanic* as the aft portion of the huge liner was alongside; moments later, the lines securing the bow of the *New York* also broke and the smaller liner was left free in the water, swinging directly ahead of the *Titanic*. Momentarily, a disaster seemed inevitable, but remedial action proved effective and the *New York* was coaxed away. The *Titanic* gingerly moved past towards open water. After clearing the *New York*, the *Titanic* stopped dead in the water. In their haste to depart, some of the workers assigned to complete the internal fixtures had been left aboard, and were now taken off by the tug *Vulcan*. This done, the *Titanic* resumed her course and arrived at Cherbourg at dusk, an hour late. Mail and passengers were duly taken on board, or placed on board the tenders for further outbound destinations. The final port of call before New York was Queenstown in Ireland, which the *Titanic* reached the next day, April 11th. More passengers and mail were loaded or unloaded. Just before 2pm, the anchors were hoisted and the *Titanic* steamed off to the south-west, the people on board anticipating landfall to a jubilant welcome in New York in 6½ days time.

Chapter 2: A Routine Crossing

Having cleared the south western coast of Ireland, the "Queen of the Ocean" thundered away, her pampered passengers taking advantage of the hospitality of the White Star Line. Apart from those few who had complained of being placed in incomplete cabins, nothing was amiss. But even so, in the first day or so after departure, a few were unhappy. And they had been given the most precious task of all; the safe navigation of the ship.

One seemingly vital piece of equipment that have attained grossly ironic status are the binoculars. Between Belfast and Southampton, the lookouts were given binoculars (or "glasses" in 1912 parlance). These had been loaned to the lookouts by David Blair[1], and when the voyage to Southampton was completed, George Hogg was asked to lock them in his cabin. This was duly done, and the key was returned to Blair by a seaman called Weller. But, as the legend retold by Blair's descendants goes, when he had departed the ship, he found the key in his possession - this was sold by auction a few years ago, and it is labelled "Crow's nest telephone." Naturally, this was seized upon by the press and fed their "nothing could go right for the *Titanic*" pronouncements. But a closer look reveals some elements that arouse suspicions; as researcher Tim Trower pointed out, the typeface used for the keytag is not the same as other, genuine examples of fonts used on other surviving *Titanic* keys. Secondly, why should a key to the "telephone" impede access to the "binoculars"? They were not stored in the same place in the crow's nest, and neither receptacle had a lock on it. Thirdly, if this key was used to lock the binoculars in a safe in Blair's cabin, it would be strange if a spare did not exist on the ship.

The crow's nest lookout team were indignant in Southampton and conferred about the lack of binoculars. On previous ships of the White Star Line, they had always been provided, although lookout Fred Fleet muttered later about their dubious quality. When the ship had departed Southampton, lookout Symons went up to the officers' mess-room and asked for glasses. He asked Lightoller, who then went into another officers' room and came out and said, "Symons, there are none." Symons went back and reported this news to his colleagues. Hogg's own story was that, after leaving Queenstown, he had approached the 2nd Officer and asked where their glasses were. Hogg did not catch the reply, but it was something like, "Get them later." Fleet would later claim that Hogg asked "several times" for binoculars.

Regardless of just how effective they could be in sighting objects, the senior officers each had binoculars and it seems surprising that one of their glasses were not loaned to the look-outs if necessary. Lightoller disagreed that the reports from the lookouts amounted to "complaints," as later suggested at the British Inquiry: "[the look-out] has the right to come and report, and there the matter ends." His version of the exchange with Symons went as follows: "I went into the Chief's room, and I repeated it to him. I said, "There are no look-out glasses for the crow's-nest." His actual reply I do not remember, but it was to the effect that he knew of it and had the matter in hand. He said that there were no glasses then for the look-out man, so I told Symons, "There are no glasses for you."" David Gittins has suggested that Lightoller used Blair's original binoculars for his own use. Why shouldn't he? They were marked "Second Officer." And while some surmise that the binoculars may still be locked up in a safe in the 2nd Officer's cabin 12,500 feet down, the truth may be as simple as this: with all the last minute work taking place at Belfast and Southampton, the binoculars - the ones intended for the look-outs and not just loaned to them - were simply overlooked. Based on the look-out's testimony it seemed very odd that the *Titanic* was the first White Star Line vessel in which they had served in which no binoculars had been provided.

One of the 1st class passengers undoubtedly basking in the glory of this new creation was none other than Bruce Ismay. J.P. Morgan's plans to accompany Ismay was cancelled due to illness. At the inevitable inquiries, Ismay insisted that he was simply an ordinary passenger; he even stated that he had not paid a fare, and he would not have paid if he was on a liner operated by a rival, such as Cunard. One presumes, despite their competitive differences, some form of entente existed.

But one piece of evidence that was not related at the U.S. Inquiry, emerged in Britain weeks later. Whilst docked at Queenstown, Ismay met with Chief Engineer Bell about the possibility of running the ship at full speed on Monday or Tuesday: "I wanted to know how much coal we had on board the ship, because the ship left after the coal strike was on, and he told me. I then spoke to him about the ship and I said it is not possible for the ship to arrive in New York on Tuesday. Therefore there is no object in pushing her. We will arrive there at 5 o'clock on Wednesday morning, and it will be good landing for the passengers in New York, and we shall also be able to economise our coal. We did not want to burn any more coal than we needed." Subject to good weather, the ship would be run at her maximum velocity for "a few hours" in a few days time. And she had two days spare coal on board, in addition to her projected consumption. All this was unknown to the U.S. inquisitors; Pitman had declared that one of the engineers, probably Bell himself, had told him that there was insufficient coal to run at full speed. Modern research has cast considerable doubt on this claim, however.

With the amount of post-disaster hatred levelled in the United States at Ismay, who had survived when so many women and children had not, failing to declare his conference with the Chief Engineer made some prudent sense, although it certainly does nothing to add to the proclamation that he was nothing but "an ordinary passenger."

On April 12th, the *Titanic* received a wirelessed message about ice ahead. Like many ships, the *Titanic* had a wireless telegraph; hers was manufactured by Marconi and was the most powerful on the sea. She was allocated the call sign "M.G.Y.", the "M" denoting Marconi to differentiate the installation from those of rival operators. Although wireless messaging at sea was comparatively new, and not every ship hosted such apparatus, the White Star Line had two operators on the ship to provide a 24 hour service. Employed by the Marconi company but signed on as members of the ship's crew, were Senior operator John "Jack" Phillips and his Junior, Harold Bride. In the strict regime of wireless telegraphy, matters pertaining to navigation were given the highest priority, followed by messages "relating to the conduct of the Radiotelegraphic Service, or to previous radiotelegrams transmitted by the station concerned", and then to "ordinary correspondence" (that is, passenger traffic. This ice warning came from s.s. *La Touraine*, and was preceded by an "M.S.G", or Master's Service Gram. This prefixed indicated a formal message that was to be delivered to the captain or the officer of the watch, for their immediate attention and acknowledgement. Captain Smith had a message of receipt sent back, but the ice was so far west and north of the *Titanic*'s location, that, even by the time she got to the longitude of the location, the ice would be of no concern.

Saturday April 13th; another day on the ocean. Passengers busied themselves as best they could; promenading, reading, writing letters, exchanging gossip. It was also the first inkling that the *Titanic*'s first crossing was to be other than routine. For, at about 1.30pm Elizabeth Lines was seated in the reception room, outside the main dining saloon when she became an unwitting witness to a crucial meeting. Seated a few feet away were none other than Smith and Ismay, with an array of coffee, liqueurs and cigars.

As Lines said later, "At first I did not pay any attention to what they were saying, they were simply talking and I was occupied, and then my attention was arrested by hearing the day's run discussed, which I already knew had been a very good one in the preceding twenty-four hours, and I heard Mr. Ismay - it was Mr. Ismay who did the talking - I heard him give the length of the run, and I heard him say "Well, we did better to-day than we did yesterday, we made a better run to-day than we did yesterday, we will make a better run to-morrow. Things are working smoothly, the machinery is bearing the test, the boilers are working well". They went on discussing it, and then I heard him make the statement: "We will beat the *Olympic* and get in to New York on Tuesday.""

And to emphasize this point, Ismay slapped his closed hand on the arm rest of his chair. And the subservient Captain Smith had not said a word. In the words of Lines, Ismay was "very positive, one might almost say dictatorial. He asked no questions." And he seemed to be very keen to draw comparisons with the maiden voyage of the *Olympic*. This information was divulged a year and a half after the disaster when legal tensions over the White Star Line's culpability were high. It is a valid question to ask why Lines had left it so late to proclaim her story. Naturally, Ismay denied that such a meeting with the captain ever took place. He also denied knowing how the *Titanic*'s daily runs compared with the *Olympic*'s on her maiden voyage the previous year[2].

April 13th merged into April 14th and everything seemed routine, with one exception: the customary lifeboat drill, normally held on Sunday before noon. Although the drill to test the watertight doors had taken place, the crew muster and inspection for the boats had not taken place. No one knew why. The weather does not seem to have been particularly bad to force a cancellation or postponement, except for one rogue entry in 3rd class passenger Jakob Johansson's diary: "...it is raining and everybody must stay inside." Everyone else described it as calm, but becoming progressively colder.

But the *Titanic* faced another problem, deep below in her ganglia of boilers, pipes and pistons; a coal fire had been burning. Knowledge of the fire seems not to have percolated up the command hierarchy: Lightoller, for one, claimed not to know of it, and that his lack of knowledge could be explained if only a small fire was burning. Prior to departure, Maurice Clarke visited the *Titanic* as the Assistant Emigration Officer under the Board of Trade; he was not told of the fire and later said, "if it was a serious fire it ought to have been reported to me."

Chief Engineer Bell must have had some misgivings. He ordered some of his men to inspect the bulkhead adjacent to the fire, and then, soon after leaving Southampton, to empty the bunker, depriving the conflagration of fuel. A fireman named Hendrickson recalled the coal fire; in his five years with the White Star Line, he had never seen one before and it imprinted itself upon his memory. It had started when the *Titanic* left Belfast (April 2nd) and was finally doused on Saturday (April 13th) with the water hose trained on the fire all the time, and "was not out much before all the coal was out".

Like Hendrickson, another crewman by the name of Dillon had been ordered to clear out the coal, but it still took "some time" to put out. All the paint in the bunker was missing and the wall was warped from the heat. To fireman Barrett, "The bottom of the watertight compartment was dinged aft and the other part was dinged forward." Barrett had been working in the stokeholds of various ships for 10 years and described the coal fire as "not ... uncommon." Hendrickson brushed off the damaged area and rubbed some black over it to give a sense of normality[3]. Had the coal fire expedited the eventual sinking? The fire was in the forward starboard bunker of boiler room 5. On April 14th, the iceberg ripped 2 feet into the bunker's wall. By that time, all the coal had been removed, leaving the bunker empty. Fireman Barrett's evidence would indicate that there was some damage in the adjacent bunker, in the aft starboard section of boiler room 6; they obviously had not worried about heat being transferred through the bulkhead to spontaneously ignite the coal in the forward bunker, as it had not been cleared of coal, unlike the one in boiler room 5.

A 21st century reappraisal by Metallurgist Dr.Tim Foecke's analysis of the coal-fire, concluded that, even if the bulkhead had indeed glowed red hot at some point, it would not have been damaged sufficiently to have contributed to the sinking. What is interesting are those who claimed to know nothing of the fire and regarded it as inconsequential. It is up to the reader to determine whether a fire in a bunker that contained several hundred tons of fuel and raged for 11 days with a fire hose trained on it at all times before it was tamed can be described as "small."

The *Titanic* proceeded apace across the Atlantic. On the morning of April 14th a Marconigram, from the s.s. *Caronia*, warned of having passed a swathe of bergs, growlers and field ice just to the north of the *Titanic*'s projected route. Captain Smith responded to this M.S.G in his usual amicable manner. The message was posted in the chart room[4].

This is the only ice warning that 4th Officer Boxhall recalled; indeed, all the ice he plotted on the navigation chart was to the north of the *Titanic*'s track. 5[Th] Officer Lowe remembered "casually" seeing a chit stuck into the frame of the chart room table with the word "ice" on it and a position. He never saw that memorandum again. Lightoller never saw the slip of paper, but did remember the captain bringing the message on to the bridge, where he was allowed to read it and made a mental note of the location of the ice. In fact, Lightoller did not notice any notation regarding ice on the chart "because [he] did not look." On this point, he contradicted himself: from the *Caronia*'s warning he claimed he had no reason to think that they were in the vicinity of ice. As he said, the officers "were continually in touch with the chart." A strange attitude for someone who later claimed that he did not look for any signs of ice. 3[Rd] Officer Pitman looked at the *Caronia*'s note, and saw that they would be in the longitude of ice, but that there was none actually reported on their track.

More time passed, and by early afternoon, another ice warning was received, this time from the s.s *Amerika*. Two icebergs had been seen just south of the *Titanic*'s track. This message was prefixed with an M.S.G but with the caveat that it was to be retransmitted to the ground station at Cape Race, where it would be forwarded to the U.S. Hydrographic Department in Washington, D.C. Despite the M.S.G, no reply was sent, although it was indeed relayed many hours later when the *Titanic* was in contact with Cape Race. None of the surviving officers recall the message. Just a few days hence at the U.S. Inquiry, Lightoller would be asked if he knew he was in the vicinity of icebergs. He replied "No" and must have been shocked when the spectre of the *Amerika*'s ice warning was raised. Although he claimed not to have seen it, he had been "caught out" lying. He had even worked out when the ice would be encountered based on his own knowledge of the ice reports he had seen.

Another Marconigram crackled across the airwaves, this one from a fellow White Star vessel, the s.s. *Baltic*. The message contained a report from the Greek steamer *Athinai* mentioning icebergs and field ice in the *Titanic*'s path, as well as information that a German oil tanker, the

Deutschland, was short of coal and was not under control. Smith sent off a cordial acknowledgement. Now there was no need to worry about how far icebergs and field ice might drift in the few days since they had been seen; here was a message warning that ice seen that very day was now south of 42° North - and potentially in the path of the ship. The delivery of this message might have been seen by Helen Ostby: "Late Sunday morning, as I was sitting on deck, Captain Edward Smith was talking nearby to a few passengers when a steward came out and handed him a message. Captain Smith looked at it, but then continued talking for a while with the passengers." The only problem is the timing; the *Baltic*'s message came in about lunchtime. Nevertheless, Ostby felt that this might have been one of the numerous ice messages received.

This ice warning may have had a larger audience. Just before lunch on April 14th, Smith approached Ismay, and handed him the *Baltic*'s telegram without saying a word (according to Ismay). Ismay glanced casually at it and put it in his pocket. Ismay claimed that being handed radio messages was not unusual, but this was the first and only (admitted) occurrence of this on this voyage. But Ismay only admitted this because it was mentioned in the press after the survivors had landed in New York. Had Ismay seen any other warnings and not mentioned them to limit his the perceived influence on the ship's navigation? Why did Captain Smith give Ismay the telegram? Ismay claimed not to be able to understand latitude or longitude. Was it, as some have suggested, a subtle appeal to slow down? Or perhaps to render aid to the *Deutschland*? Some hours passed, when Ismay encountered 1st class passengers Mrs. Thayer and Mrs.Ryerson, who were shown the telegram (from a distance of "four feet" Ismay claimed later). Ryerson asked what the message said, and Ismay replied that it warned them that they were among the icebergs. "Of course you are going to slow down?" asked a concerned Ryerson. "Certainly not," retorted Ismay, "we are going to put on more steam and run away from them." Ryerson informed her friends Mahala Douglas and Leila Meyer, from which the above information is gleaned, but Ryerson did not mention this in her affidavit just after the disaster; it is not clear if Douglas or Meyer learned of this information while on the *Titanic* or not, but another friend of Ryerson, Grace Bowen was made aware of the telegram and the mention of starting more boilers soon after Ismay and Ryerson had parted before dinner on the White Star ship. 1st class passenger Imanita Shelley also spoke later of rumours about the receipt of ice messages which were circulating around the ship on Sunday night. Mrs.Ryerson's evidence three years later was more detailed, and she submitted it in the ensuing court case to prove negligence on the part of the White Star Line: according to this account,

Ismay actually held out the telegram in front of her and said "We are in among the icebergs...We are not going very fast, 20 or 21 knots, but we are going to start up some extra boilers this evening." In contrast to Mrs.Douglas's account, Ryerson claimed that she did not ask if they ship was going to slow down, but was merely left with the impression that they were speeding up to get out of the ice. When Ryerson asked about the rest of the telegram, she was told about the *Deutschland* wanting a tow, and she inquired what they were going to do about that. Ismay replied that they were going to do nothing about it. Although Ryerson could not remember the exact words, she was left with the strong impression that the *Titanic* was going to get into New York early and surprise everybody. Ryerson's conversation with Ismay was merely out of politeness as her mind was overburdened with a family bereavement, but she was concerned about the ship getting in very late on Tuesday or early Wednesday, as they had made no preparations for an early arrival[5]. Ismay was indignant when he was questioned about this when he arrived in New York. He denied saying that he had been asked if they would slow down; and he certainly denied saying that they would speed up to evade the area of danger. All he would accede to later was that he knew the ship would be in the ice region that night. He certainly did not know what was happening in the engine and boiler rooms[6]. Years later, Jack Thayer Jr. would testify that this father had been told by Ismay on the morning of the calamity that "two more boilers are to be opened up today," which is precisely what fireman Fred Barrett claimed in 1912.

Just before noon, another message came in from the s.s. *Noordam* via the *Caronia*, but the ice was well to the north and could be safely ignored. Smith sent an acknowledgement to this message. No surviving officer claimed having seen this message[7]. An interesting school of thought has developed on some *Titanic* related internet forums; apart from *La Touraine*'s and the *Noordam*'s messages, all the ice reports described the hazards as being roughly on *Titanic*'s course. We know from shipping gazettes of the day that there were dozens of ice warnings dispatched, albeit most of these were north of the *Titanic*'s path, and only a few of which were sent to the *Titanic*. It seems odd that, of all these messages, the only ones that would reach the *Titanic* were that ones that could have hindered its navigation. Certainly, the wireless operators had no idea where they were on the ocean, and if they didn't, they certainly had no right of veto on irrelevant messages that posed no danger at all to their ship. The suspicion - and it exists without any proof - is that more wirelessed warnings were received or overheard, but the only ones that would be admitted were the ones that could not be denied. The exception to this argument is the *Noordam*'s message; it was received, and Smith sent a message of receipt back, but were it not for enquiries made at the British Inquiry, its existence would be unknown.

5.50pm came and went. Some three quarters of an hour later than planned, the *Titanic* changed course; whereas previously she had been on a so-called "Great Circle" route which took account of the curvature of the Earth, now she was on a more or less direct "Rhumb Course" which led to New York. The point at which the course was changed was colloquially known as "The Corner." Why this course was changed late is unknown. If it was to avoid ice that was reported to the ship, it was no more than a token deviation from her known navigation, as it brought the ship about ten miles south of where she would have been otherwise. It would not have provided a huge safety margin in the area of the reported ice. Whatever reason Smith had for delaying the course change was not shared with any surviving officer or crewman.

A notable departure was the lack of boat drill for the forward emergency boats. These were always kept swung out and ready in case of an emergency, such as a man overboard. Now, like the regular boat drill, this had been overlooked, or ignored. Lookout Jewell says that this drill happened only once a trip, but he may have confused this emergency drill for the regular one; quartermaster Hichens said it happened every night at 6pm, and involved a junior officer, 6 seamen and a quartermaster. Jewell put the lack of drill down to the strong breeze that had been blowing "all day" but which diminished as the sun set[8]. The truth is, no-one knows why the drill was not performed. Perhaps because of this, there is some confusion about the placing of lamps in the emergency boats. Hours later, Boat 1 left without one; Boat 2's seems to have run down, as a steward named Crawford was to recall: "An officer got into the boat afterwards. This man handed me a lamp out of the boat. I saw a lamp standing on the deck. It was ready-lit. I said, "It will be all right for us," so I stowed it in there." When queried about this, Boxhall confirmed that a lamp was lit every night and placed in the boats at 6pm, and although he initially confirmed that there was a lit lamp present, he became belligerent went pressed on the matter: "I am not going to be driven to say that [i.e. that there would be a light in the emergency boats]. I do not think they were exactly in the boat. They were hanging in the wheelhouse or in the bridge, covered over with a canvas cover - not exactly in the boat."

It became colder and just before 7 o'clock, the limb of the sun disappeared below the horizon. Preparing for the hours of darkness, the lighting in the cabins, staterooms and promenades came on, and the *Titanic* glistened like an illuminated jewel. The only place where lighting was a serious distraction was on the bridge; to preserve the watch officer's night vision, all lamps on the bow were turned off. Indeed, Murdoch told Hemming, the lamp trimmer, "when you go forward get the fore-scuttle hatch closed, there is a glow left from that, as we are in the vicinity of ice, and I want everything dark before the bridge."

The decorum and pomp of dinner was imminent, and men and women of the 1st class dressed in the finest regalia. Prior to his meal, Ismay was enjoying a cigar in the 1st class smoking room when Captain Smith approached him and asked him for the *Baltic*'s Marconi message from earlier. Explaining that he wanted to put it in the officer's chart room, Smith was given the report and he left the room. It was now 7.10, or 7.15pm. At half past seven, Ismay took his place in the dining room, with his companion, the ship's surgeon Dr.O'Loughlin. Ismay completed his meal 30 or 45 minutes later, and Captain Smith, seated at a different table, was still there. If Smith did put the *Baltic*'s/*Athinai*'s message in the chart room, it was not noticed. Boxhall was working in there exclusively from 8pm till 10pm and did not see it. He did notice a previous message about the drifting *Deutschland*, which had been there two or three days. Pitman also seemed to have recalled this message too.

About half past seven, Junior Marconi operator Bride temporarily took over from his senior, Jack Phillips. He overheard a message from the s.s. *Californian* to the s.s. *Antillian*; prefixed M.S.G., it gave a sighting of three icebergs not very far away. Despite being very busy, Bride scribbled down the details and took it to the bridge and handed it to "an officer." Initially, Bride claimed that he delivered it to the captain, but his later testimony clouds this issue. It may have been Murdoch who received the chit, while Lightoller was at dinner. Soon afterwards, the *Californian* was in contact, this time offering the *Titanic* their ice warning directly; Bride informed his counterpart that he had already overheard it and received it.

The rigmarole of ascertaining the ship's position took place at this time. With a sextant, and with the horizon still visible in the rapidly growing gloom of dusk, Lightoller and Pitman took their turns observing certain target stars in the sky. By knowing the angle that the stars made with with the horizon, and with recourse to laborious calculations and mathematical tables, one could then calculate the ship's position. Pitman started on these computations as soon as they had been collected.

If the timing is right, Lightoller came back from dinner at approximately this time to perform the stellar observations (according to Boxhall), and Murdoch went off duty again. Lightoller claimed to know nothing of the *Californian*'s message; the only news he heard was that the temperature had dropped 4° Fahrenheit (2.2° Celsius) in the half hour that Lightoller away, and was now at 39° Fahrenheit (3.9° Celsius). Did the drop in temperature indicate the presence of ice? Opinions differed. Lightoller did not think so. Neither did Richard Jones, Captain of the s.s. *Canada*. The British Inquiry quoted "*Nova Scotia (South-East Coast) and Bay of Funday Pilot*" (1911) as saying, "No reliance can be placed on any warning being conveyed to a mariner by a fall of temperature either of the air or sea, on approaching ice. Some decrease in temperature has occasionally been recorded, but more often none has been observed." But others thought differently. Ernest Shackleton testified, "if there was no wind and the temperature fell abnormally for the time of year I would consider that I was approaching an area which might have ice in it." Mrs.Crosby saw sailors taking water temperature readings on the *Titanic* on the afternoon of April 14th who indicated to her that the ship was amongst ice, and some other passengers (for instance, Mrs.J Stuart White) and crew also presumed that ship was near icebergs. Additionally, some members of the crew (lookouts Lee and Symons, Mail Clerk John Richard "Jago" Smith, steward Cecil Fitzpatrick and Assistant Storekeeper Prentice) all claimed to be able to "smell" ice. 1st class passenger Elizabeth Shute also stated that the air had "so strange an odor as if it came from a clammy cave" not long before the brush with the iceberg.

At 8 o'clock Pitman and Lowe left their watch, and were relieved by Moody and Boxhall. One can almost sense an element of glee when Pitman went off duty and handed Boxhall stellar calculations; "Here are a bunch of sights for you, old man. Go ahead." These calculations would necessarily take a long time. In the interim, Lowe had already arrived at a D.R., or Dead (short for De'd, or Deduced) reckoning position; by taking the last known ship's position, and projecting forward along the course at a known speed, a rough location, devoid of corrections for ocean-going current, could be found. This is highly dependant on knowing the ship's course and speed, and calculations by *Titanic* researcher Samuel Halpern would recreate this 8pm rough estimate as being some 20 miles ahead of her 7.30pm accurate position. Lowe himself was dismissive of the importance of his own work: it was "nothing of any great importance" and was done simply so that a position could be entered in a book containing instructions for the officers during the house of darkness. Lowe himself handed Captain Smith the slip of paper containing the location across his chart room table. However, Mrs.Minahan puts Smith in the dining room at about 7.15pm, and while it is possible that Smith temporarily left the dinner party to attend to bridge duties, we must be careful of Lowe's comments.

When was the *Titanic* expected to reach the area of ice? Based on the *Caronia*'s message, Lightoller estimated that, at a speed of 21.5 knots, the *Titanic* would reach the longitude of the eastern-most boundary (49 W) of ice at 9.30pm. It is a surprisingly good estimation: if we neglect the delayed turn at the Corner, the distance to 49 W would be 89 nautical miles, or 4 hours and 10 minutes steaming, which gives 9.10pm. Moody was asked for his own estimate, and he said 11.00pm. Lightoller came to the conclusion that Moody had based his own timing on a Marconi message other than the *Caronia* message. Assuming this is not some retrospective theory concocted by Lightoller, it is surprising that Moody was not asked for the basis of his own estimate.

The temperature was still falling, and by about 8.45pm, it was now 33° Fahrenheit (0.6° Celsius). Worried that the low temperature would cause the water in the pipes to freeze, Lightoller warned the Carpenter and the engine room.

At 8.55pm, Captain Smith again appeared on the bridge and conferred briefly with Lightoller. Remarking that it was cold, the 2nd Officer informed him of the orders given to the Carpenter and engine room. The laconic conversation revolved around the lack of wind...that it was "a flat calm"...and that it was perfectly clear. Agreeing that there would be an amount of light reflected from a berg and that the white outline would be visible from a good distance even if the "blue" side of an iceberg was presented to them, Smith headed to his quarters about half an hour later, telling the 2nd Officer, "If it becomes at all doubtful let me know at once; I will be just inside." Immediately upon the conclusion of this brief, taciturn conversation, Lightoller instructed Moody to telephone the crow's nest to keep vigilance for ice, particularly "small ice and growlers." Moody inadvertently omitted the "growlers" directive and he was instructed to phone the look-outs again, with the complete message. Moody complied. The time was now 9.30pm, exactly the time that Lightoller had predicted they would be within the ice area[9].

Lightoller's conversation with Smith is repeated in every book and film about the *Titanic*. Did it really happen? Mrs. Bishop told an interesting tale to newspapers after they arrived in New York; "Mr. Lucien Smith ... [told his wife] before they parted on the deck [that] he had seen Capt. Smith at a dinner at 11pm that night. When he left the dining room [sic], the captain was still there, although he may have gone to the bridge before the collision, it doesn't seem likely." Mr. Smith then went on to play bridge in the Cafe Parisien, which was next door to the restaurant. Strangely, Mrs. Smith did not mention this in her affidavit to the U.S. Inquiry, where she simply says that she and her husband left the dinner party at 8.45 to go to the cafe, and that "I stayed up until 10.30, and then went to bed. I passed through the coffee room, and Mr. Ismay and his party were still there. The reason I am positive about the different time is because I asked my husband at the three intervals what time it was. I went to bed, and my husband joined his friends."

In isolation, the newspaper interview may be dismissed as invention or hearsay; it was, after all, a second hand story from Mrs.Bishop reporting what Mrs.Smith had told her. Neither Mr. nor Mrs. Bishop mentioned this incident at the U.S. Inquiry. But, in tandem with other stories, it depicts a very different scenario from the one recounted by Lightoller. In this revisionist scenario, the captain and his 2nd Officer never had their conversation.

Daisy Minahan swore that Captain Smith was still in the restaurant when he was supposed to be on the bridge: "Capt. Smith was continuously with his party from the time we entered until between 9:25 and 9:45, when he bid the women good night and left. I know this time positively, for at 9:25 my brother suggested my going to bed. We waited for one more piece of the orchestra, and it was between 9:25 and 9:45 (the time we departed), that Capt. Smith left...I had read testimony before your committee stating that Capt. Smith had talked to an officer on the bridge from 8:45 to 9:25. This is positively untrue, as he was having coffee with these people during this time. I was seated so close to them that I could hear bits of their conversation."

Further circumstantial evidence comes from Charles Stengel, who testified, " I have a distinct recollection of a Mrs. Thorne stating, while talking about the captain being to dinner, that she was in that party, and she said, "I was in that party, and the captain did not drink a drop." He smoked two cigars, that was all, and left the dining room about 10 o'clock."

In court proceedings in 1915, George Rheims said that he saw

42

Ismay and Captain Smith talking together after dinner at about 9 or 9.15 [pm], taking coffee in the dining room. Rheims saw them there for about ten minutes, but did not know how long they stayed there. Rheims testimony is sadly suspect, due to memory problems in the wake of the catastrophe. The matter of whether Smith was on the bridge or not is an unresolved issue[10].

The overburdened senior wireless operator Phillips sat tapping at his telegraphic key, sending messages to Cape Race. The Marconi apparatus had malfunctioned the previous day, and after much struggle and toil, the equipment was now operating normally. Now that Cape Race was in range, the mountain of correspondence, mostly banal, from the passengers could be forwarded on, including the ice message from the s.s. *Amerika*. The junior operator, Bride, had promised to relieve his senior of this enormous task two hours early, at midnight. At about 9.50pm, Phillips received a message from a ship called the s.s. *Mesaba*. Addressed to the *Titanic* and all east-bound ships, it warned of heavy pack ice, field ice and a great number of large icebergs. With hindsight, we can now say that the *Titanic* was actually entering the ice region. The message did not have an M.S.G. attached to it, but was simply headed "Ice report." Phillips tapped out a cursory acknowledgement, and the *Mesaba*'s wireless operator sat and waited in vain for an official reply from Captain Smith. None of the surviving officers on the bridge, nor indeed Bride, recalled seeing the message.

Meanwhile, it was now so cold that Lightoller gave another instruction to quartermaster Hichens who was running errands: the order was to go and find the deck engineer and bring him up with a key to open the heaters up in the corridor of the officers quarters, the wheelhouse and the chart room. At least some parts of the officer's quarters would have respite from the Arctic conditions. This done, Hichens woke up Murdoch for his watch, and then took readings from the thermometer, the barometer and the temperature of the water[11]. Some ten minutes later, at 10 pm, there was another adjustment of the crew: Fleet and Lee relieved Jewell and Symons in the crow's nest, relaying the order to watch out for ice. Hichens took over the ship's wheel from quartermaster Olliver, who was now assigned to act as stand-by for the next two hours and 23 minutes until he was due to go off watch. Lightoller handed over the bridge to Murdoch as the 1st Officer came on duty, and informed him of messages to the Carpenter, engine room and look-outs. No ice warnings had reached the bridge, so there was nothing navigationally to report. Before the 2nd Officer retired to his slumber, Boxhall presented his newly completed calculations of the ship's 7.30pm position to him.

The *Titanic* was now running faster than she ever had. On April 10th and 11th, of the 29 boilers she carried, nine boilers were unlit. On the 12th and 13th , another boiler had been added to the propulsion system. Two or three boilers were lit on Sunday morning. Since it takes twelve hours to get a boiler up to a pressure sufficient to connect to the steam pipes etc., we can say with some certainty that, at the time of the collision, 24 out of 29 boilers (or 144 out of 159 furnaces) were being fed; indeed, there is evidence from one firemen that the three 'new' boilers fired up early on the 14th were connected up at 7pm. Instructions were passed through from the engine room to keep the steam sufficient for 75 revolutions per minute on the engines, and Scott, a crewman in the engine room, recalled this number of revolutions at 11pm. Fireman Hendrickson later told that, at 4pm on Sunday, the ship was making 76 revolutions, and Fireman Thompson said that they had actually achieved 77 revolutions of the engines that day. The amount of steam pressure generated is sketchy but indicates that some desire for great speed was in demand. The boilers were constructed in accordance with Board of Trade rules for a working pressure of 215 pounds per square inch (psi). Fireman Beauchamp said the pressure being generated was between 200 and 210, and he favoured the latter value. Another stoker, Cavell, said that there was 225 psi when he last looked at the pressure gauge. This was minutes before the collision. Of the passengers, Charles Stengel told of a report from the engine room between 1 and 2pm on Sunday afternoon that the engines were turning 3 revolutions faster than before. George Rheims may have heard a variation of that same report from a steward; when Rheims expressed scepticism, the steward took him into a hallway outside the smoking room where the strong vibration was more evident. In her autobiography, Lady Duff-Gordon remarked that, at dinner that night, Ismay was confident and that the ship would undoubtedly establish a record. We must be circumspect; no-one recalled such a conversation, and this snippet of information comes from an account written 20 years later. She does not mention it in her 1912 evidence, but there is partial corroboration in the newspaper interviews attributed to a steward named Whiteley, which are discussed elsewhere in this work.

The use of the word "record" is somewhat inflammatory in *Titanic* circles, and cynics say that the *Titanic* could never match the speed of the *Lusitania* or *Mauretania*, the latter of which had seized the "Blue Riband" for the fastest Transatlantic crossing in 1909 with an astonishing speed of 26 knots, some 3.5 knots faster than the *Titanic*'s ultimate speed. But the speculation is that the *Titanic* was trying to better the unofficial record for the fastest crossing for a ship's maiden voyage, then held by the *Olympic*.

In those halcyon days, there were two steamship routes for westward and eastward travel. Between January and August, the routes were pushed south because of the dangers of icebergs drifting south and littering the path of any hapless ship. In September 1907, the *Lusitania* had completed the westward leg of her maiden voyage in a shade over 5 days, at a speed of 23 knots despite being slowed by heavy fog. However, this was for the shorter northern route since, at that time of year, icebergs were considered less of a risk, being locked up in the Arctic latitudes. In June 2011, the *Olympic* travelled the longer southern route in 5 days and 16 hours at a speed of 21.7 knots which included four hours slowly wallowing in fog. It is clear from Mrs.Lines's evidence that Ismay was clearly interested in comparing the maiden voyage of the *Titanic* and the *Olympic*. Furthermore, both ships were on the same route and could be compared equally (ironically, if the *Titanic* had not hit the iceberg, she may have run into fog, like the *Lusitania*). We know that an estimated time of arrival in New York was published in the newspapers which would give an arrival time of 4pm on April 16th, shaving over 12 hours from the *Olympic*'s crossing. No-one is sure where this estimated arrival comes from; it may have been sent out directly by the *Titanic* herself or may have been a release from the White Star Line offices; but if one assumes that the *Titanic* would have taken the same route into New York as the *Olympic* had done, it leads to a colossal speed of 25.5 knots, well beyond the *Titanic*'s capabilities[12]. Unfortunately, as has been pointed out by David Gittins, the distance to New York as quoted by this small snippet is 1284 miles as at "2.15am" (presumably April 14th) which presents difficulties. Although the message could have been sent, the wireless having just been repaired and transmissions recommenced just before this time, at the time, the *Titanic* was not 1284 miles from New York, and she would not have reached that distance until about 2.30pm on board ship. At 2.15am, the *Titanic* was more likely about 1500 miles from port. The "maiden voyage record" may been unofficial, and not given the prestige of an award like the later Hales trophy of 1935, but it would, in the words of one film-maker, "make headlines," important when trying to entice the lucrative emigrant trade (which provided more revenue than 1st class ticket holders could generate).[13]

The vibration from the engines was noticeable; Lawrence

Beesley, whose cabin was above and aft of the engines felt it very plainly, as did Charles Stengel, on a deck above Beesley and situated between the 2nd and 3rd funnels. 3Rd class passenger Mary Glynn claimed just before retiring she was told by a member of the crew that the ship "was being thoroughly tested, all of her boilers being in use for the first time. [sic]" The increase in speed was noticeable to the ship's crew as well; Pitman was sure that the *Titanic* was achieving 21½ knots at 7.30pm and had done so for the previous 24 hours. But Hichens noted that, from 8pm to 10pm, the ship was actually making 22½ knots. And stationed far aft at the stern, quartermaster Rowe had noted that the ship had covered 260 miles from noon till the time of the collision - an average speed of 22.3 knots during that time. And yet, if Ismay's earlier statement - that the *Titanic* was to arrive in New York at 5am on Wednesday - were true, the ship would have to actually slow down to about 19.5 knots for the remainder of the trip. And she still had a full speed "trial" on Monday or Tuesday scheduled. If the *Titanic* had maintained 22.5 knots, she would have completed her crossing on Tuesday at about 10pm. She would have beaten the *Olympic*'s maiden voyage time. She certainly would have "made headlines," and in time for the next morning's editions too. It is interesting to speculate what the *Titanic* would have done in the fog that had plagued other ships as they approached the eastern seaboard of the United States.

At 11pm, Cyril Evans in the nearby tramp steamer *Californian* called up the *Titanic*. Evans's communication, "Say, old man, we are stopped and surrounded by ice," must have been a rude interruption to Phillips, working diligently relaying messages to Cape Race, for he castigated Evans, telling him to "shut up!" as he was jamming his own communication. Evans listened in to the communications between the White Star giant and Cape Race for a little while before turning in himself. 24 hour wireless was not a mandatory legal requirement. Some have said that Evans should not have acted in such a way, and should have sent an "M.S.G." prefix to ensure that his message was acknowledged. What seems certain is that, in this matter, navigational data's importance was rescinded in favour of other, less pressing concerns. Evans had not even had a chance to tell Phillips of his own location which would have warned of ice somewhere to the north and west of the *Titanic* at that point.

The *Titanic*'s lights were gradually extinguished as the passengers went to their peaceful slumber: all lights in the forecastle and 3rd class accommodation would be out by 10pm; lights in the saloon, library and companionways, including open decks, such as "A" deck would be turned off at 11pm, and red oil lamps left burning in key locations and at the foot of each staircase until sunrise; the smoking room was due to close at 12.00am and the 2nd class smoking room had received an extension to its opening hours and was due to stay open till midnight. The lights in the lounge stayed open till 11.30pm when the stewards asked William Sloper and his party to finish their card game; similarly the lights were on next door in the Reading and Writing Room while Edith Rosenbaum finished writing her letters. The lights were still on in the Cafe Parisien to accommodate a card game taking place there. The only lighting in the companion ways would be emergency lighting. Far from being a brilliantly illuminated spectacle, the *Titanic* would have shown scant lighting as midnight approached. *Titanic* steamed on into the night. The glittering stars, like a scatter of diamonds across black velvet made one feel glad to be alive, as Jack Thayer, Jr. wrote later. His world, and that of 2200 others would change drastically before the night was finished. Heroes and villains would be metaphorically born that night.

Aloft in the crow' nest and peering in a cutting chill breeze, Reginald Lee and Fred Fleet spotted an object ahead. A moment's hesitation determined its identity: "There is ice ahead." Fleet rang the warning bell three times signifying danger directly ahead, and picked up the telephone. 6Th Officer Moody was standing behind and to the left of Hichens at the helm, supervising him, when the telephone rang into life. Moody picked up the receiver. "Is there anyone there?" Fleet asked. "Yes, what did you see?" "Iceberg right ahead." "Thank you," replied Moody, and he relayed the message to Murdoch. "Hard-a-starboard" yelled the 1st Officer, and Hichens obediently spun the wheel hand-over-hand as the engine room telegraphs on the bridge rang out their orders to the engine room far below and behind the frantic efforts to turn the ship.

To Fleet, a collision seemed inevitable, and he advised his compatriot to leave the crow's nest in case of a collision. Lee started down the ladder but then turned and rejoined him companion. It looked as if the *Titanic* was actually going to clear the iceberg when a grinding noise rumbled up from far below. The iceberg striking the ship threw off tons of ice onto the forecastle and forward well deck. Murdoch rushed to the forward part of the bridge; ringing the warning bell, he then turned the lever which closed the electrically operated watertight doors below. The iceberg rushed astern into the darkness[14][15]. It was 11.40pm.

Titanic Interlude

The Iceberg: Nature Defeats Hubris

The iceberg itself is the major component of the drama on the *Titanic* and yet it is an actor which is oft overlooked. Seen as little more than an aggregation of frozen water, and deemed by some as "useless", it was a formidable foe and a stark reminder to humanity of its hubris when proclaiming its sea-bound vessels as "unsinkable."

The first major point we have to consider is how far it was away when it was first seen. If it was so distant, why was remedial action not taken till it was too late?

The question of distance is difficult, since we know little of its shape or defining perimeter, and "distance" implies a definitely known displacement between two objects. To clarify, it is known that the iceberg had at least one peak. We don't know how far the iceberg extended ahead of the peak(s). If one says that the distance from iceberg's summit to *Titanic*'s bow was, say, 1300 feet then the true distance from the "start" of the 'berg to the ship's prow would be somewhat less than this if the peak was situated at some point back on the iceberg. And, of course, we do not know how far the iceberg extended out below the waterline. Unfortunately, this is one of the unknowable variables of the dynamics of the *Titanic*-iceberg collision.

We can attempt to make a crude determination of the distance by considering how long it took for the *Titanic*'s crew to react. Since we know how fast the ship was proceeding, we can translate this timing into a distance. To do this, an analysis of situation is required.

Queried about the movement of the ship before and during the collision, Frederick Fleet, the look-out man with the reputation of having seen the iceberg, said that he estimated that he was at the telephone for half a minute, and the *Titanic* started to go to port when he looked up from the handpiece. Eventually the ship's deflection from her intended course was a little over one compass point (11¼°), perhaps even as much as 2 points (22½°). If his colleague, Lee, was correct that the ship started to veer off just as the "Thank you" acknowledgement was given,

48

then Fleet had spent a suspiciously long amount of time - 30 seconds - relaying his sighting; it also means that the ship's reaction was surprisingly fast (which we shall discuss soon). Quartermaster Hichens, enclosed in the wheelhouse with nothing to see except the illuminated compass and a board displaying the steering course, was literally "in the dark". He did say that the order "hard-a-starboard" was given[1], and the ship had turned two points when she struck, the maximum deflection being 40°;. Hichen's timings indicate that Fleet and Lee's testimony - perhaps honestly given - indicate that some time had elapsed between the "Thank you" and the ship's head swinging away from danger. Hichens did say that about 30 second elapsed between the 3 bells and the "hard-a-starboard" command; in the interim time, 6th Officer Moody had relayed the look-out's warning to the watch officer, Murdoch. Hichens had managed to get the helm over just as the crash occurred; the nature of the steering mechanism, linked hydraulically to the rudder, meant that the wheel could not be spun freely. It had to be turned, hand-over-hand, becoming progressively stiffer as the wheel approached the "hard over" position. Sam Halpern makes the following points; "to put the helm over hard requires about 4 complete turns of the wheel, something that does not take more than about 10 seconds to do. But Hichens also said that the ship had turned 2 points before she struck, which we know takes about 37 seconds from time the order to put the helm over is first received. So there seems to be about 27 seconds, or thereabouts, that is missing between him getting the wheel over hard and the ship turning two points." Just as he got the helm hard over, Hichens reported that the *Titanic* was "crushing the ice, or [they] could hear the grinding noise along the ship's bottom."

The *Titanic*'s ability to turn depended mainly on water rushing past the rudder, and this in turn depended on the central turbine which propelled the central propeller When the command was given to stop the *Titanic*'s engines, the steam to the turbine, which could be run in a "forward only" capacity was cut off, and the propeller's spin would gradually decrease. However, this propeller would be "windmilling" as its revolutions decreased, so there would still be some manoeuvrability until it stopped rotating completely. In the most favourable situation, with engineers standing by to receive orders via the telegraphs from the bridge, the reciprocating engines could be stopped and reversed within 30 seconds, with another 50 to 60 seconds elapsing before the engines would be backing hard. On the night of April 14th, however, an emergency Full Astern[2] order would have caught the engineering watch completely by surprise, so additional reaction time would be needed. The *Titanic* would still have been able to turn, albeit not as well as when the engines were going full ahead.

The report of the British Inquiry summarised the collision, thus: "From the evidence given it appears that the *Titanic* had turned about two points to port before the collision occurred. From various experiments subsequently made with the *Olympic*, it was found that travelling at the same rate as the *Titanic*, about 37 seconds would be required for the ship to change her course to this extent after the helm had been put hard-a-starboard. In this time the ship would travel about 466 yards, and allowing for the few seconds that would be necessary for the order to be given, it may be assumed that 500 yards was about the distance at which the iceberg was sighted either from the bridge or crow's nest." Obviously, the 2 point (22½°) deflection of the helm was seen as a pinnacle in timing, the gauge necessary to determine how much time had passed, and therefore the distance between the ship and the iceberg.

But there is a fundamental problem comes with numbers gleaned from the *Olympic*'s tests; they were performed with engineers ready to administer an immediate stop to their vessel. On the *Titanic*, it would have likely caught them by surprise.

These values (37 seconds, 500 yards and so on) have been repeated in numerous books. Where do these values originate?

Edward Wilding was asked about this. Wilding, a Marine Architect at Harland and Wolff, told the British Inquiry that, during tests with the *Olympic*, her engines were registering 21.5 knots, corresponding to 74 revolutions per minute. He mentioned that it took 37 seconds for the head to turn two points and that this was achieved in 1200-1300 feet. In later testimony, Wilding again provided evidence and revealed that the *Titanic* would turn 440 yards (1320 feet) forward and 100 yards laterally during a 2 point manoeuvre, this being the deviation noted by witnesses on the *Titanic*.

Let us pause to review these numbers. The *Titanic* was travelling at 75 revolutions, and 21st century researchers tend to assume that the ship was making about 22.5 knots, or a knot faster than Wilding had reported. This equates to 38 feet per second. Even the British Inquiry report states that the *Titanic* was making 22 knots. And 1200-1300 feet is actually 400-500 yards.

Where did "466 yards" come from? At the British Inquiry, the following was said: "Therefore [the *Titanic*] having turned the two points to port must have taken 37 seconds, and I do not think that I am adding too much or treating [the lookouts] unfairly when I say if you add three seconds for the report of what takes place you get as nearly as you will ever be able to get the time that had elapsed between the report of Fleet and the striking of the iceberg; that is between the sighting of the iceberg and the striking of the iceberg at most 40 seconds must have elapsed. That I think is the position of the discussion on the evidence such as we know it. Now that means this, that the furthest distance at which the iceberg was seen from the vessel was 466 yards - anything from 450 to 500 yards is the extreme distance that you can put it. I say 466 because it is two-thirds of 700 yards which I was assuming she was travelling per minute. Therefore, what we have got established is that this vessel going along at this pace, travelling at this 700 yards a minute, only sees the iceberg at a distance of 466 yards, and that that is not enough [room to evade the iceberg]."

700 yards a minute is only 20.7 knots. And an experiment by this author has shown that, from the time of the first ring of the bell to the warning being acknowledged on the bridge with a polite "Thank you" by 6th Officer Moody, a time of about 10 seconds would have elapsed, during which the *Titanic* would have moved forwards (based on 22.5 knots) 380 feet, or nearly 127 yards. 40 seconds at 22.5 knots is 508 yards. And yet "700 yards" is accepted, unchallenged by the court.

Is there any corroboration for a time between sighting and collision of more than 37 seconds? Certainly, but it was not heard in London as the witness, quartermaster Olliver only testified in America. He was on duty at the compass tower, when he heard 3 bells. He looked up, but the massive funnels blocked his view. He walked forward and arrived on the bridge in time to see the tip of the iceberg slip astern on the far side of the ship. The *Titanic* had already struck the iceberg, as he heard a grinding noise when he got to the bridge, but before he saw the 'berg[3].

His walk from the compass tower to the bridge acts as our stopwatch, from three bells to when the iceberg was abeam of the bridge. The distance covered by his walk can be covered at normal human walking speed in about 60 seconds. At 38 feet per second, this would make the iceberg 2280 feet from where the tip was seen (just aft of the bridge), or 2210 feet from the crow's nest. Even this answer may not provide a true depiction of the distance; if the *Titanic* had time to slow down even fractionally after Murdoch rang through the engine room

51

telegraph orders, then this distance could easily be slightly different[4].

But there is a conflict with Olliver's account.

Fourth Officer Boxhall was just leaving the officer's quarters when he heard the three bells. He heard the "hard-a-starboard" order and was almost on the bridge when the ship struck. How could Boxhall, from a closer location, get to the bridge as the same time as Olliver?

Boxhall's various versions of the collision varied considerably. In America, just a few days after the sinking, he said, "At the time of the impact I was just coming along the deck and almost abreast of the captain's quarters, and I heard the report of three bells. Almost at the same time I heard the 1st Officer give the order "Hard-a-starboard," and the engine telegraph rang. [It was a] slight impact...It did not seem to me to be very serious. I did not take it seriously." It was not slight enough to break his pace. A few weeks later, he told the court in London, "I heard the bells first...[I] was just coming out of the officer's quarters. [I felt the shock] only a moment or two after that...just a moment before that, [he heard the order] for 'hard-a-starboard' and heard the engine room telegraphs ringing...[I] was almost on the bridge when she struck."

His story mutated over time. In 1959 he gave a lecture and said that, he "had done a tour of the decks and had just looked into his cabin when he heard the lookout sound three bells. He immediately went out on deck again, and a few minutes later, at about 10.40 pm. [sic], when the ship struck, he felt no more than a slight tremor."

Then in 1962, Boxhall claimed that he was actually in his cabin having a cup of tea when the bells rang; it is understandable that he did not want to divulge this information at the inquiries as this would be seen as gross dereliction of duty for a junior officer even if Murdoch had allowed him to do so. During the Inquiries, Boxhall was suffering from pleurisy and the officer of the watch may have taken pity on his junior if he had this ailment during his time on the *Titanic*. Incidentally, Boxhall claimed that he did not see the iceberg passing just feet by him due to him still being dazzled by the lights from the interior of the ship.

Taking each one of these distances in turn, "abreast of the officer's quarters" to the bridge is about 45 feet; from the doorway to the officer's quarters is about 60 feet. These distances can be covered by a human in 10-14 seconds. This is the time that it took from 3 bells to collision; and yet Olliver indicates a time of about a minute.

52

If Boxhall (and if we neglect his 1962 "cup of tea" story) is correct, then Olliver had to have walked very fast to arrive on the bridge at nearly the same time as Boxhall. Or if Olliver is right, Boxhall took an inordinately long period to walk just a few feet. There is no indication in the testimony that either man ran, or dawdled along the deck. We must hark back to a previous mention of the shape of the iceberg: if we take Olliver's derived 60 second duration from 3 bells to when he entered the bridge, then recall that he said that the tip of the iceberg had just passed the bridge. The main body of the iceberg, if it extended ahead of the peak, could already have passed along a considerable fraction of the *Titanic*'s hull when Olliver saw the tip. The actual collision could easily have been a few seconds before this, and indeed Olliver said that the grinding noise had stopped when he saw the tip of the berg.

Can we decipher any other clues from the testimonies of the witnesses? It is difficult as many who could have given evidence perished. If we take Boxhall's story and reconcile it with his 1912 testimony, we can paint the following picture: he was coming out of the officer's quarters, a moment or two later he felt the slight shock of the impact. A "moment" before this he heard the "hard-a-starboard" order and the telegraphs ringing. Arriving on the bridge, he saw Murdoch operating the control to close the watertight doors. Could Boxhall have heard Murdoch's order and the telegraphs ringing from his quarters?

We know from the operating instructions of the watertight doors that a warning bell was to be rung, and then after waiting for ten seconds, the control to close the doors would be activated; the doors would start to fall and seal after 25-30 seconds. It is not clear from Olliver's statement if he personally saw the watertight doors being closed. Are there any other witnesses who can describe the temporal relationship between the closing of the doors and the collision? Many of those in the bowels of the ship perished, and of the few who gave testimony most gave conflicting estimates of time. But there are the recollections of leading fireman Fred Barrett. He heard the bell ring in boiler room 6, and had barely given the order for his underlings to deal with the boilers when the "crash" occurred. Reading his story, Barrett is clear that the word "crash" meant not the time of initial impact, but when the side of the ship opened up spewing water and foam into the boiler room. At 22.5 knots, and from his location about 230 feet aft of the bow, the iceberg would have traversed this distance in about 6 seconds, assuming a steady speed of about 22.5 knots.

If Barrett was right, the iceberg was already practically upon the *Titanic* when the warning bell was rung. Boxhall's evidence on timing is imprecise, as he perpetually used the word "moment" to indicate time. All we can deduce is the order of events. What can be inferred from the Barrett evidence is that Murdoch did not close the watertight doors until the very last second, when he was sure than an impact was likely to occur. The timings are very close; if the iceberg had indeed taken 6 seconds to travel from the bow to boiler room 6, and the warning bell to those below was rung for 10 seconds, then the iceberg was 4 seconds from the bow when Murdoch decided to close the doors.

How long would it have taken to warn the bridge of the iceberg? As described, it would have taken about 10 seconds to recreate the dialogue exchanged between Fleet and Moody. Olliver would have arrived about a minute after the initial three bells, and if this corresponded with the watertight door control being activated, then the warning bell was rung about 40 second after the "Thank you" from Moody.

If Olliver's arrival on the bridge was after the watertight door control being activated, then this whole timeline is compressed. Although he admits that he only saw Murdoch "about the [watertight door control] lever," Olliver states that he did feel the collision just as he entered the bridge. Boxhall was still on his way to the bridge when the felt the impact and he said that he saw the lever turned, which closed the doors below. But did Boxhall arrive after Olliver? Given the 4th Officer's changing story, there is no way to know exactly where he was when the 3 bells rang or when the collision happened. Interestingly, the 40 seconds is close to the 2 points (22½°) deflection time of 37 seconds that the *Olympic* recorded during post-disaster tests. Other authors have noted the problems with the testimony and how the *Titanic* seemed to be turning as soon as look-out Fleet finished on the telephone.

So how far from the *Titanic* was the iceberg? Olliver's timings suggest a little over 2200 feet. Wilding suggests about 1300 feet. This large discrepancy in the time implies that there is a hidden latency in the time line...or perhaps someone was withholding something at the inquiries?

Fred Fleet drew two sketches of the iceberg in the 1960s. As historical documents, they are invaluable. But as a record of what actually happened, they have little value, other than sentimentality. The "First Sight" sketch shows the iceberg on the horizon. This indicates such a long time between sighting and warning that it implies negligence on the parts of the lookouts. Perhaps what Fleet meant to say was that only a portion of it was above the horizon; the remaining fraction would be black against the water? Even so, this would happen such a distance from the *Titanic* that it begs the obvious question: why did the lookouts leave it so late? Then there is the positioning of the iceberg. In the doodle, is clear off to starboard. Fleet reported that it was "dead ahead."

The discussions above seem to be unable to resolve the distance between the *Titanic* and the iceberg; the best estimate is that the two were less than half a mile apart. Why was the iceberg not seen until it was unavoidable?

The insurmountable problem of the inability to see, and then take evasive action to clear the iceberg was raised at the inevitable inquiries. Lightoller surmised, "Of course, we know now the extraordinary combination of circumstances that existed at that time which you would not meet again once in 100 years; that they should all have existed just on that particular night shows, of course, that everything was against us. In the first place, there was no moon. Then there was no wind, not the slightest breath of air. And most particular of all in my estimation is the fact, a most extraordinary circumstance, that there was not any swell. Had there been the slightest degree of swell I have no doubt that 'berg would have been seen in plenty of time to clear it... the absence of swell we did not know of. You naturally conclude that you do not meet with a sea like it was, like a table top or a floor, a most extraordinary circumstance, and I guarantee that 99 men out of 100 could never call to mind actual proof of there having been such an absolutely smooth sea... it must have been a berg broken from a glacier with the blue side towards us."

The absence of moonlight to assist visibility, and the lack of breaking waves around the base of icebergs, signifying the approach of any object was, in the "Lightoller Defence" (as it has been known), the reason for the 'berg being seen so late. Lightoller himself had seen the lack of swell only twice in twenty years. One postulated theory for the late reaction is the "black [or blue] berg" theory; simply put, it is an iceberg that had capsized due to melting which changes the centre of flotation and this exposes a darkened surface to the air. One of the captains examined at the British Inquiry mentions having seen this happen when an iceberg capsized in the daytime exposing a darkened face. Witnesses to discoloured icebergs on the morning of the 15th are rare (seaman Osman said he saw a "dark" 'berg, "like dirty ice" and passenger Woolner spoke of white, blue, mauve and dark grey colours) but any deviation from the expected "white" icebergs may be attributed to lighting effects caused by the rising sun. Witnesses to a dark iceberg during the night of April 14th/15th 1912 are rare. One of them was a steward, Alfred Crawford who described the iceberg as a large black object much higher than the deck he was standing upon. At the time, he was located on the short promenade at the forward end of "B" deck, where there was very little light to illuminate the iceberg. From his position, a white iceberg, with no light playing upon it could be seen to be dark (the same argument could be said about the lookout's sighting). A similar argument applies to quartermaster Olliver who had arrived on the bridge in time to see the tip of the ice berg sliding by; he thought the 'berg was dark blue, but the lack of illumination in the area would have affected his perception of the colour. Conversely, quartermaster Rowe was at the stern of the *Titanic* and could see the iceberg with all the lights of the hull playing upon it; to him the iceberg was white, and extremely close to the hull[5]. And of those who saw the large deposit of ice that was flung on to the forward portion of the ship by the collision, none described any discoloured pieces.

The International Ice Patrol (instigated after the *Titanic* disaster to warn vessels of the menace of the ice) told author Michael Davie c.1985 that they had never seen a black berg. For this august group to deny the existence of such a phenomenon implies that they must be rare indeed. Even Sir Ernest Shackleton admitted that he had only seen icebergs that "appear[ed]" to be black on two occasions during his, admittedly, limited time on the North Atlantic; he had seen "many" in his career up to 1912, though. Recently, the International Ice Patrol confirmed that blue icebergs were very rare, and that their oceanographer could only recall one, from the 1950s, but never an iceberg that was "dark".

Perhaps the weather was slightly inclement? The night was generally described as clear with perfect visibility enabling one to see the stars setting below the horizon as the Earth revolved under them. But one of the look-outs (Lee) claimed at the British Inquiry that there was a "haze right ahead...extending more or less round the horizon...we had our work cut out to pierce through it just after we started. My mate [Fleet]... said 'Well, if we can see through that we will be lucky.' Fleet denied making such a comment, saying that the haze was "nothing to talk about." But when the iceberg was seen, Lee claimed that the haze was a serious impediment; "it was a dark mass that came through that haze and there was no white appearing until it was just close alongside the ship, and that was just a fringe at the top...one side of it seemed to be black, the other side seemed to be white. When I had a look at it going astern it appeared to be white." The haze lifted towards daybreak[6].

Lee's comments about the haze were dismissed by the court as a ploy to explain why the iceberg was not seen till so late. If there was a haze that gradually got worse during their 10-12am watch, it should be have been noticed by Murdoch on the bridge, and ideally, the speed reduced, and the captain called[7].

But running a ship at full speed until a change in the weather caused a corresponding change in a ship's navigation was commonplace, it would seem. Expert testimony was gleaned from many ships captains at the inquiries, and they came from a variety of companies operating ships on the North Atlantic, not necessarily the White Star or allied companies who could have given false evidence to support an ally in the shipping business. The captains all supported the practise of running a ship at full speed at night unless the weather was dubious, regardless of ice warnings. And the binoculars, viewed by many as essential aids to spotting obstructions, were not spoken of too highly either. The overall impression was that they were not a necessity, and were referred to in disparaging terms: they "spoil the look-out"..."they were difficult to focus"..."We see everything [from the bridge] first before the look-out men do." This seems to be the general consensus of opinion today; binoculars are good for isolating and identifying objects of interest, but in terms of generally scanning a horizon, they are a hindrance as they cut down the vision immensely. Michael Davie's conversation with the International Ice Patrol is of relevance. As he related in his book, "you can get captivated by binoculars"; the training of look-outs involves "[taking] big sweeps first with a wide field, searching for anomalies, then close-ups." But Fred Fleet demurred against the contemporary 1912 dismissal of the glasses. He was sure that if he had had binoculars, he would have seen the iceberg in time to avoid it, and his description of how he used them mirrors that of the International Ice Patrol: "We look all over the horizon...If we fancied we saw anything on the horizon, then we would have the glasses to make sure, before you reported." The binoculars would not be affixed to his eyes at all times, but would simply be a method to make sure of what was seen. Even his comrades, Hogg and Symons, describe something similar: "you would make sure, if you had the glasses that [an object] was a vessel and not a piece of cloud on the horizon." Even Lightoller had used this practise. As he said later, "I have never seen ice through glasses first, never in my experience.

Always whenever I have seen a berg I have seen it first with my eyes and then examined it through glasses."

One final matter deserves to be raised, and it again comes from Lightoller: "when it comes to derelict wrecks or icebergs, the man must not hesitate a moment, and on the first suspicion, before he has time to put his hand to the glasses or anything, one, two, or three bells must be immediately struck, and then he can go ahead with his glasses and do what he likes, but he must report first on suspicion." Such an action, based on a "better safe than sorry" approach was to be commended in his view. With 50 years of malleable memories, Fred Fleet came forth with a significant modification to his tale when he told researcher Leslie Reade what actually happened before the bell was sounded. Fleet claimed that he saw a black "thing" looming up, and being unable to identify it, he asked Lee if he knew what it was, but his friend couldn't say. Previously, the only suggestion of a hiatus between the sighting and the bell being rung was Fleet telling his compatriot "There is ice ahead" which he told the audience at the U.S. Inquiry. Now, there was even more of a suggestion that, if he had reacted more instinctively and instantaneously, the *Titanic* might have had sufficient time to swing her bow out of the way. There might be a nugget of truth in the story; Fleet admitted that he had not seen an iceberg in the last four years of his sea-going life. Lee was not asked when he had last seen an iceberg. How long had Fleet waited before he had determined the identity of the "black mass"?

Incidentally, the majority of the captains who were interrogated at the inquiries stated that they would not have increased the number of look-outs upon receiving ice warnings. These captains estimates of the first sight of an iceberg varied from 2 to 3 miles, to an incredible 10 miles. This latter value seems optimistic, but it is dependant on the size of the iceberg. A 'berg 60 or 70 feet tall would be too tiny to see at 10 miles, but a huge one, towering several hundred feet above the water may just be possible if conditions are right.

The testimony at the inquiries makes it seem implausible, even incredible, that a solitary iceberg could have got so close to the *Titanic*, with three pairs of eyes straining into the darkness. Some of the captains who provided testimony stated that the ice has a "phosphorescent", or "effulgent" appearance, and at night, the iceberg had the ability to reflect light absorbed during the day, "like luminous paint," which has been noted in various contemporary documents. One wonders what they were actually seeing, as the "air glow" phenomena does not match the known physical property of ice at all; perhaps "iceblink", St.Elmo's fire or phosphorescent algae? Scientific data tells us that icebergs would only reflect 20-40% of the light falling on them, and without a searchlight, the only source of illumination would be the stars ... and the 20-40% assumes that the light would all be reflected back to an observer. But an iceberg is naturally irregular in shape, scattering incident light in all directions. And therein lies the problem; at night, an iceberg, although white, would be practically black to an observer at a distance. The inevitable difficulty of seeing a black shape against a black sky is not a flippant question. Some researchers in *Titanic* lore speculate that the reason why the iceberg was not seen till too late was because the look-outs were peering down upon it. While it is true that a greater height about the sea gives a greater visible range to the horizon, it could be a handicap. At a great distance, the 'berg would be an insignificant, invisible speck. Close up, and from a height of 90 feet looking down at a berg of height approximately 60 feet, the "body" of the berg would be contained within the horizon and very difficult to spot against the black background of the sea. Some speculate that if the captain had placed another look-out further down than the crow's nest, the iceberg would have been much more visible, silhouetted against the stars, gradually being blocked out by the berg creeping towards them. Shackleton agreed, that it was better for look-outs to be nearer to the waterline; "[the iceberg] blends with the ocean if you are looking down at an angle like that. If you are on the sea level it may loom up." Succinctly put, if the observer were to view it from low down, looking up, it would block out the stars in the sky; but looking down at the berg, it would obscure the lights of the reflected stars in the water. The lookouts were essentially straining their eyes for a hole in the starfield: an area of no stars in a black, starry sky, or even an area on the surface of the sea devoid of the reflection of starlight.

Sir Ernest Shackleton concurred, "[One] might ... only [see the iceberg from] three miles [away], depending on the night and depending almost entirely on the condition of the sea at the time. With a dead calm sea there is no sign at all to give you any indication that there is anything there. If you first see the breaking sea at all, then you look for the rest and you generally see it." But when asked about the iceberg that had stopped the *Titanic*, he cautiously ventured a distance of only ¼of a mile in which an iceberg could be seen. He was also scathing about the ship's speed; "You have no right to go at that speed [21 to 22 knots] in an ice zone." Shackleton obviously treated ice with respect; had the other captains been so impressed that ice was a deadly force of nature? Suggestion abound in *Titanic* research that shipping captains had a "ram you - damn you!" attitude and treated ice no differently from other meteorological conditions that affected navigation, such as rain and fog[8]. Was this due to complacency? Newspapers of the era have many stories of ships encountering ice and the majority survived, with little loss of life.

What do the experts say of iceberg visibility? Researcher David Gittins quotes two sources, "*The Sailing Directions for Newfoundland*" and "*The Theory and Practice of Seamanship*"; the latter book dates from the 1960s, and he quotes from the 1980s edition. Whether opinions of iceberg visibility had changed in the intervening 7 decades is unknown. In the former publication, Gittins quotes, "On a clear, dark, starlit night a lookout will not pick up a berg at a greater distance than a ¼ mile." In the latter book, it is said that it is "unlikely that a sharp lookout will detect a berg at distances beyond about 500 metres (¼ mile)".

Further research on the pontifications of the experts has been performed by George Behe, who has found that, in the 1926, 1938 and 1958 editions of "*The American Practical Navigator*" by Nathaniel Bowditch, the reader is told that "an iceberg is rarely discernible at a greater distance than a quarter of a mile." In 1995, this was revised to "On clear, dark nights icebergs may be seen at a distance of from 1 to 3 miles, appearing either as white or black objects." The early editions of these publications are confirmation of the findings of the British Inquiry, who concluded a distance of 500 yards (¼ mile), or from Olliver's deduced timings, indicative of a distance of some 2200 feet (733 yards or 0.36 miles).

¼ mile seems a surprisingly small distance to see an obstruction, and then to avoid it. At 22.5 knots, this distance could be traversed in 40 seconds. Other effects come into play when trying to discern dark objects at night. The investigations of researcher Art Braunschweiger highlights a fascinating phenomenon; because of the peculiarities of human vision, there is a distinct blind spot directly in front of an observer, and that peripheral vision is best suited to seeing such objects looming ahead. Indeed, Mr.Braunschweiger quotes a U.S. Army Aviation manual which states that larger and larger objects will be missed as the distances increases. The technique taught by the U.S. Navy is to search and scan; hold the binoculars up to the horizon and scan, raster-like within the field of vision afforded by the binoculars while holding them prone, pausing for 5 seconds each time on each small sector being observed. Then lower the binoculars and search the area with the naked eye. This technique wasn't available in 1912, as it only came with decades of research into the problems affecting the human eye at night.

How then can this be reconciled with Captain Rostron's experience while en route to rescue the *Titanic*'s survivors aboard the *Carpathia*? He saw about six icebergs on his ship's mission to aid the sinking liner. He put the distances as 1 to 2 miles away. The last iceberg was seen at about 4am, and it was only ¼ mile off his ship, in excellent agreement with the later musings of writers and professionals on the subject. This earlier discussion that describes an observer close to the water "looking up" and seeing an iceberg silhouetted against the stars contradicts Rostron's experiences. He had placed a man in his crow's nest, and one at the very tip of the ship. He had officers on the bridge also keeping vigil. And yet, in all cases, it was the eyes on the bridge that saw the icebergs first. The *Carpathia*'s forecastle was about 30 feet high; the last iceberg at 4am was 25 to 30 feet high. The look-out on the prow should have been looking directly at the iceberg, and yet the watch-keepers high up had seen something the look-out had not. In this instance, experience mattered; Rostron knew what an iceberg at night looked like. Crucially, Fred Fleet had not see one in 4 years during his time as a look-out on the *Oceanic*, his previous ship and he was a curious choice for a lookout, as he seemed quite unable, or unwilling to provide estimates of distances or time.

Another piece of idle speculation rife in *Titanic* circles is whether the *Titanic* could have survived a head-on collision. Parallels have been drawn between the *Titanic*, and another ship, the *Arizona*, in 1879. She hit a berg directly and was left with a hole "20 feet broad and 30 feet deep" in her bows. It is impossible to compare the two vessels. The *Titanic* was travelling at 22.5 knots; the *Arizona* at 15. The Arizona's tonnage was reported to be some 5600 tons, but it is not clear what this refers to, as ship's weights are reported in different forms, namely gross, displacement and deadweight tonnage and this is lacking for the *Arizona*. The "best" indicator of a ship's mass is the displacement tonnage, and the best estimate for the *Titanic*'s is some 53,157 tonnes at the time of collision. At most, there could be a factor of over 21 times difference in Kinetic Energy (or energy by virtue of motion) between these two ships. Although Edward Wilding was sure that the *Titanic* would have survived, albeit telescoped in by 80 or 100 feet, killing all those in the front of the ship, it is clear that he had performed no calculations on this. When one considers how complicated such calculations would be, one realises why he had not attempted this. One would need to take account of the resiliency and elasticity of not only the hull plates, but all the internal structures and how they would serve to decelerate the iceberg as it ploughed into the hull, with mangled debris building up, serving to slow down the crushing effect even more. It is simply a process that has no parallel; no vessel has ever performed such a feat, and hopefully, none ever will. We simply cannot compare it to any other hull compaction. It is a calculation best suited for a computer - and these were not available in 1912. Author Daniel Allen Butler has striven to convince readers that the *Titanic* would have been shredded by a head-on crash but his calculations suffer from a number of severe failings that render them meaningless; he uses the wrong type of stress values, then uses equations wrongly, then mixes up his scientific units, and finally introduces spurious numerals that purport to convert between these units. His claims make no sense.

One other effect deserves a mention in this discussion: wind chill, or the reduction in temperature by virtue of the wind. In the *Titanic*'s case, this was generated by the forward movement of the ship herself. Unfortunately, the *Titanic* crew did not record the air temperature but fortunately, we have this value as recorded by the *Californian*, a steamship not so far away. At midnight, the air was 27° Fahrenheit (-2.7°Celsius). Modern research has shown that this gives a perceived temperature on the skin for a ship moving at 22.5 knots (25.9 miles per hour), of about 13° Fahrenheit, or -10.6° Celsius. With a chilling blast directed at the face, it is astonishing that anything was seen at all. Various websites give warnings of frostbite within 30 minutes at this wind chill, and others caution of the corneas freezing. And the lookouts were expected to stand watch for two hours in such conditions. With no binoculars to provide even temporary respite from the icy gust, it would be have uncomfortable, putting it very mildly. At least the watch officers on the bridge had the option of shielding themselves behind windows.

A discussion on what was felt during the contact with the iceberg is interesting in that it reveals the truly subjective nature of people's perceptions. The crewmen stationed near the bow provide a vivid description. In or near the seaman's mess on "C" deck, Seaman Poingdestre felt a "big vibration," as did a colleague named Brice; a few feet away, Buley only noticed a slight jar as though something was rubbing along the hull, whereas the collision nearly sent Lucas off his feet. Slightly aft, and two decks down on "E" deck, in the seamen's sleeping quarters, Symons was awakened by a grinding noise; Archer was also asleep and felt a "kind of crush" like a cable running through the hawsepipe; Clench was sleeping too and was awakened by the "crunching and jarring" sensation; Moore had turned in and heard a sound like a cable running out, but felt no shock; and Jewell was woken by the collision. Further forward, on either D or "E" decks, fireman Shiers, in his bunk, felt the shock, but it did not seem much. Fellow fireman Harry Senior said, "I was asleep in my bunk at the time of the collision. I was awakened by the noise and between sleeping and waking I thought I was dreaming that I was on a train which had run off the lines, and that I was being jolted about." Fireman Hurst was awakened by"a grinding crash," and Jack Podesta felt a "quiver" and the crash sounded like "tearing a strip off a piece of calico." However, Leading Fireman Hendrickson, on "G" deck and not far from the initial impact point with the iceberg, slept right through it, being "dead to the world"!

What of the passengers? What did they experience? Far aft close to a location furthest from the point of impact, Lawrence Beesley noticed "an extra heave of the engines and a more than usually obvious dancing motion of the mattress. Nothing more than that- no sound of a crash or of anything else, no jar that felt like one heavy body meeting another. And presently the same thing happened with about the same intensity."[9]

Hugh Woolner was in the 1st class smoking room on "A" deck, which was well aft of the collision point. He described later "a rip that gave a slight twist to the whole room" and "a heavy grinding sort of a shock, beginning far ahead of us in the bows and rapidly passing along the ship and away under our feet." Adolphe Saalfeld was also in the smoking room (he felt a "slight jar"), as was Algernon Barkworth ("we heard a grinding sound which caused the ship to tremble"). Almost directly below them, Pierre Marechal was playing auction bridge in the Cafe Parisien and recalled "a violent noise similar to that produced by screw racing." Elizabeth Shute was in her cabin, on the next deck down, almost directly below the smoking room, and she said, she felt a "...queer shivering" that ran under her and "...apparently the whole length of the ship." Further forward, William Sloper had just vacated the lounge on "A" deck and was heading down the stairway to his cabin, when "there was a lurch and a creaking crash; the boat seemed to shiver and keel over to port."[10]

To Major Peuchen, on "C" deck and just in front of the aperture for the 2nd funnel, it "felt as though a heavy wave had struck our ship. [The ship] quivered under it somewhat." Not too far away, on the port side of the ship, Marie Young mentioned a "grinding wrenching force"; next door, Mrs.Schabert was awakened by "a mighty crash", and in the adjoining cabin, Mrs.White gave the picturesque opinion that it was as though they had run over "a thousand marbles." To Henry Harper, it invoked memories of the time when he was on a ship that had ripped into a reef and later sunk; he thought the *Titanic* had simply run over a fishing smack. Looking out of the nearest port, he saw the iceberg only a few feet away and rushing aft. Below him, and further forward (so closer to the source of the strike), Norman Chambers spoke only of "[noticing] no very great shock, the loudest noise by far being that of jangling chains whipping along the side of the ship. This passed so quickly that I assumed something had gone wrong with the engines on the starboard side."

Edith Rosenbaum had just reached her cabin on "A" deck when she felt two or three jolts, the final one forcing her to reach out to her bed-stead for support. She then saw the iceberg gliding past her window. It is odd that Boxhall, walking on the deck just 10 feet above her said that the impact was slight enough not to jar or stop him in his walk to the bridge. If Rosenbaum is correct, this hints that Boxhall was not where he claimed to be. Or that Rosenbaum was exaggerating. On the other hand, the *Titanic* may have had more shock absorbency than many suspect. Elizabeth Robert, below and 30 feet forward of Rosenbaum, said that the crash was so violent that she was thrown out of her berth[11].

To most passengers, the impact was brief and consisted of a slight vibration or rumbling, enough to instil curiosity but not enough to trigger alarm. But others had a more tangible experience because some had seen ice and in a few locations, it seemed to have entered cabins and passageways. Mrs.Hogeboom, all the way forward on "D" deck recounted that, "At 11:45 Sunday night we were awakened by a terrific crash on the side of the ship where our staterooms were. I called to my sister and niece to find out what it was. In going out [into] the corridor we found many ice crystals, which had come in through the portholes." Kornelia Andrews, in the cabin opposite, confirmed this. Slightly further aft, Mrs.Kimball said that the ice came in through their open porthole, and in an adjoining cabin, Margaret Swift noticed that "...pieces of ice came through the portholes into the cabins." Charles Stengel was also told that ice had entered into someone's cabin, and Peuchen said that passengers had told him of ice being deposited on their portholes[12].

Other than these few accounts, there is surmise and speculation. Just scant minutes after the fatal collision, Clinch Smith showed his friend Archibald Gracie a small piece of ice. David Gittins writes, "This incident occurred on "A" deck. Are we to assume that Smith, a 1st class passenger, took the trouble to climb down to the foredeck, which was behind the gates defining 3rd class territory, merely to pick up a piece of ice? Was there ice on 1st class decks?" Indeed, apart from the ice in the forward well deck and at the aft end of the forecastle, the only instance of ice on deck was noticed by seaman Scarrott when he and his mates were called to prepare the lifeboats. One account says that he saw ice fragments scattered around the forward two boats on the starboard side, 4 decks directly above where Hogeboom, Andrews et al. saw ice come tumbling into their rooms[13].

Those who actually experienced the slight impulse generated by the iceberg impact felt only mild interest and confusion, and only a small number were concerned enough to brave the chill night air. But for others, particularly those who worked in the bowels of the *Titanic*, they had more of an inkling that the situation was far more serious, for they had actually seen water come tumbling into the hull. And, as we shall soon see, many professed themselves to be so in awe of the *Titanic* that thoughts of her foundering were not given any serious consideration...even by those who had seen water entering her shattered hull.

Chapter 3: A Precarious Situation

For 74 years, it had been thought that the damage consisted of a 300 foot long "gash." This was dispelled in 1986 when the first (manned) submarine survey of the newly located wreck was conducted. Although most of the area of the damage is buried in silt and sediment caused by the wreck ploughing into the ocean floor, the last fifty feet or so could be inspected. What was seen was not a continuous hole but a small separation in the hull plates caused by rivets being lost along a seam. Attention in recent years has shifted towards the role of these rivets. Metallurgist Dr.Tim Foecke has conducted analysis on steel recovered from the wreck site which indicates that some of the rivets were of a substandard material and perhaps susceptible to shearing off under an applied load; variability in the quality of the rivets may have made some more amenable to damage than others. Foecke has pointed out that knowledge of the effect of impurities in the steel in 1912 was primitive, as were quality control methods. To this author, although Foecke's work is tantalising, it's failing is that it relies on too few items of steel retrieved from the ocean floor to be 100% definitive. But his work on the rivets demonstrated that the *Titanic* steel is not a brittle material, that it is comparable to modern day steel and that its properties are not dependant on the temperature to which it is exposed as indicated by previous tests on steel and decried by Foecke.

Calculations by Harland and Wolff soon after the disaster, and duplicated using computers some eight decades later confirm that the total damage to the ship amounted to about 12 square feet, or approximately the size of a normal domestic door. Over a length of 250 feet, this gives us an average height for the damage of just ¾s of an inch. This damage was assessed to be not one continuous hole, but a series of punctures; this assessment was all but ignored in the press and enthusiasts who could not seemingly believe that the mighty *Titanic* was felled by such trivial damage. This damage was not confined to one compartment, where it could be isolated, but to at least 6, and possibly 7. Given that the iceberg was seen very close to the *Titanic*'s hull, one would normally expect more damage. David Gittins proposes a new theory to explain the lack of injury to the ship after boiler room 4, which is the furthest aft damage that we know of; based on an analysis of the testimony given in Britain about the thickness of steel used, he suggests that the central portion of the *Titanic*'s hull was stronger than the forward segment. He further suggests that the iceberg may have been in contact with the hull for much longer than is suspected, and that the lack of damage aft of boiler room 4 may be due to the additional strength of the hull, and by the action of the iceberg, which would be sliding at this point and applying a steadily applied load, rather than the "sharp impact" delivered to the areas ahead of this boiler room.

Given that the iceberg damage is buried in the sediment, is there any way that it will be ascertained, short of complicated excavations of mud and silt? An attempt was made in the 1990s by using sonar technology to peer below the mud. The echoed sound waves would hopefully tell of the location of any more gouges in the hull other than the ones visible in 1986. The results were trumpeted loudly; a series of slits, estimated to be no wider than that of a human finger in some places, were located in the first 6 compartments. These data were, and are, widely hailed as definitive proof of the damage inflicted by the berg. But this is misleading. Contemporary internet news reports from the wreck site revealed that similar sonar tests on the port side of the *Titanic*, which we know escaped the iceberg, revealed greater damage and the scientist responsible for the survey considered that the slits were caused due to impact with the ocean floor. This contrary opinion was overlooked in later documentaries and forensic reports and one must wonder why. Was it to allow the expedition to retain the gravitas of a true forensic investigation without the problems that controversial and unwanted data might bring? Certainly, diagrams showing the location of the "slits" are very hard to find, but one shows a hole in the forward-most compartment, above the peak tank. But we know from the experience of a crewman named Hemming that this area was still dry soon after the collision. The estimated size of the "slits" is very close to that calculated during the 1912 inquiries, but this may be coincidental. In this author's view the larger amount of damage to port casts significant doubt on the validity of the sonar results. How can one determine which slit(s) are due to iceberg damage and which are caused by impact with the ocean floor – unless one wants to validate a certain theoretical model? Until the unlikely day comes when the mud and silt covering the forward bow is removed, the real damage must remain conjecture.

What seems clear is how the water caused the ultimate fate of the ship; water was being forced into the hull by its pressure bearing down upon the "holes." This is dependant on a scientific measurement called "the head," or the difference in height between the water level inside the ship, and the actual water level. The deeper the holes beneath the water, the greater the initial force of fluid pouring in. When the water level inside the hull is the same as that outside, there is no "head", the pressures would be equalised and there would be no extra water cascading into the ship. But consider what would happen when this situation is applied to not just one compartmentalised area, but several, each one admitting different volumes of water. If the water inflow was sufficient, and the weight of water pulling the ship's hull down was sufficient, then there may come a point when the external water level would be above the height of the watertight compartment, leaving water to flood fore and aft into adjacent compartments, adding to the weight of water which would pull the hull down, increasing the "head" and so on. In short, the weight of water equates directly to a loss of buoyancy. Eventually, there would come a point where the internal water level could never catch up with the external level...resulting in the ship's bow sinking even further and resulting in the eventual loss of the ship. If there were any other avenues for water flow into the hull, such as open gangway doors or windows, this would add to the total surface area that permitted water to enter.

Could anything have been done to remedy the situation, to either prevent or slow the loss of the ship until help arrived? It has been suggested that a method called "counter flooding" be attempted. This entailed opening the watertight doors in the flooding compartments, allowing the water to flow evenly inside the ship and thus preventing the ship from going down by the head. The British Inquiry's report stated, "It is probable, however, that the life of the ship would have been lengthened somewhat if these doors had been left open, for the water would have flowed through them to the after part of the ship, and the rate of flow of the water into the ship would have been for a time reduced as the bow might have been kept up a little by the water which flowed aft." But a computer simulation performed in the 1990s, and replicated using a large scale model for a television documentary arrived at different conclusions. While it is true that the ship's forward list (or "trim" to use correct parlance) could have been arrested, the large amount of fluid in the base of the ship would have made the *Titanic* very delicate and prone to capsizing. Power would have been lost earlier as water flooded into the boilers required to generate electricity and the loss of lighting would have caused pandemonium. The ship would have toppled over approximately an hour before the real *Titanic* slipped below the ocean, taking with her unlaunched lifeboats and resulting in an even more horrendous loss of life.

The vibration and grinding noise alerted those on the bridge that the *Titanic* had struck the iceberg; despite Murdoch's actions, there simply was not enough time for evasive action to have been effective. The actions of those on the bridge are a conflicting and confusing mass of testimony; quartermaster Olliver had walked to the bridge upon first hearing the warning bell from the lookout; he arrived in time to see the iceberg head aft on the opposite side of the ship. Controversially, Olliver claims to have heard an order for "hard-a-port," presumably to swing the stern of the ship away from the iceberg. However, neither Hichens, at the wheel, nor Boxhall who was approaching the bridge, claimed to have heard this order when later giving evidence. Hichens, however, did confirm it to talking to a passenger on the *Carpathia* days later.

Boxhall was also to add to the confusion, claiming to have heard the order for "full speed astern" and to have seen this on the engine room telegraphs. This order is not remembered by any other survivor on the bridge, and it is also not reflected in the confusing memories of those who worked in the engine room and were lucky enough to escape the doomed ship The only other person who recalled the sensation of the ship suddenly being driven forcibly in reverse was a steward who admitted to memory problems..

Almost immediately afterwards, Captain Smith rushed on to the bridge and asked Murdoch what had happened. Murdoch reported that it was an iceberg, that he had ordered hard-a-starboard and the engines to be reversed, and "had intended" to order hard-a-port but that the iceberg "was too close." Confirming that the warning bell, and the watertight door control had been activated, Smith, Murdoch and Boxhall went to the starboard side of the bridge and peered aft, but the berg had been swallowed up in the darkness. The only obvious sign that anything had happened was a few tons of ice that had been cast off from the berg at the time of impact and which now littered the forward well deck. In a curious dereliction of duty, Boxhall decided of his own volition to inspect any sign of damage in the decks below him. He ventured down as far as he could but saw nothing (curiously, the manually controlled watertight doors on "F" deck had not yet been closed). Venturing back to the bridge, he relayed his positive report to Smith and Murdoch. During Boxhall's excursions, Olliver was standing by for orders and he recalled at the U.S. Inquiry that the captain ordered the ship "half speed ahead." The reason for this is unknown.[1]

Obviously fearing damage to the ship, Smith ordered Olliver to find the carpenter to take a draft of any water that had entered the hull; this would determine if there was any damage and if so, how fast the water was entering. The quartermaster headed below and located the carpenter already performing the task, lead line in hand. Boxhall had returned from his previously described excursions below and he too was also ordered by the captain to find the carpenter to take a sounding. Evidently, the carpenter had not finished his task yet and the captain was becoming impatient[2]. Boxhall again left the bridge and met the carpenter who came rushing up the crew's stairs with the alarming report that the ship was making water fast. Leaving the carpenter to report personally to the captain, Boxhall's journey down below was again interrupted, this time by a mail clerk who informed him that the mail sorting room was filling up. Boxhall left the bridge, again without orders, and inspected the flooding areas. He saw water rising rapidly up the staircase which led down to the mail sorting area and he could even hear it rushing in. On his way back up the bridge, Boxhall met the Second Steward, Mr. Dodd, "in the saloon companion way - and he asked me about sending men down below for those mails. I said "You had better wait till I go to the bridge and find what we can do." In an interview 50 years later, Boxhall's story had mutated slightly: he says that his route to the bridge involved going up through the "top lounge, where the band was, they were playing Alexander's Ragtime Band." This is difficult to believe. Officers were not permitted to enter passenger areas, and there is no mention of the band starting to play so early. If he was referring to the lounge on "A" deck, he must have taken a very circuitous route; the lounge was aft of any stairs he would have had to climb, and there would be no reason for him to take ridiculous detours to the bridge. Boxhall's investigations had probably concluded before midnight and there was no need for the band to start playing so soon. If, as the argument goes, the band were asked to form to console alarmed passengers, then Boxhall's "sighting" makes no sense. There is no hint that passengers had been awoken by an order from the crew, although certainly a curious few were patrolling the decks looking for the source of the strange vibration that had roused them. Secondly, and more importantly, there was little evidence so early on that the ship was mortally wounded. Indeed, perusing the testimony, one is struck as to how invincible the passengers and crew thought the ship was - until fairly later in the proceedings.

Back on the bridge, Olliver was given another task; an order, written on a sealed piece of paper to be delivered to Chief Engineer Bell, whom he found below in the engine room. By this time the engines were not revolving; the ship had stopped for good. The watertight doors that had been closed by Murdoch had been opened, evidently to allow access to the rooms that had been sealed off[3]. The Engineer informed Olliver to tell the captain that the mysterious sealed order "would be done as soon as possible." When Olliver returned to the bridge, the Chief Officer told him to get the boatswain to uncover the boats, ready for lowering. The busy quartermaster had barely returned from instructing the boatswain when the 6th Officer gave him a new order: to fetch the crewmen's boat allocation listing. The time would be about midnight.

The wheelhouse of the *Titanic* had a telephone that connected directly to the reciprocating (piston) engine room; this telephone was not used by Smith. Why not? Researcher David G.Brown has made a fascinating case based on the regulations of the I.M.M. Soon after the collision, the *Titanic* had a list of 5° to starboard. By "counter flooding" tanks at the very bottom of the ship, this list could be corrected...but such orders had to be provided in writing. However, Smith needed to know which compartments had been breached for such an order to be effective...which may explain why he had no less than three people seek the carpenter. Since neither Captain Smith nor Chief Engineer Bell survived we will never know what the true nature of the order was.

Despite not being needed on watch for over 2 hours, Chief Officer Wilde had awakened and helped with the inspection, heading off to the seamen's area underneath the forecastle before returning to the bridge area. What of the remaining officers, slumbering in their quarters? Lightoller was in bed; he had just extinguished the light and had turned over to get some sleep, but he was awake. He felt a slight bumping and a grinding noise and, after a few minutes, he ventured out onto the port side of the boat deck and other than seeing Murdoch in the distance, and the fact that the *Titanic* was slowing down, nothing seemed to be amiss. Crossing to the starboard side, he saw the silhouette of the captain standing forward on the bridge. It being cold, Lightoller returned to his bunk, thinking it was nothing serious. Reasoning that if he was required, he would be called, he turned in again for the night. It was certainly not his duty to go to the bridge when it was not his watch. In his estimate, about half an hour had passed before Boxhall came up to his room with the latest developments. "You know we have struck an iceberg," the 4th Officer said and Lightoller replied, "I know we have struck something." Boxhall then said, "The water is up to "F" Deck in the mail room." This was all the information Lightoller needed. Dressing hurriedly, Lightoller stepped out of the officer's quarters at the same time as Wilde, who told him to commence to get the covers off the boats, all hands having already been called to perform this task. As Lightoller started clearing away boat No.4, the crew started to arrive and the 2nd Officer directed them to boats on both sides of the ship.

Third Officer Pitman, who had retired earlier than Lightoller and was already half asleep, roused himself after feeling the vibration of the collision and was left wondering why they had released the anchor, as the sensation felt very similar. Three or four minutes later, he walked on deck, looked around and saw nothing. As he said later, he sat down and lit his pipe, and started to get dressed as his watch was due to commence at midnight. Boxhall came into his cabin and gave the same report to Pitman that he had imparted to Lightoller, and the 3rd Officer went on deck to assist in preparing the boats[4].

5Th Officer Lowe had no such report from Boxhall or anyone else as to the severity of the ship's condition. He was asleep at the time of the impact and was half awakened by hearing voices in the officer's quarters. Looking into the corridor, he saw ladies with lifebelts on. Rushing to get dressed, he hurried out on deck to help with the boats.[5] Boxhall did not mention in later questioning waking, or visiting Wilde's cabin.

Deep within the bowels of the ship, the mundane routine of the *Titanic*'s voyage was interrupted, and those toiling, or reclining in slumber were jolted with the realisation that things had gone awry. Seeing, or hearing strange things, word spread among the crew that the ship had been subjected to a calamity. Under the forecastle, Lamp Trimmer Samuel Hemming and John Foley (storekeeper) were in their quarters on "C" Deck. Hemming was roused by the impact and looked out of the porthole but saw nothing, surmising it to be ice as he could see no vessel nearby to attribute to the shock. Then, their attention was diverted to a nearby hissing noise. Going forward to the forepeak storeroom, they both climbed down to the top of the water tank at the prow of the ship but found nothing amiss[6]. Clambering up the ladder, they then found the source: an exhaust pipe that permitted surplus air to be expelled from the tank as water entered. The air was being forced out with such force that it was producing a whistling noise. Alfred Haines, the boatswain's mate, and Chief Officer Wilde had just arrived, and the latter asked what the noise was, and Hemming reported to him. Wilde, who had been off duty since 6pm and was due back on shift at 2am, returned to report to the bridge.

Hemming and Foley returned to their bunks for a few minutes, but were given a disturbing report by the ship's Joiner; "If I were you, I would turn out, you fellows. She is making water [in holds] one-two-three, and the racquet court is getting filled up." Then, as the joiner left, the boatswain, Nichols, came with his own report. The ship's builder, Thomas Andrews, had evidently been on a rapid inspection tour of the damaged areas, and the news was relayed thus; "Turn out, you fellows, you haven't half an hour to live. That is from Mr.Andrews. Keep it to yourselves and let no one know." Then came the order to report to the boat deck. It was now midnight. Andrews no doubt knew that the *Titanic* could stay afloat with any three of her first four compartments flooded, so he had probably seen and assessed more watertight compartments than the joiner had for him to proclaim the ship as doomed.

Many of the off-duty sailors and stokers stationed at the bow rushed out on deck to see several tons of ice that the berg had thrown onto the well deck during the collision; some claimed to have even seen the iceberg drifting astern. An early intimation that the bridge officers were more alarmed than those who ambled on to the deck comes from seaman Evans, who encountered "the 5th or 6th Officer." The officer ordered Evans to find the carpenter, and to get him to sound all the wells [holds] forward and report to the bridge[7]. Heading below to the working alleyway, Evans met the boatswain who asked whom the seaman was seeking. When told, the boatswain told Evans that the carpenter had already gone up and enquired what was amiss, and Evans informed him that he thought the ship had struck an iceberg. The boatswain departed to go up. At this time, the tarpaulin on cargo hold hatch No. 1 which was ballooning up due to the force of water entering the hold below him, expelling the air and forcing the cover up, and a curious Evans went to view it. Then, Evans heard the call to attend to the boats[8].

Had the boatswain encountered Andrews on the bridge, or on his way up there? There are no sightings of Andrews at this time; conceivably, Andrews imparted his assessment to the boatswain, who then told Hemming that they had just half an hour and then summoned the boat crews on deck. However, after returning from his trip to the engine room, quartermaster Olliver had been told to instruct the boatswain to call out the watch. If the boatswain had been on the bridge, why did the officers not tell him personally to prepare the boats? Why wait till Olliver had returned? The clues are fragmentary: the boatswain was seen minutes after the collision ordering the watertight doors to be shut, then we are told that he had "gone up" to the bridge after the small discussion with Evans during which the boatswain had asked "what is the matter?" Clearly he did not know what had happened and Evans told him that he thought they had struck an iceberg. Then there are two mentions of the boatswain in quick succession: Olliver's order for him to prepare the boats, and the "half hour to live" given to Hemming, coupled with the call to muster. Obviously some information had been imparted to him, but when and where it was given is a fertile area for debate. Such an analysis of "who heard what and when" is necessary to try and establish how quickly the *Titanic*'s fate had been determined, and more crucially, how fast the crew were to react to this news. As shall be seen presently, this is a vital concern when it actually became necessary for the crew to start preparing the boats for lowering.

The water pouring into the cargo holds attracted the attention of others stationed nearby. Going into the mess room for coffee, lookout Symons also heard that there was water in No.1 hold. He heard the water first, and then peered down through the gratings to the bottom of the ship. But now the water could actually be seen coming in a "rush", nearly up to the coamings on the hatch on "G" deck many decks below. After leaving the crow's nest at midnight, lookout Lee was also attracted by the sound of water splashing inside the ship and he peered down the cargo hatch into the innards of the ship. He saw water coming in "not so fast."[9]

The in-rush was more alarming to some crewmen.

Actually being driven out of their quarters by the rising water, some crewmen were bringing up their bags and putting them on the forecastle hatch. Lee heard the boatswain call the other watch that had just finished at midnight and had gone below; they went out to the boats too. Lee's companion in the crows nest, Fred Fleet, had already gone below to turn in and found no-one there. But while most thought of the rising water as nothing serious, other crewmen had more of an inkling. Seaman Poingdestre, returning from an excursion to see the ice deposited on deck, had encountered the ship's carpenter, who informed him that the ship was making water and that there was already a depth of 7 feet in hatch 1. The carpenter advised his friend to get up to the boats, but Poingdestre lingered where he was for a few more minutes before hearing the boatswain's call.

By midnight, the general alarm had been relayed to the crew. 3Rd

Officer Pitman had awakened, and after being told by 6th Officer Moody, who he found on the aft port side of the boat deck, that there was ice in the forward well deck, Pitman went forward to investigate. He too saw the crowds of firemen streaming up with their bags, and looking down the hatch, he saw water swirling round the cargo hatch many decks below him, a little stream on both sides of the cover on "G" deck.

The next watertight compartment aft contained cargo hold No.2 at the bowels of the ship, and it too was compromised. Leading Fireman Hendrickson returned to his quarters after seeing the ice on deck and also the 'berg far astern. His companion, Ford, came back and told him that there was water below, down one of the spiral staircases that led to a tunnel allowing the 'Black Gang' access to the boiler and engine rooms without sullying the rest of the ship with coal dust and grime. Looking down the portside stairway, Hendrickson saw water rushing about the base of the spiral steps, and practically "falling in." Alarmed at this, Hendrickson clambered up the steps to report this observation.

Since the water was seen swirling around the base of the staircase, it can be deduced that the iceberg managed to cut its way a few feet inside the hull of the *Titanic*, as the casing for the fireman's spiral staircases was ruptured allowing water inside. This casing was inboard of the hull by a couple of feet. The fireman's passage went through the length of cargo holds 2 and 3, and with no watertight door in the passage, the water was free to pour down its length. At the forward-most end of the tunnel, the spiral staircases allowed water to eventually enter the preceding watertight compartment, contributing to its rate of inflow. Putting it simply, if the *Titanic*'s 3rd compartment had been the only one damaged, and the fireman's passage had been punctured, the water would have flowed into the 2nd compartment too.

Cargo Hold No.3 presented a similar design flaw as the fireman's passage. Water was seen entering the area that had been reserved for postal staff to sort mail prior to arrival at their destination. But the stairs to the postal area led up to 1st class territory, in a corridor that had no watertight doors. If the damage was severe enough, there was nothing to stop water flowing up and then aft into compartments astern of the postal area. To summarise, water which was held in cargo hold No.3 (the fourth compartment) could possibly enter the fifth compartment. And indeed, we know from witnesses that it did.

Survivor's testimonies allow us to recreate the flooding of this small area of the ship. Boxhall had seen water rising fast, within 2 feet of "G" deck; Dining Saloon nightwatch man Johnson observed Captain Smith and Thomas Andrews headed to the engine room a little while later, and he followed the latter to the mail room, where he saw water on the deck below. He went and told a fellow crewman by the name of Wheat, and, his curiosity aroused by his friend's report, went forward and saw water "almost flush with "G" deck." This was only one deck below the lowest 1st class passengers cabins[10]. The only other witness to the water in this area was Norman Chambers, who had rushed up to the boat deck upon hearing "the jangling of chains whipping along the side of the ship." His fellow passengers who had peered out of the cabins after hearing or feeling some sort of commotion beneath them, were initially placated by the soothing reassurance of stewards who tried to convince the passengers - with some success - that there was nothing to be alarmed about. This is not mere disinformation on the part of the stewards; at this point in the growing calamity, very few knew just how serious the situation was.

Seeing nothing amiss on deck, Chambers returned to his room, and he and his wife went back on deck. His second trip being fruitless, and there being nothing to warrant alarm, they descended the stairs, when they saw "at the top of [the] stairs [leading down to the mailroom] I found a couple of mail clerks wet to their knees, who had just come up from below, bringing their registered mail bags." Looking down into the "trunk room" [the 1st class baggage room] from the landing on "F" deck, he saw water within 18 inches to two feet of reaching the deck upon which he was standing[11]. Incidentally, while standing looking down at the water, 1st class passenger Norman Chambers was joined by "three of the ship's officers - I did not notice their rank or department [who had] descended the first companion and looked into the baggage room, coming back up immediately, saying that we were not making any more water. This was not an announcement, but merely a remark passed from one to the other." Who were these people? It is unlikely that it was Boxhall as he never mentioned being joined by other officers or the venturing of opinions to others nearby when he gave testimony. Captain Smith was instantly recognisable by everyone. This leaves Wilde, Murdoch and Moody. If, as has been suggested on a *Titanic* forum, the "officers" were wearing dark blue jackets, they may have been post office workers, or perhaps even members of the engineering staff or even the purser's department. To the uninformed eye of passengers, anyone wearing such a uniform would pass for an "officer".

A fellow passenger, Mr.Harder, also located on "E" deck near

Chambers noticed one important occurrence. Like Chambers he had ventured on deck, braving the icy air to assess the situation, and at midnight (by his own estimation), he and the others were sent below to put on their lifejackets. When returning to the boat deck, he passed a group of four or five crewmen congregated around a hole in the floor of the deck. Normally covered with a metal plate marked "W.T.D", this was the location of the control to close the two manually operated watertight doors on the deck below, near the swimming pool and Turkish baths. By inserting a metal wrench into a slot and turning it, the door(s) could be sealed. Harder overheard the crewmen say, "Well, it's no use. This one won't work. Let's try another one." Whether "this one" referred to the watertight door, or the wrench is not known, as Mr.Harder did not stay long enough to observe what happened following this. Certainly, the crew did not seem alarmed and the situation was not taken seriously. Harder did relate this incident to another passenger, Mr.Bishop, but he recalled being told a slightly differently anecdote. As he said in testimony later, "immediately after the accident they saw the members of the crew trying to do something to these holes in the deck with a key such as they use in the shut-offs to the water system in cities, and placing the key down there, they failed to turn the one of that side, and they immediately went to the other side and could not close that. They said, 'There is no use; we will try the other side.'" Assistant Second Steward Wheat was apparently one of the men struggling with the door control, but he did not allude to any difficulties when later asked. Like Boxhall and his impromptu below decks inspection, Wheat admitted that he closed the doors without orders.

The rising water in the mail section and the supposed inability to close the watertight doors may not have elicited much concern, but a few decks below it was different. The stokers who laboured ceaselessly to fuel the might ship's hungry boilers had seen for themselves the spectacle of the Atlantic come pouring into the ship and swirl around their feet.

At 11.40pm leading Fireman Fred Barrett was on the aft starboard side of boiler room 6, talking to 2nd Engineer Hesketh, when the red indicator light illuminated, indicating that the bridge had signalled the ship to stop[12]. Barrett yelled out to "shut all the dampers,"[13] but before this could happen, the collision occurred, and water came pouring in two feet above the stokehold plates, and about two feet from Barrett. The leading fireman and the engineer jumped through the closing watertight door into boiler room 5, leaving the other stokers behind, one of whom was George Beauchamp, who had been close to Barrett in the stokehold. He too noticed the shock and said it was like the roar of thunder. A few minutes after the watertight door dropped, the order was given to draw the fires. Beauchamp noticed the water "coming through the bunker door and over the [floor] plates." After drawing the fires in the boilers, someone shouted "that will do" and everything in the room was shut down and he and the others went up the escape ladder. By his estimate, it took about 15 minutes to draw the fires[14]. Because of the water level, the firemen purging the boilers had to act quickly, or perhaps abandon their work prematurely, as another fireman named Threlfall remembered that he had helped to draw the fires in another boiler room and Engineer Hesketh had ordered the men to stop work at about 1.20am, or 100 minutes since the collision, well after Beauchamp's "15 minutes" (and, as can be seen elsewhere, there is a witness who said that staff were evacuated from the engine room at this precise time).

Immediately after jumping through the watertight door into the next compartment aft, Barrett noticed water rushing into the coal bunker 2 feet aft of the bulkhead; this was located on the forward starboard side of the boiler room, proof that the damage inflicted by the iceberg had slightly penetrated this room, too. The amount of water was described as a greater rush than from a fire hose. The water seemed to be contained within the coal bunker. Indeed there was no water on the compartment floor plates. Barrett closed the door on the bunker, sealing the water in, albeit temporarily, and by his estimation, about 10 minutes after the collision he heard the order from Hesketh for "all hands [to] stand by your stations". Since this meant the flooding boiler room next door, the only way to get in was via the escape ladder up to the alleyway, and then down another ladder into boiler room 6. Looking down into that room, he and engineer Shepherd saw 8 feet of water already in there. They returned to boiler room 5, where they found two engineers, Mr. Harvey and Mr. Wilson attending to the pumps[15].

Soon thereafter, an order was telephoned through from the engine room and relayed by Harvey for all the stokers to go up on deck, but Barrett was to remain. Apparently, Barrett's role was to fetch anything from the engine room that was needed. Before, it was an easy job to go through from stokehold to stokehold, but now, with the watertight doors closed, this entailed a tedious diversion up and down the escape ladders. After the exodus of stokers etc., the only people left in boiler room 5 were Barrett, Wilson and another engineer, Shepherd. Then the lights went out. Harvey sent Barrett to fetch some lamps, and at the top of the ladder, Barrett met two fireman. Deputising, Barrett passed on the order to the men, who eventually came back with 12 to 15 lights[16].

Returning to the boiler room with the lamps, Barrett found that his labours had been for nothing, as all the electricity had returned and the lights were already illuminated. Checking that the boilers had no water in them, Harvey ordered Barrett to fetch some men to draw the fires, eventually requisitioning between 15 and 20 men. In 20 minutes, the coals had been raked from the furnaces and their task done, the men were sent back up aloft again[17]. Harvey's next order was to lift a manhole plate on the starboard side of the boiler room. The room was now awash with steam making visibility difficult. Mr.Shepherd, walking across the room, fell into the open manhole and broke his leg. Barrett and Harvey carried their injured companion into the pump room near the (now closed) junction with boiler room 4, the next room aft[18][19].

Oblivious to what was occurring in the remainder of the ship, the three men continued with their work. But after about 15 minutes, the situation dramatically changed when a rush of water surged through the gaps between the boilers, heading aft from forwards, or from the direction of boiler room 6. Mr.Harvey ordered Barrett to go up the escape ladder, and without stopping to look, the leading fireman ascended. In the working alleyway, Barrett headed aft, noticing a small amount of water forward. Barrett estimated it was now 1.10am[20]

We now have evidence that the fore peak tank, cargo holds 1, 2 and 3, and boiler rooms 5 and 6 were punctured in the initial confrontation with the iceberg; this is far in excess of the redundancy afforded in the ship's design to remain afloat. The labours of the engineering staff aft of these damaged compartments continued, and with an analysis of the evidence, comes indications of yet more damage, albeit latent, to the ship.

Far aft, trimmer Thomas Dillon was in the reciprocating engine room. By his estimation, 30 minutes had elapsed since the collision, and the doors to the forward stokeholds were ordered to be opened. He and his team got as far as the juncture between boiler room 4 and 5, and the door was not opened. This was, by his timing, an hour and 40 minutes after the meeting with the fatal iceberg. When he got to the forward part of boiler room 4, he noticed that the floor plates were damp, and that a small quantity of water seemed to be coming up through the floor. His story is corroborated by another trimmer, George Cavell, who was already in boiler room 4. He was in the aft starboard coal bunker and the impact with the 'berg dislodged the coal, showering him in black anthracite. Extricating himself from the avalanche, he climbed up into the stokehold from the bunker, and then, like the situation in boiler room 5, the lights went out. Climbing up into the working alleyway he saw 3rd class passengers, some of whom were wet, with stewards shepherding them. Leaving the crowd of steerage he went to fetch some lamps and returned to boiler room 4 to find that in his absence, the lights had already come back on. In his estimation, they had only been out for 4 minutes, and he climbed back down into the room where he helped to draw the fires from the boilers. By this point, water was gradually coming over the floor plates, reaching a foot in depth. Cavell went for the escape ladder and seeing no one in the alleyway above, he decided to check on his comrades and partially descended down the ladder but visibility was poor due to the steam. He climbed back up, noting that the alleyway was dry[21].

Why were the watertight doors re-opened? Ostensibly, it was to allow easier access to the forward, unflooded stokeholds. Why was this? A greaser by the name of Scott remarked that he thought he saw four men carrying a large suction pipe, "which they used for drawing the water up out of the bilges" from one of the aft watertight compartments to the stokeholds. He does not provide any more information as to what it was used for, or whether it was used, but remembered that it was brought forward from a further aft watertight compartment behind the engines, after the doors had been raised[22]. With 6 compartments damaged and filling, and a 7th showing indications of water seeping up from somewhere below (a possible hint as to some injury inflicted to the ship's double bottom), nearly half of the water tight compartments showed signs of having been ruptured. The only recourse was to abandon ship.

Titanic Interlude

The Boats: Inefficiency And Panic

Much has been said of the interpretation of the "Woman and Children First" rule being liberally interpreted by Lightoller as meaning "Women and Children Only" - even if it meant boats leaving half full. But is this true? Lightoller only seems to have had sole authority on boat 6, and while it is true that he placed people in boat 4, the actual order to lower away came from the deck above. With the other boats, Wilde or Captain Smith were present, and Lightoller probably had to accede his authority to "lower away!" to his superior. A latter day excuse - that passengers wouldn't come out on deck - falters when one examines contemporary accounts. Cold though it may have been, this did not stop the procession of passengers on to the boat deck. It is highly likely that when boats 6 and 8 departed, there were enough men nearby to nearly or completely fill these boats.

Using estimates of boat occupancy from the inquiries, from letters and newspaper accounts, we can glean some statistics of boat occupancies on the port side. Because of the lack of definitive accounts from passengers in boats 16, 12 and 10, I have unfortunately had to omit their estimates from this table.[1]

Boat number (in probable order of lowering)	Average crew estimate of people in boat	Average passenger estimate of people in boat
Boat 8	40 women; 4 crew	21 women; 4 crew
Boat 6	38 women; 2 men; 2 crew	20 women; 2 men; 2 crew
Boat 16	50 women (?); 5 crew	?
Boat 14	52 women and children; 7 crew	56 total; including (?) 3 children, 1 man
Boat 12	45 women and children; 2 crew	?
Boat 2	27 women and children, 1 man, 4 crew	19 (including 2 crew and 1 man?)
Boat 10	60 women, 5 children, 2 men, 4 crew	?
Boat 4	40 passengers, 2 crew	35 women, 3 children, 2 crew
Boat D	20 women and children, 2 men, 3 crew	30 women and children

81

Boat 6 is interesting; its commander, Hichens, claimed to have actually counted 38 women, 1 seaman, himself, an Italian boy and Major Peuchen, the last two being ordered in to help row the boat. Peuchen contradicts this claim, as he said that a count was made for this boat; exactly 20 women, Hichens and Fleet and the boy. Also in No.6, Fleet said in the UK that there were 24 women in the boat, and he was adamant on this point. In America, he had said that no count was made.

The total in boat 14 was 48, mentioned by Daisy Minahan, was counted by Officer Lowe, and is presumably a count of everyone, not just passengers on board. However, Miss Compton says that there were two counts, the first being 58, the second being 60, though a child near her did not answer to either count. Crewman Morris also claimed to have counted the people in 14, and made it out to be 53 women and children. In boat 4, a shouted question from the top deck concerning the number of women on board elicited the answer "24". Quartermaster Bright informs us that boat "D" held 25 people when his boat left.

Of interest is that the numbers given by crew and passengers are comparable, with the exception of boats 6 and 8 and possibly 2 and "D" but a determination of these latter two's numbers is made problematic by a lack of data; these boats left with very low numbers. In these cases, the crew's estimate is in excess of the estimate given by the women and children on board; this is apparent in boat 6 when Peuchen and Hichens counted the numbers and gave different numbers; Mrs.Eloise Smith's tally agreed with Peuchen's. A genuine mistake given the dark conditions, or were the crew trying, as the British Inquiry later said, "to make the best case for themselves and their ship"? One is reminded of the testimony of Symons, in the undermanned boat 1. At the U.S. Inquiry, he had said there were 14 to 20 passengers in his boat. In London, he earned a rebuke when he admitted that he knew there was only a total of 12 and claimed that his American inquisitors had muddled him up. "There does not seem much muddling...You were asked a very plain question," said the head of the Inquiry.

Lightoller's plan to provide just 2 crew members per boat can be seen in these figures; he loaded boat 6 and was present at boat 12 too; boat 4 left with only two aboard, too, but eventually managed to acquire some more when crew men descended to the water from a vacant rope left by a departed boat and were picked up; in fact, the situation may have been worse than this, as Mrs.Ryerson said that boat 4 was lowered with just one crewman aboard. The standard Lightoller mantra of "women and children only" can be levelled at this boat; it left with just 24 women, with room for more, despite at least half a dozen 1st class men being nearby. However, it was Wilde who gave the order to lower away after being told how many were there. So, who is to blame for this boat leaving so bereft of people? Lightoller or Wilde? Boat 4 also has the worrying anecdote from Emily Ryerson that a steward named Dodd told her that her son Jack could not proceed into the boat. Mr.Ryerson reproached Dodd and told him, "Of course that boy goes with his mother, he is only 13." Dodd relented and then said "No more boys."[2] It could be argued (and it has been on one too many *Titanic* internet forums) that, in 1912, a 13 year old could be classed as "a man"; be that as it may, it seems heartless to think that any form of discrimination extended to males barely into their teens. Data is not very conveniently found for the 3rd class, or indeed, most of the 2nd class passengers, and so it is hard to say if there was a widespread policy barring males to enter boats based on their age.

Why were some of the officers so timid when filling the boats? Lightoller later claimed that he thought that the weight of the boats and personnel would cause the davits to buckle, and this may explain boats 6 and 8 leaving so empty ... the boats further aft were much more heavily loaded, but once we return, chronologically speaking, to the front of the ship, we see boat 4 leaving with few people. Any lessons gleaned from the nearly full boats towards the stern were lost. Lightoller was to claim in his autobiography that "if [they] were to avoid the unutterable disgrace of going down with lifeboats still hanging in the davits, there was not one single moment to lose," implying that haste expedited the lowering of half-full boats. But in his autobiography, he admits that he did not strongly entertain the notion that the ship was actually sinking, so why the hurry? At his testimony, he does feed the speculation that the boats were handled as fast as possible; but with boat 4 there is no attempt to search for anyone else to fill up the empty spaces, no hint that men were to be allowed on board, and certainly no hint that the ship was going to immediately founder with the boat still on the davits.

Each of the main and cutter boats had a plaque installed, which was labelled with the number of people that could be carried; 64 and 33 respectively[3]. There was no reason to be ignorant of the people that could be held when it was in plain sight.

Or perhaps the crew were wary of the limitations of the equipment? At Boat 13, the commander, Fred Barrett, heard an order from the top deck, "Let no more in that boat; the falls [ropes used to lower the boats] will break." He is unsure as to who gave the order. Interestingly, this boat was one of the more heavily laden ones, proving that the boats, davits and falls could handle the weight but by this point in the sinking, the information was of little use as only a precious few boats remained to which this pragmatic knowledge could be applied. One of them was boat 10, which, if current understanding of the boat loading sequence is correct, was attended to by Murdoch after boat 13 had departed. It too left nearly loaded to its maximum capacity.

At Boat 12, crewman Poingdestre had heard Lightoller's misgivings that the falls would not support the weight but the 2nd Officer denied later that he had voiced his misgivings publicly. Even Lowe was sceptical but was more concerned with the boat being able to take the load, rather than the davits: "Do you think the boat will stand it?" he said to seaman Scarrott[4]. But the boats could take it: on May 9th, 1911, and in the final stages of her fitting out, one of the *Olympic*'s lifeboats had weight equivalent to about 65 people placed onboard, and then raised and lowered six times, with no difficulty. And just before the *Titanic* left Belfast, Board of Trade Inspector Francis Carruthers had weights equivalent to 66 people introduced into the boats and the freeboard (the distance between the sea and the gunwale) with four oars was 2 feet 3 inches. Lightoller mentioned in his testimony that he was present during Carruther's inspection: "Yes; [Carruthers] examined the lifeboats, swung them out, lowered them down, hauled them up, and examined the equipment." This begs the question; were the boats loaded from the boat deck and lowered, or were the boats loaded from the water? And how much of the inspection did Lightoller see? If he did see a boat and davits haul the weight of 66 men, there was no reason not to be more extravagant with the loading. And if he didn't know, why was this information not imparted?

This lack of knowledge is compounded by the fact that on board the *Titanic* were nine men from Harland and Wolff, the so-called "Guarantee Group." This small team, led by designer Thomas Andrews and comprising plumbers, electricians and so on, were given the job of noting and recording the ship's performance, and repair any small deficiencies. Andrews was seen actively enticing people into the boats that left half full. Why did he not insist that the boats be loaded to capacity? Also on the *Titanic* was the very man who had designed the lifeboats themselves, Roderick Chisholm. This author has not been able to ascertain any sightings of him, but if there were any concerns, Chisholm should have been located and queried. If he was questioned about his design, there is no record of anyone having done so.

Both Lightoller and Wilde had been in attendance when some of the last few boats left the aft end of the port side. They could see that the boats and their lowering tackle could easily support the weight of some 50 or more people...so why were they letting later boats leave with barely half this number of occupants? Lightoller claimed his plan was to fill up the boats from gangway doors, close to the waterline. His idea, which seems to have been concocted at the same time as a similar plan by Murdoch (even though Lightoller never told anyone his idea) never came to fruition. He claimed to have seconded Nichols, the boatswain, and about six men to go below and open the doors. They were never seen again. This seems to have happened at about the time boat 6 was being lowered; consequently, it was noticed that there were few crewmen to man the boats at the time. It is often claimed that Nichols and his men were trapped by a cascade of water inside the hull, but it is hard to determine where this could have happened. A seaman by the name of Poingdestre saw water rush into his quarters just before the order to fill the boats was given, and this was on "E" deck, only 60 feet forward of the location where the set of doors closest to the bow were. The last sighting of Nichols is on the starboard boat deck at the time boat 1 was launched, which, we are told, was about 1.00am. It is highly likely that by the time Nichols got to "E" deck, about 40 minutes after Poingdestre's escape, that this whole area on the *Titanic* would have been flooded and he would have been unable to even reach these hatches. So what would he have done? Would he tried to open other hatches further aft? There would be no such problems with water hampering the effort towards the rear of the ship, and it would have taken mere minutes to reach them and then lever them open.

Meanwhile, orders were issued for boats to stand close by to the gangway doors...Jewell in boat 7, Pitman in boat 5, Beesley in boat 13, and Mrs.Ryerson in boat 4 heard them. Apart from this last instance, there is no mention of anyone else on the port side being hailed to remain close to the doors. An odd oversight ... unless the "plan" on the port side was merely a retrospective adoption of Murdoch's own scheme and an excuse to explain why so few were in the boats? The orders to head to the gangways were soon forgotten, or not heard (e.g. quartermaster Olliver in No.5, lookout Hogg in No.7) and the frail vessels skulked off into the darkness. If any doors were open, they would have presented a brightly lit contrast to the darkened hull, but no-one reports such a thing; boat 4 even rowed down the port side hull looking for an open door but saw nothing. Boxhall, in his 1962 revisionist interview said that when he got to the aft starboard side of the hull in boat 2, "I found that there was such a mob standing in the gangway doors, really, I daren't go alongside because if they'd jumped they'd swamp the boat. She was only a small boat, could hold about thirty five people...I daren't go along the side again, and I pulled off and laid off." No one else in the boat recalled such an event, and Pitman in boats 5 was looking at this very spot on the starboard hull; he did not think the door was open even though he had been told to "keep handy to come to the after gangway." Boxhall never mentioned being called to a gangway door in 1912, only being told to come round to the starboard side. If the doors were never really opened, what happened to Nichols? At the British Inquiry, a comment was made that the order seems to have been countermanded because "there was ground for supposing that the ship might go down rather earlier, and then, of course, the effect would have been disastrous on any boats that were engaged in taking passengers in at the gangway door."

A more prosaic explanation is possible: self preservation. Nichols had been informed very early on that the ship had just half an hour to live. Even though this is a gross underestimate, every second that was spent below decks would have increased the possibility of becoming trapped in the flooding hulk. Whether Nichols and his men were indeed somehow trapped below decks, or concealed themselves somewhere in the hope that they could fashion their own escape and not even attempting to open the doors, will never be known. After that, there is nothing. Whether he stayed on the starboard side of the ship and followed Murdoch's plan to open the gang-way doors, or he crossed over to port and was told the same thing by Lightoller will never be known.

The wreck itself offers few clues and it is difficult to determine what condition the ship was in when it slipped below the waters and what damage was inflicted upon impact with the ocean floor. The only open gangway door that can be discerned is on the port side of "D" deck, leading into the 1st class reception room. When found in 1986, it was found to be ajar and it is cited as proof that Nichols partially succeeded in his task. A concrete determination is impossible though. Logically, Nichols would probably have gone to the doors on "E" deck, which offered a better chance of disembarkation from the ship as they were close to the waterline. These doors were almost certainly inaccessible when he got there judging by Poingdestre's experiences when his quarters flooded, which was some 40 minutes earlier. Nichols then had the option of trying to open the "D" deck doors which meant straying into the taboo 1st class area (though it is arguable as to how rigidly the crew/passenger segregation would be enforced at the time) or going all the way aft to the other doors on "E" deck. All these doors were no more than a few minutes walk apart and would have taken little time from the forward "E" deck doors. The single open door on the wreck – the forward-most one in a set of two - has caused some to speculate that the sagging bow of the ship would have helped the door to open naturally, swinging freely under gravity as they were hinged on the forward edge, the same as the ones further aft. But then speculation runs amok. This door – and this door only – was opened, were are informed, because the ship's huge list to port would have enabled the hatch to swing freely open, while providing a huge handicap to those trying to force its counterpart on the other side of the ship "uphill" to be opened. But at the time Nichols and his men got to "D" deck, the list would have been negligible or non-existent. The enormous list to port did not appear till much later, certainly in time for all the hatches to be opened. In short, if this theory is true, Nichols and his men opened only one hatch – and failed to do so with any of the others. Taking the logic even further, the aft port side "E" deck hatch should have been just as easy to open. We know from witnesses that it was still closed a very short time before the end of the vessel. We must therefore ponder if the "D" deck door being open is simply an artefact of the way the ship hit the ocean floor.

That Lightoller's unilateral, and unmentioned plan to fill the flimsy craft from a much lower deck caused some consternation is evident; Mr.Peter Daly claimed that Captain Smith exclaimed, "Bring those boats back, they are only half filled!" Major Peuchen in No.6 related how, while rowing away "a sort of a whistle [was heard]...this was a call to come back to the boat." Could this have been an attempt to refill the boat with more occupants? Lightoller himself heard the captain use the megaphone to issue the "come back" order two or three times while he was superintending the forward port boats; Lightoller interpreted this as orders for the boats to be filled from hatches close to the waterline. Captain Smith was helping to load boat 8, but if he did say something about it leaving with so many vacant seats, we have no information. Certainly, when he next helped at a boat (No.2) there is a similar problem, but it is very hard to form concrete conclusions with such a dichotomy between passenger and crew estimates[5].

What of the starboard side? It has often been stated that the boats were filled with women and children, and then men were allowed in to fill the unused space. While there is some truth in this, it is far too simplistic to state this as inviolable fact. The first four boats on that side of the ship were not loaded to anywhere near their capacity, as there were very few people available to place in them. Some men escorted their loved ones to the gunwales, and then stepped away; Charles Stengel was turned away from boat 5 when it was deemed to be full and an interloper in that same boat was ordered to be put back on deck, only the immediate lowering saving him from ejection; and Washington Dodge only found sanctuary in a later boat (Mrs Dodge claimed that he refused to get in as there were women still on deck). And Jewell, in boat 7, remembered that there were instructions not to allow male passengers in the starboard, forward-most boats; this order does not seem to have been followed with any vigour though as Mrs.Bishop did not recall hearing "women first," "women and children only" or any instructions for men to stand by while she was in the vicinity. Murdoch had decided when sufficient numbers had been placed in the boats to warrant it being lowered away. On the starboard side, there were very few people left behind, and it seems that numbers on the deck were replenished as the stewards moved around the allotted quarters to waken their passengers and usher them on top. On the port side, there are stories of "many" men being left behind on the boat deck. Regarding the ladies nearby, we can make a few observation. When boat 8 on the port side departed 20 or 30 women were still on deck, and they were invited to head aft to boat 10 et al. Some of these women refused to leave their husbands, at least temporarily. At this time, the forward boat deck was almost exclusively 1st class space, and only one lady (Ida Straus) ever steadfastly refused a place without her husband. Since only 4 ladies in 1st class perished, we must deduce that the others who had refused entry presumably were coerced or changed their minds later on.

A similar analysis of the starboard boats can be performed; due to the lack of passenger data for boat 15, this set of data is omitted[6].

Boat number (in probable order of lowering)	Average crew estimate of people in boat	Average passenger estimate of people in boat
Boat 7	28 total; 12 women, 3 crew, rest men	42 total; (3 crew, 4 men)
Boat 5	39 total; about 30 women?	45 total; 8 crew, 7 men
Boat 3	34 total; 10 crew	32 total;, 8 crew
Boat 1	7 crew, 2 women, 3 men	7 crew, 2 women,3 men
Boat 9	58 total; 4 men, 8 crew	45 total
Boat 11	67 total; 10 crew, 48 women, 9 children, 2 men	58 total
Boat 13	65 total; 4 children	55 total
Boat 15	62 total; 26 women and children, 7 crew	?
Boat C	57 total; 5 crew, 6 men	49 total; 4 crew, 40 women and children

Some points should be noted; although the occupants of boat 7 were asked to count off, some did not respond. This was mentioned by Mr.Bishop, who remembered that the number "28" was sung out. Haines (No.9) was asked how many men he had in his boat, and he replied "I counted them. I guess there were about 45 to 48." This seems extremely high; the remainder of his response refers to women, and then men being allowed to fill up the empty space. Other accounts indicate only a handful of men were in the boat, so this author concludes that Haines was mistaking "men" for "women" or "total passengers". In Boat C, Rowe's evidence was far from clear. When he got to the boat initially, there 52 women and 3 children in the stern, but when the boat reached the water, there were 39 in it. This does not include 4 Chinese (or Phillipino) stowaways. Pearcey claimed the boat held an incredible 71 people, compared to its calculated capacity of 47, an absolutely impossible claim. He claims that he actually counted about 66 passengers, and these were the ones that he could actually see. Also ensconced in this boat, Ismay gave evidence that 4 male crewmen and 45 passengers were aboard. Cynics would say that he no doubt wanted "his" crew to seem as diligent as possible in loading the boats[7].

As with the port side boats, there are the inevitable deviations between what the crew and the passengers perceived. Most of the numbers are in reasonably good agreement. The discrepancies could be due to honest mistakes, genuine errors ... or aggrandizement. It is impossible to tell. If one takes the crew's estimates alone, it exceeds the number actually saved by boats under davits by well over hundred; the lack of reliable passenger estimates for some of the boats makes it impossible to determine how their numbers compares to those actually rescued.

Unlike Lightoller, Murdoch is often cited as the officer who let men into the boats where space permitted. Is this true? He was certainly eager to lower the forward starboard boats with only a fraction of their capacity occupied. What of the other boats?

Although seaman Brice said that it was loaded from "A" deck, boat 9 was undoubtedly loaded from the boat deck, the domain of 1st Officer Murdoch. It was heavily filled with women and children escorted from the crowded port side of the *Titanic*, and there was space for only a few men, and some were left behind on deck; if reports are true, they stepped back when the call for ladies and children was shouted out.

Boats 11, 13 and 15 were different altogether. They were lowered to deck "A", and it was the stewards who were responsible for loading the boat. In fact, a huge swarm of stewards, two deep, surrounded boat No.11 and only allowed women and children in. Nevertheless, a few male passengers did manage to enter the boat. Boat 13 was, again, seemingly only loaded with a few men, and Fireman Barrett did recall "The men stood all in one line when I was getting up there. I saw them standing in one line, as if at attention waiting for an order to get into the boat, against the back of the [deck] house." Abraham Hyman also noted the peculiar calm: "The women were being helped in, but the men didn't seem to want to get in. Then I noticed that it was the next to the last boat in that part of the ship. The others were all lowered, and I got a little uneasy. I climbed up onto the rail, and watching my chance, slipped into the boat just before they began to lower away. Most of the men thought they would be safer back on the [*Titanic*], and some of them smiled at us as we went down." It would seem odd if the men held back from entering boat 13, but formed themselves into a baying crowd in time for the next, and last boat in the locality, No.15[8].

Boat 15 is something of a mystery as there are so few accounts that can be reliably associated with it. George Pelham was not called to testify at either inquiry, but like all the crew, he was asked to write a deposition for the British inquisition upon arriving back in England, and his statement has survived. He recalled "40 male passengers" in the boat. A stoker by the name of Dymond was in charge, and while he does not give exact figures, 41 out of the 68 he claimed were men, either crew or passengers. Steward Nichols recalled that the order was "We can only take the women. No man is allowed to get in." Cavell was in boat 15 and also recalled that a great many women got in, with 3rd class men standing back. For these last three or four boats, great doubts remain, and stories are inconsistent about whom got in, and from where. Boat 15 is a puzzle; it may have had a lot of men in it, or it may have had a handful[9].

But one thing is certain; Murdoch may have been responsible for seeing the loading of boats 1-7 and allowed men in when space permitted, and when people were available, but for some of boats 9-15, the actual filling of the craft were mostly performed by the stewards on "A" deck, and it seems they let very few men in (boat 15 possibly excepted). The notion that Murdoch was responsible for saving all the men on the starboard side is a fallacy. How attentive was the 1st Officer in supervising the boats from the deck above? Did he order any men out of the boats less than 10 feet below? A crewman by the named of Mauge jumped into one of these boats and was nearly manhandled out by someone on "A" deck. And, if Beesley is to be believed, Murdoch did not even stay long enough to oversee the lowering of boats 13 and 15; he issued orders for the boats to stay in range of the aft gangway door, and then walked off to the starboard side (of course he may have come back after a little while, by which time Beesley was in No. 13 and did not see Murdoch; but the 1st Officer should have stayed to ensure that the ropes fore and aft were paid out correctly to prevent the boats(s) tipping up) [10].

This review highlights an unfortunate artefact of the *Titanic* and its story. Despite 100 years of testimony, letters, interviews and books from survivors, there are many unanswerable questions. Much of what happened and the numbers rescued at the aft end of the boat deck is sabotaged by our distinct lack of knowledge. Unfortunately, once we move aft from the glitterati of the forward 8 boats, it becomes very difficult to place people in certain boats. Various lifeboat passenger lists are claimed in various books, and on several websites, but these are little more than guesses, and some of them not very well educated. Many 2nd and 3rd class people are placed in boats 12-16 simply because testimony suggests that these held the most non-1st class personnel. This isn't just a matter of trivial wranglings over the minutiae of evidence; it could conceivably redevelop ideas regarding the end of the *Titanic*. But it is an impossible task. Few lifeboats had recognisable "traits" such as Hichen's tantrums (which will be discussed later); boat 13 nearly being crushed; boats 6, 8 etc. rowing off to the mystery lights of a ship on the horizon (see later); Boxhall's flares in No.2. If a witness were to mention these, assigning a person to a boat is straightforward... But what if they didn't? To the unobservant, being in boat 9 or 11 was the same as being in, say n boat 16. There isn't enough information to place people in certain boats and without that, we can't be sure of the context of their observations. To give an example, some passengers tell of stories of people being shot. There are sufficient stories in existence that make it hard to dismiss these tales as copy-selling mirages of the press. What if it could be proved that some of these reports could be attributed not to a boat that was lowered at the last minute, when panic and the use of a firearm would be logical, but to an earlier boat, such as boat 16, about which we know very little? Did the crowd in the area fuel a panic amongst the officers? If they did, the surviving officers never said anything. Perhaps passenger corroboration could help - but one looks in vain for anyone who can definitively be tied to this, or to any of the other of the non-celebrated boats. It is understandable that saving one's life

91

was far more important than inquiring about a boat number. With so little data it seems foolish to crowbar a personal account into a particular craft simply to satisfy one's own theories.

To reinforce this point, let us examine just one example, that of Daniel Buckley who was fortunately questioned at the U.S. Inquiry; his comments therefore cannot be attributed to press hyperbole or manufacture. I have placed in parentheses what boats portion of his testimony could refer to:
"When the sixth lifeboat was prepared, there was a big crowd of men standing on the deck. And they all jumped in. [There was a crowd of men inside boat 2 when it came time to fill it.] So I said I would take my chance with them. I went into the boat. Then two officers came along and said all of the men could come out. And they brought a lot of steerage passengers with them; and they were mixed, every way, ladies and gentlemen. [Could this refer to the story of steerage passengers that steward Hart allegedly placed at boats 8 and 15?] And they said all the men could get out and let the ladies in. But six men were left in the boat. I think they were firemen and sailors. I was crying. There was a woman in the boat, and she had thrown her shawl over me, and she told me to stay in there [Mary Glynn said that a man masquerading as a women was in No.13, and in No.14, Lowe found a similar person]... Then they did not see me, and the boat was lowered down into the water, and we rowed away out from the steamer. The men that were in the boat at first fought, and would not get out, but the officers drew their revolvers, and fired shots over our heads, and then the men got out [Shots were fired at boats 14, "C", "D" and possibly "A"]. When the boat was ready, we were lowered down into the water and rowed away out from the steamer. We were only about 15 minutes out when she sank [Boat "D"?]." In a letter to his mother, Buckley says that he was in the third boat lowered, and that there were 40 men in it. This could refer to one of the forward starboard boats but the use of gunfire dissuades us from this conclusion; or perhaps he was in boat 15, whose male occupancy number is disputed.

Buckley's account does not describe any boat that we know of. It seems ludicrous to suggest that he was mistaken. The spectre of doubt appears here; perhaps the experts who pontificate about who was in which boat do not know as much as they like to suggest. Perhaps false testimony was given. It is unlikely that we will definitely know. The simplest matter therefore is to disregard the evidence that does not fit as an aberration, since there is no way to reconcile such troubling testimony with our firmly established knowledge. None of Buckley's observations match any one boat. And if his recollections are true, why do others not speak of similar events in their own accounts? The crew, it is posited, could be relied upon for their silence if they wanted to work for the White Star Line and its associate companies again...and not all passengers gave accounts of their own escape. If Buckley gave an account of, for instance, boat "D"'s departure, then the chances of the people on deck surviving to relate their tales were tiny indeed given that the only ones to escape were the very few who clambered onto swamped and overturned boats[11].

The lifeboats of legend were woefully undermanned. The reality is that the ones towards the stern were more heavily loaded than their counterparts at the bow. But it is subjective; one man's "half empty" boat could be another man's "filled" boat.

Norman Chambers in boat 5 wrote that, he was "in a lifeboat which the Board of Trade registers as having a capacity of sixty people, and we were crowded, our boat being just manageable" with 3 or 4 having to stand in the middle of the boat; he placed 35 to 38 in the craft. Crewman Ward recalled that his boat, No.9, was "a full boat ... We had not room to pull the oars. [The people] had to move their bodies with us when we were rowing." In boat 11, claimed as the most overloaded boat, Wheelton said, that they "Had difficulty rowing because the passengers were so close together." In boat 13, Barrett related how people had to sit six on a thwart, and there are again reports of people having to stand. Samuel Goldenberg chaired a committee of survivors and part of their formal statement reads, "The board of trade rules allow for entirely too many people in each boat to permit the same to be properly handled."[12][13]

How does one reconcile these observations with the recollections of Dr.Washington Dodge, who wrote of the starboard boats, "not a boat was launched which would not held from ten to twenty five more person." How many could occupy a boat? The regulations on this point were clear; for a main lifeboat, a mathematical forumula provided an answer of 65 people. A further practical test was then performed to determine the number without compromising the stability of the boat or affecting the work of the oarsmen. This reduced the number slightly to 64. This still seems like an overestimate. Researcher David Gittins writes that, under modern SOLAS (Safety of Life At Sea) rules, occupants of a boat would be required to sit on the thwarts, which amounts to just 24 people. If one is flexible and allows seating around the edge, one can add another 10 people. To add anymore implies that people would have to do what was indeed reported that night - they stood, for hours on end, in the spaces between the thwarts. Alas we do not know for sure how overfilled some lifeboats were; as noted above, with the weight of 66 men and 4 oars, the freeboard was found to be 2 feet 3 inches. Barrett in boat 13 said his freeboard was half a foot. Notwithstanding Dodge's opinion, anyone seeing a lifeboat with about 30 or 40 people would think that the boat was full, and that all seating space was occupied[14].

And what of the potential crew for the boats: were the boats undermanned? Lightoller's idea was 2 crewmen to a boat, whether this meant using seamen, or substitutes (such as stewards), and two to lower the boat. His plan went awry with the claimed disappearance of the boatswain and 6 seamen. Even Peuchen noticed on deck that there seemed to be a lack of sailors at their posts, ready to man the boats; possibly the men had gone below to try and open the gangway doors. Steward Fred Ray's recollection, cited elsewhere, puts boat 9 very close to boat 7's departure time. Were there enough to man the boats? How much time elapsed between these two boats? The most respected analysis of the boats and their launch times can be found on Bill Wormstedt's website, but it has an interesting peculiarity; a large gap between the first boat on the starboard side and boat 9 (50 minutes), and boat 1 and No.9 (25 minutes). But Ray's evidence indicates a much shorter gap, perhaps 20 minutes or less during which time he returned to his quarters, fetched his coat and returned after a brief conversation with a passenger. Why so large a hiatus? One suggestion, if this gap is not due to an artefact of the analysis, is that there were insufficient men for the starboard boats; between the first four on the starboard side and the aft quartet, some of the port side craft had been lowered and men were needed for these boats[15].

The Deck crew muster lists 59 people who are listed as officers, seamen (able or otherwise), quartermasters and lookouts who could conceivably have the skills to prepare a boat for launch. Based on a discussion at the British Inquiry, where it was mentioned that the carpenter (and presumably joiner), boatswain (and his mate) and the lamp trimmer may be regarded as able bodied seamen, I have included them in this number (indeed, it was concluded that even cooks and stewards may qualify if they can prove that they had served as able bodied seamen.) Also included are the two Masters-At-Arms[16].

Based on these fairly flexible criteria, at the U.S. Inquiry 83 sailors were tallied as being on board; Lightoller said 71. Some "non-sailor" crewmen, such as Hendrickson, also claimed to have the necessary skills to prepare a boat for lowering[17].

If we take just this bare number of 59 we can perform some analysis: out of these, Hogg, Jewell and Weller departed in No.7, Olliver in No.5, Moore in No.3, Jones in No.8, Symons and Horswell in No.1 and Fleet and Hichens in No.6. Thus, after 6 boats, there are 10 sailors unavailable. Quartermasters Rowe and Bright were at the bridge, firing rockets. In Boat 16, we have Bailey, Archer and his "mate", in 14 there was Scarrott, and in 12, there were Clench and Poingdestre. This removes another 8 from our possible roster. Pitman and Lowe were seconded to boats, so we neglect them from our study. From the remaining 39, we must remove the boatswain and 6 men that were sent to open the hatches and were never seen again.

How many were seconded from other boats to assist with the boats on the aft port side, thus removing them from being able to help on the aft starboard side? Of the ones we know of, Archer had been ordered by "an officer" to help after assisting at the forward starboard side. Clench was seconded to number 16 while he was unlacing number 11. Evans assisted with the forward starboard boats, including number 1, before heading off to boat 12.

This removes one seaman from the total, as we have already taken account of Archer and Clench. While boats 12, 14 and 16 were descending, which seem to have occurred within minutes of each other, they would have needed 6 men, two at each davit to pay out the falls.

If the men who were tasked in lowering boats 12-16 were reallocated (and we know at least one – Paddy McGough – was, as he lowered boat 14 and then left in 9), we are now reduced to 31 men; enough for boats 9, 11, 13 and 15 to have been lowered simultaneously or sequentially, utilising the same crew for each boat. Of course, we do not know what all the qualified seamen did as not all were interrogated at the enquires; and even when they were, they may have inadvertently omitted some of their activities. We don't have a complete picture, and all it would require is that this number drop by a handful to force a painful conclusion: that the mighty *Titanic* was running out of men to assist with the boats. Having said this, Murdoch placed firemen in charge of 13 and 15 rather than the more usual seamen, quartermasters etc. so there may have been a local shortage of seamen with these two boats , even though lookout Lee and two other sailors were in boat 13. Concrete conclusions seem difficult to determine. But we do know that boat 9 had 4 seamen on board, boat 11 had 2 and boat 13 had 3. If we deduct these 9, and the six men left on deck to lower boats 11, 13 and 15 (the men responsible for boat 9's lowering could have entered later boats; it is impossible to tell), we have 16 men left. How many were still left on the port side of the ship to attend to the unloaded boats there, or boat "C" still on the starboard side? It may very well be that when 15 departed, there were no seamen locally available to man it; the crew seems to consist of members of the 'black gang' and stewards.

On balance, it seems unlikely that the aft starboard boats had to wait for crew to become freed from their task on the port side. And if one takes Lightoller's or the U.S. Inquiry's numbers, there were ample seamen available. What about passengers to fill the boat? Thomas Cardeza stated that Murdoch was ordering people aft, and that the first officer said people had "a better chance" at the aft boats that at the forward ones, which were then being filled; why Murdoch was ordering people away from unoccupied boats is curious. Norman Chambers also observed people being direct to the rear. However, Cardeza did head to the rear of the boat deck but soon returned when he and his entourage saw such a crowd that he didn't think they had a chance of finding refuge in a boat. The numbers in boat 9 would be bolstered by crewmen who directed people from the port side after the departure of most of the the aft boats on that that side. Curiously, as mentioned elsewhere, the loading of this boat was far more discriminate, with fewer men and more overall people on board.

So, why is there a claimed 25- and 50- minute gap? A closer inspection of the timing of the boats may suggest an answer; if the lifeboats, particularly the four on the aft port area were launched closer together, and the arbitrary 5 or 10 minute time between boats 7,5,3 and 1 were reduced, the duration between these four and boat 9 becomes, in this author's opinion, more manageable. Dr.Dodge's observations may be illuminating; after observing his wife and child leave in boat 5, "during the ensuing half or three quarters of an hour", he watched the boats on the starboard side as they were successively filled and lowered away. He eventually found himself at boat 13. Steward Walter Nichols noted that it took twenty minutes to lower his boat - number 15 - and get away. Boats 13 and 15 were almost instantaneously launched. If we take Dodge's 30-45 minute estimate and take away 20 minutes from Nichol's statement, we are left with 10-25 minutes, and if one further incorporates the time taken to launch boats 3, 1, 9 and 11, then we are left with a more palatable time. Although this requires an estimate of the time required to fill and lower the boats, the gap could be reduced to just a few minutes rather than a colossal 25 to 50 minute duration which seems implausible.

The only alternative is that, for a time span of 25 minutes, the entire operation of lifeboat launching on the starboard side completely ceased. There is no evidence that boat 9 was delayed because there were not enough women to be found to fill the boat. Boat 9 did leave with a rather large complement, but Murdoch had just come from boat 1 which had the smallest complement of any boat that night. There is no reason why he should not have done the same at boat 9 if sufficient personnel did not present themselves.

Extending the above work further, how many seamen were left on board the *Titanic* at the very end? After the very last of the aft starboard boats departed, we have about 22 left aboard. Boats 10, 4, 2, "C" and "D" remained, and these left, respectively, with 2, 2 (not including Jack Foley, a storekeeper), 2, 1 and 2. However this includes Rowe and Bright who had already been removed from our total. Taking into account this small correction, we have a total of 15 remaining, which includes the 5 officers left on board. The report of the British Inquiry proclaimed that "Very few of the deck hands were left in the ship, as they had nearly all gone to man the lifeboats, and the stewards and firemen were unaccustomed to work the collapsible boats." But the raw numbers indicated that there were enough seamen available. Certainly, when "D" was being sent off, there were so few seamen available that Lightoller himself had to man one of the falls; by this time, 2 men were working at the davits of boat "C" on the opposite side of the bridge. There must have been some seamen available because, when boat "A" landed on the boat deck, a voice from the roof of the officer's quarters yelled "Are there any seamen among you?" A positive answer was received, and according to Colonel Gracie, "quite a number left the boat deck" to assist in the preparations for boat "B". Whether this unspecified number of seamen was sufficient is open to debate, as 3rd class passenger Olaus Abelseth recalled an officer walk by him and his companions asking "Are there any sailors here?" Abelseth thought that the officer was seeking seamen to help with the collapsibles. It may also be worthwhile mentioning seaman Lucas, who departed in boat "D". He says that at the very end, eight sailors were left on board, and they had instructions to do nothing but stand by the boats and lower. If this is so, why did Lightoller feel the need to man the falls? And how many of the eight as seen by Lucas wound up on the starboard side to help with "A" before being summoned away, as heard by Gracie? This makes an accurate determination very difficult. Confounding the issue are the recollections of Mr. and Mrs. Hoyt. A rush by steerage prompted Wilde to wave his gun at the mob, and Mrs Hoyt was placed in the boat but there was a "sudden list" during the descent and the crew left them hanging in mid-air and ran to the other side of the deck "to save themselves" (or perhaps they went to assist with other boats on the starboard side?). In the meantime, Mr. Hoyt had conversed with the Captain who advised him to go to a lower deck as the boats might return to the ship. Hoyt went down, and found his wife's boat still dangling. He jumped into the sea. Meanwhile, the boat had resumed lowering and eventually came across Mr.Hoyt who was saved (his namesake, a rotund character picked up by boat 14, perished after being plucked from the water.)

In addition to the supposed lack of seamen, there is some indication that the crew did not know where to go. Assigned a boat station, and their name placed on a list, quite a few wound up anywhere. Sometimes this was due to ignorance; for example, George Beauchamp and Fred Barrett, both stokers (a breed of men unresponsive to taking part in boat drills we were later told at the Inquiries) did not trouble themselves to look at the list. Of those who did look, there are some interesting examples. Wilfred Seward knew his assigned boat was No.3 but having seen that no-one was being put into it, he went to No.5, eventually leaving in the "correct" boat. Alfred Shiers was also allocated a place in No.3 but left in No.5. Frank Morris knew his boat was No.16, but got in No.14. Charles Joughin was supposed to be the commander of boat 10 but missed his spot when that boat was deemed to be full, even though he was standing practically next to it. William Lucas was supposed to assist at boat 1 but helped with boats 2, 4, 6 and then went "right aft" and later found himself in "D", or the opposite side of the ship to which he should have been working. This confusion was not confined to seamen, stewards and so on, but permeated the officers too. Boxhall and Pitman both claimed that they were in charge of boat No.1, while Lowe professed that he simply did not know his station.

Aside from the issue of available manpower, how well were the boats equipped? They were, we are told (and as discussed elsewhere) loaded with provisions of water and biscuits. But what of the legally vital necessity of lamps? The earlier mention of Nichols and his "ship has half an hour to live" imperative brings us to the story of Lamp Trimmer Hemming, another one privy to the projected life expectancy of this ship. Concerned about the lack of lighting in the boats, Lamp Trimmer Samuel Hemming was instructed by the captain to fetch the lamps from below the forecastle and to distribute them to the boats. He claims to have brought up 14, four at a time, all lit and full of oil. He passed them on to the lifeboats on the port side that had not already departed, and also to some of the starboard ones. Hemming recalled passing them to someone in the boat himself, or putting them on the deck so that they could be lowered down the falls to boats already deployed.

Idle speculation leads to dubious conclusions. But a few important points can be deduced; Apart from the first five port side lifeboats[18] (with the exception of lifeboat 4 which had been lowered level with "A" deck and was, for the moment, inaccessible), not one of the lifeboats had a lamp within it. Crawford says that Hemming came along with a handful of lamps "long before" boat 8 departed (which was one of the first) and he saw him distributing them to other boats. Horswell claims to have put a lantern in boat 1, but no-one else recalls seeing it, lit or otherwise. It should already have had a lamp put into it at dusk. He also said that he had placed a lamp and a chronometer in boat 2; steward James Johnson also described the lamp before this boat left; "An officer [Boxhall] got into the boat afterwards. This man [Boxhall?] handed me a lamp out of the boat. I saw a lamp standing on the deck. It was ready-lit. I said, "It will be all right for us," so I stowed it in there." Why did Boxhall give him one that was already in the boat? Was it because the original lamp in there had depleted its fuel? Lamps were supposed to have enough oil to burn for 8 hours.

Many occupants of the boats searched for lamps, but none were found. Hemming was not seen to approach or hand out any lamps apart from at the forward port section of the *Titanic*. And of those who did get a lamp, many found it to be worthless, with very little oil to provide illumination. What was Hemming doing? He certainly did not deliver his lamps to any other boats. The trip to the Lamp Trimmer's store and back would take about 10 minutes (including the time taken for a lamp to be filled with oil and lit), and the likelihood is that he could have found himself drowning inside the capacious, dying hulk of the *Titanic* while performing his duty, if the ship had only half an hour to live, as he was told; this estimate of the ship's lifespan had come from Andrews, an authoritative source and could be trusted. If Hemming decided to secrete himself on the deck, thus disobeying orders, rather than risk being trapped below decks, we now have an explanation as to why he never delivered the lamps to the majority of boats, for he never went to retrieve many of the lights.

Hemming's testimony is not the only occasion when one suspects that disinformation is being ladled out. Sometimes, when perusing the inquiry transcripts, one wishes that the interviewees showed more candour. Take for instance, the incident of boat 16; Seaman Archer and steward Andrews were questioned on the same day in America and portions of their statements read like clones of one another: they were instructed not to allow any more people just before their boat was lowered. They both saw no confusion, panic or effort by anyone to gain unauthorised access to the boat. Everything was quiet. Compare this to boat 14, right next to No.16; the crewman at the tiller had to physically eject one man and repel other potential invading men. When boat 14 was lowered, Officer Lowe had to fire shots to ward off the crowd. Boat 14 and 16 left at practically the same time, and while steward Morris said that the mob was at his boat, No.14, and "not 16", one wishes that Archer and Andrews had volunteered the fact that there had been a scrummage, albeit not at their boat, but only a few feet away and no doubt visible to them[19].

How does one cope with these conflicts? It is unpleasant to label people as liars, but the strong impression is that the truth is an evasive commodity in these stories. Another one who presented dubious evidence was Fireman Hendrickson; he says that, at the aft port boats, "everything was very quiet, as if nothing had happened." He witnessed people getting into boats in the vicinity of his own (No.12) and spent "somewhere about three-quarters of an hour or an hour" lowering about five boats, before heading off to boat No.1. Officer Lowe helped at boat 1, and later escaped in boat 14, which establishes some form of chronology, as boats 12, 14 and 16 departed at practically the same time; and yet Hendrickson says that he helped to lower the aft port side boats before No.1. Perhaps Hendrickson meant to say that the boats were lowered level with the boat deck but he did not stay long enough to see them actually lowered to the water. If he had, he would have seen an unruly crowd and heard gunshots. Hardly the same as "everything was very quiet."

And so, at 2.05am, with all the boats that had been placed under davits rowing away, we have the noble and gallant vision of 1st class men mingled with those of the lower classes, ready to meet their fate. Refusing, or refused a space in a boat, the gentry would now face doom with the plebeians. But how much chivalry did the men who had been turned away display? How many accepted their fate, and how many wanted to survive? If we knew this one could argue that those who stepped back from the boats after loading their wives simply were not concerned about escaping, and that they would have perished anyway. Indeed, there are cases in the forward boats of men doing this. They had no desire to step into a boat even if they hadn't been debarred. But, in the case of the "women and children only" order, if many found their way into later boats, then it would give a strong indication that Lightoller and Wilde had decided arbitrarily who was to live and who was to die and allows us to quantify those who didn't meekly want to accept the inevitable. It is a difficult analysis as we know so little about how the 2nd and 3rd class men fared; if they were rebuffed, did they then try to enter boats on the other side of the ship, their efforts unrecorded by history? 1st class passengers are generally better represented by the data. We find only three cases of 1st class men who escaped in later boats; Messrs. Stengel, Dodge and Carter; but we must note that Dr.Dodge was pushed into a boat by his table steward. 1st class passenger Colonel Astor asked to enter a boat to comfort his pregnant wife, and he was refused; he did not try to re-enter another. Even after the ominous tilting of the bow, even after the sound of gun shots, even after the rockets exploding overheard, most 1st class men left on the decks had decided not to escape even if it meant seeking other boats.

The most tragic aspect of the foundering of the great ship is the thought that exists to this day, that given enough boats, everyone could have been rescued. It took well over an hour to launch 18 boats, and save about 670 people. With due reverence to those that night, the loading operation was neither efficient nor well planned, and about 400 spaces in the boats were wasted. It has been argued that the *Titanic* needed time to have saved 2200 people, but it also needed discipline by the crew...and both of these were lacking. This will be explored in detail later.

Mrs.Warren's statement seems to have a certain truth, when she writes of the situation when the first two boats were launched; "There seemed to be a sort of aimless confusion and an utter lack of organized effort." It seems to be a general testament to the effort of the crew that night. Some did their best, but the uncompromising conclusion is that about 400 places in lifeboats were squandered.

Titanic Interlude

Left To Die?

Most of us will have seen James Cameron's 1997 film; in that vision of the disaster, the 3rd class areas were festooned with slatted gates, called "Bostwick Gates," which isolated the steerage from the more palatial areas. But the reality is very different; when one inspects the *Titanic*'s plans, only five can be found. The first one was at a set of stairs that led up to "E" deck and thence to the 3rd class open space (a "common room") on "D" deck near the bow[1]; the second was further aft and sectioned off a corridor near the area reserved for washing potatoes. This corridor sported two staircases; going up, one would emerge near the baker's shop[2]; going down, one would eventually emerge near the stores on "G" deck. The last three gates were used to prevent any unwary personnel from falling down the shaft used to hoist goods from deck to deck.

With the fantasy that 3rd class were locked behind fictitious gates discredited, are there any genuine examples of the class hierarchy in play on the night of April 14th, a hierarchy that would give preferential treatment to the more refined passengers?

Neither the British nor the U.S. Inquiries found any evidence of class distinction. The inquisitors in America only interrogated three male steerage passengers, whereas the British equivalent did not interview any; for the most part, all of its survivor's testimony derived from members of the crew with three exceptions (Ismay being one of them). The British took testimony from two stewards who insisted that they had been part of a team that had escorted the steerage to the upper decks, and this was enough to clear the crew of any nefarious misdemeanours.

How then does one describe the survival rate for 3rd class? Taking the British Inquiry statistics, 140 out of 144 1st class women were saved, and 5 out of 6 children. In 2nd class, 80 out of 93 women and all 24 children were rescued. In 3rd class this drops shockingly to only 76 out of 165 women, and 27 out of 79 children[3]. Taking the men, 57 out of 175 1st class were saved, 14 out of 168 in 2nd class, and 75 out of 462

3rd class. Second class men fared very badly, whereas more men in 3rd class were saved than in 1st class. The shocking statistic is that despite the "women and children first" mentality, 3rd class ladies and their offspring are particularly badly represented.

Why was this? Did the geography of the ship thwart the 3rd class evacuation? The 1st class cabins were centrally located and directly below the boat deck, allowing for easy access. The 3rd class were located much further down, at the bow and stern of the *Titanic* and while this sounds as if the layout was designed to obstruct them in any escape, emergency doors were sprinkled throughout their quarters to enable the steerage to head aloft to the boats. While the allocation of cabin numbers to specific 3rd class passengers is almost non existent, we do know that single men were stationed at the bow, and single women and families at the stern. What is interesting is that the 3rd class men would be the first to know the severity of the drama, and indeed, quite a few stepped from their beds into water that was dribbling under the door into their rooms. This author has counted 389 single men that were potentially stationed at the bow; researcher David Gleicher provides a figure of 402, plus an additional 36, or 18 childless couples in the bow area. 1st class were slower to react as their cabins were higher up in the ship, and it is only when water threatened to impinge upon their areas (the rising water in the mail rooms that spilled out on to "E" deck) that anyone knew of any problem.

Let us start our assessment of the discrimination question with the three men questioned in America, starting with Daniel Buckley. The relevant part of his story is as follows: jumping from his bunk into icy water, he failed in his attempt to instil any sense of alarm in his room-mates. Leaving his room, "Two sailors came along, and they were shouting: "All up on deck! unless you want to get drowned." ... They tried to keep us down at first on our steerage deck. They did not want us to go up to the 1st class place at all...There was one steerage passenger there, and he was getting up the steps, and just as he was going in a little gate a fellow came along and chucked him down; threw him down into the steerage place. This fellow got excited, and he ran after him, and he could not find him. He got up over the little gate. He did not find him. [The gate] was not locked at the time we made the attempt to get up there, but the sailor, or whoever he was, locked it. So that this fellow that went up after him broke the lock on it, and he went after the fellow that threw him down. He said if he could get hold of him he would throw him into the ocean." It should be noted that the "gate" referred to by Buckley was not a Bostwick Gate, but one that only extended to waist height, one of many that peppered the outer decks to prevent unwanted intrusions of the lower classes into the domain of the gentry[4].

The second 3rd class man to face interrogation in America was Olaus Abelseth. He was awoken and went up on deck, where he saw ice. An "officer" informed him that there was no danger, but Abelseth was not satisfied. He roused his sister and brother-in-law and they headed aft, eventually arriving on the hind quarter of the ship. He noticed an interesting sight: "There were a lot of steerage people there that were getting on one of these cranes that they had on deck, that they used to lift things with. They can lift about two and a half tons, I believe. These steerage passengers were crawling along on this, over the railing, and away up to the boat deck. A lot of them were doing that... [the gate] was shut ... so they could not go up that way. A while later these girls were standing there, and one of the officers came and hollered for all of the ladies to come up on the boat deck. The gate was opened and these two girls went up. We stayed a little while longer, and then they said, "Everybody." I do not know who that was, but I think it was some of the officers that said it. I could not say that, but it was somebody that said "everybody." We went up." They managed to get to the port side of the boat deck where only one or two boats were left.

The third man to offer testimony was Berk Pickard, and he was one of the rarities; a single man with a berth in the mixed accommodation aft: "The only warning given to the steerage passengers after the collision was that we were ordered to take our lifebelts and go to the deck. I wanted to go back to get my things but I could not. The stewards would not allow us to go back. They made us all go forward on the deck. There were no doors locked to prevent us from going back. I did not take much notice of it, and I went to the deck. The other passengers started in arguing. One said that it was dangerous and the other said that it was not; one said white and the other said black. Instead of arguing with those people, I instantly went to the highest spot. I went and I found the door. There are always a few steps from this 3rd class, with a movable door, and it is marked there 2nd class passengers have no right to penetrate there. I found this door open so that I could go into the 2nd class, where I did not find any people, only a few that climbed on the ladder and went into the 1st class, which I did." His use of the word "ladder" is interesting, and is a point to which we shall return.

Astonishingly, when asked about allegations of discrimination; the three were unanimous. They didn't think there had been any!

Buckley said, "I think [the 3rd class] had as good a chance as the 1st and 2nd class passengers... at the start they tried to keep them down on their own deck...All the steerage passengers went up on the 1st class deck at this time, when the gate was broken. They all got up there. They could not keep them down." Abelseth said, "I think [the steerage] had an opportunity to get up." He elaborated by saying that no-one was restrained below, and there were no gates or doors locked as far as he could see. Pickard related, "The steerage passengers, so far as I could see, were not prevented from getting up to the upper decks by anybody, or by closed doors, or anything else."

This is astonishing; Pickard's statements are understandable as he did not encounter any obstacles, but the observations of Abelseth and Buckley - particularly Buckley - prove that there was some attempt at segregation. One commentator has gone so far as to suggest that steerage expectations were so low, it was "enough" to be given a lifejacket. This is slightly comical. Perhaps, 1912 values were different from today: survivors and newspapers often referred to Captain Smith as a "hero" when it was his negligent navigation that had caused such horrendous casualties!

Apart from these three, can we glean any hints of discrimination from private letters, interviews or newspaper articles? The answer is yes.

For the most part, the majority of 3rd class accounts that this author has seen are nondescript; there is no more elaboration of the route up other than "we went on deck ... and entered a boat"; men woke up and seemed to head to the aft space of their own volition; confused passengers awoke but were placated by stewards who told them that nothing was amiss and that they should go back to sleep. Lest any ulterior meaning be conveyed by this last statement, it should be noted that the same thing was happening in 1st and 2nd class; people emerging from their cabins were told not to be alarmed by uninformed stewards, and told to go back to bed.

But after appearing on their promenade decks, the steerage did experience behaviour that confirm Buckley's and Abelseth's statements. Take Margaret Devaney for instance: "the doors leading to the other decks were closed on us and we had to climb up ladders to the boat deck." Mary Glynn reckoned that, just twenty minutes before the boat went down stewards ran through the steerage shouting orders for all passengers to go on deck. There was no time for those who had neglected to even clothe themselves. The passengers swarmed to the companionway leading to the upper decks, but were held back by "officers", who said things were not ready. John Bourke and Patrick Canavan knew there was a ladder leading to the upper decks and gathering the women and girls about them they started for it. Annie Kelly owed her life to a friendly steward who implored her, 'All hands on deck. For God's sake, hurry if you would have a chance for your lives.' Kelly tells us that "they went [up]..The first thing they saw was the people being held back from going up the stairs to the second deck....they held them down to the last moment. About half an hour before the [*Titanic*] went down was the time they called the Burkes [sic - Bourkes] and the others from their berths." And here it was that the steward to whom Annie Kelly had been talking so often saw her running with her companions towards the ladder that went up to the second class deck, as the crew they were not letting the steerage passengers up the stairway. Kelly's friendly steward took her by the hand and ran her up the stairs without anyone stopping him. Confusing, she then says they were then "letting all the people up the stairs" implying that the attempt to hold the steerage back was only a transient measure, similar to that observed by Abelseth. Margaret Murphy later said, "sailors were beating back the steerage passengers...A crowd of men were trying to get up to a higher deck and were fighting the sailors...Then the sailors fastened down the hatchways leading to the 3rd class section. They said they wanted the air down there so the vessel would stay up longer." Ellen Shine stated, "people rushed to the upper deck where they were met by members of the crew who endeavoured to keep them in steerage quarters."

Katherine Gilnagh gave an account of her passage to the decks to author Walter Lord in 1955. Although it should be read with the caveat that memories could have been reshaped or confabulated over time, it is informative to compare this to Buckley's account: "Every one was just waiting around. News came that the boats were being lowered, but when she and the girls tried to go up to them, a man stopped her at the 3rd class barrier and wouldn't open the gate. They were still standing there, when Jim Farrell came up. "Great God, man!" he roared, "Open the gate and let the girls through!" To the girl's surprise, the man did then open the gate, and Kate slipped through to the 2nd class deck. Her troubles weren't over, because she still couldn't figure how to get up to the 1st class Deck, where the boats were. The 2nd class deck was now deserted, except for a single man standing all alone. He offered to let her stand on his shoulders and climb up onto "A" deck that way. She accepted the invitation and soon scrambled over the rail above and onto "A" Deck."[5] Anna Sjoblom was also one of those interrogated by Lord in 1955; "The stairway was closed. It seems that those in charge were sure that the

106

ship would be saved, and I suppose did not think it best to have more people above than necessary. ..I got talking to a young Swedish girl who was with two friends ... They knew about an emergency stairway and showed us where it was and so that is how I got up to where the life boats were; the girl too"

The stories described here apply to those who tried to leave the well decks, and head further up. There doesn't seem to have been any hindrance of the steerage getting up to the aft well deck, as there were no gates that could block one's passage. Indeed, the well decks were 3rd class territory. For the families and ladies at the stern, all one had to do was ascend the main 3rd class stairway and emerge from underneath the poop deck. The geography was fairly simple. But what happened to the men sectioned in the bow? When one examines their movements, one concludes that the steerage men acted surprisingly promptly to extricate themselves from their slowly flooding quarters.

Within minutes of the collision, many of the steerage men decided to head aft, most of them seemingly of their own accord. Fireman Charles Hendrickson was below decks soon after the collision, and he saw a large number of 3rd class men walking along the alleyway. They were seen by several people, and their descriptions tally; they were dragging their bags, boxes and "portmanteaux", and some witnesses described them as being wet. Stewards were there, guiding them aft, but still there was some confusion: Hendrickson described some of the steerage walking to and fro, sitting on their luggage. Obviously some didn't know what to do. Were they waiting for instructions? A possibility. It seems unlikely that the steerage had become lost, as they would have had to traverse this alleyway regularly to get to their dining room (in the middle portion of the *Titanic*), or to their smoking and general room, located all the way aft. They would have known the route.

A detailed analysis of Hendrickson's account put this sighting of the steerage within the first 15 minutes of the impact. How long did they remain there? There is scant evidence, but certainly fireman Cavell's claim that he saw them 1½ to 2 hours after the collision is wrong; the front portion of the alleyway would be flooded and so would any steerage accommodation forward of this. There is evidence that well before this 1½ to 2 hour period, the 3rd class passengers had left the alleyway, and they seemed to have headed aft into the mixed accommodation at the stern, and where the stairs to the deck were to be found. Baker Joughin also noticed this huge swarm of 3rd class, slightly aft of the emergency door into 2nd class; Muller, the interpreter, and two or three stewards were also there. Joughin's estimate of the time was between 12.15am and 12.30am. Steerage passenger Mary Coutts noticed "foreigners carrying all their belongings - rugs, blankets, and even small trunks - up on deck." She was located two decks below the well deck and everything was quiet when the procession had cleared. She was left standing alone in the corridor for quite a long time, with only the soothing words from others telling her that there was no danger to satisfy her. Gunnar Tenglin also describes a similar scene of the steerage exodus from forwards; "[the] Italians were greatly excited. They were swarming up on deck, in all stages of undress, carrying baggage of every description." August Wennerstrom had reason to remember them; he and companions were dancing to piano accompaniment in the 3rd class area under the poop deck when 50 "Italian" emigrants came in, carrying their bundles (the main 3rd class stairway was just outside the smoking room); "They acted like they were crazy - jumping and calling on their 'Madonna'. We made a circle around them and started a ring dance around them." Incidentally, David Gleicher informs us that there were only two steerage Italian men! [6][7]

Evidently, other men took the most direct route to the upper decks. Rather than heading aft, they walked up the stairs from their berths, past the 3rd class common room and emerged on the forward well deck. They were seen by seaman John Poigndestre about 40 minutes after the crash, as he headed back up to the boat deck from his own berth. Poigndestre noticed 50 to 100 steerage men, with 3rd class stewards intermingled, talking with them[8]. Back on the deck, Poigndestre heard the order to start placing women and children in the boats which provides us with some indication as to when his sighting of the steerage took place.

Both Poigndestre and Joughin talked of stewards mingling with the steerage, and others speak of the 3rd class men being guided aft along the alleyway. But in general, what were the crew doing to help the steerage? Few members of the ship's complement in the steerage area survived and only two were called to the inquiries.

Albert Pearcey, a 3rd class pantryman, was one of them; soon after the impact, he claims to have assisted 3rd class men from their forward rooms along the alleyway, where they were guided through an open emergency door into 1st class, and then up the Grand Staircase, to the boat deck ... and to potential safety.

There are inherent problems with Pearcey; he claims to have

remained at his post forward until there were no more steerage passengers to be seen. He appeared on the boat deck at nearly 1.30am, a time that can be established by the fact that he was in a lifeboat ("C") minutes later when a passenger remarked upon the time: 1.40am. However, this time is indisputably wrong, and it seems that the passenger was one of the few to have retarded their clocks by 20 minutes to account for westward travel; the proper time would be slightly after 2.00am. If steward Ray's evidence is correct, the water on "E" deck was already up to the level of the doorway through which the passengers were passed at the time of the first boat departure, an hour or more before Pearcey's own escape. AB seaman Poingdestre testified that the forward section of "E" deck was flooded to waist height when he went down at about 12.20am, a claim that is borne out by an analysis of the water rising up through the cargo holds and spilling out onto that deck. The forward steerage quarters would long since been vacated and under water … and Pearcey claimed to have stayed at his post for over an hour until he was sure no more men were coming through from that area. Then we have Emily Ryerson's account from boat No.4, which was launched soon before "C"; she noticed that deck "A" was only about 20 feet above the water, and that it was pouring through open ports, which would be at least deck "C". By this time, "E" deck forward would be flooded. It is a shame that Pearcey was not asked about the route he personally took to the boat deck, and whether he went up the Grand Staircase, or using the crew's service stairs which were further aft. Then we have negative evidence from the 1st class passengers. Woken by the curiosity of a "bump" or a "grinding noise" and then the cessation of movement, many ascended the Grand Staircase to ascertain the situation before returning below decks. Shortly thereafter the evacuation orders were issued and at many dozens of 1st class passengers climbed up the decks, hindered by the lack of elevators; Norman Chambers even went up twice, from his berth on "E" deck. And not one 1st class passenger or steward meandering through the companionways and passageways saw a single steerage passenger either ascend these stairs, loiter on a deck, or wait to embark in one of the lifeboats that were close to the staircase lobby. If the 3rd class men had emerged on deck, rather than wait to enter one of these enticing boats directly in front of them, they had dispersed when it came time to load the craft. Only one steerage man entered one of these forward boats where the steerage men would have emerged; a boy with an injured arm that the Captain had ordered into boat 6. Why didn't the other men try to enter a boat? To summarise, sufficient doubt exists in Pearcey's story[9].

The only other witness that proffered evidence that the 3rd class

109

were afforded assistance to the boats comes from steerage steward John Hart. His story can be recapitulated as follows: after being woken, he was ordered by the chief steerage steward, Mr.Kiernan, to go to his allocated portion of the ship and rouse his people, a total of about 58 people including about 9 married couples with children. Traversing up one deck from his bunk, he found that most of "his" people had retired for the night, but the majority were up. He saw that lifebelts were placed on the passengers, but some had so much faith in the ship's invincibility, some refused to put them on. After this, Hart noticed the procession of single men coming from forward with their bags. The afore mentioned Mr.Muller was present, trying to keep the stream of waifs quiet; somewhere in this area, Hart noticed the door to 2nd class was open, which was also noticed by Joughin. In accord with other statements, the stream of steerage men seemed to be heading for the aft well deck, via their main staircase.

Soon after, Mr.Kiernan, fresh from ensuring that other passengers in the other steerage areas had belts, reappeared and an order was passed down to take women and children to the boat deck. This was about 12.30am. Hart gathered 30 women and children and took them upwards, via the main 3rd class stairway, and then forward straight across the aft well deck, through previously closed doors into 1st class, and then up the Grand Staircase. Stewards were posted en route to show the way. Slightly xenophobically, Hart reported that he "had no foreigners" in his bunch and because of this, there were no difficulties in enticing his throng to leave their baggage behind.

Hart arrived at the station for boat 8, which was being lowered at this time. In his testimony, Hart stated that "two or three" of his entourage found it cold, saw the boats being lowered away, and thought themselves more secure on the ship, consequently returning to their warm rooms below. Leaving his crowd on deck, Hart returned below to retrieve more people, passing another crowd of women, children and men who were being escorted up by one of his colleagues, a man named Cox. On his second trip aloft, Hart managed to gather approximately 25 people[10], but this time the men wanted to come along too, and some would not come as they would not leave their "apartments." Now Hart tried a different tactic; whereas previously he had tried to impress upon the men, women and children that the ship was not damaged in any way, he now informed them of their perilous circumstances. Despite this, a very small number of women refused to accompany him despite this dire statement. The more eager men who were determined to accompany Hart were prevented from doing so by the other stewards.

Upon arriving at the boat deck with this second entourage, Hart could see no boats being lowered on the port side, but looking aft on the starboard side, he could see boat 15, at the very end of the deck. He walked along the boat deck, placed his 25 people in the boat with some others who were already there, and got in himself. It was then about 1.15am, by his estimation. The boat descended to "A" deck where it picked up more steerage: 5 women, 3 children and one man with a baby in his arms, leaving some men behind to watch as the boat dropped out of sight. In Hart's estimation, there were about 70 people, 13 or 14 crew included, in the boat when it touched the ocean.

If Hart's story was true, he was indeed a valorous hero. Not counting the few who returned below, he had brought up 55 women and children to the boats; out of 103 ultimately saved, this is a major fraction. His colleague, Cox, who was not saved, also brought up an unknown number of passengers from the deep recesses of the vessel.

Is Hart's story true?

We shall probably never know who was on "E" deck at this time; Katherine Gilnagh and her companions were almost certainly on deck when the order for lifebelts was given - they were in compartment Q, just a few passageways aft of where Hart was mustering his own passengers. Mary Coutts and her two young sons were probably somewhere on "E" deck, but it is debatable as to whether her account is compatible with Hart's own story. Coutts said that after the men carrying their baggage had disappeared from her deck, apparently heading up, she was left standing in the corridor for a long while, but when the order to put on life belts came, she found she only had two for the three of them who were sharing her cabin. From her story, there was a general shortage of belts that resulted in many running from room to room searching for this most basic of survival implements. Not even a passing officer nor anyone else knew of any spare life belts. Eventually an officer led her and her sons to his quarters were the cork vests were affixed. The most interesting part of this story is just before this, when Coutts writes, "Nearly everyone was on deck now, and we were just going when I saw the ... officer..." What does she mean by "on deck"? Does she mean the deck on which she was standing, implying that everyone had been roused from their slumber? Or does she mean up, either on the well deck or on the boat deck? What does she mean when "we were just going"? Was she about to be led up to the boat deck with the others? One searches vainly for clues or hints but none present themselves.

111

Critics of Hart's version note that no steerage were in boat 8; at the time, the 3rd class who were already on deck were congregated much further aft, around boats 10-16. But Hart does not say that he put them in this boat, which was being lowered. He simply said that he left them there and headed back down again for his second batch of evacuees. When he was in the water in boat 8, Steward Crawford heard an order for people to head to boat 10 from the vacant spot where his boat had been minutes earlier; if there were any 3rd class nearby, they would almost certainly have heeded this order, especially if, as Hart said, they were not "foreigners" and could presumably understand English. Boat 10 was part of a quartet of boats at the aft port side of the *Titanic*, a location where many 3rd class found safety in the boats.

Then there is the problem of timing. Within 45 minutes, Hart had paraded the route to the boats three times. Edward Wilding, a marine architect at Harland and Wolff, told his interrogators in London that, from the deepest recesses of the steerage quarters, it would take 3 to 3½ minutes at a slow pace to reach the boat deck. Wilding knew the *Titanic* intimately; but Hart did claim to have the plans for the ship in his head. Would he really know the way through the unfamiliar 1st class areas? He did have stewards to guide him along the route, so even if his first trip to the boat deck was occasionally hindered by the odd wrong turn, he would be familiar with the route on his 2nd and 3rd trip, and, of course, when he headed back down, he would not have any passengers to slow him down. Even if only a few minute elapsed to congregate passengers - and on his second trip, to stop the men from joining their spouses - the difference between Hart's 45 minutes and a 9 to 10½ minute journey inferred from Wilding's evidence is stark. And this assumes that Hart was accurate in his timings. Hart could see that the emergency door leading from 3rd class to 2nd class, and directly up to the boat deck was open. Why did he not use that route rather than the elaborate and circuitous path he claimed to take?

Although this author only had access to a small fraction of accounts from 3rd class survivors, one would expect some of them to corroborate Hart's account. Unconfirmed stories from a Mrs Johnson indicate that she and her two children were saved when a steward led them up on deck. Mrs.Elin Hakkarainen reputedly said that she was encouraged by a steward to join a small group of women that he was leading to the boat deck. Mrs. George Joseph Whabee also remembered "well dressed men" (stewards?) leading her and others to the boat deck. But one would expect more than these three accounts.

112

Finally, we reach the problem of boat 15. On the port side, Hart claimed not to have seen any more boats, but on the opposite side, he sees the last boat at the end of the deck. This is from a distance of some 330 feet from his location at the Grand Staircase vestibule. This does not seem possible. After leaving the area of the gymnasium and heading aft, the boat deck was illuminated by lights below knee height[11]. Dr.Washington Dodge even said, "We were in semi-darkness on the boat deck... we only knew what was going on about us within a radius of possibly forty feet." Charles Stengel had clambered into boat 1 and, as far as he could see, there were no other boats on the starboard side of the ship; he was wrong, as there were four boats further aft, which he obviously could not see from a little over 300 feet away.

The other, and much more major difficulty account with Hart is how his 25 people entered boat 15; from the boat deck he claimed. He was adamant on this point. Testimony from crewmembers Cavell and Taylor, and a newspaper account from a steward named Nichols[12], say the same thing and it contradicts Hart: only a skeleton crew of about 6 men were placed in the boat from the boat deck. Everyone else was loaded in from "A" deck.

There is one other piece of evidence to consider. Frederick Scott was one of those who toiled in the ganglia of the engines below decks. At 1.20am, by his account, he was ordered out of the engine room. Emerging on "E" deck, he and his 30 or 40 colleagues were without life jackets. Mr.Kiernan told them were they could be located, and via a long-winded route down many passageways, they were led one at a time to a locker. They then clambered up on deck, and Scott got to the boat deck in time to see not only boats 14 and 16 lowered, but a warning shot from an officer in one of these boats, and saying that if anyone transgressed into the boat they would be shot.

The interesting point is that during his foray into the sleeping quarters of the steerage to find a life jacket, Scott never saw one passenger, just some stewards getting belts. He admits that he did not look, but he would have noticed corridors full of men, women and children standing around waiting to be escorted up. Critics may point out that Hart's time of 1.15am when he entered the boat with his band of steerage is slightly before the 1.20am time when Scott left the engine room and saw very few in the corridors nearby. Perhaps the few people that Hart left below had dispersed in the interim time? This all depends on their timings being right. The British Inquiry puts boat 15's departure some twenty minutes later than Hart's claim...or precisely the time when Scott should have seen the corridors choked with steerage. We know where the life jacket locker was, and his route from the engine room emergency door would have taken him on a perfunctory, but comprehensive tour of 3rd class space on "E" deck, where he saw stewards but none of the people under their care.

The timing issue is of paramount importance to this discussion; if Scott, and his inferred evidence is true, then there was hardly anyone left on "E" deck. If Hart is right, he left some on that deck. Scott had no reason to lie; Hart may have felt the need to protect himself from accusations of negligence.

Sufficient doubt exists to make some researchers feel that Hart's story is a fiction. Certainly he said nothing that could not be gleaned from talking to his fellow crewmembers after being rescued. And, until we unearth stories from women and children escorted up, there is nothing to verify his claims.

What ultimately happened to the 3rd class on deck? There is testimony that alludes to "hundreds" and "big crowds" of 2nd and 3rd class congregating around the aft four boats on the port side. Some little time later, when Scott and Ranger dropped into the water from this very location, they saw no-one at all[13]. Evidently, the crowds had moved forward, as there are reports of steerage in the very last boats to be filled, all the way forward. It is certainly surprising that Lawrence Beesley did not notice a hoard of people surge round to his side of the ship from the other side of the ship, given that the boats in his vicinity left some time after the ones on the port side, and which were surrounded by "hundreds" of people. If anyone did venture to Beesley's side of the Titanic, they would have seen empty falls, not knowing that the boats had not gone, just lowered down to "A" deck. Conversely, some enterprising passengers may have found a way down to "A" deck to join the complements of the boats on the opposite side. The lack of information from boats 13 and 15 prevents us from reconstructing the steerage movements on deck. As discussed elsewhere, very few people can unambiguously be placed in these boats and their stories do not always conform.

The biggest indication that the steerage were hampered during their escape come from testimony and a later book written by 1st class passenger, Archibald Gracie. Leaving crewman to tend to the final boat on the starboard side, he and his companion Clinch Smith turned to head aft, but "We had taken but a few steps [from the boat] ... when there arose before us from the decks below, a mass of humanity several lines deep, covering the Boat Deck, facing us, and completely blocking our passage towards the stern. There were women in the crowd, as well as men, and they seemed to be steerage passengers who had just come up from the decks below." These people were cast into the sea by a wave that came surging up the boat deck. This account is often repeated but never analysed.

Evidently, Gracie saw many people appear in front of him, but was he accurate in his comments? We know where Gracie was when he saw this "mass of humanity", and from his vantage point he couldn't possibly have seen if the throng had come up from below decks. All he could have seen was men and women emerge from the 1st class staircase lobby and perhaps from round the deck houses, aft of the gymnasium. So, where did they come from? Leaving aside the emotive issue of helpless passengers suppressed by thuggish seamen below, answers present themselves in the testimonies of survivors. It seems likely that, rather than "surging up from below", the steerage were already there, on deck.

Lamp Trimmer Hemming had clambered down from on top of the officer's quarters where he had prepared boat "B"'s descent to the deck. On his way from the port to the starboard side, he saw that there were one or two hundred men, but no women as far as he could see. Captain Smith yelled out for everyone to move to the starboard side; the ship had developed a precarious list to port, and by moving weight to the opposite side, Smith evidently hoped to correct the list. Researcher Samuel Halpern has calculated that the ship had a 10° list at the time boat 10 was prepared, and this was some time before Hemming heard Smith's order. Were the "two hundred" people on the port side merely obeying Smith's order? The quickest route to the starboard side was through the ship - through the 1st class lobby and emerging just where Gracie saw them moments later. Another possibility is one mentioned by Assistant Cook John Collins; he was on the port side when he heard that a boat was being launched on the starboard side and that "all women and children were to make for it." However, Collins' testimony may be too early for Gracie's sighting; he arrived in time to see the boat falling to the deck from the roof above; when Gracie saw his "mass of humanity" the boat had been there for a little while already and this was before he saw the crowd surging "up" [sic].[14] Another possibility is that the mob on the port side had just seen boat "B" land uselessly upside down on the deck. It was obviously of no use to anyone, and the crowd may have rushed to the opposite side of the deck to see what was happening there...and just in time to meet Gracie.

Gracie tells us what was happening on the starboard side at the very end, but there are very few accounts from the port side at this time; Harold Bride was washed into the sea with the overturned boat "B" from this side of the *Titanic*. A steerage passenger named Victor Sunderland was somewhere nearby. Although his newspaper interview deviates slightly from what we know, he does state that, "The ship had begun to list to port by that time and the boats on the starboard side were nearly all gone. The passengers rushed to the port side, but were crowded back by the crew to keep the boat even. The captain ordered all boats to row away from the ship. The ship began to sink by the head and by then the boat deck was clear of all but Lightoller, two firemen and myself." Even though we know that Lightoller was on the roof of the officers quarters and wheelhouse, rather than on deck, Sunderland's account seems to confirm that everyone had moved to the opposite side of the *Titanic* and were prevented from returning. Interestingly, at about this time, Jack Thayer Jr. who was on the starboard side, recalled that the ship shifted back on an even keel; that is, it had righted itself. Does this seem likely? Could a few hundred people have shifted the balance of the ship, restoring it, even temporarily? Edward Wilding was asked about this, and he calculated that 800 people moving 50 feet would cause a shift of 2°. His interrogators seemed to think this was negligible, and indeed, it would be insufficient to correct a list of 10°. But Wilding's calculations seem to be based on a virtual *Titanic* that was buoyant, on an even keel and in no danger of instability caused by the ingress of water. Author Leslie Reade speculated that Wilding may have over-estimated the *Titanic*'s stability. Without recourse to a computer simulation, there is no way of knowing at present if a few hundred people shifting on an increasingly tender ship could effect a gross restabilisation as stated by Thayer. But there is more evidence of a ship whose stability had become very precarious; as the boat deck sank below the waters, it temporarily emerged, as if trying struggling to stay afloat, before slipping under again, this time for good. It could be that as the unfortunates on board ran towards higher ground, the shift in weight aft precipitated a "see-saw" like effect tipping the stern down slightly and the bow up. If so, the flooding was too severe inside the ship for this effect to be anything other than transitory.

Is there anything that could be said about any remaining passengers that did not make it to the boat deck? Crewman Dillon found himself on the aft well deck, with a "great number" of men, but only two women, whom he helped chase up the ladder when a cry went out for more ladies as the last boat was leaving. Dillon clambered up to the poop, where there were "many" male passengers; he was still there when the ship foundered. The stern and poop seem to have been the last refuge for many of the steerage.

Does the issue of discrimination extend beyond the confines of the steerage? The 2nd class are one of the great neglected areas of *Titanic* study; much attention has been focussed on the 1st and 3rd class, and the 2nd class don't fit into the stereotypes of "the glitterati who were rescued while the impoverished were left to die" or "the down-trodden members who struggled to survive against the odds." The 2nd class fall between these two categories; not one single 2nd class survivor was called at the U.S. Inquiry, whereas three steerage and many more 1st class were called. Much of what we know about the fate of the 2nd class comes from Lawrence Beesley's book, plus a few scattered letters and articles. Reading the few survivor's stories, it is hard to believe that the 2nd class were the subject of any directed campaign of segregation. Rather they seem to have been caught between the orderly procession of the 1st class into the boats, and the worry about a possible stampede to the boats by the steerage.

Robertha Watt was a 2nd class passenger. She clambered up the crowded 2nd class stairway; she refers to the elevator "not running" so we can at least deduce that she went up the forward stairway that led to the boat deck (the aft one simply went as high as the promenade on "B" deck). She noticed "the master at arms stood with a pistol in his hand, threatening to shoot steerage passenger men who attempted to come up the second cabin stairway."[15]

Here was one 2nd class passenger who did observe some attempt to keep steerage below, regardless of whether Joughin and Hart had seen the doorway that led to this stairway open "early on". Watt places this time as about 1 o'clock, but timings seem to be very flexible that night.

Diverting from this discussion slightly, Beesley was witness to an incident that may be of relevance: he saw two ladies approach the gates that separated the 2nd class from "1st class" promenade [sic - actually the

117

engineer's promenade] only to be stopped by an "officer" who barred their way, telling them "No, madam, your boats are down on your own deck" and he pointed to "A" deck below, where some boats were hanging. The ladies turned and headed to the stairway. Who was this "officer"? It is impossible to know. Someone with no recognition of the crew would mistake anyone wearing a blue woollen suit for an "officer." We do know that Purser Hugh McElroy was near boat 9 when it was being filled; it may have been him, one of his staff, or someone about whom nothing else is known.

But the *Titanic*'s geography had a strange quirk that handicapped the 2nd class. While the boat deck was segmented into areas for 1st and 2nd class, engineers and officers, "A" deck was completely 1st class territory - from start to end. The 2nd class staircase did not open onto deck "A", were it was surrounded by the 1st class smoking room forward, the verandah and palm court to port and starboard, and a fan ventilation system to the stern. There was no direct route to "A" deck for the 2nd class.

Astute readers will remember some references to "ladders" when we discussed the 3rd class segregation. It seems likely that they were the sole source of hope for some 2nd class passengers too. Safely housed in boat 13, Beesley chatted to two ladies who told him that they had to come up one of "the vertically upright ladders that connect each deck with the one below it, meant for the use of sailors..." Others faced the same impediment, including one lady who was inactive and only served to delay the people waiting to ascend.

Sylvia Caldwell was one of those. She too found herself in boat 13, and told Walter Lord in 1955, "Several of us were ordered to go below several decks as they were not going to fill the boats to capacity on the boat deck. The men went down about three decks - none of the other officers knew we were there so locked the door - later some officer on the deck above shouted that there were people down on the lower deck they lowered [sic?] a ladder & all crawled up except my husband, baby and I [when we] finally heard an officer say "My God! There is a woman down there." "

Mary Hewlett was another passenger trapped below decks: "...there [was] an officer was ordering people to climb up a ladder on to the upper deck so I went with the crowd & when I reached the top there were eight or ten stewards there who said I must get into a boat that was on the davits - however they insisted & I was put into boat No.13."

118

If Caldwell was right, the 2nd class entrance on the boat deck was locked, barring any easy access to the boats at all. When was it locked? Bertha Watt made it to the 2nd class promenade on the boat deck and eventually found her way into boat 9, the first of the four of the aft starboard side to be lowered. She does not mention seeing any boats, but does describe a "crowd" which would possibly have obscured them. We also do not know how long she waited on deck before getting into No.9, and as we know No.9 left after boat 14 on the port side. We do not know how long Caldwell and her family were trapped, but it seems to have been a little time before boat 13 left the ship. By this time, the pandemonium around the aft port boats had subsided. If it was decided to seal the door at this time, lest any further panic ensued, it would make sense, but only from a crowd management point of view. From a humanitarian point of view, hundreds could have been isolated below with only four pairs of ladders to afford access to the boats.

The staircase described by Watt et al. opened up on to the 2nd class promenade on "B" deck, where their smoking room was located. This seems to have been a haven for people; if 3rd class were forced to climb ladders, this is the deck they would have to pass, and indeed, it seems to be this area that the steerage talked about when referring to "locked gates." Crewman Thomas Ranger's work in the innards of the ship completed, he ended up on this small 2nd class area of "B" deck the *Titanic* with 20 crewmen, mostly firemen, and no women or children. This promenade may have also been the haven for steerage in their attempt to get as high as possible - and to safety. Boat 15 was lowered past this very 2nd class promenade, and by crewman Cavell's account, the majority of the boat's ultimate occupants were taken in from this deck. They were all 3rd class women and children and although there were men there, they were not taken on. His fellow crewman Taylor could not corroborate the location of this loading; as he said, "I could not see, because we kept the boat off the ship, to keep from rubbing down her side." Steward Nichols did not mention this loading from the lower deck at all in a newspaper account[16].

With passenger accounts now exhausted, we now examine crew accounts. Are there any examples of members of the ship's crew being kept away from the boats? Surprisingly, yes. Lightoller himself admitted that some "stewardesses" were turned away from the boats. Nellie

O'Dwyer suggests a reason: "There was some trouble with the nurses [sic - stewardesses?]. They were supposed to place lifebelts on the people. A few of them tried to escape. But the officers shouted at them, and they came back to their work."

Major Peuchen told his inquisitors in America that, before the boats were lowered, "When I came on deck first, on this upper deck, there were, it seems to me, about 100 stokers came up with their dunnage bags, and they seemed to crowd this whole deck in front of the boats. One of the officers - I do not know which one, but a very powerful one - came along and drove these men right off that deck. It was a splendid act." He may have over exaggerated the number. 1st class passenger Helen Candee also saw these men, and recalled that they obeyed without a "murmur or protest" even though the officer had previously said words to the effect that he would like to see them overboard[17]. This act has been attributed to Chief Officer Wilde.

Charlotte Collyer also reported on suppression of the firemen from the upper deck: "Suddenly there was a commotion near one of the gangways, and we saw a stoker climbing up from below ... I saw 1st Officer Murdoch place guards by the gangways to prevent others like the ... stoker from coming on deck." Surprisingly - or perhaps not, given the fear of being blacklisted by the White Star Line after giving damaging testimony - there is a lack of corroboration for these sightings. Stoker Harry Senior says that Captain Smith ordered the firemen to be kept below, on the well deck[18].

John William Thompson later recalled that, "after he and some other firemen had gone on deck after the collision, Leading Fireman William Small ordered them back below, apparently to go back to the boiler rooms." Then, Wally Hurst, another fireman, wrote to Walter Lord in 1955 stating that after the call to muster, they were told by a quartermaster while on the forward well deck "not to come on the boat deck until later on." Both Hurst and Senior said that they went onto the boat deck upon seeing boat No.1 being lowered; by leaning out over the side of the well deck, boat 1 would have been easily observable. Although a few lucky stokers, trimmers and greasers did get in early boats, the majority seem to have departed in later boats. The early leavers were on the starboard side, well away from Wilde. Why were the stokers treated in such a callous fashion? Charles Stengel's evidence may give some answers: "I heard that explained afterwards by an officer of the ship, when he said, "Suppose we had reported the damage that was done to that vessel; there would not be one of you aboard. The stewards would have come up" - not the stewards, but the stokers - "would have come up and taken every boat, and no one would have had a chance of getting aboard of those boats.""

There is only one other case of crewmen held below; Paul Mauge, secretary to the a la Carte restaurant chef told his story in London. Through a sometimes impenetrable grasp of English, he regaled the inquiry thus; "I said to the other cooks to wait for us. After that we had been by the 3rd class deck just at the back, and we have been trying to go on the 2nd class passenger deck. Two or three stewards were there, and would not let us go. I was dressed and the chef was too. He was not in his working dress; he was just like me. I asked the stewards to pass. I said I was the secretary to the chef, and the stewards said, "Pass along, get away." So the other cooks were obliged to stay on the deck there; they could not go up. That is where they die...They let me pass, Me and the chef, because I was dressed like a passenger. I think that was why they let me pass... I think all the members of the restaurant were there...perhaps 60...Anyway they could not pass because I stood on the 2nd class passenger deck for half-an-hour." Mauge got on to the boat deck in time to jump into one of the boats at the aft end of the boat deck. He was nearly manhandled out of the boat but evaded this attempt. Steward Johnson talked of the restaurant staff but his account adds little; "I saw [all the restaurant staff] all bunched together, but everyone was bunched together at first; but after that I only saw one, and he saved himself."[19]

Many have claimed that this occurred at the restaurant's staff's quarters on "E" deck, but it is clear that the stewards were preventing anyone from going up to the 2nd class area from the well deck ... where so many other 3rd class were inhibited from climbing up...and where even 2nd class were temporarily ensconced with a sealed stairway door and having to find recourse in a crew's ladder.

That there was some attempt to prevent certain persons from reaching the boat deck seems to be without dispute; how widespread and how "official" the orders were and who instigated it are unknown. As grandiose as the claims in cinematic depictions are, the suggestion that certain people were indeed inhibited from escaping is inescapable, but how many of the stories we have discussed here can be ascribed to discrimination and how many to negligence?

Chapter 4: Impending Catastrophe

The scene on the boat deck was one of pandemonium; dozens of sailors busied themselves unlacing the covers of the lifeboats, coiling the ropes (known as "falls") that would lower the boats and their precious cargo to the sea some 60 feet below and so on. No-one thought to equip any of the boats with compasses, as prescribed by the law at the time, and few left with lamps. The calm night was only interrupted by the deafening roar of escaping scene that only added to the unreal scene: a little time after the collision, the surplus steam from the boilers had been automatically vented from valves atop the funnels for safety reasons, lest there be a pressure build-up. Fortunately there were few, if any passengers on deck to interfere with the preparations for the escape. From a distance, it must have seemed that nothing was amiss as the *Titanic* lay on the "flat calm" sea beneath thousands of twinkling stars. Granted, the bows of the ship were slightly lower in the water than usual, and the roar of steam being belched implied some mishap, but there was no gaping hole in the ship's hull above the waterline, and no torrent of water surging into the ship; in brief, there was nothing obvious that suggested disaster.

The crew's continual labour with the boats attracted the attention of the only bridge officer who had managed to sleep through it all; 5th Officer Lowe, and his reaction to the confusion on deck is interesting. He armed himself with his gun because, as he said later, "You never know when you will need it". At some point, the senior officers must have had similar thoughts as they too sought the protection of firearms. Unlike Lowe, the pistols that Lightoller, Murdoch, Wilde and Smith equipped themselves with were company property; they were brand new and still coated in grease.

When did the other officers arm themselves? On the starboard side, Charles Stengel saw two fellow male passengers jump into lifeboat No.5, containing his wife. Stengel reports hearing the officer on the deck say, "I will stop that. I will go down and get my gun," who then left the deck momentarily. This should be compared with the comments of Henry Harper, who left in boat 3, the next one after boat 5; "four of five stokers or some such men came along and jumped into the boat... 'Huh!' [The officer in charge of lowering] said: ' I suppose I ought to get my gun and stop this.' But he did not go and get any gun, and neither did he order the stokers out."[1]

Lightoller's unreliable memoirs puts the retrieval of the weapons just after boat 6 was lowered to the sea, when the Chief Officer came over from the starboard side (where no one else claimed to have seen him) and asked where the firearms were. Murdoch, despite being the officer responsible for weapons, did not apparently know where they could be found (possibly due to his demotion in Southampton during which he had moved cabins) and Lightoller led his fellow senior officers to the 1st Officer's room where the revolvers were dispensed. In 1912, Lightoller would write about obtaining "some articles" from Murdoch's room - an allusion to weapons - but puts it closer in time to the attempt to free one one of the boats from the roof of the officer's quarters...and a time frame when we know that Lightoller used his weapon according to the later testimony of passenger Gracie that we will describe presently. [2]

The officers were now all awake and were assisting on deck, and following an inspection below decks to the damage to the hull, Captain Smith returned to the forward boat deck and the bridge, where he spent the rest of the evening (in fact, almost exclusively on the port side). The ship's fate had now been ascertained, and she would surely founder, taking half of the people on board with her to the bottom of the ocean, 2½ miles below. Only now, with this knowledge confirmed, did the steward's demeanour change: rather than informing passengers to "go back to bed" or that "we will resume our voyage in a few hours," now their directive altered. Still polite, the insistent message was for passengers to go on deck wearing their cork-lined life jackets. Each steward had been allocated a section of ship, and now they moved from room to room in their areas checking that everyone was up, that everyone was attired with lifejackets, that no one had been overlooked, and then politely directing them to the boat deck.

Many of the stewards were asleep at the time of impact, and were mostly roused by the subtle vibrations and shuddering of the engines. Some thought that a propeller blade had been dropped. But, in those first few minutes afterwards, while curious heads peered out of dormitories and portholes, events occurred that were far from ordinary. While the impact of the collision had been more alarming to those stationed at the bow, the stewards, located amidships and on the port side, were not unduly alarmed by the faint sensations coming from a long way away...until word started filtering along, and samples of ice from the forward well deck were passed round. In short, the stewards were understandably slow to react. This may explain the reaction of one person overheard by passenger Charles Stengel who expressed the opinion that the stewards were not doing their duty in summoning passengers on deck. Major Peuchen backed up Stengel; he had later encountered two ladies who had not been awakened by the stewards but by a neighbour. But analysis of the testimony and survival figures shows otherwise, at least as far as the 1st class passengers were concerned. The stewards seemed to have been efficient in rousing the passengers.

The steward's stories are interesting, as they shed light on the rising tension in the crew's quarters. Bedroom Steward Henry Etches was one of those slumbering, along with 18 others in his quarters. He was next due on duty at midnight. Between 7 and 10 minutes after the crash, he heard a loud shout which he recognised as the boatswain's voice, yelling, "Close watertight bulkheads." Looking out of his room, Etches saw the boatswain running from fore to aft, with a seaman following him. Etches partly dressed and again peered into the corridor where he saw 3rd class passengers heading aft, carrying their belongings. Another one who apparently heard the boatswain cry was 1st class steward Edward Wheelton. After looking out of the port, and chatting to some of his colleagues, he clambered back into bed when he heard, "watertight doors." 3rd class pantryman Albert Pearcey may have been one of those who carried out these orders. He was on "F" deck, outside the pantry when he felt a small motion. He next heard the order "All watertight doors to be closed," which he and several other men did, closing the doors aft on "F" deck, as well as the ones leading to his pantry. John Hardy, the Chief 2nd Class Steward, had also received an order from Mr.Barker (a purser) to close the doors and rouse the passengers "as a precaution". The doors on "F" deck were duly closed[3].

It was about this time that the ship's band decided to play, ostensibly to allay fear and panic. An inspiration to passengers and generations to come, they played till the last minute without any attempt to enter a boat or to save themselves. Since they all perished we shall probably never know if and when they were summoned on deck with their catalogue of inspiring and calming songs. Jack Thayer jr. claimed to have heard them play in the lounge a little time after 12.15am by his estimation, where he wrote that "[they] were playing lively tunes without apparently receiving much attention from the worried moving audience" who crowded into the room. Thayer does not mention this fact in any of his other writings; the mention of the band comes 28 years after the disaster, and his placement of the band is intriguing. Pre-collision, the

124

lounge had been the domain of impatient stewards who were imploring passengers to leave in order for them to tidy up and lock the room up for the night. Interestingly, Thayer says that the order had been given to put on lifejackets before he saw the band. Since the desire was to congregate the passengers on the boat deck, would they have sought to delay people by playing within the ship? Archibald Gracie makes an interesting point in his posthumous book; seeking ladies to fill spaces in the boats, he journeyed the length of "A" deck going from aft forwards, but saw no-one except in the 1st class smoking room[4]; the lounge was located on the same deck. Gracie's narrative is confusing, but it would seem to be about the time that Thayer purportedly saw people in the lounge. However, William T. Sloper said that he was told by people who were the last to leave that they found the orchestra playing in the lounge. Stewardess Annie Robinson remembered hearing the band three quarters of an hour after the collision when she was heading up to "A" deck to summon the other stewardesses. Although this author is sceptical of people's opinions of timings, Robinson's story provides some credence to the notion that the band were playing inside the ship at some point. The steam was still blowing off from the funnels and she would not have been able to hear the band if they were on the boat deck, indicating that the musicians were somewhere near the staircase that Robinson ascended, and probably still within the ship.

The only other witness who reported seeing the band playing earlier was Boxhall in his revisionist interview of the 1960s but his account is peppered with doubtful details. Immaterial of when they started, at some point, the band eventually took up a position on the port side of the ship just aft of the foyer to the Grand Staircase where an open location in the ship's deckhouses would allow them to play without interrupting the evacuation process. They may have played somewhere on "A" deck, as passenger Pierre Marechal saw them "between decks"; he was in the first boat to leave. Quartermaster Rowe remembered hearing the band as he walked to the bridge on the port side of the ship at about the time this first boat departed. Mrs.Futrelle also heard the band play inside the ship but it is unclear when and where this happened.

As usual, interesting and conflicting data can be found in the record; 2nd class passenger Lawrence Beesley saw the cellist come from the 2nd class entrance, heading down the starboard boat deck, the spike of his instrument dragging along the decking. Beesley puts this after the first rocket was fired (and hence after Marechal's boat departed). If the timing is right, the other bandsmen must have started without cello accompaniment. It must have been a struggle getting the instrument from his cabin 5 decks below on "E" deck to the boat deck as none of the passenger elevators were running. There is also no easy way to get from the lounge on "A" deck to the 2nd class boat deck entrance without taking significant detours.

With many passengers now on deck and waiting to embark, the focus of the drama shifts from the interior of the ship to the exterior. Consequently, reports from inside become less frequent and few of these refer to the flooding of the now useless hulk. One of these stories comes from Laura Francatelli whose cabin was on the lowest deck of 1st class accommodation. Francatelli would later write of her alarm at seeing water inch towards her along the 1st class corridor on the starboard side. Franctalli rushed up four flights of stairs to her employers to report what she had seen; she was said to be "in hysterics." This water seemed to have originated from the area of the mail sorting rooms which Boxhall, Chambers et al. had earlier seen was flooded. Soon afterwards, steward Wheat descended to his quarters near the Turkish bath; by this time, the water had flowed so far aft that it had now reached the base of the Grand Staircase and was now cascading gently down the stairs to the deck below where his room was. The stairs down to his quarters were located further aft, and just slightly off the main corridor where Francatelli had seen water, indicating that the water was slowly progressing deeper into the hull. At about this time, another crewman, by the name of Ray, noticed that the port side of the ship was also flooded (discrepancies in their statements will be discussed elsewhere). Also on this lowest deck was Miss Kreuchen, who reported to her employer, Miss Robert that the baggage room was underwater. When told that she needn't worry and that it would be all right for her to return to her cabin because of the ability of the fabled watertight compartments, Kreuchen went back and returned promptly with the news that her room was flooded. Yet, Kreuchen, Robert and Miss Madill and Miss Allen (the other members of their party) left the ship in one of the very last boats, implying that they did not think the flooding was serious. There is no mention of anyone's reaction when Kreuchen came back and said that her own cabin was now flooded[5].

Seaman Poingdestre's experience was more dramatic: taking a brief break from assisting in readying the boats, he returned to his quarters to fetch his rubber boots. By his own estimate, this was 30-45 minutes after the collision. As he was leaving the quarters, a wooden bulkhead ruptured, and he found himself deluged up to his waist in icy cold water.

Amidst much decorum and unpractised routines of evacuation, the passengers marched up from their warm beds to the cold upper decks. Some 1st class tried to retrieve their valuables from the purser's safes only to be turned away. Stewards ferried cargoes of bread as nourishment for the intended crews of the lifeboats, but it is doubtful that any found their way into the boats; the barrels containing the food was left as piles on deck, where frustrated passengers and crew found themselves tripping over the abandoned, but much needed, supplies. A large spectrum of human behaviour was enacted; some passengers smuggled their pet dogs into the boats (one was left locked in a cabin when its owner went up on deck!), some complained that they didn't have time to "do" their hair, and at least one lady gave a steward the task of locking her trunks in her cabin.

The passengers were mostly oblivious to the unfolding drama, and many simply regarded the instructions to enter the boats as a highly inconvenient drill, or that it was a matter of precaution, that they were simply going to row away while for a little time while the damage was fixed. At any rate, many expected to be back on board for breakfast. Only on a few occasions did the possibility of calamity enter the minds of the unwary. Dr.Washington Dodge had gone forward to view the tons of ice deposited on the well deck, and while there, he engaged in conversation with two stokers who had slipped into 1st class space. "Do you think there is any danger, sir?" asked one of the firemen. Dodge replied that if the vessel had sprung a leak, the stokers would know more about it than him, to which he was told in an alarmed tone, "Well, sir, the water was pouring into the stokehold when we came up." However alarming this news was, it did not seem to have worried Dodge unduly as he deposited his wife and child in one of the very first boats but did not enter himself. Why he did not is not known, but he later wrote that as he saw his family's boat descend he was "overwhelmed with doubts as to whether or not I was exposing them to greater danger, than if they had remained on board the ship." This seems to have been many people's concerns: why risk exposing oneself to the dangers of a little row boat when the mighty *Titanic* seemed far safer?

Other incidents where the intimations of catastrophe were inadvertently revealed to the men, women and children of the three classes are rare; these include Charlotte Collyer who saw a stoker, whose fingers of one hand had been severed, blood spattered on his face and clothes, and who told Collyer in response to a query about the danger

127

that "Its 'ell down below. Look at me! This boat'll sink like a log in ten minutes" before collapsing on deck, resting his head on a coil of rope. In response to a query from an "officer", Elizabeth Shute was told that there was no danger of any kind, but, not trusting the reply, listened to what the man said upon entering a nearby cabin; "We can keep the water out for a while." The 3rd class already knew of the danger; as related elsewhere, the forward cabins were flooding.

The crowds on the boat deck were growing in number but curiously, the number on the starboard side was never as large as on the port side. Mrs.Dodge offered an explanation: "I supposed all the women were congregated on the port side because it would naturally be the highest side, and the safest because [it would be] the last to go down." Indeed, the list in its earliest stages provided the highest vantage point on the port side, and, if this author's experiences with vertigo are any hint, people would naturally tend to accumulate at a location that would prevent one falling over the side of the precipice into the sea. This can only be part of the solution to the question of why there were fewer on one side than the other; when the list shifted to port, the number to starboard was still less than to port. There is a suggestion that the crowds on the port side when boats 6 and 8 were being filled had become excessive, and the deck too crowded; one 1st class passenger noted that the door on the port side that led from the staircase foyer to the boat deck was locked, and he had to go to starboard. There are reports of passengers standing on the coiled falls for the lifeboats, and looking at the deck plans, space does seem to be lacking in this area. Dr.Dodge offers an alternate explanation; "the captain was in charge of the launching of the boats on the port side. Now in times of danger, the captain always draws a crowd. The more notable men on board, who were known by sight to the other passengers, knew Captain Smith personally and remained near him. These men attracted others. In this way the crowd grew on the port side, while at no time was there anything like a crowd on the starboard side."

With the boat covers being unlaced and then the boats themselves swung out over the ship's side and lowered in line with the deck, a matter that needed to be resolved was where were the passengers to be loaded into the boats? The boat deck was easiest as the boats did not have to be lowered very far even though this entailed people stepping down into them, and some accounts do exist of people losing their footings. The alternative was clambering in from "A" deck over the solid railing and through the windows, an approach that was less cumbersome. And indeed, this seemed to have been the adopted plan: on the port side, boat 4 was lowered level with "A" deck...but the windows were closed and a suitable spanner to lower the glass panes could not be obtained for about an hour; in the meantime, the officers and crew moved on to other boats, leaving frustrated passengers to traipse back up to the boat deck and wait in the cold, and then head back down to "A" deck when entry was possible. And indeed, Captain Smith was heard by passenger Hugh Woolner[6] to say, "I want all the passengers to go down on "A" deck, because I intend they shall go into the boats from "A" deck." Woolner reminded him that the windows were closed, and Smith remarked, "By God, you are right. Call those people back." This left the lifeboat temporarily inaccessible. Prior to this, Colonel Gracie had delivered some ladies under his charge to 6th Officer Moody and some of the other ship's crew on "A" deck who blocked the progress of men towards the boats. The "women to the lower deck" was heard by Henry Harper on the starboard side before he escaped in boat 3, and he saw some ladies head down, others being escorted by their husbands. On the port side only one boat (4) was loaded from "A" deck. On the starboard side, it was slightly different. Perhaps the problem with the closed windows had been recognised from an early point, only the aftermost boats (11, 13 and 15) had people placed in them from "A" deck, which were located so far aft that there were no windows at that location that required opening. Indeed, Lawrence Beesley recalled that "an officer came along from the 1st class deck and shouted above the noise of escaping steam "All women and children get down to the deck below and all men stand back from the boats."[7] This was at about the time that the boats nearby (9, 11, 13 and 15) were swung out, and before the first rocket was fired; while it is difficult to be sure, this was probably before the fiasco with boat 4 had occurred.

And, while there was a crowd on the forward port side, there was never enough people on the other side of the ship to completely fill the boats there, perhaps because of the desire mentioned above to head for "the higher ground." Karl Behr escaped in boat 5, the second one lowered, and later wrote that they were "evidently" the last passengers on the top deck, and that it was later explained by the fact that the passengers were "ordered to go to "A" deck, while we had gone above that. There were other lifeboats on our side, but they must have been filled later from the lower decks." Were people redirected to the wrong deck and missed out on a space in the early boats, or had Behr heard about the abortive plans on the port side? If so, the situation had been remedied when boat 1 was being lowered, as 5th Officer Lowe stopped the boat and asked them to look on "A" deck, and no-one was there. The only witness to this was Lowe himself, however. Interestingly, Norman Chambers, who also escaped in boat 5, remarked that, upon approaching the starboard side from port, a steward was directing people aft! He and his wife stepped behind the vestibule awning and waited until no more people were emerging from the lobby and the steward had moved away. They then headed towards the forward boats, in time to enter boat 5. And, before boat 1 was lowered, the few people who were on the boat deck, "disappeared", apparently heading aft; this boat was located being a solid railing and unless one cared to look, it would seem that there were no boats available in that sector of the deck to admit people...hence, people walked off, looking for other boats, and leaving few to enter this boat.

Further aft, on the starboard side, Lawrence Beesley also heard a strange order from "an officer" which was given to ladies who had tried to pass through a gate into the 1st class promenade space. These ladies, 2nd class passengers, were stopped and told that their own boats were on their own deck; they turned and headed back to 2nd class space. The orders that Chambers heard may have had a similar basis; by the time he heard them, boat 7 was gone, and boat 5 was in the process of loading. The only boats forward of these were in the promenade space reserved for the ship's officers; a space that was normally off limits to passengers, but accessible in an emergency. Without examples of further accounts, it is difficult to be sure, but a reasonable suggestion is that the people herding the passengers on the starboard side were not aware of the impending disaster and simply kept the class structures, demarcated by gates and barrier, intact. This does not seem to have been the case on the forward port side, but there is a suggestion of class structures still being maintained aft. Early after the order to load with women and children, the forward boats on this side were the domain of the 1st class. The aft 4 boats were surrounded by "hundreds", and, if appearances are or any merit, they were predominantly 2nd and 3rd passengers. Why did they not head forward to see if there were any boats there, away from the crowd?[8]

Some other examples of conflicting orders abound in books, letters and evidence given after the accident. Lawrence Beesley, after hearing the two ladies sent back to their own deck, heard a story among the men on the top deck that male passengers were to be taken off on the other side of the ship; all the men crowded to the port side, leaving the starboard side almost deserted except for two or three men. This would be about the time that the large crowd was growing around boats 10, 12, 14 and 16. The source of this "men to the other side" report is not known. It left Beesley practically alone on the starboard side, and no doubt any man who ventured across the deck after receiving this report would have been dismayed to find out that the order here was "women and children only."

This "men to the port side" order is curious as it conflicts with other evidence; John Thayer Jr.'s writings twice refer to women being called to the port side; this order seems to have been issued very early on in the evacuation. Corroboration does exist in some other private accounts: Dr.Washington Dodge gave an address in which he said, "I learned afterwards that the order was given by the officers, for the women and children to go to the port side of the vessel." Martha Stephenson's and Elizabeth Eustis's version has "women and children to Boat Deck and men to starboard side" but it is impossible to place this order in any chronology of events. Steward Wheat's evidence confounds the issue slightly; he had heard that women were to disembarked from "A" deck on the port side. The timing of this order is not clear, but it seems to have been fairly early after he and his colleagues were given lifebelt orders for the passengers. Mrs. May Futrelle wrote that "The women were ordered to go on deck 'A' on the promenade deck...the officers said, 'Women and children will go to the promenade deck. The men will remain where they are.' No man was supposed to be on the boat deck."[9] This could corroborate Gracie who was not allowed near the boats on "A" deck either. The ladies of the Fortune family heard a variation of the order heard by Futrelle; at the stairway to the boat deck, Mr.Fortune and his son were stopped by a group of officers, who told them they would not be permitted further, although the women were allowed up to the boats. This story - if true - seems to be an exceptional case, as there seem to be no other cases of 1st class men being barred from accessing the boat deck.

Perfunctory as the crew were in being called to prepare the boats, how dilatory were they in placing people within them? Sadly, this is another contentious issue in *Titanic* circles. Some say that the first boat left at 12.25, some say 20 minutes later. Reconciling these opinions prompts much bickering in debates. As noted in a previous section, the order to uncover the boats was a little before midnight. The clocks on board ship were due to be put back by 23 minutes at midnight to compensate for westward travel, and many crewmembers has set their own timepieces back before this. Therefore, one could ask if the boat order was given at 12.00am, or 12.23am in adjusted, retarded time. The problem in constructing a chronology is this: the captain's movements before the boat muster are reasonably well known. There would seem to be no opportunity for him to leave the bridge and ascertain and inspect the damage for himself, which means that, if he went below, it would have to be after midnight. The only dissenter was night watchman James Johnson. He was due to go off duty at midnight and during his shift, he saw the captain and Thomas Andrews head down the stairs to the engine room. This would seem to be impossible if it was before midnight. A 23 minute clock change can be invoked to explain this conundrum: if Johnson, like so many others, had expected to work an extra 23 minutes, then he could have seen Smith and Andrews as late as 12.23, in unadjusted time. We now have extra time in which to place the captain and the designer below decks. With at least 43 minutes latency from the collision until the "artificial" 12:23 "midnight", we now have time for the captain to get the boats swung out, and get the passengers on deck. But one cannot help but feel from the various accounts that there was a delay between the order to uncover and prepare the boats, and then, to load them ready for the evacuation and also send out a wirelessed distress call. One ponders why this is so.

Logic can explain the tardiness in transmitting anything over the airwaves. Few crew and even fewer passengers knew that the ship was mortally wounded, and the order for the boats could attributed to being a very inconvenient boat drill, a "straggler" from the previous day when one should have been held. This midnight "boat drill" could then be dismissed as a quirk or foible of the ship's captain and people would be unaware of to the real reason for the orders to take to the boats. While this limitation of bad news could be compartmentalised within the *Titanic*, orders to summon help with the wireless were different. Dozens of ships and ground stations could hear the distress calls, and the false pride that existed in the "Queen of the Ocean's" "Unsinkability" would be open to ridicule, especially if an incorrect and premature distress call sent out. It makes sense therefore to wait to give the order to abandon ship and transmit help as late as was practically possible when it was known with certainty that the ship would founder.

A problem arises with this scenario. The boatswain was telling fellow crew men within the first 20 minutes that the ship had only half an hour to live, and this came from Thomas Andrews himself. Evidently, Andrews was wrong. By the time Smith and Andrews went below to ascertain the damage (and were seen by Johnson), a fair amount of this "30 minutes" had been eaten up. This seems incredible. Why was there not more urgency? Andrews is not reported to have been afraid to expedite people who were dallying over the evacuation. How insistent

132

would Andrews be in imparting his fears to the captain? Had the boatswain exaggerated the danger and Andrew's message? A possibility; but with an order from the captain to prepare the boats, there should have been no need to provide an impetus.

It is a pity that this hypothetical "impetus" was not given to the sailors who toiled preparing the lifeboats. As already stated, there were 20 lifeboats on the ship; two were stowed on the officer's quarters roof[10], and two were swung out at all time for emergencies. This gives us 16 for the men to work on. Boat D was overlooked and its covers not even taken off until Hichens had finished at the wheel at 12.23am[11]. Boat 9 was not even swung out and lowered until the first boat (7) was in the water (according to Ray Dent)...and Beesley seems to indicate that boats 9, 11, 13 and 15 were being worked on at the same time. And it seems that boat 10 was not even swung out until well over an hour into the evacuation process. The report of the British Inquiry puts boat 7 as leaving at 12.45am, and the most respected analysis of lifeboat timings, compiled by Messrs. Wormstedt, Fitch and Behe slightly modifies this time to 12.40. The call to muster the boats was a little before midnight. Even allowing for the fact that available crewmen were called twice (once before midnight to rouse the already off-duty crew, and then to summon the crew who had just gone off duty at midnight, such as Fred Fleet who went down to his quarters and, having found no-one there, was instructed by a quartermaster to go to the bridge[12]) this is an enormous 40-45 minutes before the first boat departed the sinking hulk of the *Titanic*. Why was there such procrastination? Some researchers claim that there wasn't one, and point out that many passengers and crew place the time of the first boat being launched as being about 12.25am. 3[Rd] Officer Pitman was one such person; he got to boat 5 at about 12.20 to find it being uncovered. Within 10 minutes, he claimed, his craft was in the water. This seems insufficient time to even place people in the boat (a possible dissenting voice is his colleague, Harold Lowe, as we shall soon see) and it is obvious that he was estimating the time, as did most of the passengers. Even if Pitman was right, by 12.20am, or about 20 minutes after the muster call, here was one boat that was not only hadn't been swung out, it hadn't even been unlaced. In this author's opinion, the perception of timing estimates is subjective, and is discussed in detail elsewhere. If the passengers were on deck sometime about 12.15-12.25 as some claim, they witnessed the boats not ready to depart, but still being readied. Mrs.Bishop, who escaped in boat 7, watched the crew for 10 minutes preparing the boats. Norman Chambers arrived on deck soon after the order to don lifebelts, and saw the crew unlimbering the equipment on the port side; crossing to the

133

starboard side, he saw the men coiling ropes up on the deck; his wife was not impressed by what she saw: "No officer was directing, and few sailors were in sight. Things were being done, but in a haphazard, unsystematic fashion. There was no evidence of the least familiarity on the part of the crew with the routine of lowering the boats." Henry Harper's description concurred: "Presently a number of stewards and other men of the ship's company began to fuss with the tackle of a couple of lifebelts near where we were on the upper deck. I say 'fuss' with them, but I might as well say 'make a mess of them.' They seemed quite unused to handling boat gear. They took away a section of the deck rail near each boat and then climbed into the boat and hoisted away on the falls so as to swing the boat clear...very slowly, and stumbling here and there, the people began to get in." John Snyder wrote that as soon as the boats were ready, people were told to get into them[13]. Beesley heard the order for everyone on deck with lifebelts on, and, after being on deck for some little time saw, not boats ready to take on passengers, but crew "arranging the oars...coiling ropes on the deck" and then turning the cranks to swing the boats out.

There is no indication that these passengers, who were among the first on deck and departed in the first boats (Beesley excepted), lingered on their way up top. They seem to have arrived promptly...and the boats still weren't ready in twenty minutes.

So, we now have some form of evidence that at least some of the boats had been overlooked until well after midnight, and a few others were being "fussed over" while the passengers waited. Why did it take so long to prepare them? Were there too few sailors? We shall presently see that the estimate for the number of sailors on the ship, who could work on the boats, was between 59 and 83; the numbers vary because of the imprecise definition of the term "sailor." Basic arithmetic puts the average number of men for 16 boats at 4 to 5 men; this average goes up if one allocated the same number of men among fewer boats. This is more than enough to unlace the covers, swing out the boats, coil the ropes ready for lowering, arrange the oars and masts and so on. Major Peuchen was surprised at how few sailors there were on the forward port side; as described elsewhere this may be because some of the men had been seconded to open a gang-way close to the waterline to facilitate easier loading of the boats. Because of the lack of available man power, Peuchen was asked to help remove the masts from the boats to make more room. The slow pace in handling the boats was endemic on the *Titanic*. And, to give another of the chronic shortage of men, a steward and Captain Smith personally attended to the one of the falls of boat 8.

It might be instructive to ponder how long it would take a crew to attend to the boats. Seaman Buley said, "The next order from the Chief Officer, Murdoch, [sic?] was to tell the seamen to get together and uncover the boats and turn them out as quietly as though nothing had happened. They turned them out in about 20 minutes...I was over on the starboard side at first...I helped lower all the starboard boats [level with the boat deck]."[14]

Lightoller testified that, "it would take us from 15 minutes to 20 minutes to uncover [boat] No. 4; then to coil the falls down, then to swing out and lower it down to "A" deck would take another six or seven minutes at least." Lowe's answer to a similar question was as follows: "I should say, from the start to finish of putting a boat over [including taking the covers off], until you get her into the water, it will take you somewhere about 20 minutes." This included the time taken to uncover the boats. Lightoller said that it took this long just to take the canvas tarpaulin off! Was he simply padding the time to explain or excuse the slow response by the crew? It seems likely.

Others commented on the time required: Horswell said that the boats on the forward port side were cleared away in ten minutes, but Jewell gave a contrary story: although they were "in a hurry", it took half an hour at most to get his boat (7) prepared and lowered to the sea. Pitman's response only seemed to detailed the swinging out of the boat; "It struck me at the time the easy way the boat went out, the great improvement the modern davits were on the old-fashioned davits. I had about five or six men there, and the boat was out in about two minutes...I thought what a jolly fine idea they were, because with the old-fashioned davits it would require about a dozen men to lift her, a dozen men at each end. I got her overboard all right, and lowered level with the rail." Pitman's description of "two or three minutes" is perfectly in line with tests performed by the British Board of Trade, who managed to swing a boat out in under two minutes, but Pitman's testimony prompts more questions: without a drill, how familiar was the crew with the davits? Unfortunately, this author only has incomplete data with which to work, but we know that, out of the deck crew on board, 17 of them had come from the *Olympic*, which was fitted with the same style davits. Many came from another White Star ship, the *Oceanic*, dating back to 1899 and fitted with "old" davits, and whether any of these crew had served on the *Olympic* at any time in the past or had experience with the davits from other ships is not known to this author. One can only ponder on just how difficult it would have been to adapt to the Welin davits, if all one had used in the past was a more cumbersome arrangement. It does appear that, if only the crew had performed a full lifeboat drill that Sunday, things could have been very different.[15]

It is often stated in *Titanic* discussion forums that the *Titanic* having more boats would not have made more difference; the ship had a lifespan of two hours and forty minutes (or two hours and 20 minutes if one neglects the first 20 minutes before the boatswain was called to muster the crew), and that only 18 out of 20 boats were launched successfully. "What the ship needed was time, and she didn't have it," was one argument on a discussion forum. What this author suggests is that "what the ship needed was an efficient crew, and she didn't have it." If the crew had shown more alacrity, then less time would have been taken to prepare the boats that they did have; by the time the passengers had started to arrive on deck (perhaps 12.25am?), boats "D", 5, 3, 9 and 10 were in a state of unreadiness, and no thought had been given to retrieving the apparatus that would have lowered boats "A" and "B" safely from the deck house roofs to the deck. This effectively means that, out of 16 boats that were under davits and could have been lowered, 4 of them had not been attended to in the 25 minutes since passengers had started to spill out on to the deck, which was three quarters of an hour after the "prepare boats" order was given ... and a full hour after the collision. And if Beesley is correct, that the aft starboard boats were swung out at the same time, we can add boats 11, 13 and 15 to the tally of craft that were not been sufficiently prepared.

It may be said that Lightoller's evidence (21 to 27 minutes to get a boat down to at least "A" deck) is a deliberate over-exaggeration to explain why the process of launching was so slow. Lowe's statement disagrees with this: " It was not the launching of the boats that took the time. We got the whole boat out and in the water in less than ten minutes. It was getting the people together that took the time." Presumably, "getting the boat out" did not include the removal of the tarpaulin, but he raises a valid point: gathering the people took the time. The accounts we do have suggest that this would not have hindered the evacuation, as there were already passengers available at the boats that were ready to go. There are very few cases of people placed in them complaining of waiting inordinately while extra incumbents were sought. For the forward-most boats, which left with approximately 30 or 40 people, one must ask how long it would take to assist such a number into a 30 foot long craft? One final point: at the British Inquiry, retired Captain John Pritchard, who had retired as commander of the Cunard Line's *Mauretania* at Christmas 1909, was asked how long it would take

136

for his boats to be got out, with the covers off and swung out. With a properly disciplined boat crew, his reaction was immediate: "six minutes." And yet it is claimed that it had taken 15 to 20 minutes just to get the *Titanic*'s boat covers off.

How concerned were the crew who worked on the boats that disaster was imminent? We have only the word of those who were asked, and this is a small fraction of the total who toiled on the boats. It is an important question; a concerned crew might have worked faster, with more urgency, rather than a crew who regarded it as merely a matter of routine. The answers that we do have are somewhat illuminating.

3Rd Officer Pitman did not think the situation was serious. Before he left the *Titanic*, Murdoch shook hands with him and bade him good bye and good luck. It struck Pitman that Murdoch might have thought that the situation was serious when this farewell occurred. Steward Hardy later found himself walking aft with Murdoch (Hardy himself left in one of the last boats) a little while after Pitman had gone, and the 1st Officer said, "I believe she is gone, Hardy." This made his companion realise, for the first time, that the ship was doomed. Lightoller knew that it was serious when he was in his bunk and informed on the water entering the mail rooms. But even he did not think the ship was going down, a fact confirmed in his unreliable memoirs. Of all the surviving officers, Boxhall was the only one to directly enquire about the condition of the ship. He was unsure as to when this was, except that it was in the early part of the evening after the order to clear the boats has been issued. "Is it really serious?" Boxhall asked the captain, who replied, "Mr. Andrews tells me he gives her from an hour to an hour and a half." By inference, neither Boxhall nor Smith shared Andrews diagnostics with anyone. But Boxhall later said that, when he took to his boat, despite the ship being down by the head, and despite being told of Andrews' proclamation of the *Titanic*'s doom he was "undecided" whether the ship would indeed founder. One wonders why Boxhall found Andrews story unconvincing...unless false evidence was being given at the testimony. Andrews knew the ship better than anyone else aboard. It also means that Andrews had revised his estimate of the ship's lifespan from "half an hour" to "an hour to an hour and a half."

Of the seaman who worked on the boats, one is hard pressed to find anyone who thought that the *Titanic* would founder. If the boatswain was indeed telling only a select few, such Hemming, that the ship would not survive for much longer "and not to tell anyone," the lack of urgency becomes understandable, for no-one knew that they were in the midst of a crisis. Hichens is one exception; upon reaching the water, he urged his fellow crew to hurry as the "boat" was going to founder; his fellows thought he meant their tiny craft, but he was referring to the *Titanic* herself. Hichens assessment is suspect, as he seemed to have been in an anxious and frantic state anyway. He had been on the bridge when the collision occurred and his observations while stationed there may have sparked his apprehension. As we shall soon see, his prognostications of doom and disaster continued even after his boat had managed to achieve a safe distance.

More remarkable are the crewmen who had seen or heard water rushing in to the hull, or had seen the effects of the ingress; namely, water flowing rapidly into the cargo holds which was forcing air out, causing the protective tarpaulins over the hatch coverings to balloon upwards. Crewman like Buley, Clench, Hogg and so on even describe the level of confidence in the ship being so high that no-one thought it was going down. When comparing these unconcerned and nonplussed observations, Hichens behaviour seems out of place.

There was no sense of panic or confusion on deck, and the soothing music of the band only served to allay people's fears. In the first boats loaded forward, one finds comforting words that it was no more than a drill, albeit a peculiarly scheduled one, or "a precaution." There are no instances of this decorum being shattered, or the very fine division between instilling urgency and creating pandemonium being crossed. One gets the feeling that in the first few boats, neither urgency nor pandemonium availed themselves upon the patient crowd.

But compare that to what was happening at the port side aft end of the boat deck. There was panic and a surge for the boats that forced a gun to be fired to quell the rising crowd. This part of the boat deck was the domain of the 2nd and 3rd class and it seems unfair to suggest that the panic was caused by their social upbringing with a greater "desire to survive" ingrained into their psyche. One obvious suggestion for the consternation in this location comes not their nurture but their recent experiences; although statistics are not known, a large proportion of men in this location would have been steerage men, and some of those knew that the ship was flooding. Some had even felt the water come under the door to their room. Did they act in such an unruly fashion because they had seen proof that the ship was doomed? One 3rd class man remembers a crewman coming along his corridor urging everyone on deck unless they wanted to be drowned. With such a directive, one would be under no illusion that the ship was seriously injured. As we have seen, the 1st class did not seem unduly concerned even when told of water inside the ship.

But, if there was any ignorance as to the mortal peril everyone faced, it was dispelled when, at sometime before 1am, the first distress rocket was sent aloft. Fired from a tube near emergency boat No.1, these small metal cylinders were ignited by pulling on a lanyard; the projectile leapt 600 to 800 feet into the air and exploding with a deafening report, sending down a cascade of white stars.

Like nearly everything else in the *Titanic* story, the time of the first rocket and the number launched is still debated 100 years after the event. Although peripheral to the *Titanic* story, a nearby ship, the tramp steamer *Californian* saw the *Titanic*'s rockets, and the first one was timed at about 12.45am on that ship. As can be seen elsewhere, an argument has been made that the *Titanic*'s clocks were 2 hours and 2 minutes ahead of New York time, and we know that the *Californian*'s were 1 hour and 55 minutes ahead. This would put the time of the first rocket at 12.52am on the ailing ship, well over an hour after the collision. If Boxhall's UK evidence is any hint, he did not wait for orders from the captain to procure the rockets: "I had sent in the meantime for some rockets, and told the captain I had sent for some rockets, and told him I would send them off, and told him when I saw this light. He said, "Yes, carry on with it.""

The "light" referred to by Boxhall was a ship that was seen only a few miles ahead of the *Titanic*, its twinkling mast and navigation lights plainly visible off the port bow[16]. The rockets were sent up to attract its attention. The *Californian* saw 8 rockets, but estimates of those on the *Titanic* range from 6 to 12 fired, with one person saying they went up at "minute intervals."[17]

When was the "mystery ship" first seen by the *Titanic*? It was not there when Fleet and Lee were in the crow's nest (or so they claimed), but rather, it was seen "by the other lookout," which places it between 12 midnight and 12.20 when the lookouts descended, if one accepts their 20 minute estimate as the time they spent in the iron cage on the mast. Sadly, the lookouts were not asked about this when interrogated at the inquiries. Seaman Buley said that the lights were seen when they were turning the boats out, "ten minutes" after they struck the iceberg. His timing seems to be off, as the crew were sent to swing out the boats 20

139

minutes after the strike. Boxhall however, does hint at an "early sighting" in his testimony: " I was unlacing covers on the port side myself and I saw a lot of men come along - the watch I presume [at midnight]. They started to screw some out on the afterpart of the port side; I was just going along there and seeing all the men were well established with their work, well under way with it, and I heard someone report a light, a light ahead. I went on the bridge and had a look to see what the light was." The boats on the aft portion of the port side of the boat deck were indeed being prepared about midnight: passenger Beesley saw an officer starting to uncover boat 16, and Pitman found Moody there a few minutes later. But we should also remember that Boxhall also said that he took a look at the mystery light when he was working out the ship's position for the wireless men- and we know from ground stations that this was received at 10.35pm New York Time. 2 hours and 2 minutes ahead of this is 12.37am; rockets would not be sent up for another 15 minutes. Meshing this with Boxhall's other comment is difficult, as it implies that the boats were being swung out and attended to very late, perhaps nearly an hour after the collision. Were the crew really this slow?

But if the mystery ship's lights were indeed spotted in the first 40 minutes, then why wait till nearly 1am, or another 40 minutes, before sending up the rockets? This hints at laxity on the part of the *Titanic*'s crew, or that no-one bothered to inform an officer that a promising opportunity for help existed...The converse argument is that if the crew had indeed acted promptly, and rockets were sent aloft earlier than the claimed time of about 12.50 am then the 2 hours and 2 minutes New York time difference is not correct.

The rockets are intimately involved with two gentlemen who found themselves located at the aft end of the ship. Quartermaster Rowe was stationed on the poop when the impact occurred; he had seen the iceberg gliding along the starboard side of the ship and initially mistook it for a "windjammer with all sails set." He seems to have been completely overlooked. His relief, another quartermaster named Bright (and who was one of the very few who had been informed that the ship was going down by the head) was late in relieving Rowe, who expected, like Hichens, to go off duty at "12.22" [sic - 12.23?]. Soon afterwards, Rowe observed a lifeboat in the water and telephoned the forward bridge, where a surprised Boxhall picked up the receiver. Rowe asked if the officer knew that there was a boat in the water. This was news to Boxhall; before he went to the bridge, all he had heard was the order to "clear away" (that is, prepare) the boats to leave the ship; he had not even heard the directive to fill them with people. The 4th Officer asked the caller if he was the 3rd officer, but when told that he was the quartermaster on the poop he was ordered to bring detonators, used to fire rockets to the bridge. Rowe and Bright acquired the relevant boxes from a nearby locker and headed forward, whereupon they helped fire rockets and use the Morse lamps to signal for assistance.

When analysed, this story introduces dubious aspects: Boxhall claimed that he received the telephone call after sending a rocket up. Indeed, he claimed that he had just put the firing lanyard inside the bridge[18]. But Rowe's statements in the decades to come mostly contradict this; only on one occasion does he say that rockets were going up when he was still aft. His comments and interviews are almost universally clear; nothing was seen or heard, other than steam venting, before he went to the forward bridge. Indeed, he even says that all "was quiet" before he went to the bridge. Perhaps we should seriously question - for the first time - the truth of Boxhall's comments. This would not be the first time that his statements arouse suspicion. Boxhall's comment to the Captain that he had "sent for" the rockets suggest that the rockets were not stored locally, but had to brought to the bridge from a remote locale.

Although Boxhall confirms Rowe's "boat in the water" story, Bright did not mention this when questioned. Indeed, he said that upon arriving on the poop, "[Rowe and I] stood there for some moments and did not know exactly what to do, and rang the telephone up to the bridge and asked them what we should do." Conversely, Rowe does not mention Bright in his statements, and one only wonders whether he was indignant about being left for an undisclosed amount of time in the cold when he could have been tucked up in a warm bed, while he paced back and forth waiting for his relief to arrive. This does not seem likely as it sounds extremely petty. However, Rowe does sound as if he did everything himself.

Rowe's observation about the boat he saw is interesting. He always assumed it was No.13, but this left a long time after he had vacated the poop. What boat he saw is not known, other than it was a starboard one. From his vantage point, Rowe would have found it difficult to see along the ship's hull to ascertain which boat it was. He could almost certainly see that No.15 was still on board, and may have assumed that the next one forward, No.13, was the one he had seen.

Then there is the issue of timing. Rowe puts the time of the first boat at 12.25am, but in later years moves this to 1.00am. He was

141

wearing a watch and he timed the collision as being 11.40pm. It is tempting to speculate that he had reset his watch to compensate for westward travel, but in the ensuing decades, he denied this, and even said that he did not think of, or even look at his watch; it may be that his timings post-collision are estimates. If he had adjusted his watch, this would make the unadjusted ship's time as being 12.48am, which is close to the time (12.45am) that is generally accepted as being when the first boat did indeed leave...but it also confirms that the rocket firings did not commence until suspiciously late in the sinking; approximately an hour after the collision, when every second did, quite literally, count. Having been told that the ship had an hour to an hour and a half to live, the perennial question remains: why on earth was so much time allowed to pass?

Boxhall claimed to have fired the rockets until the very last minute when he was ordered away by the captain. There is some evidence that once the 4th Officer departed, the captain himself superintended the rockets, until finally ordering Rowe away in the penultimate lifeboat that was under davits. The problem in this scenario is that Rowe himself said that he left the bridge to get into the boat at 1.25am, and that the *Titanic* sank, by his estimate, 20 minutes later after his craft had spent 5 minutes rubbing down the hull on account of the large list. The *Titanic* sank at 2.20am by nearly all accepted accounts, or nearly a full hour after Rowe claimed he left the bridge. If we add on the 23 minute time retardation, we get 1.48am, which is only half an hour before the ship went down, which is a better fit to the testimony. Further confirmation of this point comes from the *Californian* which placed the last pyrotechnic at about 1.40am. This equates to 1.47am on the *Titanic*, further confirmation of the 2 hours and 2 minutes time lag between the *Titanic* and New York and that Rowe's timings are offset by 20 minutes...but still the problem of the delay in using rockets remains.

The most serious departures in evidence between Rowe and Boxhall comes after the detonators were delivered to the bridge. Rowe (and Bright) assisted with the firing, and Rowe was tasked with using the Morse lamp to try to establish contact with the mystery ship. Although some were convinced that the other ship was flashing a reply back, a check with binoculars proved that it was simply the mast light flickering.

As per instructions from Captain Smith, rockets were sent up every five or six minutes, in accordance with the regulations that signals were to be sent up "at short intervals." However, Rowe claimed that after

142

firing the first two rockets, Boxhall was nowhere to be seen; the 4th Officer later claimed that in addition to helping with the rockets, he was helping out on the port side with the boats, but no-one else remembers him. He explicitly remembers that he did not help with the lowering of the boats, but assisting "to get people along there." Boxhall also claimed that he went to find the lamp trimmer, after consulting with Chief Officer Wilde after mentioning to him that there were no lanterns in the boats. The trimmer was found after some effort, and the lamps were brought up and placed in the boats. This is not what Hemming, the trimmer, said; he claimed that the order came directly from the captain himself.

It is known that Boxhall has pleurisy during the subsequent inquiries, and while there is no evidence that he was ill during the disaster, the suspicion is still there. His desire to get out of the cold is understandable; he claimed in the 1960s that he was having a cup of tea in his cabin when the iceberg struck, which is at variance with his 1912 testimony. If the 4th Officer "disappeared" during the rocket firing, we may have an explanation.

Much time was seemingly squandered in that first hour; everything from the boats to the rockets were dealt with at a precariously slow rate, as though there was little sense of urgency. By 1.00am, 5 or 6 lifeboats had already left the *Titanic*. They were occupied by about half of their normal rated capacity. 14 or 15 boats remained on board, as were about 2000 people. Who would live and who would die? And who would choose?

Titanic Interlude

Timings and Tribulations

2 hours and 40 minutes elapsed, so we are told, between the collision and the sinking. Equally authoritatively, we are given an impressive battery of timings, bolstered by references to testimony and private accounts. Can we be this dogmatic about the sinking? In this author's opinion, No. There is simply far too much variation in witnesses statements to create a completely cogent and accurate schedule of events that happened on board the *Titanic*.

A fine example is the water level on the stairs leading down to the mail room, as discussed elsewhere; one of the initial witnesses has it reaching higher into the ship than later observers which is impossible. This is not the only problems facing researchers, and there is a prevalence to pick and choose evidence that fits ones one pet theory, a condition endemic to many facets of the *Titanic* tragedy. For instance, dismissing Pitman's time of the first boat lowered (about 12.25-30am he claimed) and then derive a "correct" time of actual launching by subtracting the amount of time Pitman said he had been on the water ("about an hour and a half") from 2.20am to get a more palatable answer of 12.50am. What about Karl Behr, in the same boat as Pitman, who puts the time as two hours? Why isn't he given much credence? The subjective estimation of time is obvious in other accounts, and we shall discuss a few of them here.

Steward C.E. Andrews claimed he left the *Titanic*, in boat 16, at "about half past 12." He claimed that the accident happened "about 20 minutes past 11," or twenty minutes earlier than the accepted time of collision. A confounding aspect of the night the *Titanic* sank is that the clocks on board were due to be set back to account for westward travel. If one surmises that the 20 minute discrepancy is due to him altering his timepiece, what he implies is that he left the *Titanic* 1 hour and 10 minutes after the collision, putting his time of departure, in unadjusted time, at 12.50am. This seems far too early for this boat. Another example comes from Boat 1, where lookout Symons remarked about the duration between lowering and the foundering. He said, "Well, I should think myself if I say it was within half-an-hour I should not be far out. It

144

may have been less." In the same boat, Hendrickson puts the gap between the lowering and the demise of the *Titanic* "about three-quarters of an hour"; yet we are told that the actual timing was about 80 minutes. Emma Schabert puts the time between her boat leaving and the sinking at half an hour, which is far too late. Lawrence Beesley estimates the time he left the *Titanic* as being 12.45am, and he even says that when the ship foundered, they had been afloat "an hour and a half." These estimates would seem to be incredibly awry. Then, what of Seaman Lucas, who estimated that the water was up to the bridge an hour and a quarter after the collision - an hour too early. He also said that "about an hour" elapsed from the time he started on the boats till he finished with the last one; again, a severe underestimate. Steward Hart says that he left in boat 15 at about a quarter past one, which again is too early, or so we are informed by the cognoscenti of *Titanic* researchers. What makes accounts such as these any more accurate or otherwise than any of the others that are cited in books and articles?

Admittedly these are ludicrously extreme examples, but they do show how people's estimate of time, no matter how adamantly maintained and honestly believed, can be wildly inaccurate.

Perception of time was subjective, it would seem that very few people looked at a watch after the collision. And even if they did, do we truly know how many of them had adjusted their watches? To give a possible example, Margarette Spedden's diary has an entry labelled "April 15 - 12.30A.M. At sea in one of the *Titanic*'s lifeboats!!" But she was in boat 3 which we are told left a good 20 minutes later[1].

The best examples of inaccuracies in timings comes from two *Titanic* crewmen. I will summarise the relevant portions of their testimony here:
Steward Fred Ray was ordered on deck, and, after acquiring a lifebelt for the second steward, he went to his allocated boat, No.9. It had been uncovered and was just being swung out. Ray then went to the rail and saw the first lifeboat lowered on the starboard side. Feeling the chill night air, he retired to his room briefly. While down there, he noticed that the forward part of "E" deck was underwater; the working alleyway was so full he could "just" manage to get through the doorway which led to the 1st class grand staircase[2]. He "leisurely" walked up, exchanged a few words with Mr.Rothschild, and appeared on "A" deck, then went onto the "open deck" [the boat deck?] where he proceeded to No.9 which was just being filled with women and children.

Now compare this with another steward, Joseph Wheat:

Receiving an instruction from Purser McElroy to get all his companions to their stations, Wheat went from "E" deck down to "F" deck to discover everyone was gone, and noticing water running rather quickly down the stairway. Proceeding back up, he noticed that the working alleyway was "quite dry," and that the water was coming from the starboard side of the ship, up the staircase that led up from the mail room. Via the service stairs, he proceeded from "E" deck to "B" deck, and met Latimer, the Chief Steward, whom he assisted putting his lifebelt under his big coat. From there, Wheat proceeded up the forward stairway to the boat deck and saw that No.9 boat was just being filled.

The curious point here is that both witnesses wind up at boat 9 at almost the same point; even if they were off by just a few minutes, it seems impossible to believe that the alleyway could go from being "dry" (Wheat) to being "flooded" (Ray) in a very few minutes. If the rate of flooding was that fast the *Titanic* would have sunk in minutes. It is clear from their testimony that both men did not dawdle (though it is admitted that both men did spent a few minutes talking to passengers or compatriots); for Ray, his route required ascending and descending 5 flights of steps, and then walking laterally about 500 feet, a journey that would have taken less than 10 minutes, which seems plausible for a boat going from "being swung out" to "filling." Wheat's journey would require a small walk aft from his quarters, up 5 flights of stairs, then a walk forward to the Grand Staircase and then aft again. The journey is comparable to Ray's. How can they both describe the same alleyway, at about the same time, in different stages of flooding? The above extracts mention two boats, number 7 (the very first) and number 9 launched a while later. This provokes debate on the issue of timing. A respected chronology of *Titanic* lifeboats puts the timing between the first boat and No.9 as being a colossal 50 minutes. Assuming that Ray was correct in his statement that he saw the first boat lowered, and even if we generously say that some time passed between Ray and Wheat getting to boat 9 and it ultimately being lowered, we are still left with a huge gap in the timing that does not reconcile itself with Ray being below decks for only about 10 minutes even if one posits that the loading and eventual lowering of boat 9 was delayed for some reason. Steward Ward's testimony can perhaps be used to confirm this hypothesis at boat 7, he saw some women and men enter the craft, and then headed aft to No.9 boat where he assisted to unlace the cover. Another steward, Widgery, also went to No.7 at first. He said, "When I got up there, it was just about to be lowered. The purser sent me along to No. 9. They had taken the canvas off of No. 9 and lowered it [level with the boat deck.]" There

146

is no indication that a huge hiatus or procrastination occurred. If there had, why not go and help with other boats? One should also mention the testimony of a greaser named Ranger as his testimony exacerbates the gulf between the "wet" and "dry" alleyway. Ranger was in the electric workshop the night of the collision, repairing some fans. He felt a slight jar, and two minutes turned to look at the turbine engine and noticed that it was stopped. After 15 minutes, he was ordered to stop all the stokehold fans, which were consuming large amounts of unnecessary power. With 45 to shut down, it took (he claimed) about 45 minutes, and he would have to walk down the alleyway on "E" deck, and then into each individual fan room on "F" deck. During this time he had not seen any water. Basing our analysis on his estimate of timings, he time would be 12.47am, which relates closely to the the 12.45 or 12.50 time given by Wheat when he went to fetch any stray personnel for the boats - it was soon after this that he noticed the water. There is one other person to consider; Laura Francatelli. She saw water coming along her corridor on "E" deck; it had obviously come from the area of the mail room. She rushed up to the cabin of her employers, the Duff-Gordons, in time to hear the order to put on life jackets. They then went on deck in time to see the first boat lowered. Her story, and timing, corroborates Wheat.

So, whom does one believe? Ray or Wheat? And why discount one over the other? Even if the water inside the ship had sloshed in response to the change in list from starboard to port, it would still have been contained in the port and starboard corridors, and thus, still visible.

Other instances of faulty timings can be teased from the testimonies, but they require a patient assessment of people's actions and then correlating what happened, and in what order. For instance, let us take quartermaster Olliver: he was sent on an errand down to the engine room, and while he was there, he noticed that the forward watertight door to boiler room 1 was open; he even saw someone go into the dark stokehold. When he returned, he helped to muster the crew for the boats and even gathered the crew assignments for 6th Officer Moody. This was a little before midnight and we know this as the crows nest bell rang to signify the time. But then we have fireman Hendrickson's evidence: he went to report that the force of water rushing into the cargo hold was causing a tarpaulin to billow up in the fore part of the ship, and went to the engine room to report this. While there, he noticed that the watertight doors were closed. When asked to estimate how long this was since the collision, he replied, "something like three-quarters of an hour." But Olliver's evidence puts this at well before 20 minutes had elapsed. There is no evidence that the doors were closed again in the interim time.

Then we must consider the flooding in the boiler rooms. Fred Barrett fled boiler room 5 when water rushed in. He put this at about 1.10am[3] and noted when he climbed the escape ladder into the working alleyway that there was a little water, coming from forward. It clearly was not up to the level of the emergency door that Ray had passed through, as the escape ladder from the boiler room was forward of the door, and Barrett would almost certainly have testified of having to wade through water, or even of water falling down onto him as he climbed up. And yet Wheat said the alleyway was dry at about 12.45 or 12.50. At about the same time, Ray says there was so much water he had difficulty getting from the alleyway to 1st class quarters.

We have other accounts of the working alleyway at claimed points in the sinking. A crewman by the name of Dillon had helped to raise the afore mentioned watertight doors and when he got as far forward as boiler room 4, he "knocked about" and observed that the floor plates were damp. Working his way aft, he was then ordered out of the engine room about 1 hour and 40 minutes after the collision[4][5]. Another person who slaved below decks was a gentlemen named Cavell; he was in boiler room 4 and saw the water rise over the floor plates, eventually reaching a foot in depth. Evidently, this was after Dillon's sighting of a simply "damp" floor. What is fascinating are Cavell's impression of times, perhaps among the most extreme examples of misperception that night. Cavell was in the bunker when the ship struck and found himself beneath a cascade of falling coal. Dusting himself off, he had just clambered back into the boiler room when the lights went out. He went up to the alleyway and saw 3rd class passengers clambering aft. This was an hour and a half to two hours after the impact, he said[6] [7]. Briefly rushing off to fetch some lamps, Cavell returned to the boiler room to find the lighting restored; he says the lights had been off for a few minutes. Then, he says he ultimately left the boiler room and, by his own estimate, entered a lifeboat 2 hours after seeing the passengers. That gives a total of 3½ to 4 hours, and the *Titanic* hadn't even sunk by this stage yet. The *Titanic* is generally accepted to take 2 hours and 40 minutes to sink[8]. But we are not finished with Cavell yet. Vacating boiler room 4, he entered the alleyway and sees no water. If he had left the room after Ray's sighting, he would find himself swimming into a pool of water in the corridor. Unless the alleyway was subject to a complex tidal system, with water ebbing and flowing, surging and receding along the corridor, then Barrett had to have left boiler room 5 (at 1.10am according to him) after Cavell left room 4 [9][10].

148

Timing problems exist in other accounts, but while they do not confound an attempt to form a chronology, they invoke new mysteries. For instance, there are the issues of latencies, or "unknown" time. Stoker George Beauchamp assisted in emptying the boilers of the fiery cinders, and then went to boat 13. From his testimony, it sounds as if nothing happened in the meantime. But if the currently existing ideas as to the timings of lifeboats are correct, there was a whole 90 minute gap between these two events. What happened in the meantime? Another example: John Collins was an assistant cook on the *Titanic*. He went up to boat 16 and saw firemen and sailors with their bags ready. He made it clear that this was very soon after the collision, and he went on deck in response to the order to assist with the evacuation. An acquaintance of Collins described in 1985 that his friend had said the boat was then lowered. But boat 16's lowering occurred a long time after the collision. Collins then hears of a boat "getting launched" on the starboard side; this was collapsible "A" which is touted as being prepared quite a while after boat 16. So, there are sizeable gaps between going on deck, seeing boat 16 ready for loading, and then then going to boat "A". One wonders what he was doing in the meantime. Probably nothing happened in the mean time, but one wishes that this was made clear in the testimony. Did these witnesses happen to see anything important?

In summary, one should not just accept timing estimates blindly. When one sees a steward, say, stating that he was ordered on deck 5 minutes after the collision...or 15 minutes...or 30 minutes one should always be cautious.

Two established facts propagated as truth are that the *Titanic* collided with the iceberg at 11.40pm and sank at 2.20am. To question these amount to heresy. But the *Titanic* story is full of tiny fragments that, when integrated, question basic tenets of the sinking. Some of the doubts concern the collision and sinking times.

As stated, the *Titanic*'s clocks were regularly retarded to compensate for the successive decrease in the time difference between the ship and her eventual destination, New York which was 5 hours behind Greenwich time. The *Titanic*'s clocks were due to be altered at about midnight, so that in accordance with rules in the I.M.M. (International Mercantile Marine, the owners of the White Star Line) handbook, by noon the following day ship's clocks were correct, allowing for a very slight correction when navigational sightings were taken at first light.

On the night of the sinking, the *Titanic*'s clocks were to be set back 47 minutes; 23 minutes between 8pm and midnight, and 24 minutes between midnight and 4am. The ships clocks, controlled in the chart room and relayed to all other ship-based timepieces automatically, would then be correct at noon and correspond to the longitude of the predicted 12pm position. This means that those on duty from 8pm until midnight would be on duty for another 23 minutes; those on duty from midnight till 4am, an extra 24 minutes.

Were the ship's clocks set back? Nearly all the passengers put the time of collision in the 11.35-11.45 time range. Allowing for the fact that people's personal timepieces may be out of sync just a few minutes, this is in impressive agreement with the accepted time of 11.40; indeed, one survivor's account is illuminating. Eleanor Cassebeer's letter to her brother mentions her watch was set at dinner that night to ship's time by Purser McElroy. It showed 11:44 when the crash came while she was brushing her hair before retiring. McElroy's watch would undoubtedly be set to ship's time, and Cassebeer's letter does not mention her adjusting her clock by 23, or 47 minutes. Also, the "11.44" is reasonably close to the time of the collision as noted by Hichens and Rowe[11]. We also have a group of passengers in the 1st class smoking room who had elected to stay up so that their own watches could be set when the ship's clocks changed. They noted the time of collision in the 11.40-43 region. But in 2nd class Marie Jerwan related something quite different: she said that after a hymn service, she consulted a clock to set her own timepiece back by 50 minutes for the next day and her companion, Mr.Bateman, did the same. They retired at 10.30pm. At a quarter to midnight she felt the shock of impact. Here was one passenger who was saying that the clocks had already been set back before the collision. Furthermore, the 2nd class clocks, like the ones in 1st class, were linked to a master chronometer. They would all have been showing the same time. William Sloper claimed that he looked at his watch at 1.45, and five minutes later, the ship sank. One might think that he had reset his own timepiece...but in the same interview, he notes that the collision occurred at 11.40. It is unclear whether he gleaned this timing of impact from his own watch too. If so, had he set it between the time of collision and foundering? Margaret Swift, rescued in boat 8, claims that the ship struck at 11.45, that it was between 1 and 1am when she left, and it was 2.20 at the time of sinking. She showed her interviewer the watch that she had used on board ship, hanging from her neck like a pendant.

Seemingly, her determination of timings would be definitive? But no, for she then admits that she had not changed her watch to midday on Sunday. She was adamant that despite this, the time of sinking would be no more than a minute or two out, but if her watch was still keeping Saturday's time, her timings would be 40 minutes out compared with the ship's own chronometers.

If the reader is left confused by this miasma of contradictory evidence, it is deliberate and this author apologises. But it exposes the brashness of researchers who insist confidently that the elements in the story of the sinking forms a cohesive whole with few deviations from a strict narrative. The *Titanic* story is laced with confusion, but they are rarely mentioned.

Also, if the *Titanic* had steamed for an extra 23 minutes, or even a 47 minutes (supposing that all the time was taken off the clock in "one go" at midnight), then the *Titanic* would have steamed on for another 8-17 miles. From what we know of the *Titanic*'s navigation that night, this would have placed the ship well to the west of the location at which the wreck lies.

The analysis of the timepieces for the crew is slightly more complex as it is difficult to note whether the times they mentally recorded were seen on personal watches and clocks or ship's clocks linked to the master chronometer on the ship. Although the majority of crew members put the time of the impact as being about 11.40, some put it about 20 minutes earlier. Evidently they had set their clocks back so that when they awoke, their own clocks would be synchronised with ship's time, ready to start their duty shift at the correct time. Even boatswain's mate Albert Haines remarked on the time retardation when he testified that, "The right time, without putting the clock back, was 20 minutes to 12." Here was one crewman who was sure that the clocks weren't set back, but another one wasn't too sure; Dillon, stationed in the engine room, said later, "I noticed the clock, but I did not take any particular notice what time it was. The clock was put back about 20 minutes, I think."

It seems likely that the clocks were not retarded before 11.40pm. But had they been adjusted in the 11.40 to midnight interval? It is not too easy to answer this. People's perceptions of time gleaned from the ship's clocks (as opposed to passenger time, from personal timepieces) are very fleeting. One such example comes from lookout Symons; he heard the call to muster on deck to turn out the boats and it was just before midnight, "because, as I was on my way to the deck, so they struck eight bells in the crow's-nest." But was this 12.00am, or 23 minutes later? Fleet and Lee had expected to be in the crow's nest for about 2 hours and 20 minutes from 10pm. The iceberg was struck at 11.40, and they were relieved "About a quarter of an hour to 20 minutes after." This comes from Fred Fleet and we must be cautious as he was unable to offer any estimate of the time from first sighting of the berg till the impact. Still, we can only presume that Fleet knew the difference between 20 minutes and 40 minutes till the end of his watch. It seems remarkable that his successors in the crow's nest felt the impressive duty to go on watch 20 minutes early, in the biting cold[12].

Another crewman who expected to do another 20 minutes was quartermaster Rowe, who was standing a solitary watch at the stern of the ship. He fixed the time of collision at 11.40pm by actually looking at his watch. In later years he claimed that he did not retard it, but there is some indication in his contemporary statements that he did. He claims to have left in a boat at 1.25am, and was in the water at 1.30am. The ship sank 20 minutes later, or 1.50am by his own time. This is still some 30 minutes too early by conventional understanding of the sinking. A watch change of 20 minutes puts it closer to 2.20am, the accepted time. If this is what happened, his clock was altered between 11.40pm and 1.25am (or 1.45am approximately in unadjusted time).

Another quartermaster, Hichens, was standing at the wheel and was relieved at 12.23am. Whether he saw the time on one of the two ship's clocks mounted nearby, or he had a wristwatch, or just assumed that it was "12.23" because that is the time he was replaced at the wheel cannot be stated with certainty. He later said, "I do not know whether they put the clock back or not...I did not notice it." It seems clear that he was basing "12.23" on the time that he knew his duty shift would end. Comparing his statements with his scheduled successor at the helm (quartermaster Perkis), and those who helped at, and ended up in his lifeboat (Major Peuchen and Lookout Fleet), it is impossible to say with certainty whether the ship's clocks had been adjusted or not. But if he had left the helm at midnight (in adjusted time) when the 8 bells were sounded in the crow's nest and when the seamen were ordered on deck, his chronology looks odd. The first task he did was to unlace the covers of collapsible boat "D", a process which would only have taken minutes. He was then ordered to boat 6, which had been swung out and passengers were taken on board. We do not know with certainty when boat 6 was finally lowered, but it seems to have been close to 1am. If Hichens had started to load passengers in boat 6 circa 12.10am, giving

10 minutes for him to unlace boat "D", then the boat lay dormant for the better part of an hour before it disembarked. However, a time of 12.33am, neglecting the 23 minute time change, seems more palatable.

Certainly, analysing other witness accounts provides little evidence whether the clocks were put back between the 11.40 and midnight time frame. Following his journey to the engine room, Olliver was told to inform the boatswain to uncover the boats and prepare them for lowering and then fetch the boat's muster list. Thanks to Symon's account, we know that the men were summoned on deck just a fraction before midnight. But which midnight? With or without 23 minutes added on since the collision? Olliver's excursions could be done in 43 minutes...but they could also have been done in 20 minutes too. And it was after that the boats order was dispatched to the boatswain.

Pitman's comments are salient. When asked if the clocks were set back, he said that they weren't, because they "had something else to think about." As certain as this might seem, one could ask how could Pitman know? He wasn't on duty at the time of the collision; if he had been told that the clocks had not be retarded, who told him and when, and why did he not mention from where he gleaned this vital information? Did he compare his watch with someone else's? We do not know. But regarding the "something else to think about" argument, another pertinent point to emphasise is that once the ship had finally come to a stop, there was no reason to change the clocks as the ship was obviously not going to reach the expected longitude for noon on Monday. This final cessation would be about 10 or 15 minutes after the covers of the lifeboats had started to be removed, as seen by Lawrence Beesley. But if the clocks were to be altered at midnight, and the ship was proceeding - albeit very slowly - after this time, then someone on the bridge thought that the ship could resume her course, implying that a change of time was perhaps necessary. Only a moving ship could reach her anticipated noontime location.

Ascertaining the time of the sinking also produces the same problems. There is a peculiar mix of times, usually different by 20 to 30 minutes, undoubtedly caused by the perceived time change.

Take the comments of stoker Beauchamp as an example. When he was queried how long it had taken for the ship to slip under the waves, he replied: "About 2 hours and 10 minutes. Someone in the boat had a watch because it was between 20 and 25 to 12 when she struck, and it was just after 2 the gentleman said that she went down, or just about 2, somewhere handy 2 o'clock." Beauchamp was in boat 13; also in that boat was Lawrence Beesley. He was to write, "All accounts agree that the *Titanic* sunk about 2.20am: a watch in our boat gave the time as 2.30am shortly afterwards." Lookout Lee, also in this boat, heard a woman state that it 2.30 by her own watch; this was after the ship had disappeared.

Several in the lifeboats noted the time of the *Titanic* sinking; it may be a valid question to ask how they could see a watch in near pitch black conditions as very few of the boats had lamps.

Other accounts present problems: Annie Robinson, a stewardess, claimed, "Well, I looked at my watch when the ship went down and it was twenty minutes to two. That was by altered time when we were in the boat, and I do not think we were in the boat more than three-quarters of an hour." If Robinson's story is true, and the 2.20am time is correct, she had adjusted her clock the full 47 minutes. One wonders why there aren't more stories like this amongst the crew: if one expects to come on duty after 4am, adjusting a clock to only one half of the planned clock alteration could possibly lead to a crewman arriving on shift at the incorrect time.

Barber August Weikman was washed overboard at 1.50am, and his watch stopped at this time. It seems that his watch was had been set back too. His account has been misinterpreted by some researchers who claim that this reinforces a 2 hour and 10 minute elapsed time. But his affidavit to the U.S. Inquiry is not clear on this point. He said, "I was sitting in my barber shop on Sunday night, April 14, 1912, at 11.40pm, when the collision occurred." He doesn't say that he obtained this time from his own watch; it could have come from information gathered afterwards. He certainly doesn't say whether the source of the collision timing is from his own watch, later to be stopped in the water. There could very easily be twenty minutes difference between a hypothetical unaltered ship's clock and his own hypothetical altered watch[13]. The matter is fertile for confusion.

The majority of times of the foundering, either deduced by stopped watches, or by people looking at the time while in a lifeboat, point to 2.20am, with an error of a few minutes either way, and allowing for the fact that people ejected into the water when the bow of the *Titanic* submerged were dry and afloat for a slightly less time than those clinging to the stern. In the midst of all this confusion, Jack Thayer Jr.'s account stands out; he had seen the time the ship had struck with his

154

own eyes, and his own clock marked when he went into the water, which could not have been anything but a few minutes before the *Titanic* disappeared. The collision was at 11.45; his watch stopped at 2.22am. There is no reason to suppose that he adjusted his own watch, and if we change his time to coincide with the commonly accepted 11.40, then he went into the water at 2.17am[14][15].

This discussion over trivial minutiae might seem irrelevant. To an extent, this would be correct. In this author's opinion, as long as one uses a consistent time frame, and does not mix up passenger with ship's time like Beauchamp did, one can form some deductions. This is not mere semantics: if one were to analyse the watertight and floatation capabilities of the *Titanic*, then one would necessarily compare the state of the ship with elapsed time. To elucidate this point further, let us consider Pearcey's evidence. He claimed that his boat, "C", had left at 1.40am because one of the passengers had stated the time. This nugget of information could then be married with the observations made at that time that the *Titanic*'s forward well deck, but not the forecastle, was awash; but if this time was 20 minute early, this would help to generate incorrect deductions. In this case, the *Titanic* would appear to be less buoyant than she actually was at this time. It also does not jibe with other evidence. The British Inquiry determined that "C" left at 1.40 and boat 4 15 minutes later. If so, then something peculiar must have occurred. Bluntly putting it, the *Titanic* must have reacquired some lost buoyancy. For, when boat 4 departed, deck "A" was 20 feet from the waterline. Hugh Woolner's evidence tells us that boat "D" left minutes after "C" - and "A" deck was flooding. The "C/1.40am" evidence is that "A" deck was flooding, but 15 minutes later, was now above the water.

Pearcey's comment also had a tragic consequence for the Carter family. As noted, the British Inquiry puts boat "C" as leaving before boat 4, in which Carter's family were placed. Both Mr and Mrs Carter gave statements to the press soon after arriving in America, with Mrs Carter even stating that her husband placed her and their children in the boat. Sadly, the British Inquiry's determination of lifeboat timings led to the Carter's divorce in 1915. Walter Lord reported Mrs.Carter's allegations of the "cruel and barbarous treatment and indignities to the person" that she claimed to have suffered: "When the *Titanic* struck, my husband came to our stateroom and said, 'Get up and dress yourself and the children.' I never saw him again until I arrived at the *Carpathia* at 8 o'clock the next morning, when I saw him leaning on the rail. All he said was that he had had a jolly good breakfast, and that he never thought I

155

would make it.' Mrs.Carter's 1912 statements would contradict her divorce statement, and yet, it would seem, the British Inquiry's incorrect deductions had altered her perceptions. Sadly, Walter Lord compounds the error made by the British Inquiry by repeating the launch sequence times, with the implied hint that Mr.Carter was indeed a self-serving coward who would abandon his wife and two children.

Allied with the initial and concluding times of the calamity, another controversy over timing exists; what was the time difference between the ship and New York? The difference between Greenwich and New York was 5 hours, and ship's time was gradually reduced each day until ship's time matched those of the clocks on land. As we have heard, the time on board was schedule to be reset between 8pm and 4am. At the various inquiries and court cases, three time differences were offered; 1 hour 33 minutes at the U.S. Inquiry, 1 hour 50 minutes at the British Inquiry, and 1 hour 39 minutes at the hearings into the White Star Line's liability for the disaster. The last one of these can be discounted as it corresponds to the transmitted longitude of the sinking; obviously the *Titanic*'s crew did not think that at noon they would be at the sinking location. The second of these time differences has no basis in any evidence that was heard, and its longitude is at a point reached in the early evening of April 14th; it is nowhere near the extrapolated locations of the *Titanic* at noon on either April 14th or 15th. The first of the time differences has at least some evidence to corroborate it. Lightoller gave evidence about the time of the foundering and the corresponding time back in England, saying "5.47 - 2.20 - 5.47 Greenwich mean time: 2.20 apparent time of ship" which gives us a 1 hour 33 minute time difference with New York. How he came by this knowledge is not known, but it is the same timing as given by the *Carpathia* to the *Olympic* when the latter ship was given particulars of the tragedy; as researcher Sam Halpern has noted, the longitude for 1 hour and 33 minutes was sent by the *Carpathia* at 3.15pm New York Time on April 15th. It is the *Carpathia*'s own location; 45 minutes later, she sent another message, but this one included their New York time difference, not the *Titanic*'s. The time is for the *Carpathia*'s longitude. The simplest explanation is that a mistake was made, mixing up the *Carpathia's* current location with the *Titanic*'s.

Lightoller may have based his evidence on this simple confusion as the "1 hour 33" is too much of a coincidence. But it can be proven to

156

be wrong. At the time of collision, the *Titanic* was within a few miles of where the wreck is located. From the longitude of the wreck to the "1 hour 33 minutes" meridian is about 81 miles. At 22 knots, it would have taken 3 hours and 40 minutes of steaming, or 3:20am in the morning. Even if one factors in the possible clock retardation, this is still some 9 hours shy of noon time. Or, to put it another way, to cover 81 miles in 12 hours and 20 minutes would mean that the *Titanic* would have to slow down from 22 knots to 6.6 knots! Lightoller's statement in America confirms the standing instruction to bridge officers, but it contradicts his "1 hour 33" comment; "The clocks are set at midnight, but that is for the approximate noon position of the following day. Therefore Sunday noon the clocks will be accurate." We are therefore left with the following options: the *Titanic* was scheduled to actually slow down on Monday; that the officers did not know where the *Titanic* was; that they did not obey the rules as stipulated by their employees; or, deliberately or inadvertently, they had given false testimony.

So, what was the time difference between the *Titanic* and New York? If the I.M.M. rule book was followed, and the ship's time was not retarded, the clocks should still have been set to match noon on April 14th. Knowing the total distance travelled and the course, we can extrapolate backwards and hence the ship's longitude at noon on April 14th can be ascertained, and hence, the apparent time. This gives a time difference of be 2 hours and 2 minutes for the *Titanic*. This ties in with Harold Bride's testimony where he said that, thanks to the two clocks in his wireless cabin, he could see that the time was "about" two hours ahead of New York. As a word of warning, Bride was not the most reliable of witnesses, and the 2 hours and 2 minutes does have some implications when fitting in the distress signals into the ship's apparent timetable. Further comment on Bride's statements and the impact they have on this deduced time difference and the timing of the wirelessed distressed signals can be found elsewhere in this work.

To conclude this necessarily complicated interlude, while it is certain that the *Titanic* did indeed hit the iceberg at 11.40 and went to the bottom 2 hours and 40 minutes later, the timings between these events are not definitive. While it is often thought that nothing could go right for the *Titanic* and her passengers and crew, the same could be said about modern day researchers who find themselves inundated in a welter of confusion over the times on the ship that night.

Titanic Interlude

Andrews And Ismay: The Good And The Bad?

Following the collision, Thomas Andrews, the designer of the ship, acted swiftly to assess the damage. Shortly afterwards, and well before midnight, he had voiced his concerns to boatswain Nichols, and told him that the ship had only half an hour to live[1]. While Andrews' job was undoubtedly to provide an analysis of the wound inflicted to the *Titanic*, a fair portion of his job was undoubtedly to avert a panic, and this meant placated the passengers with soothing platitudes and to allay their fears. For instance, Mrs.Eleanor Cassebeer talked with Andrews on deck, and he assured her that they were safe, affirming his conviction that the ship was unsinkable and that she could break into three parts, each segment being able to float indefinitely. If her account is correct, this was soon after the collision. There are no other sightings of Andrews in any of the passenger areas at this point.

Captain Smith obviously would have sought the designer's advice as he gathered data on the extent of the damage inflicted to the ship. It seems providential here to describe how the two men, Smith and Andrews reacted in the first hour, and how information filtered to the passengers.

Helen Ostby was one witness to the captain's impromptu inspection and assessment. As she ascended the grand staircase, Captain Smith and one or two other officers were coming down it. They didn't stop to talk to the passengers at all, and looked "sober." Either she didn't recognise Andrews, or he had not yet joined the captain's party.

At least one person was proactive in gathering information from the captain. One of the men in Mrs.Bishop's party, Colonel Astor, approached the captain as he descended the stairs: "The captain told him something in an undertone. He came back and told six of us ... that we had better put on our lifebelts. I had gotten down two flights of stairs to tell my husband, who had returned to the stateroom for a moment, before I heard the captain announce that the lifebelts should be put on."

158

Mr.Harder saw the Bishops and Astors at approximately this time, and the small crowd seemed to be of the opinion that there was no danger. Harder continues; "A little while after [seeing the others] an officer appeared at the foot of the stairs, and he announced that everybody should go to their staterooms and put on their lifebelts." However, we should not instinctively grasp the implications of these inherent timings without more thought and comparison with other testimony, as the stories do not quite tally. Mr.Bishop said that he only saw Mrs.Astor and this was just before the order to put on the lifebelts. Mrs.Bishop describes how they [she and her husband?] were reacquainted with the Harders just minutes before the lifeboats started to be lowered. If they were indeed reunited with the Harders at such a late point the captain's whispered notification about the lifebelts did not invoke much concern in the group! Such a late timing seems difficult to countenance, as Mr.Harder mentions the officer giving the lifebelt instruction after meeting the Bishops, and Mrs.Bishop said that the boats started to depart soon thereafter.

Whatever the circumstances, we can determine that two sets of orders were given; an informal one to a select few that was then relayed to others, and an official order a while later. It is hard to differentiate between these orders. And even so, there are only a few hints as to when the order(s) were distributed. In this respect, the recollections of Mrs.Ryerson may help. At approximately 12.10am a passenger ran by her cabin calling to everyone to put on their lifebelts and come up on deck. This man told Ryerson that the orders had been given by the captain. What seems certain is that before this, passengers had started to put on belts; after the ship struck, steward Andrew Cunningham showed six or seven ladies how to put on the belts, and this was before the order had been given to put them on. After the call to the boats, lookout Symons noticed that when he arrived on deck to labour over the boats, there were passengers on deck, and they had their lifebelts on (even though Symons timing of when he went on deck - midnight, as evidenced by the ringing of the ships' bell - is central to our understanding of what happened, we must be wary as very few passengers would have been on deck at this time.)

The Bishops saw Captain Smith on "A" deck. When Smith arrived on "D" deck he had been joined by Thomas Andrews who was slightly ahead of him: night watchman Johnson was on duty in the dining saloon and he saw Andrews come down the Grand Staircase, pass through the saloon and then go down to the engine room, via the "working staircase" (a convenient route for stewards et al to pass from all decks between the

159

boat deck and "E" deck)[2]. Three or four minutes later, he saw the captain following Andrews' route. Johnson waited, and Andrews returned a minute later. An inquisitive Johnson followed Andrews, who proceeded down to "E" deck where water was seen in the mail area, two decks below them.

The captain's conference with the engineers and his inspection of the damaged areas complete, he returned to the bridge. Charles Stengel was on "A" deck when he saw the captain come up the stairs: "He had a very serious and a very grave face."

Andrews obviously lingered below decks while the captain went back to his command post. Recollections of Andrews being seen deep inside the ship are fragmentary: Johnson mentions seeing him reassuring a group of 1st class ladies in the corner of the reception room, which was just outside his duty station. This was after Andrews had been to see the water in the mail room[3].

A crewman by the name of Etches gave another impression of the seemingly omnipresent Andrews. By Etches impression, it would be about 20 minutes past 12 when Andrews stopped him on "B" deck and asked him if he had woken all the passengers in Etches area of the ship. Having been told that they were up, Andrews instructed Etches to go down to "C" deck with him, telling him to be sure, and make the passengers open their doors. Etches was to tell the passengers under his care that the lifebelts were on top of the wardrobes and on top of the racks, and to assist them in every way he could to get them on. On "C" deck, Etches met the purser who was standing outside of his office, surrounded by a large group of ladies. The purser was asking them to go back in their rooms and not be alarmed, but as a preliminary caution, to put lifebelts on. Mr. Andrews said, "That is exactly what I have been trying to get them to do," and, with that, he walked down the staircase to go on to "D" deck.

While Smith rushed up to the bridge to give orders, Thomas Andrews remained below to expedite the rousing of the passengers and to ensure that they were attired with life belts. Evidently, Andrews made his own way up to the boat deck, but it is difficult to determine when this occurred. William Sloper refers to "The designer of the *Titanic*, who was on board, [who] came rushing up from below at this minute, and although he said nothing about the seriousness of the trouble, one look at his face convinced me he was worried." Then Sloper writes about being ordered to put on life preservers, and eventually finding himself on

160

the top deck where the boats had had their covers removed and had been swung out. Sloper was to leave in the very first lifeboat.

Mrs.Frank Warren's story is similar; "[After the collision], we then went to our rooms, put on all our heavy wraps and went to the foot of the Grand Staircase on "D" deck, again interviewing passengers and crew as to the danger. While standing there a Mr. Perry [sic- Andrews?], I think his name was, one of the designers of the vessel, rushed by, going up the stairs. He was asked if there was any danger but made no reply. But a passenger who was afterwards saved told me that his face had on it a look of terror. Immediately after this the report became general that water was in the squash courts[4], which were on the deck below where we were standing, and that the baggage had already been submerged. Just at this point a steward passed, ordering all to don lifebelts and warm clothing and go to the boat deck at once, saying that this move was simply a precautionary measure." Dorothy Gibson told a friend that, "The steward assured us as he passed in the corridor that the *Titanic* simply couldn't be sunk. Just then I saw one of the designers of the ship, coming up the stairs, three or four steps at a bound. His face was pallid. When I tried to make further inquiry of him, he simply couldn't speak, from his excitement. " Moments later, she heard the command for people to don lifebelts.

There are, unfortunately no accounts of Andrews being seen on the bridge at this time. Soon afterwards, as heard by crewman Poingdestre and Major Peuchen, Smith gave the order for the evacuation of the women and children to commence.

Stewardess Robinson's recollection of Andrews is touching. After she had been on "E" deck and had seen the water for herself in the mail area, Mr. Andrews approached her at the foot of the stairs and said to her, "put your lifebelt on and walk about and let the passengers see you." She replied, "It looks rather mean," and he retorted, "No, put it on," and then after that he said to her, "Well, if you value your life put your belt on." In her estimation, this was 45 minutes after the collision. Barber Weikman also portrays a similar altruism. After examining the flooding, he went upstairs and met Mr. Andrews who was giving instructions to get the steerage passengers on deck. As he went along "B" deck he again met Andrews, who was opening the rooms and looking in to see if there was anyone in, and closing the doors again. Stewardess Mary Sloane Went round to her passenger's rooms and Andrews came along. She read in his face that "he was a man whose heart was broken". He told Sloan to make sure passengers had lifebelts on, and to get one

161

for herself and to go on deck. An hour later, she saw Andrews helping women and children into the boats, imploring them not to hesitate: "Ladies you must get in at once. There is not a minute to lose. You cannot pick and choose your boat. Don't hesitate. Get in, get in!"

The calm demeanour that Mrs.Cassebeer described previously had now gone; she had donned a belt, and upon arriving on the boat deck, she met Mr.Andrews who took her by the arm and deposited her at lifeboat No.5, the second to leave. He motioned to her to get in, and she asked if he would also enter join her. "No, women and children first." Andrews persistence never faltered. Mr. Albert Dick, who left in No.3, said that Andrews gave encouragement when he must have known that calamity was near: "[Andrews] was on hand at once and said that he was going below to investigate. We begged him not to go, but he insisted, saying he knew the ship as no one else did and that he might be able to allay the fears of the passengers. He went. As the minutes flew by we did not know what to do or which way to turn ... Captain Smith was everywhere doing his best to calm the rising tide of fear ... But in the minds of most of us there was ... the feeling that something was going to happen, and we waited for Mr. Andrews to come back. When he came we hung upon his words, and they were these: 'There is no cause for any excitement. All of you get what you can in the way of clothes and come on deck as soon as you can. She is torn to bits below, but she will not sink if her after bulkheads hold.' It seemed almost impossible that this could be true ... and many in the crowd smiled, thinking this was merely a little extra knowledge that Mr. Andrews saw fit to impart."

To invoke the cliche, Mr.Andrews then disappears into history as sightings of him cease. But he has one last hurrah, incorporated lovingly into the *Titanic* legend.

Soon after the sinking, John F. "Shan" Bullock wrote an account of Thomas Andrews's life. Labelled by some as a hagiography, it includes the famous statement; "Some fifteen minutes were left ... Later, an assistant steward saw him standing alone in the smoking-room, his arms folded over his breast and the belt lying on a table near him. The steward asked him, "Aren't you going to have a try for it, Mr. Andrews?" He never answered or moved, "just stood like one stunned."

It has been accepted as fact by everyone. But did it really happen?

162

The steward had been identified from contemporary newspaper accounts as John Stewart. Stewart was in boat 15, according to a crewman named Rule; but then there is his admission that his memory was affected by the disaster. At the British Inquiry, Rule testified that Stewart himself was in charge of the boat, which contradicts the known evidence which states that a fireman named Dymond was in command. Stewart was not called to testify at the inquiries, but if he was in boat 15, he was in a position to see into the 1st class smoking room and potentially see Andrews, and could have rushed in to speak to him, but this would have been far too early in the *Titanic*'s death throes; the "unknown" steward imploring Andrews to try to save himself occurred shortly after 2.00am. Boat 15 left at least a quarter of an hour or more before this. Of course, we must be cautious of any claimed timings, but it would seem likely that the sighting of Andrews was not at "the last minute"; indeed, it seems to have happened well before 2am.

But the more one delves, the more one finds contrary evidence: for instance, there is the testimony of Frank Evans. He says that one of the people that boat 14 picked up from the water after the *Titanic* had sunk was "the steward, young Stewart." There was only one steward on board by that name, and he was indeed "young" (27). He is also listed as a "Verandah Steward". The Verandah and Palm Court was right next door to the 1st class smoking room, where Andrews was supposedly seen, a perfect place to have noticed the disconsolate Irishman. Again, if Stewart was on the ship till the end, he could conceivably have encountered Andrews. But obviously, he could not have been lowered to safety in boat 15, and then be rescued from the water hours later. A suggestion has been made in some circles that Evans testimony was misheard, and that he actually said, "the steward, [a] young steward." Given the appalling acoustics present in the British Inquiry Hall this must be a possibility.

Shan Bullock's book sometimes associates accounts of Andrews behaviour that can definitely be attached to real people (e.g. Mary Sloane, Etches account of Andrews tireless work before the collision), the other later sightings of him in the book (Andrews taking a lifebelt to the bridge; Andrews toiling in the engine room; Andrews throwing deck chairs overboard to provide flotation for the swimmers) have no way of being verified that they ever happened. They have been ignored in favour of the smoking room anecdote which even Bullock states was not the last time Andrews was seen; many authors ignore this fact to accentuate the heroic demise of the ship's designer. Could it be possible that all the accounts are fabrications? Steward Cecil Fitzpatrick saw Captain Smith conversing with Andrews on the bridge; straight after this,

163

Fitzpatrick headed over to the starboard side to where boat "A" was being prepared. Like Captain Smith, Andrews jumped overboard as the bridge was inundated. This was when many claim that Andrews was supposed to have been staring into space in the smoking room, unresponsive to the suggestion to save himself.

Whatever the truth, there is no mention anywhere of Thomas Andrews attempting to gain entry to a lifeboat. The same cannot be said for Joseph Bruce Ismay, who did manage to escape. Like Andrews, there are many accounts of his actions in the first hour or so after the disaster ensues. Then, he disappears for a long time before reappearing just before the death of the *Titanic*.

Ismay himself claimed that he was asleep in bed when the impact occurred. He presumes that the jolt woke him up. After a moment or two's confusion, he went into the corridor and met a steward but was unable to find out what had happened.

Putting on a dressing gown and a pair of trousers over his pyjamas, Ismay hurried off to the bridge, the first occasion he claimed to have been there. This was about ten minutes after the crash. He was seen by Colonel Gracie who had embarked on a round-deck inspection just before midnight. He wrote in his posthumously published book, "I descended to ... Deck "A", port side...Entering the companionway I passed Mr.Ismay with a member of the crew hurrying up the staircase. He wore a day suit and...was hatless. He seemed too much preoccupied to notice anyone. [I] regarded his face very closely...it occurred to me that he was putting on as brave a face as possible so as to cause no alarm among the passengers."[5]

On the bridge, Ismay found Smith, and asked him what had happened. The captain said, "We have struck ice." "Do you think the ship is seriously damaged?" asked the Chairman and Smith replied, "I am afraid she is." If the timing is right, this would be during the initial assessment of the damage[6]. No one who survived recalled seeing Ismay on the bridge at this time; this conversation between Smith and Ismay presumably occurred when the report from the carpenter had come back about the water entering the hull. Leaving Smith on the bridge, Ismay headed down, where he met Chief Engineer Bell on the companionway. Bell provided a little encouragement; the ship was indeed badly damaged, but he was confident that the pumps would keep her

164

afloat. At no time was the true severity ever mentioned to Ismay, to the best of his recollection anyway. He went off to his room for a short while, but soon after returned to the bridge[7] in time to hear the order for the boats to be got out (or, in conflicting evidence, he may have heard the order to lower the boats). He walked along the starboard side of the ship where he met an officer, whose name he could not later remember[8]. Despite him having no capacity as anything other than a passenger, a slip of the tongue at the U.S. Inquiry may reveal something of Ismay's true role that night: "I told [the officer] to get the boats out." Is the use of the pronoun "I" significant?

The next sightings of Ismay demonstrates that, like Andrews, he was keen to ensure that the evacuation proceed promptly. Dorothy Gibson remembered him helping to fasten her lifebelt on. At this time, Pitman was standing by boat No.5 which was being uncovered and he was approached by a man who quietly muttered, "There is not a moment to lose." Pitman was unsure as to who the stranger was. The strange character remarked to Pitman to get the boat filled with women and children, to which the officer replied, "I will await the Commander's orders." The stranger remarked "Very well," leaving Pitman with the feeling that this was the White Star Chairman that he was addressing. Pitman went to the bridge, and saw Captain Smith, and told him what had occurred,, voicing his thoughts as to the interloper's identity. Smith's reply was to "Carry on." Returning to his boat, the 3rd Officer started to place people in the craft with Murdoch's and Ismay's help. A lady came up to the boat and Ismay asked her to jump in. "I am only a stewardess," she said. "Never mind, you are a woman, take your place," she was told and she clambered in. Richard Beckwith's paraphrased account is as follows; "Ismay was near the mate. Both of them gave orders for families to keep together and said everyone could go as there was room for all." When asked if the men could come too, Mrs.Beckwith was told by Ismay, "Why certainly." George Harder's experience at No.5 is similar; "I have been told that Mr. Ismay took hold of my wife's arm - I do not know him, but I have been told that he did - and pushed her right in. Then I followed." But Ismay's persistence in placing passengers in the boat did not work in one instance. Emma Schabert mentioned afterwards that he tried to get her to enter a boat but she refused. He said "You made a great mistake not to get into that boat." "It does not matter, I prefer staying with my brother," she replied.

Karl Behr contradicts Ismay's claim that he was not in control of the loading; "Mr.Ismay himself directed the launching [of boat 5] splendidly...we got into the boat and then Mr.Ismay asked if there was

165

anybody else to get in and there was no one left around there. Fully three minutes he waited, for others to come along, before he gave orders to launch the boat, having sent in two petty officers and two or three seamen."

Eleanor Cassebeer made an interesting observation; "A fact that is not generally known is that it was very hard for men to coax the women into the lifeboats...it almost became necessary for Mr.Ismay and Mr.Andrews to use force in making some of the men get into the boats with the womenfolk so that they might be saved." Then steward Etches commented that, "[Ismay] was asking the gentlemen to kindly keep back, as it was ladies first in this boat; and they wanted to get the boat clear first. The gentlemen were lined up, those that were trying to assist, and Mr. Ismay said, "Kindly make a line here and allow the ladies to pass through"; and I think it was Mr. Murdoch's voice that was calling out, "Ladies, this way; is there any more ladies before this boat goes?"" This confusing testimony makes it clear that although Ismay did help in some capacity, exactly what he did, and his manner, whether imperious or conciliatory, seem uncertain.

But, as boat 5 was descending the 60 feet to the water, the aft end falls became hung up leaving the boat at a precarious angle. Ismay shouted out to Murdoch to stop, and the situation was remedied. Lowe was the seaman attending to the aft falls of this boat and found Ismay's presence intolerable, as the impatient Chairman was waving his arm in a circle and saying, "Lower away! Lower away! Lower away! Lower away!" and hanging on to the davit. Lowe retorted, ""If you will get to hell out of that I shall be able to do something. Do you want me to lower away quickly? You will have me drown the whole lot of them." Ismay walked off forward to boat 3; at the time Lowe did not know to whom he was speaking[9].

If anything, Ismay's attitude betrayed a zeal that may have originated from any number of sources; guilt, for pressing the speed of the ship, sheer panic, or frustration at the speed of the evacuation. If so, he was the only one who was alarmed at how slow it was proceeding. If his testimony is accurate, he certainly did not think the ship was going to founder.

2Nd Class passenger Charlotte Collyer claims to have seen Ismay at the aft boat deck prior to her departure in boat 14; "A man in plain clothes was fussing about [the boats] and screaming out instructions. I saw 5th Officer Lowe order him away." Based on newspaper accounts,

Collyer surmises that it was Ismay she had seen, but there is no other evidence that he made it this far aft, and the incident with Lowe was on the other side of the deck.

Ismay was next seen at boat 3, as the first rocket detonated, as Lowe remembered seeing him illuminated by the explosion, but Ismay did not stay to watch boat 1 being readied. Instead he made his way to boat 9 and joined Murdoch and Purser McElroy. The male passengers and crew were standing in a circle round the boat and as women and children appeared on deck, he asked the men to make way for them. Edith Rosenbaum recalled seeing Ismay at this boat; the Chairman expressed horror that she was still on board and thrust her down some nearby steps, getting into the next boat to be lowered, No.11.

And Ismay seems to disappear for a protracted period of time. While it is true that he did help in the disembarkation, he never seems to have progressed beyond boat 9 on the starboard side.

Ismay reappeared not long before the *Titanic* foundered. A little while before he was ordered away, Boxhall was going to the chart room when he met Ismay standing by the wheelhouse door. He recalled Ismay asking him why he did not get the people in the boat [No.2] and get away; Boxhall's response was to tell him that the boat and its crew were ready. Immediately afterwards came the captain's order to load the boat. The next sighting of Ismay was a few minutes later, when he was seen trying to entice ladies to enter boat 2, but he ended up herding them round to the starboard side, where the last boat on that side under davits, "C", was being prepared.

The source of much controversy is Ismay's departure from the *Titanic*. Many felt that he, as Chairman of the White Star Line, should have remained on board and sacrificed his life. Ismay's own description of his escape was tacit; "The boat was there. There was a certain number of [crew]men in the boat, and the officer called out asking if there were any more women, and there was no response, and there were no passengers left on the deck...and as the boat was in the act of being lowered away, I got into it." Without exception, the crew of the *Titanic* who were in a position to see what had happened, defended Ismay and one would have thought that the boat deck at the location of boat "C" was a scene of tranquil serenity, without any commotion or fuss, and with few people in the vicinity. Lightoller claimed that Wilde bundled Ismay into the boat but conveniently could not remember who told him this information. Ismay denied that this was the case, and that he got into the boat of his own volition. Barber Weikman may have been the source of this information, as he said, "He was ordered into the boat by the officer in charge. I think that Mr. Ismay was justified in getting in that boat at that time." But again Ismay denied it, and his story was backed up by 1st class passenger William Carter, the only other male passenger in the boat. Ismay's version has been accepted as truth and repeated many times.

The story is completely at variance with the stories told by passengers in the vicinity; lest it be thought that they had some motive for generating scandal, most of the accounts come from 3rd class passengers who would have little or no idea that the boat they were witnessing was soon to hold the White Star Chairman; they simply provide a picture of a mad, desperate jostle to enter the safety of the lifeboat (similar to what was happening exactly opposite at boat "D"), with men being thrown out of the boat, guns being fired - and women and children overlooked in the crowd. Researcher Paul Lee has compiled a list of these accounts, and the chasm between the crew's stories and passenger accounts is striking. These stories are not buried in the files of newspapers either; Hugh Woolner described the frantic scene at the U.S. Inquiry but his inquisitors failed to realise that he was talking about the very boat that Ismay was in, and whose description of departure did not tally with that of the Chairman.

Jack Thayer Jr. described a crowd around the boat in 1912, again contradicting Ismay, but in 1940, this description (he saw Ismay push his way into the boat) and location (he said Ismay got in on "A" deck) had changed which makes one suspect that his memory had become tainted. Again, it comes down to a simple question: does one believe the crew, Ismay and Carter, or the other passengers in the area? And if there was a crowd surging to get into the boat, how did Ismay and Carter manage to fight their way through it at the expense of other people's survival? Were they given preferential treatment? Ismay's family were forbidden to talk of the *Titanic*, but a few scant morsels of information have emerged; he claimed that he was ordered into the boat by an officer as his evidence would be vital at the inevitable inquiry. Ismay never mentioned this at the inquiries as he felt he wouldn't be believed, and he may have had a point[10]. More worryingly, if crewman can, and did, adjust the truth to make the boss's departure as benign as possible, it makes it likely that they would also lie about other events that occurred.

Chapter 5: Acceptance of Fate

By about 1 o'clock in the morning, the rockets had kindled some instinct that something was amiss but even so, many still believed in the *Titanic*'s invincibility.

"Anybody knows what rockets at sea mean," wrote Lawrence Beesley later, and an officer of a nearby ship noted laconically that "A ship is not going to fire rockets at sea for nothing." But still, many people preferred to take their chances on the *Titanic* rather than a little row-boat, susceptible to the changing weather of the Atlantic. No one spoke of any formal warning and it seemed that few were pressurised to enter the boats. "Molly" Brown was one exception; she was told that "[she] was going, too", picked up and dropped into a boat. Lady Duff Gordon and her secretary were pounced upon by two sailors who wished to drag them to the boats and only their protestations ended the squabble. In this small area at the front of the boat deck, there are indeed a number of people who complained of being pushed into the boats. Such instances were rarities in the first half hour of boat lowerings when there was indeed a struggle to find people to enter the frail craft.

The behaviour of some of the ship's officers in the crisis has ignited much argument and confusion since 1912, and Captain Smith's is the source of the largest bewilderment. Well liked by the travelling public, on the morning of April 15th, his personable demeanour seems to have deserted him. Rather than inspiring confidence, he limited himself to the officer's quarters at the front of the boat deck, where he was hardly seen. And some of his decisions - and his ability to govern - are curious.

Take boat 8, on the port side. This was one of the first two boats to leave that side of the ship, and Captain Smith had given orders for its crew to row to the mystery lights on the horizon, deposit its passengers on the unresponsive stranger and then return to rescue those still on the *Titanic*. It would have been obvious that the other ship was at least a few miles away, and, if Boxhall's claims that Smith told him of the *Titanic*'s truncated lifespan were true, just getting to the other ship would have entailed more time than the *Titanic* had left. Rowing the boats was an arduous task, and those in boat 8 were inexperienced at the task. According to the Countess of Rothes, the occupants steadily rowed for three hours for the light[1].

It seems impossible to envisage that Smith thought that such a feat was possible; but he may have been so desperate as to grasp any chance[2].

If Smith's act was one of desperation, boat 8 is also indicative of another emotional trait in humanity: self preservation. Mrs.White observed later, "before we were cut loose from the ship [the stewards in the boat] took out cigarettes and lighted them on an occasion like that! That is one thing that we saw. All of those men escaped under the pretence of being oarsmen. The man who rowed me took his oar and rowed all over the boat, in every direction. I said to him, "Why don't you put the oar in the oarlock?" He said, "Do you put it in that hole?" I said "Certainly." He said, "I never had an oar in my hand before." I spoke to the other man and he said; "I have never had an oar in my hand before, but I think I can row." Those were the men that we were put to sea with at night - with all these magnificent fellows left on board, who would have been such a protection to us. Those were the kind of men with whom we were put out to sea that night." Mrs Emil Taussig's account to the newspapers is similar, but just as damaging to the conduct of the crew: "When we came on deck," said Mrs. Taussig, "Capt. Smith was preparing the eighth [sic - number eight?] boat to be let down. There was only one seaman in sight, but a number of stewards had rushed up between the crowding men and women. The captain turned to the stewards and asked them if they knew how to row. They answered 'Yes' hastily, and four of them were allowed to jump in. Only twenty women were near the boat, and these were put in. My daughter Ruth was among the first, but I said that I wouldn't go if my husband did not accompany me. There was room for fourteen more after the last woman had found her place, and they all pleaded to let the men take the empty seats. But the captain said that he would not allow it. I was frantic. There was that boat, ready to be lowered into the water and only half full. Then the order came to lower. The men were pleading for permission to step in, and one came forward to take a place next to his wife. I heard a shot and I am sure it was he that went down. Then the boat swung out from the deck. I was still with my husband, and Ruth had already disappeared below the deck. I gave a great cry---I remember perfectly calling out the name of my daughter---and two men tore me from my husband's side, lifted me, one by the head and one by the feet, and dropped me over the side of the deck into the lowering boat. I struck on the back of my head, but I had furs on, and that fact probably saved me from greater injury. The terrible thing was that we had so much room left for the poor men who were snatched away. When we got to the water the four stewards

170

who had told the captain they could row couldn't row at all. There was only one seaman to command the boat and an English woman whose name I cannot now remember took an oar and rowed until we were half a mile from the *Titanic*. My daughter also had furs on. The sailor took them from her. 'You'll not need them,' he said, and we never saw them again." Apart from the somewhat spurious mention of a gunshot, another point should be remarked upon. Mrs.Taussig left her husband behind on deck, and while her indignation may be the result of her having to forcibly leave her spouse behind, the same cannot be said of Mrs.White, who was only travelling with her maid. She had no anger to direct at losing a loved one. It is interesting that Mrs.Taussig speaks of the men who pleaded to be allowed admittance; the general consensus amongst latter day researchers is that men did not attempt or beg to enter the boats. Interestingly, steward Crawford has just come from boat 5 on the starboard side where he had seen men allowed to enter the craft, but seemingly because of compartmentalisation of duties, he never told anyone near boat 8 that a less restrictive entry policy was in force on the other side of the ship. If he had, one can only guess as to how many more men could have been saved.

Granted, there did seem to have been a shortage of trained seamen to man the boat, due to Lightoller's claimed instruction to send men below to open the gangway hatches, but the stewards who volunteered exhibited the perfectly natural desire to save themselves, and were prepared to lie to achieve this. How endemic was this tendency to exaggerate one's abilities to gain access to a boat? Mrs.Futrelle recalled in her boat that the men, all crew, who seized the oars were "perfectly helpless" to handle them. She was immediately struck that they were unfamiliar with the handling of a boat, being cooks and stewards. She finally asked one man why he was in the boat if he couldn't row, and he replied in a tense, strained voice, "I want to save my life as much as you do yours." Henry Harper had departed in an earlier boat (No.3), and had a similar story to Futrelle: the men at the oars clumsily struggling to impart motion, while the man at the tiller managed to run the boat in a semi-circle, ending up heading back towards the ailing *Titanic* at one point. The man at the tiller was, incidentally, an able bodied seaman!

Immediately in front of boat 8 on the deck was No.6, and by some happenstance of fate, it contained two of the gentlemen intimately involved in the liner's fate; lookout Fred Fleet and quartermaster Robert Hichens, who had by now surrendered the wheel of the world's largest ship for something more modest - the tiny wooden tiller of a lifeboat. In the ensuing hours, he distinguished himself in various uncomplimentary ways.

This boat faced a conundrum; there were only two sailors nearby who were free. Captain Smith seized a boy by the arm and said: "Here's one." But the boy proved to be useless at rowing, for he had a broken arm. An officer - probably Lightoller - gave instructions for the boat to row to the mysterious ship, deposit its human payload and then return to the doomed liner[3].

Descending to the ocean, Hichens yelled up to the boat deck that he could not manage his boat with only one seaman (Fleet). Up on deck, there seemed to be no-one available to spare, and so Lightoller appealed to the male passengers in the crowd. Major Arthur Peuchen stepped forward and declared that he was a yachtsman, and that he could handle a boat "with an average man." His offer to help was taken up, but the plan to enter the boat via the "A" deck promenade was swiftly aborted; the windows were closed (this was to act as a barrier to the filling of boat 4 which languished just in front of No.6). Boat 6 was now many feet below and jumping was not an option; the only solution was for Peuchen to lower himself, hand-over-hand down a rope into the waiting vessel.

When he turned around and looked back into the boat, Hichens was surprised to see this new interloper. Quickly adhering to the quartermaster's order to make sure that the plug[4] was in place, Peuchen was admonished for taking too long while fumbling in the dark; "Hurry up. This boat [i.e. - the *Titanic*] is going to founder." Hichens emphasised the point to the others, "You must row for your lives. If we are not a half mile away in 20 minutes, we will be sucked down with the ship." He evidently vacillated at some point, for he told everyone that rowing away was futile, as everything for miles would be drawn in by the suction, and if they were lucky enough to escape this fate, "the boilers would burst and rip up the bottom of the sea, tearing the icebergs asunder and submerging them all." Whenever anyone's efforts flagged, Hichens would remind them of the dreaded suction.

Boat 6 cut loose and headed off into the night; its mission, like boat 8, was to row to the twinkling lights of the strange ship on the horizon. A little way off, a whistle was heard and Hichens ordered the boat to stop so that he could hear it. The boat was being called back to the *Titanic* and the crew of the small vessel thought they should return but the quartermaster refused; "No, we are not going back to the boat.

172

It is our lives now, not theirs", and he urged his reluctant crew to pull further away. The women at the oars diligently pulled and boat 6 slipped away[5].

The "disagreeable" quartermaster at the tiller rankled Peuchen who described him as "talkative" and "swearing a great deal." The two had one row and Peuchen thought that Hichen's sighting of a buoy - in 12,500 feet of water - to be absurd, and the Major informed the ladies not to argue with the man at the tiller[6].

The reciprocal attitude of the passengers to Hichens was more charitable. Espying a silver flask of brandy, he asked for a sip but was refused; he was however given two blankets which were eagerly wrapped around the shoulders of this "shivering aspen." But generally, Hichens behaviour was deplorable, and his granddaughter Sally Nilsson suggests that he may have been suffering from shock. Regardless, Hichens stayed at the tiller all night, refusing to surrender his bastion of power. Goaded by the ladies into helping to row while one of them or the injured boy be allowed to navigate the boat, the quartermaster refused, reminding everyone that he was in command. When boat 16 briefly tied up alongside, a stoker was transferred to No.6 and Hichens became belligerent when Margaret Brown suggested that the new arrival row to keep his blood circulating. When the two boats parted, Hichens moved to prevent their separation but Brown told him that if he tried he would be thrown overboard. A reassuring hand was placed on her shoulder and as Hichens became increasingly impertinent, the new stoker yelled in a thick cockney accent, "Oi, Soy, don't you know you are talking to a loidy?" Hichens retorted, "I know whom I am speaking to and I am commanding this boat!"

Certainly the most controversial, if not the most shameful, aspect of the evacuation was that of emergency boat No.1, which was on the starboard side of the bridge. Nominally, it had a capacity of 40 people. That night, it held but 12[7].

The hint of scandal was emphasised by the fact that of these 12 people, it held three 1st class men, two 1st class ladies, and seven crew men. Of the five passengers in the boat, two held esteemed titles of the British gentry - Sir Cosmo and Lady Duff Gordon. Had privilege eclipsed the nobility of "women and children first"?

How the boat came to have so few is an interesting study in

itself. The accounts of sir and Lady Duff Gordon and her secretary, Laura Francatelli mesh very nicely; they said that sailors had asked them a few times to go to boat No.3 and, when this tactic failed, they then tried to drag the ladies away from Sir Duff Gordon. Pleading with the sailors, they were released. By this point, the three full sized lifeboats from the forward starboard portion of the boat deck had gone and everyone who was nearby departed leaving the threesome in front of boat 1. In response to his wife for directions, Sir Duff Gordon pronounced "We must wait for orders." It was then that he asked a nearby officer is they could all enter the boat. "Please do," he was told, and they were hoisted in[8].

If one is pedantic, Francatelli wrote that the officer in charge of the boat ordered them in. It is at this point, if her summary is accurate, that two 1st class men and the 7 members of the crew got in the boat. It is a mere quibble that an affidavit that she wrote claimed that the "officer" ordered the stokers in; she further claims that the officer saw the two ladies and ordered them in, but they said that they would only go if Sir Duff Gordon could accompany them. "I should be pleased if you would go," replied the officer. As they began to lower, the two other male passengers got on board too. One of them was Charles Stengel; he claimed that when he arrived at boat 1, there were only three people aboard - the Duff Gordons and Francatelli, and that he asked the officer for admittance. Stengel jumped onto the railing and rolled in, prompting a laugh from the officer and an exclamation that "That is the funniest thing I have seen tonight." However, his testimony does not mention when the crew entered the boat; it was dark, as he said. The crew may already have been there; he did admit to entering the boat as it was getting ready to lower. Fireman Hendrickson stated that he and his 'black gang' compatriots got into the boat only after the superintending officer had yelled for any more women to come forward, a hail that went unheeded; at the time, the only crew in the boat were two sailors - Symons and Horswell. A fireman named Taylor concurred; when he got into the boat, there were passengers already seated within in.

The evidence of Symons, the man in charge of the boat (or as he pompously titled himself, "The master of the situation") provided a contrary, and highly damaging account of the loading of boat 1.

The forward starboard boat deck had been left deserted, save for the few crewmen who were attending to the boat and its descent to the water. Ordered to No.1 by Murdoch, Symons affirmed that he had already been assigned to the boat, and was told to see if the plug was in the bottom. A crewman by the name of Horswell was also assigned to

No.1 and he too was told to jump in. Soon after, five firemen also entered. It was now that Symons noticed two ladies come running along the deck and asked Murdoch if they could get in. He replied affirmatively, and said the same thing to three men who also came running up and asked if they too could enter. This version of the story was rejected by the Duff Gordons when they provided testimony. On the other hand, fireman Collins recalled Murdoch ordering the passengers in.

After a wait of a few minutes, and with no one else visible to man it, No.1 boat was lowered. Safely ensconced at the stern, and clutching the tiller, Symons was issued his instructions by Murdoch; to make sure that those in the boat obeyed him.

As the boat was being lowered, seaman Evans, who was feeding the ropes through the davits, recalled the captain coming out and passing comment to "a tall military gentleman ... with white spats on."[9]

5th Officer Lowe may have been in the area, helping with the descent of the boat; he certainly later recalled the distress rockets that were being sent up from a position very close to him, as they were deafening him[10]. He also stated that he bundled Lady Duff Gordon into the boat. Lowe did not, he claimed, have any time to waste in searching for anyone else to fill the boat; for one thing, there was another boat inboard of boat 1 that needed to be fitted up to the davits, and this required that boat 1 had vacated the falls. While No.1 was departing, crew were fussing around the canvas covers of this inboard boat (collapsible "D") which would also be the subject of controversy later when it carried Ismay to safety.

But no sooner had the boat reached the next deck, than it became ensnared and the craft had to be cut away from its unwanted moorings with an axe; Francatelli claimed that the boat was released by a length of steel which was dropped on to the obstruction, jarring the boat free.

Lowe claimed that he stopped the boat at "A" deck for the men to look for any more people to take on board; no-one else remembered this. Lowe also claimed that there would be 22 men in the boat and 3 to 5 women, or twice as many as were placed on board; Symons made a similar claim which earned him a rebuke at the British Inquiry. One wonders whether Lowe exaggerated to make the low occupancy less woeful. He also claimed to have shouted down to the water "Who is that in the emergency boat?" when it was afloat, "knowing" that there was a quartermaster on board, which we know is wrong. Again, no-one else recalls this. Lowe claimed that he told all the boats, excepting Pitman's, to remain in hailing distance after they had been lowered. Again, Symons denied this[11]

Francatelli's order of events puts the "officer" giving an order to row away for a distance of at least 200 yards. Symons recalled his orders were simply to pull away from the ship but remain close and stand by if they were called back. Although this does not completely tally with Francatelli's recollection, his memory of the distance they did attain - 200 yards - is the same. Horswell's memory is slightly different; their boat was to "lay off" a little way from the ship and come back when called. Collin's story is a variation of this; he too heard that the boat was to "lay handy for further orders" when they reached the water. He thought they rowed away 100 yards. Hendrickson too remembered the order to stand off a little way and come back when called, eventually getting 150 to 200 yards away. Taylor also heard this, and the command to stand by for readiness at a distance of 100 yards he thought. In his estimation, they pulled slightly further away to escape any anticipated suction, to a total distance of 150 to 200 yards. Another crewman in the boat, Pusey, put the distance at 200 yards. Sir Duff Gordon's impression is that boat 1 was to follow the other boats and to row as fast as they could for the first 200 yards; tending to his sick wife, he affirmed that he might not have heard the order to stand by and be ready to return. When the *Titanic* sank, they were 1000 yards away but provided a caveat that, because he only had one eye he was presumed not to be a judge of distance. Lady Duff Gordon only recalled that they were instructed to row away quickly for about 200 yards but denied that they were told to come back if called.

The boat did not stay long. Symons claimed that the boat pulled a little further away to escape the suction but kept his opinion that the *Titanic* was doomed to himself; he seems to have been one of only a few people who thought that the *Titanic* was actually going down. Stopping and starting occasionally, the small boat's crew pulled at the oars, until they were about a quarter of a mile away, in Symons opinion. His would not be the only boat to disobey orders to remain in proximity[12].

These are but isolated stories in the great drama. In general, once the boats were deemed sufficiently full and ready to be lowered, the davits - and men - worked efficiently in the evacuation process.

There are a few exceptions; Boat 5 was lowered so sloppily that one end tipped up and threatened to ditch its human cargo into the sea until the situation was repaired...and when the boat reached the sea, the release mechanism for the falls did not work and a knife was used to cut the ropes; boat 4 also tipped up[13]; boat 2 also needed a knife to cut the falls, as did boat 6; in boat 3, Henry Harper noted that the men didn't know how to cast them loose and "fussed and fiddled" with the release mechanism; and, as stated previously, boat 1 became entangled in some overhanging projection on the way down, necessitating a delay while the obstruction was severed[14]. It is not known whether the incidents of the inability to release the falls was due to the lack of knowledge on the part of the boat's crews, or failure of the disengaging equipment. Unfamiliarity with the equipment was a handicap in at least one other case; not knowing that the plugs in the collapsibles were already in place, Lightoller and Lucas spent 10 minutes rummaging around in the bottom of boat "D" looking for one, before concluding that such boats weren't equipped with a plug. Lightoller blamed his failure on his inexperience with the collapsibles.

Boat 13 was safely lowered to the water, but a condenser discharge from the ship's engine room was thrusting a huge column of water near the bow of the boat, forcing her backwards...and directly underneath boat 15 which was coming down on top of them. Cries to stop lowering the boat were unheard. Again, the release mechanism for boat 13 failed, but the passengers and crew were saved when a convenient knife was found that allowed the ropes to be cut...and boat 13 drifted free. Murdoch seems to have been in charge on the starboard side and if he had been supervising the lowering from the boat deck he would have seen this incident and halted boat 15's 60 feet drop to the sea[15][16].

There were also problems with boat 14. The boat pitched up at an angle of 45°, and the falls became entangled during the descent, and the only solution was to actually release the boat while it was still suspended in mid-air, 5 feet above the ocean. The boat hit the water with such force that it started to leak, according to some accounts.

This boat also has several other distinctions. In a superb example of how the structure of command failed that night, Lowe manned boat 14 without an order from a superior officer. As he later said, "I saw five boats go away without an officer, and I told Mr. Moody on my own that I had seen five boats go away, and an officer ought to go in one of these boats. I asked him who it was to be - him or I - and he told me, "You go;

I will get in another boat.""[17]

The other notable "feature" of the loading of this boat is that it is one of only two officially recorded incidents in which a gun was used to quell a near riot. As Lowe himself said, as he and his boat commenced their drop to the sea, two men jumped into the boat; both were quickly expelled, but as he dropped down below each deck, he was forced to use his revolver to ward off any other attempts to charge into his boat by, in his own words, "a lot of Italians, Latin people ... [who] were all glaring, more or less like wild beasts, ready to spring". He claimed to have only fired horizontally, along the ship's side (although steward Crowe claimed he fired upward or downward). Before Lowe had arrived at the boat, "foreigners" had tried to rush the boat and all the crew could do was to fend them off with the tiller[18].

But what could Lowe do to prevent such calumny? If he hadn't used his gun, there would have been a stampede. If he had only let a few men on board to fill up the already scant places left, those left on deck would surely have surged around the boat, attempting ingress.

Charlotte Collyer paints a slightly different picture. A young lad, hardly more than a school boy, climbed into the boat at the final minute. Despite being hidden under the ladies skirts, Lowe dragged him out and thrust his revolver in his face, saying "I'll give you just ten seconds to get back on to that ship before I blow your brains out!" With a shift of compassion, Lowe dropped his weapon and said, "For God's sake, be a man! We've got women and children to save. We must stop at the decks lower down and take on women and children." Elizabeth Davies also mentions that her son asked for permission to enter a boat but was told he would be shot if he tried to get in. He was only 19.

Although boat 14 did not stop at any lower decks - probably because of the "wild Italians" clustered along the rail, the young boy climbed back out of the boat, and was not saved. Collyer's young daughter provides a contrary account to the accepted story of boat 14. She actually alleges that Lowe actually shot a man. 3[Rd] class passenger Laura Cribb also told how she saw an officer on the "2nd [class] deck" with his revolver in hand threatening to shoot any man who attempted to enter a boat before the women. "And he shot three," Cribb concludes. What do we make of such stories? It is hard to dismiss them, but it is hard to give them more credit, without more evidence[19].

Lowe's exhortations during all this are interesting, even if some are mis-remembered half quotes: "We want no dirty work here. I'll shoot two at a time," he said as he pulled out his gun; "If anyone else tries that this is what he will get," indicating his gun after a man had been hauled back out; "Stop or I'll fire!" "Stand back! I say, stand back! The next man who puts his foot in this boat, I will shoot him down like a dog", and "Anybody attempting to get into these boats while we are lowering them, I will shoot them," all said to ward off the creatures intent on causing upset to the boat. Lowe's machismo - and the gun - worked, and no one else tried to jump in with him and his precious cargo.

It is now that a myth needs to be dispelled. One of the most sanguine tales in *Titanic*-lore is that all the engineers died at their posts. This is not necessarily the case. Buried in the British Inquiry transcripts are the words of Frederick Scott who laboured in the innards of the ship. Released from duty, he climbed up the ladder to the boat deck. Joining him were the firemen and about eight of the engineers who had been on watch below. His timing puts this slightly before boat 14 was lowered as he recalled Lowe waving his gun to fend off the unruly mob.

Some men were undoubtedly required below; the emergency dynamos that furnished power still needed steam, and that meant that boilers needed to be tended to. Two boilers in each of boiler rooms 2 and 4 were normally utilised at sea to provide electricity. While we have some information about the coals being dredged from the boilers in room 4, there is no information for room 2. Regardless, it did not require a full complement of engineers, stokers etc. to work these furnaces. It makes sense for any superfluous crew to be relieved of duty, but unfortunately it slightly tarnishes the myth that the engineers all died below decks, at their posts. This is not an attempt to denigrate the reputation of these oft-proclaimed "heroes". Like the musicians, none of them attempted to gain admittance to a lifeboat.

5 of the engineer's bodies were later fished from the ocean, leading one to wonder whether the remainder were still working below or had not had a chance to don lifebelts. The only engineer that Scott recognised and whom he thought was the one who ordered him and his compatriots on deck, Mr.Farquharson, was not retrieved.

On the ocean, those in the boats faced being marooned until assistance arrived; biscuits and water were necessarily provided for them, and Chief Baker Charles Joughin claimed to ensure that the supply of freshly baked bread were made available, sending up thirteen bakers with four loaves apiece from the galley to the boat deck. But these loaves never seem to have reached the boats, although "barrels of bread" were reported to have been taken up by stewards and left on the deck, ready to trip up the unwary. Joughin's claim that his men took the bread up is repudiated by one of his underlings, Burgess, who said that at least some of his colleagues were in their quarters after the collision and refused to get up. They were still there when he went down a long time later, just before he departed in boat 13. Lightoller declared that, of the 13 boats recovered by the *Carpathia*, each had an ample supply of biscuits and bread and two casks of water; he had taken umbrage with Lawrence Beesley, who had insinuated that the boats had departed with no supplies. Beesley attributed his "mistake" to the fact that it was difficult to find such items in a dark and crowded boat. His argument makes sense, and of those who complained of no food, one wonders how hard they looked, if indeed they even bothered, as Jewell in boat 7 said. Of the remaining boats, evidence is scant; Hendrickson in boat 1 said he had no biscuits and Lucas in "D" also stated he had no provisions or water, while Jones in boat 8, Haines in No.9, Pitman and Shiers in No.5 and Evans in No.10 declared that they indeed had stores on board[20]. Even where evidence of provisioning, or lack thereof, is available, it does not always tally; Daisy Minahan in boat 14 said there was no bread or water, even though she describes stumbling over "huge piles of bread" lying on the deck, but steward Morris and seaman Morris disagreed. Indeed, the latter crewman even recalled drinking some of the water. Additionally, Lightoller's claim is suspect; two of the boats he had inspected were numbers 1 and 2, which he confirmed at the inquiry did not have any water or food on board. Incidentally, boat 14 was not picked up.

Joughin's allotted boat station was No.10 where he was allocated the role of "captain" on the crew listing, but those in charge of filling the boat thought that it was sufficiently full and he did not enter it. This boat had proved to be a burden to fill; the ship had developed a list to port which made the boat swing out a distance from the side of the *Titanic* and people had to be thrown, or jump across the gap; women and children had to be forcibly brought up from the deck below; and, finally, a lady had fallen between the boat and the *Titanic*'s hull. She was caught and pulled into deck "A" from where she returned to the deck above and tried to re-enter the boat. This time, she succeeded. Obviously feeling in need of something relaxing, Joughin retired to his cabin five decks below, for a half tumbler of liqueur. By now, the list was so severe that water had reached his cabin[21].

Seated on his settee, it entered his room and covering his feet as he sipped his drink. His thirst relinquished, Joughin left his room, noticing two men toiling at a manually operated watertight door in the corridor outside[22].

In our narrative, it would be very close to the end of the mighty leviathan, "The Queen of the Ocean". Now only four boats remained, two of them on the roof abreast of the first funnel. Their total capacity would be some 240 people. There were still approximately 1600 on board.

If one examines the official verdicts, one would be forgiven for thinking that the last two boats under davits were launched with the minimum of fuss. Boat "C", containing Ismay, left with the deck bereft of passengers if we are to believe his story. Other accounts, only one of which entered the official records, talk of a scramble and gunfire; astonishingly, this account has never achieved the prominence it deserved. A similar story of a scuffle is to be found with boat "D" which dropped into the sea at practically the same time as "C" but from the other side of the bridge. Lightoller recounted that he called for women and children and could not get hold of any. Even when some had been found, there were no women "within [his] sight or hearing" to fill the boat, although there were plenty of men. After repeatedly calling for ladies, some women were found and entered the boat; men who had climbed into the boat to take up the vacant spaces now climbed back out again, according to Lightoller; the order was splendid and there was no rush. There were, he claims, a number of Phillipinos or Chinese who had got in and stowed away under the thwarts; apart from these men, no other males entered the boat. His memory may be tainted, as a number of Chinese were found in boat "C", not "D"; also, a steerage man was allowed in the boat with his family, seemingly at the behest of Captain Smith. Quartermaster Bright, in charge of the boat, thought that there was room for 10 or 12 more people in the boat, but when asked why these spaces were left empty, he only replied later, "I had nothing to do with putting them in." Steward Hardy testified that the Chief Officer asked Lightoller if the boat was full, and he was told that it was. Astonishingly, Hardy says that there were no women, children or male passengers on deck and that there was no member of crew at the aft davit to lower the boat; Lightoller himself stepped out of the boat to take charge of the davit and allowed another man to take his place in "D". Boxhall had been ordered into boat 2, which left from the same davits as, and a few minutes before "D"; he said that there were "not many" people on the boat deck, and that there were some around by "the other boat."[23] This prompts an interesting observation: more than one witness at boat 2 describe a group of men (16 or 18 "stokers" one said) who filed by and got into it. "Get out, you damned cowards, I'd like to see everyone of you overboard," said Chief Officer Wilde and the men quickly, and meekly got out. What happened to them? Are we to believe that they dispersed without making any more effort to escape the doomed ship? If Seaman Lucas is to believed, they were still in the area when boat "D" was being made ready. He puts their number at about 40.

As "D" began its descent, Seaman Lucas saw two women left behind on deck, and he placated them by telling them that the boat next to the funnel ("B") was going to be put down for them.

The quixotic Gracie, instrumental in rounding up stray women, provided an account that corroborates elements of Lightoller's story; shortly before "D" was being filled, he and his friend Clinch Smith ran along the port side boat deck yelling for more women; his cries were in vain. Gracie remembered an order yelled by the 2nd Officer for everyone to go to the starboard side, presumably to correct the list to port that threatened to capsize the ship in some people's mind. While on the starboard side, Gracie was horrified to meet two ladies whom he had earlier entrusted to an officer on to be placed into the safety of a boat. He then heard a member of the crew pass by saying that the last boat was being loaded and there was space for women in it, and Gracie marched the ladies off to the other side of the ship, but his progress was stopped by a line of crewman who barred his progress and would only allow ladies to pass through the cordon. Eight of them did, two of them being Gracie's charges. Despite this, one of Gracie's companions, Miss Evans, could not be enticed to enter the safety of the craft - and became one of only a handful of 1st class women to perish that night.

In private, Lightoller told Gracie a slightly different story: some of the steerage passengers tried to rush the boat, and he fired off a pistol to make them get out. Gracie provided a caveat that this was "hearsay" and that he only saw the "most heroic" conduct when he was at the bow on the port side. 1st class passenger Caroline Brown also said that, "When we were leaving the steamship, an officer did display a revolver and threatened to shoot anybody who dared to try to leap into

182

our boat. He did fire one shot into the air to back up what he said", she claimed. Moments later, Hemming's observations seems to back up the "no women" claim: when he was climbing up to the roof to attend to boat "B", he saw one or two hundred men nearby, but no ladies[24].

Others decided to take their chances in this last boat. Hugh Woolner and Mauritz Bjornstrom-Steffanson had helped to quell the riot at boat "C"; they then headed down the nearby crew's staircase and passed directly under the bridge to the opposite side of the ship. Looking aft, Woolner noticed that the "A" deck promenade was empty and that the lights were glowing "a devilish red" colour. In front of him, boat "D" was passing by the windows, and he and his friend leapt into the boat just as water cascaded over the bulwark onto the deck. The rush of water over the railing was so swift, if they had hesitated a few seconds more, they would have been pinned to the roof by the inflowing tide.

2Nd Officer Lightoller had directed his men to extracting boat "B" from the lashings on the roof of the officer's quarters and it had fallen upside down to the boat deck, which was now awash. A few minutes earlier, boat "A" had been hoisted down from a similar position on the starboard side roof, but here it landed upright and the crew were frantically trying to attach it to the davits; at this time, the starboard side of the deck was still dry. Seeing that boat "B" was useless, Lightoller passed to the other side of the ship and from his perch on the roof watched the determined effort to ready boat "A". With the ship only having minutes to live, one would have thought that the panic to find a precious place in one of the last two boats was palatable. Far from it, if Archibald Gracie's recollections are any hint. He described neither a commotion nor any affray, just the crew struggling to ready the boat while others nearby watched.

The water was now up to the level of the forward bridge bulwark and the water was gurgling up the forward stairway, causing consternation to all on the starboard boat deck. Gracie and his friend Clinch Smith finally decided that the time had come to save themselves and they headed aft, their progress blocked after a few paces by a swarm of people who rushed out ahead of him, blocking their passage.

Further forward, the water had now spilled on to the deck itself and passengers and crew found themselves ankle deep in water. Inexplicably, the ship seemed to struggle to maintain equilibrium, as the water level fell leaving the area dry once more before surging aft with renewed force in a huge wave that negated any need to fumble with the possibility of boat "A" being launched. Now the struggle was not to launch the boat, but to cut its moorings as it could float off the ship and become a raft, albeit full of water but still buoyant - barely, anyway.

Gracie and Smith were trapped between the rising tide and the bewildered faces presented before them. The water rushed forward enveloping everyone in its maw, but Gracie eventually managed to grab a railing on top of the officer's quarters as he was scooped up. Looking around, the water had engulfed his friend and the mass of humanity he had seen just moments before. Gracie had a temporary respite from the relentless foam of water, as he was sucked down, his lungs straining to bursting point. Only his frantic struggle and determination to reach the surface saved him from plunging to the depths below.

Young Jack Thayer Jr. and a friend were near the gymnasium when they too decided to abandon ship; Thayer jumped out, but his friend slid down the side of the hull. Their different methods of escape no doubt decided their fate; Thayer survived, but his friend, Milton Long, did not. His body would later be recovered. In this area, cook Collins was also swept into the sea. Like Gracie, he found himself trapped underwater for a seemingly impossible length of time[25].

There are precious few anecdotes about comparable scenes on the port side of the *Titanic*. Harold Bride had helped to hoist boat "B" down to the next deck and he climbed down to rejoin this source of salvation. The surging Atlantic swell dictated otherwise, and he and the boat were swept into the ocean. Finding himself temporarily under the boat, Bride regained his composure sufficiently to swim out and then away, where he witnessed the vista of the *Titanic*'s demise. Victor Sunderland claimed that the boat bumped onto a railing near his location and he clambered aboard.

The water was now level with the roof of the bridge, and Lightoller simply stepped into it; the icy sensation was "like a thousand knives" as he later described it. Regaining his senses, he espied the crows nest directly ahead of him and swam to it before revising his plan and headed back to the starboard side, where water was pouring through the gratings of a large ventilating "blower". The grating was a clear path down to the bowels of the *Titanic* and if the wire mesh were to fail, Lightoller would be sucked into the depths of the ship, from which no escape would be possible. Pinned down and held underwater, he was finally freed by a mysterious blast of warm air from below that propelled him away. The source of this air is a matter of speculation as the boiler rooms were already flooded. Perhaps a boiler that had not been completely emptied of its fiery contents had disgorged its contents, the mixture of freezing water and hot coals providing a jet of steam enough to save Lightoller from death? These vents led down to the fans on "G" deck which had been turned off a long time before by a crewman named Ranger; these vents discharged through trunks leading to the boiler room(s) just below. It is hard to envisage where the fortuitous blast of air came from.

The gust propelled the 2nd Officer a considerable distance away but he soon found himself in a similarly helpless position. At the base of the first three funnels were gratings that allowed air to circulate from the boiler rooms out on deck via so-called "fidley trunks." Again, water was cascading down this ingress into the innards of the ship but Lightoller managed to effect an escape. He was never able to understand how. A 2005 expedition to the wreck site revealed that the starboard fidley grate had been pushed upwards, the bars distorted as though something "had been forced through the grating." Whether this is connected to Lightoller's extraction from this area is unknown.

Gasping for air, he came to the surface close to the boat he had helped to hoist from the roof; it was still upturned but it offered a haven from the cold water. Somehow it had drifted from the port side to the starboard side. He gripped on to a convenient handhold when he and the boat were thrown 20 feet away: the forward funnel had collapsed and missed him and the boat by inches. Others weren't so lucky and were directly underneath the funnel as it teetered over and smacked the water with colossal force.

As a matter of historical record, it is incredible that more people did not witness the falling of this funnel; Jack Thayer may have seen the first, or perhaps the second funnel collapse, Percy Keen makes mention of funnel 2, and Emily Ryerson refers to the forward two funnels "leaning" but the only other unambiguous source of data about the forward funnel disintegrating comes from Victor Sunderland who was atop boat "B" when it drifted over to port[26]. Richard Williams may have seen the first funnel fall, but his accounts are contradictory. Patrick Dillon refers to the last funnel canting aft and falling towards the aft well deck in the last few seconds. This author knows of no accounts that refer to the fall of funnel 3; odd, as this smoke stack was located centrally where the ship itself broke apart[27].

By the time Lightoller had recovered from this third miraculous escapade, he found himself alongside boat "B" again, and half a dozen men have found refuge balanced on top of it. Understandably, Lightoller's recollections at this point are confused; by this time, the *Titanic*'s lights had gone out and even though he was level with the 2nd funnel, he could not be certain he could see it, and would not even vouch that the 3rd funnel was clear of the water[28].

The *Titanic* now presented a gargantuan black shape, blotting out the stars. The cacophony of the foundering of the ship was indescribable; many spoke of "explosions" which was attributed to the rupture of boilers as cold water and hot metal mixed, but which was probably the sound of the instantaneous shredding and shattering of thousands of tons of steel plate. However, some descriptions veered from this norm; close by, in boat 5, Seaman Etches said that "she went down with an awful grating, like a small boat running off a shingley beach"; in boat "D", quartermaster Bright heard a sound "like a rattling of chains" and Hugh Woolner described "a rumbling roar". Bright's rocket-firing colleague Rowe, in boat "C" said that, "It was not an explosion; a sort of a rumbling...more like distant thunder"; he elaborated on this four decades later when he wrote that it was "like an immense heap of gravel being tipped from a height." Lawrence Beesley in boat 13 provided a verbose description; from a distance of one-half to 2 miles away, he later wrote: "And then as we gazed awe-struck, she tilted slowly up, revolving apparently about a centre of gravity just astern of amidships, until she attained a vertical upright position; and there she remained - motionless! As she swung up, her lights, which had shone without a flicker all night, went out suddenly, came on again for a single flash, then went out altogether. And, as they did so, there came a noise which many people, wrongly I think, have described as an explosion...it was partly a roar, partly a groan, partly a rattle, and partly a smash, and it was not a sudden roar as an explosion would be; it went on successively for some seconds, possibly fifteen to twenty...[it was] prolonged, more like the roll and crash of thunder." Strangely, Beesley is the only one who described the lights coming on for a single flash; this tiny detail is repeated in all the accounts of the ship's demise despite no other confirmatory accounts.

For 73 years, it was heresy to suggest that the *Titanic* sank in any condition other than intact, bar a missing funnel or two. That tidy status quo was shattered on September 1st, 1985 when the wreck was finally located and filmed. Much to the expedition's surprise, the entire stern was found to be missing and was ultimately located nearly 2000 feet to the south of the 470 feet long bow fragment. There was reason to suspect that some kind of break-up had occurred before this pivotal moment and indeed, *Titanic* patriarch Walter Lord changed his mind between his first writing on the subject (in 1955) and 1985. He partially based his opinion on the debris that lay scattered on the water; debris that was not just confined to the flotsam and jetsam that would be expected when any ship sinks (life buoys, deck chairs and so on), but fragments from deep within the interior that couldn't possibly be explained via any process other than the ship fragmenting and splitting apart. The debris included carved wood from the 1st class lounge, cabin fittings, white painted woodwork, cabin sofas, bedding, staircase newel posts and curved bannisters, wardrobe drawers, cabin doors, pilasters and so on. Even the door to the wheelhouse was later seen. This is too varied a catalogue of debris to be expected from the simple expulsion of items from deck houses, even if we assume that the ship suffered damage on the way to the bottom due to the increasing water pressure imploding areas of the wreck[29][30].

Researcher Bill Wormstedt has performed an analysis of the testimony given at both 1912 inquiries, and he found that the majority of the witnesses who described the final few moments of the dying liner expressed an opinion that the ship broke up. Another researcher, Paul Lee, has extended this work to include observations not officially given in evidence, but through a succession of letters and other accounts. Again, the preponderance of evidence is that the majority described seeing the ship disintegrate. Some boats were too far away to tell, and evidence is confusing; boat 6 was one of those who had rowed quite a distance and Major Peuchen, despite thinking the ship had gone down intact, thought that "the decks had blown up with the pressure" and that the explosions he heard were sufficient to dislodge the red and white barber's shop pole from its location deep within the ship - he remembered seeing it in the floating wreckage after being rescued. Likewise, the inhabitants of boat 8 were too far away to discern anything other than the lights being extinguished and the sound of "explosions."

Paradoxically, one can find no clear conclusions either from those in the water or perched on boats "A" or "B", who were undeniably the closest to the wreck. Thomas Whiteley was an exception; he mentioned that the sides of the *Titanic* were blown away, and that "she broke in the middle." Edward Brown was also in the water and he recalled the after part of the ship tremble, making him think that the bow had fallen off. William Mellors also opined that the ship parted in the middle. Jack Thayer Jr.'s thoughts varied, but at one point he was sure that the whole superstructure "appeared to split...and blow or buckle upwards." As one researcher has suggested, with a few exceptions, the few survivors who lived to reminisce were simply too close to see, let alone comprehend what was happening to the huge black mass before their eyes[31].

If we combine the majority of eyewitness reports, a very clear description of the final moments can be ascertained. When the *Titanic* reached a certain angle, she split apart somewhere in the vicinity of the 3rd and 4th funnels. Freed from the weight of the now severed bow section pulling the ship forward and down, the stern fell back level, on an even keel on the surface of the water. It too filled with water and was pulled back vertical before it succumbed to gravity and foundered; the weight of the water plus that of the engines, now at the exposed area of the tear, plus perhaps a final impetus from the last vestiges of connectivity between the bow and stern may have helped to pull the stern upright; estimates of how long it stayed upright vary between seconds and minutes.

An often cited voice against the chorus of unanimity of "the stern fell back on an even keel" was provided by the baker, Joughin whose account is of interest as he was on the ship to the very last, or so he claimed. After throwing deck chairs into the water to aid his buoyancy during his own escape, he went to the pantry, just below the boat deck, to take a drink of water. While there, he heard the people above him rushing aft to the perceived sanctuary of the stern, which was now lifting high above the oily black water. Intermingled with the hubbub of the surging crowd, he heard a crash, as if something had buckled ... like the iron was parting.

Keeping out of the crush as much as possible, Joughin followed the crowd towards the poop, but just as he got down towards the well deck, the *Titanic* gave a huge list to port, throwing everyone except himself into a heap; Joughin clambered on the side of the ship and found himself walking on the starboard hull plates and managed to grab the railings lining the poop deck. Standing solitary and aloft on the highest part of the remnants of the "unsinkable" ship, Joughin found himself wondering how to proceed. Tightening his belt and transferring his possessions between his pockets, where he noticed the time as being 2.15am, the ship suddenly glided away and slipped beneath the waters,

188

its lights still on. The baker paddled away without getting his head wet, he believed.

Joughin's story does not jibe with the other evidence that the *Titanic* settled down, practically level with the water, after heaving her aft end high in the air; he also denied that the stern went vertical. Those on board the ship to the last, including Frank Prentice and Thomas Dillon, never mentioned the huge list to port. Also, there is widespread agreement that the lights went out before the ship sank below the waves. Impairment of memory caused by alcohol has been mooted, but simple exaggeration by Joughin seems another likelihood. Indeed, just days after the sinking, Joughin told a newspaper that he remained on board until the *Titanic* began to sink, and then he jumped. He did not mention his perilous walk along the hull; any journalist would be remiss in not reporting such an exciting tale to his or her readers. Some corroboration comes from steward Walter Nichols, who heard many tales from survivors, which included one from "the ship's baker" who "jumped from one of the top decks into the water just before the big explosion" given how few bakers survived, this must be Joughin. His tales must, in this author's opinion, be seriously suspect, along with many others whose stories have been accepted as true for 100 years.

So, with so many vivid mental impressions recorded as testimony, letters or newspaper interviews, why did both the American and British Inquiries in 1912, not to mention every cinematic release, piece of art and book until 1985 conclude that the *Titanic* sank intact? Two of the officers (namely Lightoller and Pitman) were adamant that the *Titanic* sank intact; a view reinforced by two popular books written soon afterwards by Lawrence Beesley and Archibald Gracie. But Beesley was anything up to 2 miles away and Gracie was under water. The proclamations of the two officers, plus marine architects supported the contention that the *Titanic* went under in one piece. Lightoller was perhaps too close to see what was going on, but an account by Victor Sunderland provides a clue that the 2nd Officer was not quite telling the truth. According to Sunderland, Lightoller told the people in the water while he was on boat "B", "Make for the stern; it looks like she will float." Why say this if the stern and bow were still one connected entity? It was obvious that the ship was imminently going to founder, taking the stern with it if the two were still conjoined. Pitman was only a few hundred yards away and insisted that no break-up occurred. Can his observation be explained? There is some evidence that the detached stern swung around which would have presented the very aft of the poop deck to Pitman whereas previously he had an excellent broadside view of the ship while it was illuminated. Jack Thayer Jr stated that the before disappearing, the deck turned away from them - he was facing the starboard side at the time - and that the propeller and rudder went over those on boat "B"; Richard Williams also talked of the ship seeming to twist in a semicircle; Eugene Daly said the ship seemed to be swinging around, making him think that it would fall on top of him. These last two were on boats "A" and "B" respectively. Interestingly, it now seemed that these boats which originated at the bow of the ship had now wound up at the stern.

Boats 5 and 7 had tied up together, Pitman being in the former. Of the few survivor's accounts in these boats that were available to this author, only one spoke of the ship breaking apart, though many do talk of the "ship" (not necessarily the broken off aft end) attempting to right itself by falling level with the sea. Pitman may not have been in a position to see the end. And one might argue that, with ones eyes temporarily dazzled by the lights and which were now slowly adapting to "night vision", how much could one really see?

The White Star Line, indeed British seafaring and ship-building had been dealt an embarrassing blow by creating an "unsinkable" ship, only for her to succumb to nature on her first voyage. The further revelation that the ship had broken up would have raised question about the robustness and stability of British ships. The *Titanic* was in the worst possible condition that a ship might find herself in, and its disintegration, in hindsight, and with much computer aided analysis, was both obvious and inevitable. The argument is that, rather than admit to further damaging "failures" a decision was made to obscure the truth about the final few minutes.

Wilful blindness may be one key to the mystery of who saw what. 5[Th] Officer Lowe claimed that the *Titanic* sank at angle of about 75°; this was from 150 yards away. Although the majority claimed the ship (that is, the "stern") attained the vertical, Lowe's perspective, and the lack of light may have obscured what the 5th Officer saw. Lowe did deny that the afterpart came back on an even keel. Stewart Crowe and Seaman Scarrott in the same boat as Lowe described the stern falling back to the sea[32]. Others in this boat even spoke of the *Titanic* breaking apart.

The mental images that we have of the stern high in the area, fostered by decades of imaginative artwork and films seem to be spurious too. Computer simulations have suggested that the ship attained a fairly low angle before it broke up; certainly nothing like the reconstructions in cinema and art; no ship could withstand the pressures of raising the stern, weighing tens of thousands of tons, to such huge angles.

The forensics of the wreck itself demonstrate a few salient facts; the bow section is broken just in front of the third funnel, the boat deck angling down just aft of the second funnel and resting on the boilers in boiler room 2. The stern is a tattered mass of junk, having suffered from implosion damage during its descent, the hull plating blowing out upon impact with the bottom, and the top decks collapsing down upon the engines. The poop deck is peeled back, indicative of the destructive force of escaping air. The forward set of engine cylinders are snapped off. There is a large "missing" portion of hull between these engines and the location of the 3rd funnel. This portion is now little more than steel fragments strewn across the ocean floor. The double bottom underneath boiler room 1 is absent from the hull, and was eventually found in two pieces some distance away, evidently having stayed in one piece until fairly close to the seabed; the configuration of bends in these two pieces is consistent with a bending of the hull in this region. With this double bottom gone, the boilers themselves spilled out. Recent analysis of the wreck has led to the conjecture that the ship failed from the bottom-up, the fragmentation starting at the keel, or very near it, and propagating catastrophically up the hull.

As many writers have pointed out, this is the very place where a natural weak spot is present; the skylight for the reciprocating engines, the cavity for the fourth funnel uptake (leading down to the turbine engine room) is in this very area, as is the aft 1st class Grand Staircase, and all descend many decks. Aft of the 2nd funnel on "E" deck is the 1st class restaurant, and adjoining galley. On the next deck down is the similarly massive 3rd class dining saloon. To summarise, there are plenty of open spaces with little in the way of structural support. To tilt the ship, with the pivot point located in this very area, would certainly have resulted in the rapid disintegration of the *Titanic*. And so it proved on April 15th, 1912.

Titanic Interlude

C.Q.D. ... S.O.S. ... M.G.Y.

With the *Titanic*'s predicament confirmed, and the obvious peril forced by the lack of space in the boats, the only other option was to summon help. Succinctly, this meant rockets and the Marconi wireless system. The use of the latter system obviously necessitated the calculation of the ship's position, and this was duly obtained and transmitted across the ether.

The historical record has the problem that two positions were transmitted that night, and when compared to the wreck's location determined 73 years later, neither of them were correct.

The first distress call was made at 10.25pm New York Time and was heard by a ship called the s.s *Mount Temple*; the position was 41 44 N, 50 24 W in the standard notation for latitude and longitude in degrees and minutes[1]. The coordinates specified a location 1000 miles east of New York. At the same time, the land station at Cape Race heard the same location used.

This position was also received three minutes later by another ship called the *Ypiranga*. By 10.35pm, the "official" position of 41 46 N, 50 14 W was first heard and this was the position exclusively used thereafter. This is just to the south and well to the west of the *Mount Temple*'s originally received location, the total distance being 7.7 miles.

Why two sets of coordinates? Fortunately, the two positions transmitted were fairly close, but what if there had been a discrepancy of many miles, and not corrected till fairly late? It is fortunate for those in the boats that this did not happen.

We are left with a few options about the origin of the two locations: the *Titanic*'s wireless operator mistakenly sent out the wrong position; the ships and land station misheard the numbers; or that two co-ordinates were indeed transmitted.

The first two possibilities seem faint; "44" in Morse is ....-....-,

192

and "46" is ....--....; "14" is .----....- and "24" is ..---....- and it is not clear how the numbers could have become so garbled, thus implying a transcription error. Perhaps Senior Wireless Operator Phillips misread the numbers on the chit he was given? And while a Morse code "1" could be mistaken for a "2" if one of the dashes was mistaken for a dot, the code difference between "4" and "6" is so significant as to preclude any mishearing. Also, would three different receivers make the same mistake at the same time? No other ships heard the original coordinates after 10.35pm implying that a correction was made at the source.[2]

Other suggestions - that Phillips was tired due to a heavy night of relaying traffic to Cape Race (he was due to retire for bed at midnight but had stayed on), or that he was so shocked by the news that the *Titanic* was sinking and made mistakes - do not seem tenable.

Who provided the wireless operators with the co-ordinate(s)? Phillips did not survive, so we are left with the sometimes confusing testimony of his junior, Harold Bride, who wrote in his report to the Marconi company, "Mr.Phillips [asked the captain] if he should use the regulation distress call 'C.Q.D'[3]. The captain said 'Yes' and Mr.Phillips started in with 'C.Q.D,' having obtained the latitude and longitude of the *Titanic*." Bride confirmed in testimony that, "The captain gave [Phillips] the latitude and longitude of the "*Titanic*," and told him to be quick about it or words to that effect."

In 1912, Boxhall testified that he took the calculated position along to the wireless cabin on a piece of paper, and not wishing to disturb the operator who had the headphones on, handed it to him and it was sent out "immediately". In other questioning, Boxhall mentioned that both Phillips and Bride were present when he submitted his new calculations, which dispenses with the notion that Bride was absent relaying reports to the captain and was thus not present when Boxhall arrived at their cabin. Bride did not mention Boxhall's visit. It would seem from this testimony that the captain and Boxhall were responsible for the two differing locations, and it is assumed that Smith worked out the first set.

While on the sinking *Titanic*, Boxhall, unlike some of the other officers who acted independently, sought the captain occasionally to elicit information (finding out about the ship's lifespan) or informing him of his own decisions (that he had ordered rockets brought up to the bridge). It would be thought that Boxhall would have asked Smith about the wireless, and indeed, this seems to have been the case. Boxhall stated that, "I submitted the position to the captain first, and he told me to take it to the Marconi room." Boxhall made no mention of the captain telling him that not only had he performed the calculations but that they had already been transmitted.

But in 1962, the story had changed significantly. The alterations are worth discussing in detail.

In 1912, Boxhall had said that when he had returned from seeing the mail room flooding, he reported this to the captain who walked off and left him without saying "anything to [him] that was fixed in [his] memory." The next order that Boxhall heard was to prepare the lifeboats to be cleared away for lowering.

Compare this to the 1962 version, when Boxhall arrived back on the bridge: "... the captain said, "I've already sent a distress signal." "What position did you send it from?" [Boxhall asked and the captain replied] "From the eight o'clock D.R. [Dead, or deduced reckoning position calculate by Lowe]." "Well," [Boxhall] said, "...she was about twenty miles ahead of that sir[4]. If you like I will run the position up from the star position up to the time of the contact with the iceberg." And because, I said, she was about twenty miles ahead of our position, amended this position and took it down to the wireless room, and Phillips the wireless operator [who] was bending over his instrument, the telephone [sic] ... [said], "I'm in contact with the *Carpathia*." Well I put the amended position down on the desk, and I said, "Now send that amended position. Do you understand?" He said, "Yes." "Well," I said, "send that off right away." And that was the position the *Carpathia* came to." The *Carpathia* was in contact at 10.35pm, which is indeed the time that a new location was transmitted.

Like much of what Boxhall said later, we must be cautious that time has tainted his memory. If the suggestion that he had provided the corrected location is true, then how does this relate to events on the doomed ship? His 1912 account is that he went out to help with preparing the boats, but after this he becomes hazy in the order of events: "after seeing the men continuing with their work I saw all the officers were out, and I went into the chart room to work out [the ship's] position... It was after that [that I saw the light of the other steamer] because I must have been to the Marconi office with the position after I saw the light" It was then that he submitted his location to the captain who told him to take it to wireless operators. Then, in answer to further questioning, he agrees that he "then" saw the lights of the nearby

194

steamship. It is hard to know just when the mysterious ship was seen in relation to the transmission of the distress co-ordinates, but it was clearly about the same time as the two events were connected in Boxhall's mind.

The 1962 account simply muddies the situation; in this "new" sequence of events the first procedure was sending out the distress call, then going to help with the boats, and only then did he hear about the other ship from the "crow's nest". It is at this point that he began sending up rockets. In 1912 Boxhall never knew the source of the information about the other ship; any report from the crow's nest, as claimed in 1962, would have come before 12.20am which is when the two lookouts left their post. As is noted elsewhere, it then takes another 30 minutes (at least) for rockets to be sent up to attract the other ship. Charitably put, Boxhall's 1962 account deviates so wildly from the known aspects (particularly contemporary 1912 accounts) of the *Titanic* disaster that its value is questionable.

With reference to the two locations sent out, Boxhall does not mention the captain telling him that he used the D.R. position at the 1912 inquiries. If it is true, Smith was an imbecile. He had been given the accurate 7.30 position by Boxhall personally, and the captain had even put it on the chart. Why use the less accurate 8pm position? One possible answer is that Smith was never on the bridge at the time, was never given the position, but was elsewhere, perhaps at the dinner party being held in his honour in the restaurant.

Thanks to the labours of a French/American team of oceanographers in the summer of 1985, we know the location of the *Titanic*'s wreckage; it is 2 miles to the south of Boxhall's famous S.O.S./C.Q.D. location, but 12.7 miles to the east. The "Smith" C.Q.D. position is some 7.7 miles further to the south-west of the Boxhall one.

How Boxhall determined the incorrect final stopping point is an interesting exercise. Sam Halpern suggests that the timing of the star observations was off by 1 minute by misreading a chronometer. Since the resultant computations are very sensitive to the time, this would filter into the calculations...and Halpern has demonstrated that, if one corrects for this minute discrepancy, one can derive a location that is within 3 miles of the wreck's location. Researcher David Gittins suggests another possibility. The distress location, like the 8pm position, was calculated by taking the known movements of the ship and then extrapolating them forwards in time. To assist in this calculations, mariners used "traverse tables", which could be quickly used to determine the change in latitude and longitude for a ship on a specific course and travelling a certain distance. However, Gittins demonstrates that if Boxhall misread the tables (a very easy mistake to make when one considers the density of data presented in the tables), he could have been off in his calculations, and, working backwards, one finds that a "corrected" calculation yields a position extremely close to the wreck site.

How did Smith derive his position from the 8pm D.R .location? If Boxhall had performed his calculations correctly, his answer would have been a very short distance from the actual location of the *Titanic's* fractured hulk. And if Smith had done exactly what Boxhall had done, then his answer would have been based on an initial position that was 20 miles to the east of the 7.30 position determined by star sightings, and would only have included 3 hours and 40 minutes worth of steaming, rather than 4 hours and 16 minutes from 7.30pm (Boxhall assumed that the collision was at 11.46 rather than 11.40 and a speed of 22 knots). Quantifying this, 4 hours 16 minutes at 22 knots gives 93.9 miles steaming from the 7.30pm location. From the 8pm location, 3 hours 40 minutes of steaming gives us 82.5 miles. And since we know that the 8pm derived location was 20 miles behind the one at 7.30pm, then the distance behind the wreck site (that is, to the east) is 31 miles. And yet Smith's position was west of Boxhall's, which in turn is west of the real wreck site.

Sam Halpern's reconstruction of the *Titanic's* route allows us to determine the 7.30pm location which had been lost to history. From this 7.30 location and subtracting 20 miles, we get about 129 miles from Lowe's 8pm position to the Smith distress location. If we assume that the *Titanic* had travelled 3 hours and 40 minutes to 11.40pm, we get an average speed of 35 knots, far in excess of anything the ship was ever designed to achieve. A 23 minute time change at midnight, gives a speed of nearly 32 knots for a total time of 4 hours and 3 minutes, and a "full" time change of 47 minutes yields a little under 29 knots for 4 hours and 27 minutes. The actual speed of the *Titanic* was about 22.5 knots. Whichever way one looks at the Smith position, it is clear that no numerical manipulation can get to it. Simply put, Boxhall's position is definitely incorrect ... and Smith's position, starting from a much more distant starting point and allowing less time for steaming is demonstrably worse than Boxhall's!

196

Employed by the Marconi company, but signing on as actual members of the ship's crew, Jack Phillips and Harold Bride had, for the last four days, pandered to the paying whims of the passengers in sending missives, occasionally punctuated by the imperatives of navigational messages and ice warnings, very few of which, we have seen, reached the bridge. Out of range of land, the operators relied on other vessels to relay messages when they had established contact with a ground station. It was inevitable that subsequent inquiries would investigate the use of the wireless equipment, and this necessarily required the testimony of the sole surviving operator, Bride. Sadly, his comments leave much room for doubt as to what really transpired.

Let us examine his prevarications. His first interview was taken just minutes after the *Carpathia* docked in New York on the evening of April 18th, 1912. Summarised, his story is as follows: Bride claimed to have not felt the shock of impact, and emerged from the sleeping quarters having heard Phillips engaged in sending traffic to Cape Race. Bride was due to take over the watch and he told his senior to go to bed, but the appearance of the captain in the wireless cabin altered their routine. Smith informed the two men that the ship had struck an iceberg, and that he was having an inspection done. He advised Bride and Phillips to be prepared to send out a call for assistance, but to wait until ordered to do so. This came after about 10 minutes when the captain returned and he told them to send "the regulation distress call," or C.Q.D. The captain then vanished again, and they made light of the disaster.

After about five minutes, the captain returned and asked what they were sending. "C.Q.D," replied Phillips. Bride interjected with an attempt at humour that made them all laugh, including the captain: "Send S.O.S. It's the new call, and it may be your last chance to send it."

The steamship "*Frankfurd*" [sic] was the first to respond, then the *Carpathia*. Under instructions from Phillips, Bride went to tell the captain of this good news, and after fighting through a mass of people to get to his cabin, the news was passed on. Returning to his cabin, Bride finally had time to change from his pyjamas. Every few minutes, it would seem, Phillips sent him on errands to inform the captain of the state of other ships; this seems to have been mainly messages from the *Carpathia*. Eventually, the wireless seemed to be getting weaker and the captain returned to the operator's cabin to tell the men that "the engine rooms were taking water and that the dynamos might not last much longer." This too was sent to the *Carpathia*. By now, a visit to the boat deck by Bride confirmed how close it was to the water. The *Olympic* had established contact in the interim period.

Out on deck, Bride helped to heave "a collapsible boat" down from the roof, and then went back to the Marconi shack. The last raft had gone, he told his superior. Then came the captain's voice: "Men you have done your full duty. You can do no more. Abandon your cabin. Now it's every man for himself. You look out for yourselves. I release you. That's the way of it at this kind of time. Every man for himself." The captain took his leave of the two men.

Bride briefly left Phillips temporarily to absorb the situation on the boat deck, which was now awash. Still, the sense of duty had not abandoned Phillips, and he kept sending for another ten or fifteen minutes after the captain had released them. The water was then coming into the cabin. By this time, Bride had returned from his inspection and went into their cabin to collect Phillip's money for him. Phillips was so immersed in his duty that he did not notice that a stoker had entered the room and had started to remove the senior operator's lifejacket. Bride stated, "I did my duty. I hope I finished him. I don't know. We left him on the cabin floor of the wireless room, and he was not moving." This provided the final imperative to leave the room, and both men ran out on deck, where Bride saw the collapsible boat still on deck. Bride was assisting when a big wave tore along and washed the boat, with the junior Marconi operator holding tight of an oarlock, into the sea.

It was a thrilling tale. How much of it was the product of a journalist's desire to exaggerate the story? At that time it was difficult to tell; there had been no word from the *Carpathia* about the nature of the disaster other than basic survival statistics, the time of the sinking and a list of the names of those saved. There was nothing to corroborate the headline-making story. The only element of the story that might have aroused suspicion could have been gleaned from a study of the deck plans; it would have been impossible for water to have entered the radio room without the forward boat deck being completely submerged. One may also wonder how Bride and Phillips could even have left the room if the ship was so flooded. Even more surprisingly, Bride was very candid about the scuffle with the stoker. Accusations could have been levelled that amounted to a charge of murder.

But other information seemed verifiable; from other ship's wireless logs, there was indeed a half hour gap before the first C.Q.D. transmission and the first use of S.O.S. and this was about 20 minutes after the *Carpathia* responded. Bride's story provided an irreverent reason why the distress call been altered after a little while.

Two days later, Bride testified before the U.S. Inquiry. His story mostly amounts to a repeat of his newspaper interview; he was asleep when the impact came and was not awakened by it. Emerging from the sleeping compartment he is told that Phillips had just finished with the Cape Race traffic. In a slight contradiction to his newspaper account, it was now that Bride gets dressed and was told by his senior that "He told me that he thought she had got damaged in some way and that he expected that we should have to go back to Harland & Wolff's." Bride took over the wireless key as Phillips went to his bed, but his planned sleep was interrupted by the captain, telling them they had better get assistance "at once." Phillips took over the Morse key again.

This is the first significant deviation between the two accounts. Now, Smith only visited the wireless cabin once, and there is no mention of any delay while an inspection was being performed. The next time Smith was encountered was when Bride delivered the news of the *Frankfurt*. Smith was found on the boat deck and wanted to know her location; Bride promised to obtain it as soon as possible. Soon after, the *Carpathia's* message was also given to the captain, and Bride found him in the wheelhouse. Both men returned to the Marconi room and the captain asked what other ships he had, to be told that he was now in touch with the *Olympic*. That there was sufficient time for Bride to leave the wireless cabin, find the captain and return in time for the exchange with the *Olympic* is corroborated by the wireless logs, when 20 minutes between these two sets of communications is evident. From these timings, Bride obviously had a little difficulty in finding the captain.

Phillips then went outside while Bride briefly took over the Morse key and headphones. There is no mention of the levity about the use of C.Q.D./S.O.S. In fact, Bride's testimony only ever mentioned "C.Q.D." and he said at one point "We could not send anything more than C.Q.D." when asked about the strongest language that could be transmitted to indicate an emergency. Bride could read what his senior was sending and he surely would have noticed S.O.S.?

And now Bride helped with the collapsible only after leaving the radio office for the last time. Interestingly, he was not asked, or volunteered information about the attack on the stoker.

About a week later, Bride wrote his report to his superiors at the

Marconi Headquarters in New York. In this version, there is also no mention of the captain having an inspection made, or the order that the wireless men were to wait until the results were known. The captain was now to be found "engaging in superintending the filling and lowering of the lifeboats" when the *Frankfurt*'s and the *Carpathia*'s welcome news were passed on; later Smith would come to tell the two men that the ship was sinking fast and "could not last longer than half an hour." The report does confirm the account of the captain releasing the two men from their duties. The altercation with the stoker is now described as "a general scrimmage with the three of us," and the man "without a doubt" sank in the Marconi cabin as they left him. The collapsible boat is now hoisted from the roof after the two men left the stoker in their cabin.

There is reasonably good agreement between this report and Bride's testimony. There are a few minor contradictions: the captain was now superintending on deck rather than being in the wheelhouse; and his newspaper comment mentioning the captain's report that the engine room was flooding is now replaced by the news that the ship was sinking and would not last longer than half an hour. There is no mention of the change from C.Q.D. to S.O.S. and one may question whether he would put it in an official report. Certainly, the misplaced levity could be frowned upon, if the newspaper story is true. Or it could be a simple "improvement" by a journalist to sell the story.

The British Inquiry added little; Bride awoke to find all the traffic to Cape Race had been cleared. Once again, the captain did not tell the men that he was having an inspection made. He simply asked the operators to send out the call for assistance and gave them the latitude and longitude of the ship. When giving the captain the welcome news that the *Carpathia* was on the way, the captain is now found on the starboard side of the boat deck, superintending the loading of the lifeboats, which contradicts other witnesses who observed the captain exclusively on the port side at this time. Several messages from the *Olympic* were not delivered to the captain because they felt he was busy and "he would be worried". Worried about what? The state of the *Titanic*? But in general, Smith kept in communication with Bride and Phillips. Either they went to him, or he went to them; in one instance, he told them, as per his newspaper account that the engine room was flooded and the ship would not last very long. Little elaboration is provided on the scuffle with the stoker. Bride forced the man away and this attracted Phillip's attention, who came to assist his junior. Bride held him as Phillips hit him.

On the other hand, Bride's testimony does not mention the *Titanic* being in contact with other ships in the drama, such as the *Mount Temple*, the *Asian* or the *Ypiranga*[5]. He exclusively mentions the *Olympic*, *Carpathia*, *Baltic* and *Frankfurt*.

Despite lapses in Bride's memory, the hints of murder and near comical buffoonery (such as "The *Frankfurt* Incident" - to be referred to later), the heroism of these two men have stood as a monument for nearly a century. That their efforts saved many is undeniable; cynics would say that there is little outstandingly heroic in two men who were simply doing their jobs.

Readers will recall the debate that exists regarding the time difference with New York; some claim 1 hour and 33 minutes, other say 2 hours and 2 minutes. It is of obvious importance when applied to wireless messages; because New York provided a constant time, irrespective of clock changes on board the ship as one moved east or west, obtaining the time difference allows the various wireless messages to be reconciled, assisting our knowledge of what was happening on the *Titanic*. Without the determination of the time difference, one could claim that a certain message was transmitted half an hour earlier, or later, than it actually was. And the time difference could have serious ramifications on our knowledge of not only how prompt the ship's crew were in ascertaining their perilous state, but also influence our understanding of when the ship sank (and by inference how long she stayed afloat). An appreciation for the true ship's time would also assist in the creation of a timing context as to when orders were given to the operators by the captain.

Do we know when the first call was transmitted? Debate ensues as to the actual time on the *Titanic*, but we know that it was picked up by the *Mount Temple* at 10.25pm. For a 1:33 difference, this would make it 11.58pm on the *Titanic*, at about the time that the order to uncover the boats was given. Some have speculated that, upon Boxhall's return to the bridge after his second inspection below, Captain Smith, who had turned away without giving a word, made his way to the wireless office. Superficially, this makes sense, except that Smith had no way of knowing definitely how bad the damage was at that point. All he had was the word of the mail worker and Boxhall who had seen the mail room flooding, plus whatever information the carpenter had imparted to him.

As we have discussed elsewhere, Smith and Thomas Andrews headed to the engine room, but there does not seem to have been time before midnight for him to get back to the bridge before the order to fill the boats. Would Smith send out a distress call without knowing the full damage to the ship? Once he had ordered a call sent out, the "cat would be out of the bag" - and Smith and the White Star Line faced humiliation if the urgency afforded to the distress messages had been misplaced.

How does a 2:02 difference reconcile with this evidence? This puts the first call at 12.27am, which to many seems unpalatably late. But then, we do have the first lifeboat being launched at about 12.40am, and the first rocket some ten minutes later. This hints as to some form of latency in the proceedings; and perhaps, if one may venture the opinion, some failure on the part of the officers to act far quicker after learning of their fate. A "late" C.Q.D/S.O.S call meshes nicely with the general lack of urgency on the *Titanic*.

Bride's evidence does not help the argument for either time difference, due to his vacillation. In his first newspaper interview, he gives no clue as to the amount of time between the collision and the first call except to say that the captain told him that he was having an inspection made; this was when Bride was telling his senior to go to bed. Bride's Marconi report also mentions that Smith entered the cabin as Phillips was preparing to retire. By this evidence, Phillips was due to go off duty at midnight. In his evidence before the American inquisitors, Bride put the time of his awakening at 11.45 or 11.55pm but then conceded that he had "no recollection of the time these various incidents took place, but [he could] give ... a fairly good estimate of the times between the incidents." In further questioning Bride puts the time that the captain came in to see the Marconi men at "ten minutes" after Bride had been awakened...but then Bride becomes confused, as does his audience, when he says that the captain visited ten minutes after the collision. A few weeks later, when questioned on this same point at the British Inquiry, Bride was asked if he could estimate how long it was after he had come to relieve Phillips that Smith ordered them to get assistance. All the junior wireless man could apologetically say was, "I do not think I could."

Perhaps the most forgiving thing that can be seen about Bride and his evidence comes from the man himself, in his report to the Marconi company: "I regret to say my memory fails me with regard to the time of the occurrence or any of the ... incidents; but otherwise I am sure of all my statements."[6].

202

Can Boxhall provide illumination on this issue of when help was first summoned? Taking the two timing offsets that have been proposed and given the time that "41 46 N 50 14 W" was first heard, we get, respectively, 12:08am and 12:37am. But the first rocket - sent up to attract the strange steamer - was sent up, so we are told, at 12.50am give or take a few minutes, and this was after Boxhall's trip to the Marconi office with the new position which was sent out "immediately." Boxhall should - and probably did know - that for a ship to to send out a wireless call for assistance indicated a dire situation; at some point he had even confirmed with the captain how long the ship had left to live. And yet Boxhall waited for between 10 and 40 minutes[7] to send up rockets. The "later" time of 12.37 seem plausible when one remembers that Bride himself reported that after communication with the *Carpathia* had established that she was en route (approximately 10.40pm New York Time), he went and told the captain this heartening news. Smith was found on the boat deck, superintending the loading and lowering of lifeboats. 12.08am - corresponding to 1 hour and 33 minutes - is less than 10 minutes after the call was made to ready the boats and half an hour after the collision. It seems impossible to countenance that the passengers could have been assembled and already leaving the ship in this time[8].

Regardless of how hard Bride and Phillips had toiled to summon assistance, and if one neglects certain statements of dubious veracity, one interesting fact of the night of April 14th/15th 1912 is that some ships simply were unable to contact the doomed ship. It is not a simple matter of blaming it on failing power, or that certain ships had wireless installations capable or receiving weaker signals: the rated power of the equipment is relevant only to the ability to transmit and is immaterial of its receiving prowess. The answer may lie in the number of stations transmitting, causing "jamming" or due to atmospheric conditions[9]. The second of these possibilities may explain the messages received from hundreds - if not thousands - of miles distant. This is an important point to ponder when one considers the time of the last message from the *Titanic*, another point of deep division between researchers as we shall soon see.

That some ships could not contact the *Titanic* is evident from the wireless logs. For instance, at 11.45am New York Time, the *Olympic* asked the *Titanic* what weather he had, and was told "clear and calm."

But transmissions by other ships around this time are noted as having "no answer", "no reply" or "signals unreadable." A few messages did get through - *Olympic* at 11.47am, *Carpathia* at 11.55 - but to nearly all stations, there was only silence; even Cape Race remarked in their wireless log that they had not heard the *Titanic* for half an hour, and that "his power may be gone." This places the last message they heard at 11.35am.

And then comes the puzzle. The s.s. *Virginian* apparently heard the *Titanic* calling "very faintly" at 12.10am, and noted that "His power [was] greatly reduced." and then 10 minutes later, "Hear two 'V's' signalled faintly in spark similar to M.G.Y. [the *Titanic*'s 3 letter call-sign]. [He was] Probably adjusting [his] spark." 7 minutes later comes the following; "[*Titanic*] calls C.Q. Unable to make out his signal. Ended very abruptly as if power suddenly switched off. His spark rather blurred or ragged. (Called [*Titanic*] suggested switching to emergency set but no response)." Did these *Virginian* messages originate from the *Titanic* and can we deduce when the last undisputed message from the ailing liner was transmitted?

At the U.S. Inquiry, Bride recalled that, right at the very end, Phillips "gave another call of C.Q.D., I believe, and, had an answer to it...I could not say whom the answer was from. I could hear what Mr. Phillips was sending, but I could not hear what he was receiving...I do not think there was an answer, because he would have told me if there had been." This was the last C.Q.D. call, and both men were of the opinion that their equipment was not getting "a full spark" to transmit and that the power was being impaired all the time.

Bride's report to the Marconi company is somewhat more detailed; "Again Mr. Phillips called "C Q D" and "S O S" and for nearly five minutes got no reply, and then both the *Carpathia* and the *Frankfurt* called. Just at this moment the captain came into the cabin and said, "You can do nothing more; look out for yourselves." Mr. Phillips resumed the phones and after listening a few seconds jumped up and fairly screamed, "The ----- fool. He says, 'What's up old man?'" I [Bride] asked "Who [was it]?" [and] Mr. Phillips replied [that it was] the *Frankfurt* and at that time it seemed perfectly clear to us that the *Frankfurt*'s operator had taken no notice or misunderstood our first call for help. Mr. Philips reply to this was "You fool, stdbi [stand by] and keep out."[10]

Bride's report continued, "We had nearly the whole time been in possession of full power from the ship's dynamo, though toward the end

204

the lights sank and we were ready to stand by, with emergency apparatus and candles, but there was no necessity to use them." If the timing is right, this would be about 11.55-12.00am in New York; indeed, at this time, the s.s. *Caronia* had heard both the *Frankfurt* and the *Carpathia* working with the *Titanic*, the latter ship receiving news that "the engine room [was full] up to the boilers"[11]

The Marconi report is partially corroborated by evidence in London: after telling the *Frankfurt* to keep out, the *Carpathia* was again in contact, and "to the best of [his] recollection [Phillips] told the *Carpathia* ... we were abandoning the ship, or words to that effect." Phillips called once or twice more, but the power was failing, and there were no more replies to his hail.

The testimony of the *Carpathia*'s officer, Cottam, confirms that the last message, which mentioned the flooding engine room, was received was 11.55, but another he one sent a few minutes later elicited no response.

If the universally accepted time of foundering is correctly placed at 2.20am, and the time difference with New York is indeed 2 hours and 2 minutes, this places these *Virginian* messages at 2.12am, 2.20am and then 2.27am; the last two of these present an impossible conundrum as the *Titanic* could not possibly have been transmitting whilst on her way to the bottom of the Ocean, which was after 2.20am in the morning.

An important point needs to be mentioned here. At only one point in the evening was the *Virginian* ever in direct contact with the *Titanic*; this was at 11.10pm, previous news of the disaster having been obtained from Cape Race. Thereafter, and unable to directly reach the doomed ship, the *Virginian* was forced to receive messages relayed from other stations, and likewise, use them to pass information to the *Titanic*. Is it likely that the *Virginian* did receive the final messages from the *Titanic* when the power was failing? It would seem odd if the messages least likely to propagate did indeed receive an audience on this ship...but only the *Virginian* heard these "last" three messages. Harold Cottam on the *Carpathia* thought that these three final transmissions could not have come from the *Titanic* and he even said the *Titanic*'s signals were good to the very end.

Proximity was no guarantee of improved reception; there are a few mentions of "atmospherics" (distortions) affecting the operation of the wireless equipment. At 11.10pm, the s.s. *Baltic* notes "Jamming bad,

205

but hear *Titanic* very faint, calling *Olympic* - latter strong, freaky" and tells the *Caronia*, "I don't appear to reach [the *Titanic*]." The *Olympic* had recently left New York and was heading eastward; she was about 500 miles away from, and on the other side of the *Titanic* to the *Baltic*, and yet she was heard much more clearly; there is no hint that the *Titanic*'s power was affecting the Marconi installation at this point in the sinking, which would be approximately 1am New York Time. The *Caronia* had been relaying messages from the *Titanic* and was some 700 miles to the east at the time of the calamity, and could initially hear the *Titanic* perfectly well, this ability vanishing after 11.35pm; however, the wireless logs are not clear if the messages from the *Caronia* to the *Titanic* were ever received as they do not seem to have been acknowledged. Meanwhile, the *Baltic*'s sporadic communication lasted for about 25 minutes.

Other examples of messages being heard over a great range are even more extreme: the s.s. *Megantic* had just left Portland, and, 14 hours later, heard garbled messages from the *Titanic* from many hundreds of miles away. The s.s. *Birma*, close to the wreck site, was in contact with a steamer called the *British Sun* at 3.20am local time - which had called into Thameshaven on April 10th and was now docked safely in Antwerp!

And in the midst of all this, we have the *Virginian*, 170 miles north of the distress location and unable to establish contact for most of the evening. Cape Race could hear the *Titanic* until 11.35am from a distance of just over 300 miles away and, as demonstrated above, other stations much further away had no such difficulty in hearing the *Titanic*.

Could the *Virginian* have misheard another station and mistaken it for the *Titanic*? In 1914, Marconi General Orders for Wireless Operators gave instructions that a receiving station was to transmit "dot dot dot dash dot" twenty times during which time the requester adjusts his set, to fine-tune it for reception. The Morse code letter "v", as heard at 12:20, is "...-" ; if the *Virginian* only heard two of the "dot dot dot dash dot" but neglected to detect the final "dot" it could well have been misconstrued as a "v"...but what station would be "tuning up" at midnight, New York Time (5am in Greenwich)? This is something that is now impossible to answer, but it is perfectly likely that the *Virginian* mistook another station for the *Titanic*.

Neglecting the *Virginian*'s claimed message, we are left with the conclusion that the final, verifiable round of messages between the

206

Titanic, the *Carpathia* and the *Frankfurt*, can be timed at 1.57-2.02am if the 2 hours and 2 minutes hypothesis is correct. This is very close to the foundering time, and gives enough time for the operators to try to save themselves. This raises the ire of the 1 hour 33 minute proponents; the *Virginian*'s last message at 12.27am plus 1:33 gives 2am; again, more than enough time for the escape from the wireless room. But this has serious implications for the rest of the evidence, for it indicates that the last communications with the *Carpathia* and the *Frankfurt* would be about 1.30am on the *Titanic*; and this means that Captain Smith had released Bride and Phillips from their duty a full 50 minutes before the ship went under. This seems impossible to believe.

Is there anything else in the wireless evidence that can be used in the "1 hour 33 minutes vs. 2 hours 2 minute" controversy? Possibly; Bride's report includes the following: "Mr. Phillips then went outside to see how things were progressing, and meanwhile I established communication with the *Baltic*, telling him we were in urgent need of assistance. [When he returned] Mr.Phillips told me the forward well deck was under water." This is corroborated by his evidence in London.

The *Baltic* first heard the distress calls at 10.40pm from the *Caronia*, but a direct call to the *Titanic* five minutes later yielded no response. The *Caronia* repeated the message at 11.03pm, and at 11.10pm, the *Baltic* heard a faint message from the *Titanic*. This was sent to the bridge and after 10 minutes, the *Baltic*'s 2nd Officer had joined the wireless operator in time to hear, direct from the *Titanic*, a plea to "Get all your boats ready, [we are] sinking." Five minutes later, contact was again lost, and the *Baltic* asked the *Caronia* to tell the sinking leviathan that they were making for her. At 11.35, the Baltic again heard directly that passengers were being put off in the boats, but was unable to contact the *Titanic* and again the *Caronia* was asked to relay the heartening news that help was coming. After ten minutes, the Baltic hears that the engine room was "getting flooded." Finally, between 11.47 and 11.50, the *Baltic* contacts Phillips and tells him that they were rushing to the *Titanic*'s aid.

Bride's evidence establishes that two-way communication was in existence between the *Titanic* and the *Baltic*. The existing wireless logs do not allow us to say definitely when this was, as we do not know definitely what messages were received directly, and not relayed by other ships. Three windows of opportunity exist; the first is 11.20, the next is 11.35, and the final is 11.45-50; the first of these seems too early.

207

The point of this excruciating minutiae is that, regardless of which *Baltic* time one uses - 11.20, 11.35 or 11.45 - adding 1 hour 33 yields 12.53am, 1.08am or 1.18am. Evidence of the condition of the *Titanic* at these times are not conclusive, but it seems likely that the well deck was not under water this early on and that this only happened within the last half hour of the sinking. On this basis, the 1 hour and 33 minute hypothesis falters as it describes a *Titanic* that had sunk considerably more than had actually occurred.[12][13]

Such debates, pro or con, 1:33 or 2:02, simply lead to many unpleasant debates. Despite having the same data, both sides of the argument often claim definitive and different conclusions. Caveat Lector.

Chapter 6: Salvation

The night's horrors had not concluded. As the last of the stern disappeared into the blackness, those trapped on board were cast in the lethally cold water. Disparate cries for help, prayers and screaming emerged from various locations, before becoming one incessant, wail[1].

The agonised chorus surprised some in the boats, who were convinced that everyone had managed to escape. The piercing cries drifting across the water meant only one thing: that people were in peril. The situation called for a humanitarian, pragmatic approach.

It never happened. A few boats were too full to have taken any more on board. But this still left about a dozen boats that could have participated in a rescue, and we must remember that about four hundred places in the lifeboats were left unoccupied. Now, surely, these empty seats could be put to some good use? Away from emotive reasonings, the practicalities of a rescue were all too apparent; anyone entering the thrashing crowd would immediately seize the attention of the swimmers. The boat would act as a focal point for the throng, and would almost certainly have been capsized. It is a difficult question to ponder, especially in retrospect. Would one risk the lives of 30-40 people safely housed in a flimsy wooden vessel to save a handful more? Two boats had supremely good experience of this conundrum. Boat "A" was besieged by the seething mass of people trying to seek refuge, and boat "B" had to turn people away; these boats were practically in the middle of the struggling mob.

Officer Pitman in No.5 suggested that they at least try. But the cries of indignation from his passengers, chiefly the ladies, aborted that plan, and the oars were pulled back in; indeed, Mrs. Cassebeer alleges that the passengers "grasped the oars and interfered with the proper handling of the boat so that the seamen were finally forced to give up their efforts." At least one cynic, Mrs.Washington Dodge, noted that, "After the crying died down, two or three of the women became hysterical - about what I don't know; they were missing none of their people." Her comments, while harsh, do have an air of reality about them. The majority of married women in the boat had their spouses with them, and the protests against going back to help the dying could partially have been engendered by the attitude that they didn't care about others, as long as they were safe. It is a sombre thought to speculate how many other boats would have turned back to help if those on board knew that their husbands and loved ones were in peril. However, the residents of boats 4 and 8 also protested against going back, and some of their men folk had been left behind; many in these boats however had no spouses to forsake. The situation became too much for Mrs.Dodge in boat 5. To escape from the hysteria, she switched to boat 7, moored alongside[2].

Some of the other boats resorted to praying, singing or cheering to drown out the unimaginable sound of the desperate souls struggling to survive. The cacophony from the wreck site left an unwanted imprint upon the mind of some of those huddled in the boats; in boat "C" Frank Goldsmith Jr. wrote that it reminded him in later life of a stadium's spectators erupting when a home run was hit at a nearby baseball stadium. John Thayer Jr. mused that the screams were reminiscent of locusts on a midsummers night. To steward Walter Nichols in boat 15, it seemed as if a kennel of dogs was being fed.

Boats "A" and "B" were practically alongside of the *Titanic* when she foundered and people were allowed on board until they were either full or in danger of capsizing. Of the other boats which had departed some time previously, only two boats did their best. One of these was boat 4 which had been rowing down the hull of the *Titanic* after receiving orders to head for an open hatch, ostensibly to pick up more people. This proved futile; no hatch was to be seen, but crewmen Scott and Ranger on the boat deck saw a chance for escape and took it. Lowering themselves down the ropes attached to the now vacant davits for boat 16, they dropped down the falls; Ranger dropped into the boat, and Scott went into the water nearby but was soon picked up. Their arrival was a godsend; boat 4 had left severely undermanned, but now there were two more men to help man the oars. They were joined minutes later by Lamp Trimmer Hemming, who had adopted the same tactic as Scott and Ranger[3].

"Pull for your lives, or you'll be sucked under," came the cry and the occupants of the boat started pulling at the oars, but there was no necessity. Despite being very close (6 ships lengths, or about 5400 feet, according to one witness,) there was no suction. The anticipation was that the sinking hulk of the *Titanic* would suck water into open windows and doors, pulling everything for a considerable distance towards her, possibly even down with her. After the *Titanic* had slipped from view, boat 4 returned to the wreck and picked up 4 or 5 more people; this was despite the protests of those safely ensconced in the craft who appealed to the crew not to do so[4].

It appears that they were just in time, as the cold water had a numbing and in some cases, devastating effect on those lucky enough to be retrieved; a Trimmer named Dillon became unconscious when he was pulled in but later woke to find two bodies on top of him; steward Cunningham survived but a colleague named Siebert died not long after being plucked out from the ocean. Assistant Storekeeper Prentice had jumped from the stern with a co-worker, Ricks. Prentice found his friend in the water who had been injured when he landed on debris and soon perished, but Prentice survived and found sanctuary in boat 4. Mrs Ryerson said afterwards that, "many were raving and moaning and delirious most of the time." Of the 7 or 8 picked up from the ocean, two perished[5].

After the last man was picked up, the cries, diminishing in intensity, stopped. Soon after, other lifeboats in the vicinity were detected and boat 4, a true harbinger of heroism, went to join the others.

The only other protagonist to attempt any rescue was 5th Officer Lowe in command of boat 14. Even before the *Titanic* sank, the desperation and wailing of the ladies in this boat was serving only to induce anguish in its commander: "Don't cry, please don't cry. You'll all have something to do than cry. Some of you will have to handle the oars. For God's sake stop crying. If I had not the responsibility of looking after you I would put a bullet through my brain," he said at one point. His other comments allegedly include a suggestion that they sing "Throw out the Life Line", and that he said to his human cargo, "I think the best thing for you women to do is to take a nap."

Well after being rescued by the s.s. *Carpathia*, Lowe was in a more humble mood, stating that the only thing he regretted was "the oaths" (the harsh language?) used towards the ladies in the boats, and that he would give his life to have any one of the perished husbands restored to his wife. However, he also said that, "'they' saw to it that, among those who were saved would not be any of the rich nabobs ... We saw to it that they would take their chances with good men." This invites speculation. Who is "they"? Had "they" made an agreement to ensure that the wealthiest men were hindered in their passage to the boats, taking their chances with those who made no attempts to save themselves? It is unlikely that the truth of this statement shall be known.

Lowe was present on the forward starboard boat deck when 1st class men were admitted, but then again, he was working under senior officers (Murdoch and Pitman) who were more lenient in the loading of the lifeboats.

The accepted story is that, after the *Titanic* sank, the 5th Officer corralled five other boats ("D", 4, 10 and 12) and after confirming that no other officer were on board, he tied them together and distributed his passengers in boat 14 to the other craft so that he could return to the wreck site to pick up as many survivors as he could fit into his now near empty boat, bereft of all but a small crew of volunteers to man the oars etc. But the trans-shipping of people was a slow process and an exasperated Lowe bellowed to Daisy Minahan, "Jump, God damn you, Jump." It was while performing this that Lowe noticed a figure who was "too eager" to get into the other boat; pulling his shawl over the figure's head, Lowe found himself staring into the face of a man (an Italian, he said later), and pitched him into the boat. But the slow transferral of passengers had an important effect, as Lowe felt that a delay in attempting a rescue was prudent. Like the other boats, Lowe was wary of rowing straight into the mass of screaming humanity, which would have been suicide, so he decided to wait until it had quietened down. Between an hour and two hours after the *Titanic* had gone down, he decided it was safe to proceed. But waiting that long meant that nearly everyone in the water would be dead from exposure.

Only four were found, one of whom (William Hoyt) died not long afterwards[6].

Another survivor was a Japanese who had lashed himself face down to a piece of floating flotsam. Despite only being 20 yards away, it took half an hour to push through the bodies and wreckage. Strangely, not one female body was seen in the debris. Dawn was now breaking. A sail was erected and by now, the bright lights of a steamship could be seen on the horizon. Not wanting to be overlooked, Lowe and his small crowd were "bowling along nicely" at about 6 knots when two further boats were seen; "D" (the boats had cut free from each other soon after Lowe had departed) and "A". "D" was taken in tow, but "A", was in a precarious state and beyond rescue; the boat had sunk so far that the people had to stand all night with freezing up to their knees. All Lowe could do was take on its collection of survivors.

The above account of the marshalling of the lifeboats and the two rescues by boat No.14 comes from Lowe's testimony but when one peers closer at other people's descriptions of the rescue, one wonders who is right. Some of the accounts are so contradictory it raises the brief suspicion that the survivors witnessed different incidents. For instance, Seaman Evans said that his boat (10) was tied up to three boats, when, an hour later, Lowe in 14 came over. Lowe claimed at the British Inquiry and in affidavit written in New York in May 1912, that he collected boat 12 soon after leaving the *Titanic* and took it 150 yards away. He then went back and forth between 12 and the ailing liner, collecting other boats until he had five in total. This contradicts the accounts of other occupants in the other boats, particularly boat 4 which was already engaging in its own rescue attempt. Another problem concerns just who Lowe took with him during his rescue attempt; he and his crew indicate that 7-9 people were in the boat, including champion racket player Charles Williams - the only man whom Lowe voluntarily let enter a boat from the *Titanic* to assist in rowing. Esther Hart, in boat 14, also said that it went back empty. But Charlotte Collyer gave a very detailed account, particularly that of the rescue of the Japanese man, strongly implying that she was in the boat[7].

Interviews with 2nd class survivor Edith Brown indicated that she was in boat 14 during the rescue too. May Futrelle wrote that she saw a man in the water whom she thought was her husband and was heart-broken when she found out it wasn't; her account strongly indicates that she was present when the man was plucked out of the water[8]. Also in boat 14, Mrs Compton writes of the rescue of the swimmers: "We found one man with a life preserver on him struggling in the cold water, and for a moment I thought that he was my son." The language is very indicative that she was present during this rescue.

Ellen Walcroft claims to have been in boat 10 and wrote that "six [men had been] picked up but one man was mad. He shook the boat and we were afraid it would capsize." The use of the word "we" is interesting. Boat 10 never picked up anyone, and her account sounds like boat 4. This objection aside, it doesn't make any sense for any passengers to have been in Lowe's boat. They would have taken up valuable space that could have been utilised for anyone rescued.

Then we must ask; who instigated the initiative to go back to the wreck? Lowe's evidence is that it what his plan. Daisy Minahan said otherwise: she claimed that some of the women implored the 5th Officer to divide his passengers and go back, but Lowe disapproved, saying, "You ought to be damn glad you are here and have got your own life." He ultimately changed his mind. Ellen Walcroft's story confirms Lowe's. Miss

213

Compton said that the women protested about being so close to the *Titanic* before she sank, and Lowe acquiesced, agreeing to pull away a little distance. In other accounts, she describes how her companions "insisted" that the officer head back. Steward Crowe's story is that the ladies protested at the idea of going back again "with these people in the boat."

Although it is definitely certain that the unfortunates on boat "A" and "B" weren't collected until much later, there are some accounts from Lowe's armada that some contact was made with these boats. Collyer said that they picked up a large number of men from the wreckage, and found a boat floating bottom up; they rescued twenty of those perched atop it and four dead people were cast into the sea. Mrs. Furtrelle also says, "Within minutes Lowe had picked up those who had tumbled out of the collapsible boat. He had issued orders to the other boats and they were rapidly picking up all the swimmers who had been able to keep their heads above water." Imanita Shelley gave an affidavit to the U.S. Inquiry stating that "after the sinking of the ship the boat they were in picked up several struggling in the water and were fortunate enough to rescue 30 sailors who had gone down with the ship, but who had been miraculously blown out of the water after one of the explosions and been thrown near a derelict collapsible boat to which they had managed to cling. That after taking all those men on board the boat was so full that many feared they would sink, and it was suggested that some of the other boats should take some of these rescued ones on board; but they refused, for fear of sinking." Shelley is suspected to have been in boat 10, which neither assisted in picking up the swimmers nor helped to take on the occupants of boats "A" or "B". Her account indicates that she intimately knew what was taking place during the rescue. Caroline Brown also indicates that she and her colleagues came across boat "B" before tying up with the others. She says that they could only take on 8 or 9 out of the 30 people, one of whom was the fourth or fifth officer [sic] and that they beckoned to other boats to take off the balance. Brown was in boat "D" and her story displays signs of confusion, which doesn't bode well for her claim that a shot was fired near her boat as she departed the stricken *Titanic*[9].

Also in boat "D", Hugh Woolner wrote a letter in which he stated that an order was given to lighten boat 14, so that it could go and rescue people on an upturned boat, which was faintly visible in the distance. These men, about twenty in total, were picked up, having balanced for three hours up to their ankles on their boat. Woolner's letter then talks about the later encounter with "A", so he is obviously differentiating

214

between two different craft. Woolner's testimony partially corroborates this; "An officer came down and said he wanted to empty some of the people out of his boat, because he wanted to go and rescue some people who were on what he called a raft." He then says that "we" went in the direction of the swamped boat, but contradicts himself seconds later when he says that he didn't go as his boat was too fully laden. But he does distinguish between this swamped boat, and "A" which he referred to later.

Martha Stephenson's and Elizabeth Eustis's monologue on the sinking is interesting. She describes how Lowe ordered the boats to go with him towards the wreck, but hers (4) was the only one to stir. They then went and took on the people standing on the upturned boat. The authors of this piece are obviously confusing boat 4's rescue of "B", which occurred after Lowe had left them, but the writing of the piece is confusing; it does sound like the boatload were saved during the night, during Lowe's command. Stephenson and Eustis do talk of the people pulled in from the sea, before they tied up, so this may just be a simple case of confabulation.

Hemming, in boat 4 recalled that upon picking up people from the water, his boat got together with another, and only picked up two more boats, which was when dawn broke[10].

We must simply ascribe these accounts to some form of mental confusion which does not bode well for the rest of these survivor's accounts. It could well be that they had become confused with the rescue of "A" hours later but the "upturned" ("B") rather than "swamped" ("A") nature of the boat they describe does not conform to this theory. The people who talked about Lowe rowing to the upturned boat were passengers who could not possibly have known what was happening once boat 14 left the small armada of boats and plunged into the darkness. Still, enough witnesses provide evidence that the reason for going back was to rescue the occupants of either "A" or "B"for us not to dismiss the possibility. Revisionist historians will likely pounce on these heretical descriptions and form conclusions saying that Lowe had changed his mind in picking up the unfortunates standing on the boat(s)...but he had no qualms when he met up with "A" a little while later. We will return to the rescue of those on boat "A" and its associated confusions presently.

Hearing the wails and pleas of those struggling to survive, a suggestion was made in boat 8 to head back and haul some of them out of the water, but this humanitarian suggestion only met with indignation by some in the boat, forcing seaman Jones, the leader of the contingent, to announce, "Ladies, if any of us are saved, remember I wanted to go back. I would rather drown with them than leave them." The ladies of Boat 8 and Jones grappled with the oars, 1st class passenger The Countess of Rothes sat at the tiller, and all while the contingent of idle crew puffed at their pipes, telling their leader that "if [he] didn't stop talking through that hole in [his] face there will be one less in the boat."

The situation was diametrically opposite in boat 6. Like boat 8, several ladies had been forced to abandon their loved ones on the decks of the doomed ship, but here they wanted to respond to the eerie cries that drifted over the water. Why the responses of boats 6 and 8 were different is debatable; it may come down to class, nationality, psychology (with one or two dominant people swaying the rest) or just different feelings of self-preservation. Regardless, boat 6's efforts were scuppered by the garrulous quartermaster at the tiller. Hichens refused to return saying that there were "only a lot of stiffs there," and that entering the thrashing crowd would simply result in their own boat being swamped. Standing before his captive audience, Hichens stood trembling in the cold, "with an attitude like someone speaking to the multitude, fanning the air with his hands, [and told the others that they were] likely to drift for days...there was no water in the casks and no bread, no compass and no chart. No one answered him," recalled Margaret Brown. They were, as Helen Candee added, at the mercy of the elements, and that they would be helpless in a storm.

After a little while, the moans ebbed, and eventually ceased altogether. Survival time in the water is generally placed at between 15 and 30 minutes, although a few with more hardy constitutions would have survived a little longer. But in the darkness, it would have been an exceptional man to differentiate between the "dead" and the "unconscious". In a little more time, those who had succumbed to hypothermia would certainly have perished. Lifejackets or not, prolonger exposure to the sub-zero water would rapidly have sapped anyone's energy and determination to survive[11].

Amongst the undoubted tales of heroism, some instances of exaggeration stand out, possibly in an attempt to over inflate one's contribution to the *Titanic* tale. Take boat 12 as an example; seaman Poigndestre claimed that he pulled away to a distance of 150 yards, and after the ship had slipped beneath the water, the boat was pulled back towards the area of the wreck. He never saw anyone, let alone any corpses despite pulling in the direction of the cries. Spending a quarter of an hour searching, all he saw were several hundred deck chairs. In his estimation, Poingdestre never got closer than 100 yards from the source of the cries. It was only then, after speculatively calling out for other boats in the area, that his craft was tied up to some others; first 4, then 14[12].

Seamen Clench provides a different story. On the way down to the water, he claims that boat 12 was given instructions to keep an eye on No.14 and keep together as much as possible; they all stopped together after rowing about a quarter of a mile away. Clench never saw anyone, or any wreckage in the water either; to console the women in the boat he told them that the loud cries for help were "men in the boats shouting out to the others, to keep them from getting away from one another." His description of the boat's action do not match Poingdestre's.

Another example of "over-egging" ones achievements comes from boat 7, under the command of lookout Hogg. According to his story, he transferred some of his passengers to one boat, and then on the way back to the wreck to pluck any survivors from the water, he met another boat, who told him, "We have done all in our power and we can not do any more." Then, according to Hogg, he rowed around in search of other people before they could reach the wreck. One man said: "We have done our best. There are no more people around. We have pulled all around," and Hogg replied, "Very good. We will get away now."

The truth of the matter is this: boat 7 had been attached to boat 5, under Pitman's command for most of the night and some incumbents transferred to the adjacent craft. Although some of those in the boats were unclear as to when this happened, Pitman said that the two were lashed together before the *Titanic* went under. No one else in boat 7 recalled going back to look for any survivors. Pitman also claimed that the two were still joined until about 2.30; but others put it close to the time the *Carpathia* was seen, just before dawn...or after 4am. With boats 5 and 7 joined, it would have been impossible, given the reluctance in Pitman's boat, to head back to the wreck site. The evidence for a third boat joining them is scant[13].

Hogg's tale appeared during the U.S. Inquiry, but his testimony in London a few weeks later at the British Investigation did not cover the disputed activity of boat 7[14].

Hogg himself raises suspicion too. Mrs. Bishop in No.7 had this to say about Hogg; "One man lost his brother. When the *Titanic* was going down I remember he just put his hand over his face; and immediately after she sank he did the best he could to keep the women feeling cheerful all the rest of the time. We all thought a great deal of that man." 'That man' was Hogg. And he had no brother on the *Titanic*. This seems like an attempt to generate sympathy, for unknown reasons.

The actions of boat 2 are suspiciously contradictory. The customary story is that a suggestion was made to go back to look for survivors, but this was vetoed after howls of protest from the women in the boat. Elizabeth Allen demurs here: she says that they did go back but saw no-one. Then we must consider the movements of the boat; by all accounts, it seemed to have ended up on the far side of the *Titanic*, furthest away from its point of departure. Launched from the forward port deck, it wound up a fair fraction of a mile away on the aft starboard side of the ship. A steward named Johnson said that Captain Smith had ordered Boxhall, the commander of the craft, to row for the mystery light off the ship's bows. After "a good half hour", and at a distance of 1½ miles, the boat turned around and headed for the *Titanic*'s stern. Johnson claimed that the boat only had two oars but could move easily through the water; others speak of many more joining in the task, lady passengers included, but that it was laborious as no-one knew how to row. One might ask if 1½ miles in 30 minutes is possible. Johnson says that they did not go back to the wreck site after the *Titanic* had foundered. Then we have Boxhall, who said in America that, "I pulled around the ship's stern and was intending to go alongside, and tried to see if I could get alongside of the ship again. I reckoned I could take about three more people off the boat with safety. I did it of my own accord." Seaman Osman told the U.S. Inquiry, "I said to the officer, "See if you can get alongside to see if you can get any more hands, to see if you can squeeze any more hands in." So the women then started to [get] nervous after I said that, and the officer said "All right."" A few weeks later at the British Inquiry, Boxhall contradicted himself and Osman by claiming that he heard an order to head round to the starboard side. No one else in the boat seemed to recall this order, yelled through a megaphone, or an order to head for the mystery ship, and indeed, no one remembered boat 2 returning to the vicinity of the sunken liner to search for swimmers. One wonders why there is so much deviation in testimony, and boat 2 is a perfect example. The lack of cohesion certainly confounds and thwarts those who attempt to create a cogent account of the final hours of the *Titanic*[15].

218

As stated, after the *Titanic* sank and hearing the horrendous shrieking of those cast in the freezing waters, the response of those in the lifeboats was worse than lacklustre. Admittedly, some boats were too full to even consider heading into the desperate mob. But some boat's inactivity bordered on inhuman. One of these was boat No.1. There is no coherent explanation as to what transpired in this boat, even after all these years. We are left with confusion and contradiction. "Master of the situation" Symons thought that it would not be safe to go back at that time although he admitted that there was room for 8 to 12 more people. His story about possible coercion not to return to help those in the water is non-committal ("[He] would not doubt [hearing a male passenger in the boat] saying it was dangerous"..."[Lady Duff Gordon] may have said [that she was afraid of the boat being swamped if they rowed back]") but it seems that he did not hear anyone else venture an opinion or suggestion that they should return which he found surprising; but his story, stuck to steadfastly is that he claimed to have heard no conversation whatsoever. Those in the boat simply lay on their oars and listened. Horswell claimed agreement with Symon's version; he did not remember anything being said. Neither did fireman Pusey. The only thing that Collins recalled that there was a mention from a crewman that the boat was to pull for a short time to escape the suction. Pusey only remembered the order to clear the ship and make sure that Symons was obeyed. Fireman Sheath likewise only recalled the directive to pull away from the *Titanic* but nothing else. Sir Duff Gordon likewise did not hear anything about rescuing the swimmers or any objections to returning and neither did his wife. Charles Stengel also confirmed this; "we were quite a way away, and the suggestion was not made...I do not know why we did not." It is sufficiently interesting to note that two men who were suspected of having done nothing, or allegedly enticed others to do nothing, pushed the distance of boat 1 well beyond the 200 yard figure agreed by many, to 1000 yards; Symons, who as "Master of the Situation" and had done nothing to order his men to go back, and Sir Duff Gordon, who some thought had agreed with his wife's suggestion not to return[16].

To confound this tidy impression of No.1 boat as an unfeeling carrier of humans ignorant to the plight of those in distress, we now present Hendrickson. In deep contrast to nearly all of fellows, he claimed that he had proposed that they should go back on a rescue mission, but the female passengers objected to this plan, the crew remaining silently aloof. Lady Duff Gordon was evidently not a good sailor and spent a lot of the time reclining in the boat on the unused oars and sails, but she did rouse herself temporarily from occasional bouts of vomiting to state that she was scared for fear of being inundated by the crowd in the water, and her husband, tending for his sick spouse, upheld her views. He certainly recognised Duff Gordon's voice, for Sir Cosmo had declared "One man take command of the boat" when down in the water, which was a repetition of Murdoch's parting instruction. The attitude of the Duff Gordons seemed to dispose of any inclination towards a rescue, in Hendrickson's opinion. Taylor also confirmed Hendrickson's story, with the added detail that, in addition to a lady condemning the rescue suggestion, two men in the boat shared her thoughts, one saying "We shall be swamped if we go back. It would be dangerous to go." Taylor was seated on the same thwart as Sir Duff Gordon and according to the fireman, he was not one whose voice acted to dissuade the others. No crewman spoke up. No one else remembered the Duff Gordons stifle any potential rescue attempt.

The hint of a bribe has been levelled against Sir Duff Gordon. Although he denied anything sinister, salacious crumbs of gossip were played out at the British Inquiry. Duff Gordon claimed that 20 to 30 minutes after the *Titanic* had sunk, a man said to him, "I suppose you have lost everything?" Duff Gordon confirmed this and his fellow in the boat remarked that he could get more. When he replied that he could, Duff Gordon was told, "Well, we have lost all our kit and the company won't give us any more, and what is more our pay stops from tonight. All they will do is to send us back to London." Duff Gordon remarked, "You fellows need not worry about that; I will give you a fiver [that is, £5] each to start a new kit." Pusey remembered the gist of this. In his story, Lady Duff Gordon said to Francatelli, "There is your beautiful nightdress gone" about three quarters of an hour after the cries had finished. Pusey gently rebuked this unfeeling statement with the comment, "Never mind about your nightdress madam, as long as you have got your life"; soon afterwards there was mention of the lost kit, the stopped pay...and a payment to start a new kit. Lady Duff Gordon's 1932 autobiography confirms this exchange.

One looks fruitlessly for contemporary mentions of these stories. Collins heard nothing being said about money, and the general impression that one gets from the testimony is that the crewmen where quite surprised to receive a payment order a few days later while on the *Carpathia*. All Hendrickson remembered is that before No.1's occupants landed safely, Duff Gordon said that he would do "something" for the men, mentioning that he would get their names and send a wireless message home to their families if he could. As we have heard, Taylor was seated next to Sir Duff Gordon, and all he remembered is the men mentioning that they had lost their clothes, and the promise by Duff Gordon to inform their families of their safety by wireless.

Charles Stengel proffered some illuminating comments in a newspaper interview soon after he docked in New York. The crew wouldn't stick to the oars, he said, but lit cigarettes, laid down in the bottom of the boat and yelled jokes at each other. Sir Duff Gordon told them, "You take care of us safely and I'll make you all a present." His wife added that she had quite some money too. Unfortunately for those who revel in scandal, Stengel said nothing of this when called to give evidence in America. All he said was that when the last lights on the *Titanic* went under, he remarked that there would be suction and they should pull away, the other passengers agreeing[17].

In fact, Stengel claimed that he and Sir Duff Gordon decided which way to go, something denied by Sir Cosmo. But, oddly, Stengel's mention of "a present" does have some resonance with other evidence, as we have discussed.

The contemporary opinion among the crew probably was that their pay would end when ship went down. But it was a different matter in reality; for instance, on 30th April, 2nd class steward James Witter received an account of his wages, and the date of discharge was given as 15th April 1912; he was paid for the six full days at sea, not 5 days and a fraction. His account also listed that he was given a 13 day bonus, to account for the time he spent in New York and also for the time taken during his return to England aboard the s.s. *Lapland*. Other crewmen, such as George Moore, received a bonus; he was paid for 26 days, including the few extra days on account of him being called to testify at the U.S. Inquiry. To further denigrate the fable that the pay would stop immediately when the water washed over the last of the *Titanic*, researcher David Gittins notes that the crew had been informed by Ismay that their pay would not cease on the 15th April, and they had been told this by April 22nd Gittins also says that, "[The] White Star [Line] offered to pay the crew an extra week's wages but, after discussions with the unions, it was decided to pay the surviving crew for the entire time spent away from England." Some of the crew had also managed to acquire a pre-sailing advance, and Gittins points out that, "Since all the surviving crew received a bonus of at least 13 days' pay, none would have returned to England to find themselves owing money to White Star, even had they received an advance. The predicament of those who received advance pay may well have impelled the unions to insist on payment of a bonus. Bruce Ismay granted their request, after some argument."

Perhaps in the back of the crew's mind was the *Olympic/Hawke* collision 7 months previously. After three days laid up in the Solent, the *Olympic* returned to Southampton, and her certificate of sea worthiness revoked. The crew were discharged, and given just three days pay, amounting to their time while on the ship. Two members of the crew, including future *Titanic* seaman William Weller took the White Star Line to court to claim for a full month's pay. Simply put, he argued that, since he was not at fault, why should he be penalised? The discussions centred on whether the *Olympic* could be classed as a "wreck", and one colourful definition mentioned in court was that "A wreck is a vessel which has touched the ground." This was essential as the White Star Line claimed that, according to the law, "when the service of a seaman terminates before the date contemplated in the agreement, by reason of the wreck or loss of the ship... he shall be entitled to wages up to the time of such termination, but not for any longer." The matter was settled when the presiding judge decided that the *Olympic* was effectively a wreck as she could not proceed to sea, her laboured journey back to Belfast for repairs not included, and before which the hull had been temporarily patched up. The gamble to claim the full £1 payment was dismissed.

Regardless of where it was promised, either at sea, or on the *Carpathia*, the £5 "gift" provided a welcome recompense for the 7 crew men's losses.

Whether being placed in the boat by accident or design, the green flares, which formed part of the White Star Line's night-time pyrotechnic identification sequence, had been a providential inclusion in the inventory of Boxhall's boat, and he fired off one periodically[18].

Since receiving the *Titanic*'s distress call, the Cunard steamship *Carpathia* that had been bound for Gibraltar, had turned to the north-west and became one of many steamships that were heading for the radioed distress location. Since about 3am, Captain Rostron had been observing the occasional light from Boxhall's green flares almost directly ahead providing a location towards which he could aim. Thinking the *Titanic* was still afloat (despite the final Marconi message received being a call that the engine room was flooded [sic]) this source of coloured

222

incandescence on the dark night provided a modicum of hope.

The *Carpathia* had been steaming at a presumed speed of 17½ knots, given the computed distance (58 miles) and the time required to traverse this course. But this speed is a mechanical impossibility for a ship whose engines were old and tired. We now know that the *Titanic* was some 13½ miles to the south and east of her distress location, thereby reducing the distance the *Carpathia* had to travel and bringing her speed closer to her maximum of some 14 knots, and more manageable that 17 knots. The influence of the eastbound North Atlantic Drift is also likely to have placed the *Carpathia* some miles east of her deduced location, fortuitously putting her on almost direct line to the wreck site when she turned around. It is to be wondered what would have happened if Boxhall had not fired his flares. Conceivably the *Carpathia* could have steamed at full speed through the region littered with lifeboats with horrific consequences.

To placate the *Titanic* that help was imminent, Captain Rostron ordered rockets to be fired and night-time Cunard identification signals to be displayed[19]. Contemporary 2012 commentators have criticised his orders to use rockets, as this was contrary to an international agreement that such pyrotechnics were to be used only for signalling distress when on the high seas. Such commentators have also remarked on Rostron's full speed dash through an ice region knowing that the *Titanic* was in a precarious situation because of icebergs. These commentator ponder on the risks that Rostron was taking with the lives entrusted to him. It seems that history rewards those who take chances, if such risks are mitigated by success. Whatever the pontification of modern day historians, criticism of these "misdemeanours" is lacking from the 1912 record.

The green flares provided an almost unifying source of hope for the lifeboats too; many of those rowing for the mystery light on the horizon now made for this promising green beacon. Soon afterwards, the sight of rockets bursting many miles away provided a distraction and respite from the chill night air with the realisation that a ship was coming.

Very soon, mast lights of a steamship edged over the horizon, followed rapidly by the illuminated superstructure. Those in the lifeboats rejoiced and now rowed with renewed vigour towards this source of hope. Some created make-shift beacons, such as burning hats or paper. Other than this, all was silent apart from the gentle lapping of water at the base of a nearby iceberg, and the gentle sob of the widows and bereft in the 20 lifeboats, left bobbing in the steadily increasing tide.

The *Carpathia*'s lights offered hope and reassurance, but Hichens in boat No.6 ordered that his boat drift. Mrs. Candee appealed to her fellow passengers, "Where those lights are lies out salvation; shall we not go towards them?" The others voiced their approval and recommenced pulling at the oars, but only Hichens was dismissive. Asked if the *Carpathia* was there to pick them up, he simply said that she was there to pick up bodies.

Hichens was later to take umbrage at the accusations of his gross behaviour. In his opinion, Peuchen was not in the boat more than 10 minutes before he desired to take command. a Mrs.Meyer inflamed Hichen's anger when she suggested that he was drunk, swore and taking the blankets in a newspaper interview. The reason for Meyer's tirade? According to the helmsman, it was because he had spoken "straight" to her. He would, he said, rather than be pulling than steering, but there was no-one there to take over, especially with all the "nervous" ladies. He did admit to telling Peuchen that he had been put in charge of the boat and the Major was to do what he was told to do. Hichens denied remembering that the ladies had implored him to return to rescue the swimmers; it was impossible anyway, he claimed, as without a compass, he did not know what course to take to return to offer assistance which led to a pointed remark at the British Inquiry that, "I should have thought your ears would help you better." He claimed that he was offered a tablespoonful of whisky or brandy, and that he was given a half wet blanket, neither of which accords with other statements. As stated elsewhere in this book, his estimate of the number of people on board does not match with a count of people as seen in a photograph of boat 6 approaching the *Carpathia*. He also claims that his boat was not taken aboard the *Carpathia*, but was set adrift, which is untrue.

The crew on the *Carpathia* had occasionally slightly deviated from her course to avoid the icebergs that littered her route, but her speed never slackened. Soon after 4am, another of Boxhall's green lights was seen, tantalisingly close - but no sight of the *Titanic*. An iceberg loomed ahead and the *Carpathia* turned to avoid it. Minutes later, boat 2 was alongside and the occupants helped aboard the small Cunard vessel. The news was swiftly delivered; the *Titanic* had sunk.

Daylight was approaching, and as the sun ascended the heavens transformed from a pitch black through gentle shades of pink, orange and then to blue, revealing a beautiful sight; icebergs of all shapes and sizes were scattered around the horizon, and about five miles to the west, a huge low-lying icefield stretched from to the north-west to the south-east as far as could be seen, glistening in the new dawn. Had the *Titanic* not met the iceberg, she would have encountered this unbroken stretch of ice. However, given the large number of icebergs that could be seen it is impressive that she last as long as she did before her fatal impact.

As afore mentioned, Harold Lowe had done all he could in his search for survivors. Returning from his excursion to the wreckage with three survivors and one corpse, and his mast billowing nicely in the breeze, Lowe encountered boats "D", which he had left earlier. Upon boat 14's - and Lowe's - departure from the flotilla of four boats, "all" the ladies from "D" were transferred to No.12; this was due to fears that the collapsible would capsize with all the people loaded into it during the boat 14 trans-shipment[20].

But "D" was still perilously low in the water, caused by the extra weight imposed upon her by the trans-shipment of people, and was now wallowing pitifully in the swell. Lowe took it in tow, and in the distance, "A" could be seen with people balanced on top.

The dozen or so occupants of boat "A" had been standing in water all night; the canvas sides had not been erected and the boat, in a perilously swamped condition, had drifted off the forward starboard boat deck at the very end (this was the boat that Murdoch had been struggling with). Now the boat provided an uncomfortable refuge for the men - and the only woman to be plucked from the sea, 3rd class passenger Rhoda Abbott. According to reports, she and her two young sons had been waiting for a place at boat "C" but Abbott preferred that they all remained together, as she was concerned that she would be given a place in the boat, but not her sons. When the wave washed along the deck, she and her two children were separated forever. Only one of the bodies of her sons were later recovered.

Rene Harris in boat "D" describes the situation as her tiny convoy of boats approached "A": "I saw a revolver pointed at the boat. 'The woman first' said [Lowe's] voice. 'I will shoot the man who tries to get ahead.' He swung her into the boat [and] she sank to the bottom like a drowned bird. The young officer still held the revolver pointed at the men in the sinking boat. 'One man at a time...death to the man who makes a rush.' So they were taken into the boat one at a time."[21][22]

Lowe collected the fragile survivors and after checking that the bodies left on board were extinct of life, he resumed his passage to the *Carpathia*. Lowe's primary concern was with the living, as he said later, "I am not here to worry about bodies; I am here for life, to save life, and not to bother about bodies." But he obviously found the concerns of his passengers to be tedious. Someone implored Lowe to wait for the *Carpathia* to come to them, and to avoid the ice at all costs. Lowe snapped back, "I've taken command here. I intend to keep command because no-one seems to have sense enough to do it. Now, shut up. We will go to the boat. We can't expect her to come to us." And so saying, boat 14, its sails flapping in the breeze and with a boat in tow, made for the *Carpathia*[23].

The remainder of Lowe's small flotilla had become separated despite his order that they should remain together. In charge of No.12 was Poingdestre and he asked a fellow seaman, Lucas, in "D" to assist him rowing. Shortly afterwards, boat 12 seemed to have parted company from "D" and 10, and at one point, had boat No.4 in two. These two craft were slowly making their way towards the *Carpathia* when their inhabitant's attention was diverted by shouts, and then two blasts of a whistle which alerted them to a sorry predicament; in the daylight, they could a dozen men on top of something, a little distance away. Hemming thought it was ice, some one else thought it was a funnel. The men that they could now see were positioned uncomfortably on their tiny raft; some were standing, some crouched, some resting on the limbs of the compatriots, and some lying half in the water. As boats 12 and 4 approached, they realised that it was a lifeboat, the overturned boat "B", that the men were standing on. Among its number were Lightoller, Bride, Gracie and Joughin and over a dozen others.

The heavily laden boat 12 then delicately ambled over to the ailing boat where the men were struggling to maintain balance. Some of those on boat "B" were gingerly aided in No.12, which became heavily overloaded; estimates of the number on board range from about 50 to 80, all the way to an unbelievable 90. This merciful act of saving others had put No.12 in grave peril. As Poingdestre said, every time someone moved, the starboard gunwale went under water, and a slight breeze would have been the end for all of them. The ocean swell, which started about half an hour after the *Titanic* had sunk and had gradually deteriorated, cannot have been any help in this matter. Even so, not all the shivering individuals on "B" could be taken on board No.12;

fortunately boat 4 assisted by taking off the balance. Jack Thayer Jr. could now stand upright after hours spent kneeling, someone else hunched above him clasping his shoulders. Harold Bride's feet could thankfully be extracted from an uncomfortable position of being partially underwater, wedged between the slats of the craft. Baker Joughin claimed to have been in the water for two hours before seeing "B"; he was denied entry to the boat as it's equilibrium was dubious, and held onto the sides of the boat, supported by a colleague named Maynard. After half an hour, Joughin saw the two welcome boats, and he released himself from "B" and swam over to them. But for a few on board, it was too late. One of them was taken on board No.12 and Colonel Gracie tried in vain to retrieve a last vestige of life before realising that rigor mortis had already set in.

Spread over an area of four or five miles, the 18 lifeboats that were under control now congregated on the *Carpathia* which dodged about the ice and debris strewn sea to collect the flimsy craft and their human cargo. By about 7.45am, the *Carpathia* stopped to pick up the last lifeboats and the flotsam of the great ship became visible; there was surprisingly little debris left by the hulk of the *Titanic*. Within a few short minutes, the boat's crews were hauled aboard and Charles Lightoller became the last survivor to ascend the rope ladder to safety.

At about this time, the tramp steamer *Californian*, which had been stopped nearby in ice, hove to and exchanged semaphore messages with the *Carpathia*, promising to keep looking for any survivors. It was a forlorn expectation and for days afterwards, rumour buoyed hope that other ships had rescued passengers and crew. But for the majority of the ladies who crowded the *Carpathia*'s railing hoping that "the next boat" was to provide a happy reunion, it was clear that this would not to be. The boats had been accounted for, 13 of them being hoisted aboard and the remaining 5 left to drift and sink, boat "A" and "B" having already been abandoned. All that was left were the the *Carpathia* and the *Californian*, in a choppy sea of scant wreckage of lifebelts, tables, chairs, pillars, red cork fragments ... and one body that idly floated by[24].

With a memorial service organised on his ship, Rostron had decided that there was nothing more to be done and that the best recourse was not to proceed on his original intended voyage; he entertained ideas that his ship should attempt to reach closer ports - Halifax, the Azores or Boston, but settled on a return to New York. The ship's stores could barely hope to cater for the more than 700 people added to their roster. The *Olympic* had been steaming all night to the wreck site after receiving the Marconi calls for help, and, although she was still distant, there was a suggestion that she, should take on the survivors. This was met with horrified indignation as the *Titanic*'s sister would be seen as little more than a grim reminder of the calamity of the previous night.

And so, with many hundreds of stunned survivors, too stunned and numb to sob, the *Carpathia* turned around with "its cargo of woe" and steamed off to New York. The Marconi apparatus began to crackle the names of the survivors to any receptive station, refusing all requests for information on the calamity, instead sending only cursory details to the bemused and bewildered audience. In three days, the world would know and the *Titanic*'s legacy would be a litany of the heroic, the cowardly, the mundane, and an abundance of confusion and disinformation.

Titanic Interlude

The Fate of Heroes

The *Titanic* story has an ample share of heroes and cowards, many sacrificing themselves for the sake of "duty" or "honour." But not everyone was impressed at the disaster's glorification in the ensuing decades. Boxhall himself said that "he thought that some of the male passengers would have cheerfully locked their wives in their cabins so that they could go first [into the boats]." Harsh revisionism, from a surviving officer no less, makes us question the basic tenets of the disaster. Is all we have learned simply been an attempt to preserve the mystique and the romanticism of the doomed liner, its decks filled with men who stepped back and allowed the ladies to pass, the wireless men and engineers working till the last moment?

We have seen in these pages instances of pusillanimity; Hichens' crazed commands of boat 6 and the apathy over the drowning (particularly boats 1 and 8) are immediate examples. Stories designed to exaggerate the conduct of certain people were lovingly accepted by the press, while contrary evidence has lain dormant, only there to be found if one has the inclination to look (as an example, the fable that all the engineers perished below decks).

Some individuals undoubtedly wanted to be hailed as heroes. There are a number of accounts given by survivors that cause one to raise one's eyebrows when details of an escape altered. For instance, crewman Alfred White claimed to have been peering down from a position on the fourth funnel as he saw the ship engulfed and then break-up. In other accounts he said that he lowered himself down a vacant lifeboat fall and was picked up after he was ordered on deck to check on the situation, and saw all the boats gone and the ship's bows buried in the water. Other examples include fireman George Kemish (he claimed in his later years that he jumped into the sea and was rescued by boat 9, which no-one on the boat remembered), Mr.Carter (who undeniably was lowered into the sea in boat "C" even though he claimed in one newspaper account that he too jumped into the ocean) and Joseph Duquemin (who claims that his companion Bert Denbuoy was sucked down with the *Titanic*, and that he was rescued by boat "D" where he in

229

turn helped to pull Walter Williams from the water; however Williams has been placed in boat 13, and besides, there is ample information to suggest that only one man - a Mr.Hoyt - was picked up by boat "D"). Interesting data collected by Tad Fitch and Peter Engberg-Klarstrom on those who claimed to have been "plucked from the sea" casts considerable doubt on 25 people who stated that they had been in the sea.

Why would people lie about such a matter? Assuming that these stories are not the product of a journalist's imagination, it is inevitable that some people may want to over-exaggerate or manufacture their stories to emphasise their heroism. Then there is another matter: shame. There is at least one story of a man who was accosted by a widow on the *Carpathia* demanding to know "how was it that you were saved?" Mrs. Helen Candee tells how men would have to account for and justify their survival once rescued. Margaret Brown similarly writes how each man tried to explain how they came to be saved, "with an expression of apology as though it were a blight on their manhood." She related how she met two men on the *Carpathia* who were so extremely embarrassed at simply surviving when so many women had been made widows that they kept out of sight except to come to the dining room as they asked themselves "what women's place in the lifeboat did they fill." The men told Brown "in an apologetic manner ... how they inadvertently ... caught the last boat being lowered half empty." The men - Messrs Calderhead and McGough (who Mrs.Brown mistakenly called Bough) - were correct that the boats they entered were indeed half-full, but were wrong about their manner of departure. They escaped in boats 5 and 7, not "the last boat" as they claimed, but two of the first!

Also, one must not forget Major Peuchen; Lightoller suggested that Peuchen might need written "proof" that he was ordered into a boat, to fend off later opprobrium, which indeed later happened. Lightoller provided the Major with a small certificate describing his escape.

It is easy to dismiss those dubious claims of heroism, or of being plucked from the sea with bombast and certainty. But many aspects of the *Titanic*'s story become unfocussed when examined in greater detail, and some dearly held beliefs repeated for decades simply disintegrate. On those "25" suspicious claims alluded to earlier, less than a handful challenge our own knowledge of what really happened that night. Take Bernard McCoy as an example. He was a 3rd class Irish immigrant, travelling with two sisters. The ladies found refuge in a boat but Bernard was barred and eventually he found himself in the ocean. Although details are contradictory (one account says he had been in the water for half an hour, one account says he jumped and landed near his sister's boat), the basic gist is that his siblings were restrained from assisting their brother into the lifeboat, and the sailor in charge struck at Bernard's hands with an oar. With help from sympathetic people, and with one of the sisters holding the "sailor" back, Bernard was hoisted in. On the face of it, this seems preposterous. There are no independent accounts that this happened, not from aghast or indignant passengers, or from crew, but then, one must ask if a miscreant sailor and his lackeys would admit to such behaviour. Still, the stories of Bernard's treatment were consistently repeated by the press, and although there is no corroboration, we must admit that there are some boats about which nearly nothing is known and we must ask if the "incident" happened at one of these. The McCoy incident is reminiscent of a claimed incident with another Irish lad, Thomas McCormack, who swam to a boat and was hit on the head, his hands torn free from the gunwales. Swimming to another boat, he received the same welcome but was pulled in by two Irish ladies despite the efforts of the crew to keep the interloper out[1]. McCormack's ordeal was raised at the British Inquiry, where it was swiftly dispensed with[2].

One can only ponder on the truth of such accounts. Do they belong relegated to a pile of deceitful tales or could there be a glimmer of truth in them? The lack of corroboration is perhaps telling.

These instances aside, the press lauded certain individuals over their conduct. The band played till the end, Jack Phillips was lost, the captain did not survive, and Chief Officer Wilde, 1st Officer Murdoch and 6th Officer Moody all perished, the latter two being on the bridge at the time at the collision with the iceberg, and with their passing scholars of the disaster have had to endure an unceasing barrage of arguments and speculation as to what really happened prior to the collision. These debates rely on the myriad of contradictions of ship's timings, headings and the barked orders of the officers, confounded by the stories of the remaining crew who did survive, and whose accounts do not always mesh.

Captain Smith was universally pronounced as a hero, regardless of the fact that his ship hit the 'berg while travelling at excess speed in an area which he knew was infested with ice. His conduct after the collision, where he sequestered himself in or near the officer's quarters is telling. The plaudits given to the captain seem hardly deserved, in this author's opinion. Then we have Murdoch, long touted as the officer who let men into boats when space was available; but we know that he was only too eager to let the forward starboard boats be loaded and lowered half empty rather than seek out potential occupants. It is debatable as to how much control he had over the boats further aft which were filled on the deck below him by stewards. Wilde, as suggested in other chapters, was keen to uphold the "Women and children only" embargo on the boats, with only a hint that he bundled Ismay into one of the last boats. Ismay, of course, was his employer.

Can we speculate upon the fate of some of these "heroes"?

Captain Smith's behaviour that night is a conundrum. His command did not seem to be inspired, particularly in the seething crowd around boat 14 where an appearance by his well respected persona may have quelled the riot without recourse to weaponry. Smith seems to have been happy ordering Quartermasters Bright and Rowe to use the Morse lamp to communicate with the mystery ship on the horizon, and so on. As noted, his officers chose not to consult with him about various important matters (the alleged plan to off-load people from gangways near the waterline and so on) and he did not volunteer information about the ship's projected longevity.

Sightings of the captain towards the end are fleeting, and his ultimate fate is not known, as his body was not retrieved. Steward Edward Brown struggled to prepare boat "A" for launching and recalled the captain walking past him with a megaphone, saying, "Well, boys, do your best for the women and children, and look out for yourselves." Other accounts put Smith's last words as "Be British" or "Every Man For Himself." Smith walked onto the bridge, which seconds later was swamped as the bow dipped under. Hemming saw the captain as he came down from helping with boat "B", where Smith ordered everyone to move to the starboard side to correct the massive list that had plagued the lowering of the boats. Hemming helped with "A" and by the time he had made his own mind up to escape and crossed back over to starboard, Smith was nowhere to be seen. At about this time, as he was hoisting boat "B" from the roof to the deck, Harold Bride saw the captain dive from the bridge into the sea. This was after Hemming had descended from the roof where "B" was located; he probably missed the captain as he headed through the bridge because Smith had temporarily moved to the starboard side unseen, and where Brown heard him utter words of encouragement.

We must be wary of disinformation, particularly those that seek to provide a heroic end where evidence is lacking. August Wennerstrom's account says that, "Coming out of the deck, again, we met a Swedish woman from Chicago. She had, if I remember right, 4 small children and had not gotten them dressed in time to get in the lifeboats. We helped her with the children and I carried one of them. We met Capt. Smith, he picked up one of her children, but said that our time was coming, and before he finished the words, one of the boilers in the engine room exploded, and threw us all apart. This was the last I saw of the woman and her children from Chicago." These accounts are, again at variance with Bride, and the timing of the "explosion" is, again, irreconcilable with the Junior Wireless Operator's story who reported no "explosions" when he was on deck helping with boat "B".

There are a few accounts of Smith being seen swimming in the water, reaching boat "B"; these are generally dismissed as apocryphal. A tale exists that Smith swam up to the overturned boat and delivered a baby to the occupants, before refusing any help himself, telling the encumbents that he was going to follow the *Titanic*. Fireman Harry Senior seems to be the main source of this tale and he consistently told his stories to the press in the United States and England, but today his story is regarded as a journalistic invention to give a suitably heroic end for Smith. Certainly, no one on the boat remembers being handed a child. In one variation of this tale, two little children remained at Smith's side until the bridge was awash. Taking hold of one girl under his arm, fireman James McGann, the alleged source of this story, took the other child, but the shock of the cold water released his hold on the child, and he thinks the same had happened to Smith too. McGann claims that Smith did not reach boat "B"; Likewise, Walter Hurst, who was perched on "B" was sure that Smith did not reach this boat, but he did think he might have been a gentleman that had earlier kept cheering them on with shouts of "Good boys, good lads". This man had the voice of authority, but as Senior reached out to the man with an oar, it was clearly too late for him, and "he turned around like a cork."

Jack Phillips' fate is unknown too. Like Smith, his body was never found. Phillips is sometimes listed as being one of the men on boat "B" who perished during the night.

The last definite sighting of Phillips was soon after the two Marconi men abandoned their cabin. In one of the very first newspaper interviews, Bride said that after leaving their equipment, the two men came out on deck, and he went over to "B" which had been hoisted from the roof. Phillips then walked aft. This story is suspicious as it mentions that Bride was one of those who helped to lower boat "B" to the deck below, then went inside to find Phillips still transmitting, and then they both come out on deck to find the same boat in the same location. In actuality, Bride never returned inside after the boat had been shoved off the roof. Testimony at the U.S. Inquiry adds little ("I saw [Phillips] walking aft as I was helping to get the collapsible onto A [sic] deck.") as does his report to the Marconi company ("Leaving the cabin, we climbed on top of the house comprising the officers' quarters and our own, and here I saw the last of Mr. Phillips, for he disappeared walking aft."), and his story alters in front of the British Inquiry, where he simply says, "We climbed up on top of the Marconi cabin and the officers' quarters. The last I saw of Mr. Phillips he was standing on the deck-house."

Why do some think that Phillips managed to scramble onto boat "B"? Bride's first newspaper interview says that a dead body that he passed climbing up the ladder to the *Carpathia* was Phillips, supposedly expiring from exposure and cold. However, previously he had said that the "last time" he saw his senior was on the boat deck of the *Titanic*. Questioned in America, Bride could only say that he "had heard" afterwards that his friend was buried at sea from the *Carpathia*. Lightoller couldn't help with this riddle; he testified that Bride had told him that Phillips had been on the boat. But it is clear that Bride did not know, and he was repeating a story that he gleaned from another source. 22 years later, further evidence emerged from Lightoller's unreliable autobiography and it paints an altogether different story. Now, we have Phillips not only standing close to Lightoller, but also telling of the various ships that were en route to rescue them. Phillips passed away soon after a lifeboat was spotted in the distance, and Lightoller insisted on taking his body into the boat when they were picked up. However, in 1912 Colonel Gracie made it clear that the information about help rushing to them came from Bride, and that Lightoller was in contact with the junior Marconi man, lying prone at the stern of boat "B". Both Lightoller and Gracie were sure that the body transferred was not Phillips, but another unidentified member of the crew. Furthermore, in his report to the Marconi company, Bride writes, "I called Phillips several times, but got no response, but learned later from several sources that he was on this boat and expired even before we were picked off by the

234

Titanic's boat. I am told fright and exposure was the cause of his death. As far as I can find out, he was taken on board the *Carpathia* and buried at sea from her, though for some reason the bodies of those who had died were not identified before burial from the *Carpathia*, and so I can not vouch for the truth of this." This was written in late April 1912. If Phillips was on the boat he would surely have heard his friend calling for him, just a matter of yards away especially if Phillips was lucid enough to tell Lightoller of the ships coming to their aid. The bodies buried at sea by the *Carpathia* were examined for identification, and Phillips' corpse was not among them. As researcher George Behe says, the only person in 1912 who claimed to have seen Phillips on the boat was a steward named Thomas Whiteley, who we definitely know was on, or near, boat "B". Whiteley's story was that he floated in the water and at sunrise, saw the overturned collapsible (other interviews claim that he spent some of the night on top of debris - a wardrobe - with four other men who passed away). Swimming over to the boat, Lightoller told him "It's 31 lives against yours, you can't come aboard. There's no room," and someone swung at him with "an oar." This tallies with other accounts; that the boat was loaded so precariously that some in the water had to be turned away. Whiteley pleaded to be let on board, but to no avail. Finally, someone passed away, and Whiteley was allowed to clamber on.

Later accounts confuse the story: Phillips had a conversation with Whiteley, who chafed his hands to help the circulation, and was told that the he had been in exchange with the *Californian* and the *Frankfurt*.[3]

Of interest is the fact that Phillips related to Whiteley that this latter ship only transmitted "What's up, old man?" which crops up in Bride's later stories. Whiteley's account also includes the old fable that Captain Smith was last seen trying to place a baby in a boat but when the ladies tried to save the old mariner, he cast off instructing them to save yourselves. Smith went under water, and never resurfaced. It is debatable as to whether Whiteley heard these stories first-hand, or gleaned them from press coverage in America. Whiteley's other tales include him being told by two of the lookouts that ice had first been seen at 11.15 (discussed elsewhere in this work) and that Murdoch shot himself because of his failed responsibility to the ship and its passengers and crew. All the look-outs survived and none of them were on boat "B", but to be fair Whiteley's mention of this anecdote could have come later after the rescue. These last two elements feature prominently in some of the fables that have been nurtured since 1912.

To return to Phillips; Whiteley claimed that the senior Marconi man was dead when they took him on board the *Carpathia*, and despite the use of brandy and other restoratives, it was too late, and he was buried at sea with three others. But another interview with Whiteley states that Phillips was in one of the boats that Lowe had lashed together, and that he died soon after, his body being washed overboard, which doesn't tally with any of the known accounts of anyone in boats "D", 4, 10, 12 or 14. None of the bodies in these boats, hoisted from the frigid waters, were Phillips.

Whiteley's stories seem to be embellishments, and it is now impossible to know which, if any, are true. Two years after the disaster, Whiteley tried to sue the White Star line for negligence, but his case never made it to court. Some speculate that he was paid off to keep quiet about whatever information he had learned[4].

Following the disaster, the heroes of the disaster (Smith, Phillips, the engineers) were commemorated by a multitude of plaques and inspiring speeches. The bandsmen were also recipients of similar heroic platitudes. Playing till the end, only a few of their bodies were fished from the Atlantic. A reverence exists among *Titanic* researchers for these musicians, and only the coldest cynic would decry their efforts, like the wireless operators as "only obeying orders," or that their soothing tunes allayed people's fears sufficiently to make them doubt the unfolding grave disaster on the *Titanic*. To these "cynics", the band's actions are not worthy of praise, and that they helped to perpetuate the sense of calm on the boat deck, stopping people from entering the boats. With the small orchestra, questions do remain, but they are incidental to the undoubted lack of concern the men showed for their own safety.

These questions form the basis for many of the arguments that pervade *Titanic* forums. For instance, What was the last tune played? The commonly held belief is that it was "Nearer My God To Thee," said to be one of two hymns that band leader Wallace Hartley would want played at this funeral. Long dismissed as a fantasy, there does some to be some validity to this tale. Astonishing evidence comes from the tireless work of researchers such as George Behe, and their accumulated data indicates that the hymn was indeed heard on the morning of April 15th, 1912. Many in the lifeboats heard it being played, and their recollections cannot be dismissed as newspaper inventions, for the song was being referred to whilst en route to New York, before the press had any attempt to distort the issue. It also does not seem credible that survivor's recollections were being tainted by bogus tales on the *Carpathia*, either, or by memories of the sinking of the s.s. *Valencia* six years earlier when the hymn was sung.

Many were adamant that it was played. And with the boat deck settling rapidly into the sea, one could easily believe the notion that the band - whose repertoire of soothing, cheerful, patriotic and uplifting music - switched to sombre selection(s) knowing that the end was near and all the boats had gone[5].

The endorsement by the band-leader himself, plus the statements from a surprising number of people support the notion that this tune was played at some point. There are problems, however, and they are significant. "Nearer My God To Thee" has quite a few different variants, and the tune differs depending on nationality, and religious denomination; David Gittins claims that there were as many as eight different versions of the tune. There is no consensus at to which of these was heard, and the hint by some researchers that only U.S. passengers and crew would only have familiarity with the U.S. arrangement is laughable; it is possible that people may have been familiar with many of the versions. This uncertainty on the actual tune have catalysed those sceptical of "Nearer My God To Thee" to pounce on another "last tune" candidate to support their contention that the *Titanic*'s small ensemble only played light hearted melodies. *Titanic* aficionados have long drawn from a newspaper account given by Harold Bride, in which he stated that after leaving the prone stoker on the floor on his office, he heard the band playing rag-time, somewhere aft. And then he heard a tune he called "Autumn". The band were still playing this song as he swam away from the sinking ship after he had been washed overboard with boat "B".

Bride's evidence seems superficially conclusive. The band were not playing a hymn at the end, but this "Autumn" tune. But, as ever, problems become apparent when the evidence is analysed. "Autumn" is indeed associated with a hymn, but the name is not given to the title of a song, but the tune, and author Walter Lord suggests that it is unlikely that Bride would have identified the song via its arrangement. Indeed, hymn's names are usually given a title gleaned from the first line, but even so this mysterious "Autumn" tune does not conform to this convention. It would have been called "God Of Mercy and Compassion" and there is no hymn by this name. But, according to Lord, a waltz named "Songe d'Automne" ("Dream of Autumn") is the most likely candidate; it was popular in London but less so in America, where the

"Autumn/hymn" association was more prevalent. Furthermore, "Songe d'Automne" was abbreviated to just "Autumn." Lord's research unearthed survivors who had heard the waltz "Autumn" that night.

And despite what some apologists say, the tunes of "Songe d'Automne" and the variants of "Nearer My God To Thee" are not remotely similar. A former colleague of Hartley told a newspaper that the version his friend wanted played at this funeral would be "Sullivan's version" - more commonly known as "Propior Deo", the variant sung by Methodists, the denomination to which Hartley belonged. Of course if it was indeed this version that was played, obvious questions arise; would Hartley's bandmates know the arrangement of the tune? Would the passengers recognise it? It should be noted that certain sections of the "Propior Deo" tune are reminiscent of "Bethany", which was used in the 1953 and 1997 cinematic depictions of the Titanic's demise. There is an obvious opportunity for confusion here.

How long did the band play? Bride's tale is that the last time he heard "Autumn" was when he was in the water. For this to have happened, the surging torrent of water coursing along the boat deck would have had to have passed the point where boat "B" had been hurled to the boat deck, as Bride was clutching at this boat when he - and it - were swept into the sea. Given how fast the water was cascading aft it is surprising that the band could play for much longer if they were located at their customary location, which is next to the 2nd funnel on the port side, and less than 90 feet from where Bride was washed overboard. There also does not seem to be enough time for the band to stop playing "Autumn" and commence "Nearer My God To Thee" before the surging tide engulfed them. Then one wonders how long the orchestra could play on an increasingly slanting deck; and there is also the effect that the chill night air had on their bands men's ability to hold and play their instruments as the cold nibbled at their fingers.

Revisionist historians contend that, the slope of the deck not withstanding, no tunes were played at the finale, because the band had dispersed. The heroism of the band may be sacrosanct, but there are witness to the band laying down their instruments[6].

The first of these witnesses is the seemingly omnipresent Archibald Gracie who saw the band lay down their instruments "half an hour" before the *Titanic* sank. This detail was given at a lecture two weeks before he died, but is not mentioned in his book. This is no indication of anything; Gracie's book ends abruptly and it is possible that

238

he may have included this detail about the band if his tragic demise didn't force his book to be understandably truncated. The other witness is Algernon Barkworth. His newspaper account states that when he came on deck, the band were playing a waltz but when he next passed the spot, the bandsmen had thrown down their instruments and were nowhere to be seen. Although some researchers have associated Barkworth's story with Gracie's timing of "half an hour" before the end, Barkworth's account gives no indication when he saw the abandoned instruments.

Steward Edward Brown was on the forward starboard side of the boat deck when the sea came roaring over the bulwark. Seconds before that, he heard the band playing on the boat deck forward companionway (presumably the port side). It would be only a few moments before boat "B" was carried out to sea...and Bride heard "Autumn". If Brown and Bride's memories are believable, the small orchestra had returned for their final selection.

So, if the band did abandon their instruments, why did they do so, and did they later return? George Behe contends that they may indeed have temporarily put down their instruments; Pierre Marechal reported seeing the band "between the decks ["A" deck?]" and none of them were wearing lifebelts; Marechal left in the very first boat. A stewardess by the name of Gold stated that she later saw the band with their lifebelts beside them. Behe suggests that the band may have temporarily departed to fetch their belts, but another statement by Gold disputes this, for she says that the cork-filled belts were brought to the band. If the band did not want to stray outside 1st class territory but wanted to play where their soothing tones could dispel panic, they had two options: to venture to the starboard side, which does not seem to have been the case, or to go to the deck below where a small band of passengers were waiting to enter boat 4. All the others boats in the area had either departed, or were not yet ready to disembark[7]. Although her accounts contains much that is dubious, May Futrelle mentions that the band ventured out on to the boat deck at a fairly late point in the evening. She had just seen the tender parting of the Astors at boat 4 and noted that the orchestra had come out on the boat deck at "about the time they launched the fourth boat" [No.4 ?]; just before this, she says that she was seized and was dumped into "D". Sadly, she mentions that there was a piano out on the deck which makes her story even less credible; it is absurd to think that a large upright piano from the Grand Staircase vestibule could be manhandled through two sets of vestibule doors and over a coaming at the base of the door frames!

Although her newspaper account has much that seems inaccurate, Caroline Brown's comments may offer a solution to where the band played. According to her, they were marching from deck to deck.

For what it is worth, this author posits that "Nearer My God To Thee" was the last tune played and Harold Bride's reference to "Autumn", coming from a newspaper interview riddled with dubious anecdotes, is inaccurate. He may have heard "Autumn" at some point, perhaps when he went out to occasionally relay reports to the captain of steamships responsive to their wirelessed distress calls, and the music became confused in his mind.

Can any inspection of testimony or stories provide clues as to what happened to the lost bridge crew? Again, none of their bodies were found, and some of these gentlemen's fate is associated with an event which, if it did happen, provokes repugnance amongst researchers: the alleged shooting of passengers and subsequent suicide of an unnamed officer.

According to popular fable, as the bridge dipped under the water, the scene on the starboard boat deck switched to one of unbridled chaos; people fighting to extract themselves from the water and crew still struggling with the cumbersome boat "A". As the legend proceeds, the attempt to scramble into the frail craft was too much for one officer. Pulling his gun forth, he shot some of the interlopers before turning the gun on himself.

Such a scene translates into good headlines and controversial set pieces in cinematic depictions of the tragedy, but one must ask if it really happened.

Titanic detectives Bill Wormstedt and Tad Fitch have collected all available reports of this incident to try and elucidate the truth. Their research has provided some genuine surprises. For, though many told of the shooting and suicide, they mostly amount to rumours or stories circulated by others. Wormstedt and Fitch have found only four survivors who have first hand knowledge of the suicide incident, and some of these are suspect[8]. There are more accounts which tell of bullets finding human targets, but precious few stories of an officer's suicide. Even when we find examples of human victims, we must be careful of embellishment by the press. For instance, Mrs.Mark Fortune told one newspaper that "When the ship struck several men in the steerage tried to rush the officers in charge of the lifeboats. At first the officers were able to keep them off by slugging them, but the passengers grew more terrified. Them the officers made use of their revolvers, first to fire in the air, and then to aim at the bodies of the men." This scandalous morsel does not appear in other interviews claiming to originate from her (the contradictions may be due to the fact that she was in a state of anxiety due to the wreck).

Starting with those in the Wormstedt/Fitch list, Eugene Daly was a 3rd class immigrant, and his reasonably consistent story was first told on board the *Carpathia*, so it is not a lurid invention of the gutter press upon arrival in New York. He said, "After the accident, we were all held down in steerage. Finally, some of the women and children were let up, but we had quite a number of hot-headed Italians and other peoples who got crazy and made for the stairs. These men tried to rush the stairway, pushing and crowding and pulling the women down. Some of them with weapons in their hands. I saw two dagos shot and some that took punishment from the officers." Daly finally made it to the bridge where the crew struggled with a boat, ostensibly identified as "A". The deck dipped beneath his feet as he helped to cut the ropes securing the boat to the ship and both he and the craft floated free. Daly later elaborated on this and said that two passengers were shot and then the same officer turned his weapon on himself a minute later. A letter to a family member confirmed this. As Daly himself wrote, "At the first cabin [deck] when a boat was being lowered an officer pointed a revolver and said if any man tried to get in, he would shoot him on the spot. I saw the officer shoot two men dead because they tried to get in the boat. Afterwards there was another shot, and I saw the officer himself lying on the deck. They told me he shot himself, but I did not see him. I was up to my knees in the water at the time. Everyone was rushing around, and there were no more boats. I then dived overboard."

Note that Daly did not actually say that he saw the officer shoot himself. He may also have become confused as boat "A" was not "lowered" unless he was referring to it being brought down from the roof; this may be too early for the "shooting" as there were plenty of people in the area, none of whom recall gunfire at this point.

Daly later gave evidence in litigation against the White Star Line. Unfortunately, his testimony has vanished, but the gist was reported in the newspapers: "...when he attempted to get into [a boat] an officer threatened him, although the boats were far from full. He said he heard two shots at this time, and later saw two men lying on the deck, and was told that they had been shot." One must be cautious and question how much has been omitted by the reporter in the newspaper article; for instance, Daly did not mention actually seeing two men shot in the write-up, just their bodies. There is no mention of the officer's body, either.

But then problems arise with the interpretation of the evidence. Daly's letter to his relatives in Ireland include the following: "Maggie [Daly] and Bertha [Mulvihill] got in [the boat] and I got in. The officer called to me to go back but I got in. They told me to get out but I didn't stir. Then they got hold of me and pulled me out...The officer in charge pointed a revolver and waved his hand and said that if any man tried to break through he would shoot him on the spot." The letter then continues with mention of the two men being shot and the officer lying on the deck. Researcher Susanne Stormer has speculated that the "officer" was Moody, and the boat mentioned was No.15, as the two ladies referred to are customarily placed in this boat. According to Stormer's theory, Moody is said to have shot himself at No.16. But, there are problems: Hemming recalled Moody working at boat "A" just moments before water started creeping on to the bridge - and the struggle with "A" was after Boat 15. We do know that Moody was at boat 9, and then almost certainly at 11, 13 and possibly 15. These four boats were launched after boats 14 and 16 - when we are told that Moody was dead. Then, Maggie Daly's and Bertha Mulvihill's accounts are too patchy to determine exactly which boat they left in. If they did depart in boat 15, the next - and last - one would be "C"...where shootings are known to have taken place. We certainly are not aided by the paucity of survivor's accounts for boats 15 and 16!

Finally, we have another account from Daly, where he says that the ladies' boat was lowered and went off, and he then went to the 1st class portion of the boat deck, along with steerage and 2nd class passengers. It was at a boat in this area of the *Titanic* that the shootings occurred and even here, his story is slightly different: "I saw [the two men] lying there after they were shot. One seemed to be dead. The other was trying to pull himself up at the side of the deck, but he could not. I tried to get to the boat also, but was afraid I would be shot and stayed back." Further confusion is added to the mix when he says that, after the shooting, he rushed across the deck - to where boat "A" was being fussed over. If his "rushed across" statement is correct, the use of weaponry took place on the port side, the opposite side to the customary location of the suicide.

The next "witness" was Laura Francatelli, who was in boat 1, launched approximately an hour before the "shootings". From a distance of 200 yards she saw, "The dear brave officer [who] gave [us] orders to row away from the sinking boat ... shot himself. We saw the whole thing, and watched that tremendous thing quickly sink...." One may raise concerns as to how Francatelli could see anything from 200 yards away, but, if she is correct, she may have been gifted with keen eyesight; or the story may be bunkum. It is not likely that we will ever know. The officer to whom she is referring was unquestionably Murdoch.

Then we have Carl Olof Jansson, a 3rd class passenger, who wrote privately that he saw the "Chief Officer" "place a revolver in his mouth and shoot himself. His body toppled overboard." But Jansson said that this happened *before* the last boat was launched; he himself waited till it had gone before he leapt into the sea. Taken literally, this cannot be a reference to boat "A" which, of course, was never lowered. As we shall see with the final witness below, the suicide could be construed as occurring not in the last frantic seconds when the boat deck was awash, but minutes before that. Jansson not mention the suicide in press interviews soon after landing in New York only that he heard "the sharp reports of several shots."[9]

The final witness is George Rheims, who wrote a letter to his wife the day after arriving in New York. In it, he claims, "While the last boat was leaving, I saw an officer with a revolver fire a shot and kill a man who was trying to climb into it. As there remained nothing more to do, the officer told us, "Gentlemen, each man for himself, good-bye." He gave a military salute and then fired a bullet into his head. That's what I call a man!!!" The mention of the "last boat ... leaving" seems to be confusing, as boat "A" did not technically "leave" the ship; a similar point is made by Daly[10].

Rheim's story was consistent, however, and a version appeared in the newspapers. Strangely, Rheims did not mention this shooting in 1915 during litigation against the White Star Line, only that he heard shots "about 40 minutes before [the *Titanic*] sank" and he also claimed to have jumped into the water about 25 minutes after this. He did admit to losing his memory for two months after the disaster which may make his story suspect[11].

Rheims, Daly and Jansson found refuge on top of the last two collapsible boats; at the time of the shooting, they were supremely well sited to

243

view any "suicide."[12]

Why are there so few first-hand reports of the suicide and the shooting of hapless passengers? The obvious answer that may be proffered is that these incidents simply didn't happen. But another reason is that the likelihood of anyone being suitably placed and then being saved in a lifeboat were small. Still, it is surprising that concrete declarations of shootings are not more forthcoming as many of those in the vicinity of boat "A" found refuge on the two useless collapsibles in the water. These people were well located spot to witness the shootings and suicide. All we have are a smattering of first hand reports, many second or third-hand stories, or rumour. The silence is bewildering. If it did happen, who shot themselves? Apart from the unmistakeable countenance of Captain Smith, the candidates are Sixth Officer Moody, Chief Officer Wilde and First Officer Murdoch. Conceivably, unless one was personally acquainted with the officer, anyone in a dark blue woollen uniform could have been mistaken for a "bridge officer"; one is reminded of Norman Chambers peering into the water in the mail room when he was joined by unknown, unnamed "officers." The last name in the bridge officer's list - Murdoch - is oft cited as the primary "suspect" with the reason given that he may have felt unimaginable guilt at causing the catastrophe in which hundreds died. But Lightoller, who was atop the wheelhouse when the "suicide" is supposed to have occurred, says that from his vantage point, he saw Murdoch and those struggling with boat "A" in the water as the forward boat deck dipped into the sea. Lightoller does not mention any use of a firearm, but there is a suggestion among researchers that he may have been telling a sanitised version of what happened, to spare Murdoch's family from embarrassment and shame. But suspicions of a benign "cover-up" by Lightoller do not amount to proof. Similarly, many in the area of boat "A" do not recall hearing any gun shots, but, like Gracie, they may have been too absorbed in saving their own lives to absorb the true horror of what was taking place in the vicinity. The suicide and shootings are a genuine mystery, probably one without firm resolution. They add greatly to the mystique, but introduce new facets the *Titanic* story; that is, how panicking humans react in desperate circumstances. If the deadly use of weapons to suppress humans really did happen, it seems to be abhorred and rejected by many *Titanic* "buffs", regardless of any evidence that is presented.

Afterword

Spawning much speculation, the *Titanic* disaster has generated much debate on the retrospective issues that led to the loss of life; the lifeboat provisioning; the lack of response by the strange ship on the horizon; the excessive speed; the design of the ship; the initial reaction to the iceberg, and so on. Most, if not all, of these points can be attributed to human failings, usual incompetence or overconfidence.

Naturally, following the disaster, regulations were improved regarding the provision of lifebelts, and the use of wireless signals and distress rockets to summon help. The formation of the International Ice Patrol with its dedicated fleet of aircraft and ships that survey the sea lanes, has been of inestimable value, saving many lives that might have been claimed by ice.

The most recognisable alteration of regulations following the foundering was the increase of lifeboat coverage, and the incredible rush to equip existing ships with boats required the immediate requisitioning of literally anything that was available, particularly collapsible boats and rafts that only served to turn ships into "floating boatyards" as one writer put it. The *Olympic* could carry the extra lifeboats, but other, older vessels could not find the space; thus, their crew and passenger complement - and hence their earning capability - were reduced.

The public were baying for "boats for all" and this meant that any lifeboats were press-ganged into service to fulfil the rabid desire for safety, sometimes with embarrassing public relations consequences. For instance, 200 stokers of the *Olympic* mutinied when they alleged that the hasty stampede for more boats resulted in the pressing into service of old and unseaworthy craft. The officials who inspected the boats disagreed, and only the removal of the entrance gangways to the *Olympic* prevented other crew from leaving their posts and joining their 'black gang' compatriots. A truce was called after suitable boats were procured to the satisfaction of everyone, but the *Olympic*'s voyage was eventually cancelled because in the time taken to placate the wary of the condition of the new boats, "unsuitable" crew had been enlisted provoking the fury of original crewmen, some of whom argued that the replacement crew were non-union personnel. In this case, the mutineers were arrested, and were eventually found guilty in court, but were let off.

The *Olympic* later returned to Belfast for extensive modifications to extend her double bottom and watertight bulkheads well above the waterline. The solid bulwarks on the boat deck that separated the forward and aft boats were ripped out and replaced with a long, unbroken line of davits and boats that now stretched over 500 feet. Finally, common sense had prevailed, but 1500 people had to die for sane heads to sheepishly admit the "boats for all" maxim. Other countries followed this example.

If the White Star Line had acted on its own discretion rather than an adherence to "the letter of the law" and had provided suitable lifeboat coverage, could everyone have been saved? Bearing in mind, the *Olympic* class vessels as originally built had four banks of four pairs of davits, located at each corner of the boat deck, giving 16 boats under davits, with four additional boats included. Given this configuration, could the boat deck have been utilised to provide space in the boats for all?

The *Titanic* sailed with about 2220 people, but her maximum complement was 3547 people. If we take the boats under davits (14 "full size" and 2 wooden cutters, or emergency boats) as a basis, we find that they can accommodate 990 people. How many more boats would be needed to rescue the remaining 2557 if the ship was solidly occupied? This is a question that depends on the type of boat required. A 30 foot long craft had a theoretical capacity of 65 people though many on the night of the disaster thought the boats unwieldy with this many on board, and modern safety regulations would never allow this total in a boat of such size. An additional 40 full-size boats would be needed, or a total of 3.5 boats per pair of davits. Now, the issue of arranging these extra boats becomes evident. The boats were 4 feet high, and the maximum height of the davit arms was some 13 feet above the boat deck. Conceivably, a nested stack of 3 boats could be arranged between the davits, with the upper boats resting on chocks inside the lower ones. This does not seem to be desirable, an opinion shared by Harland and Wolff marine architect Edward Wilding, who suggested that extra boats should be arranged "in-board" of the davit arms, not encompassed between them. This means that about 3 boats were to be placed next to the boat held under davits, on the deck. A cumbersome arrangement such as this would be an obstacle to managing the boats; they would have to be lashed down, one on top of the other to prevent movement in the high seas and. Even if one considers arranging them in such a way that (say) two boats were nested, and the extra ones were placed nearby, difficulties arise; in some cases, there would not be room to place them side-by-side on the deck. Even just stacking three boats one on top of the other would mean that the deck near the boats would be practically impassable in some areas, such as near the officer's quarters. Storing boats in the central portion of the *Titanic* between funnels 2 and 3 and then dragging them up and down the decks to waiting davits is a comically ridiculous proposal; there were railings that separated the various promenades which would have preventing the boats being manhandled to their stations. Perhaps a prescient designer could have incorporated removable railings to facilitate the ad hoc movement of boats from a central repository to a required davit? In retrospect, this is a possibility, but "as built", the *Titanic* did not have this feature of modular and removable railings.

What we can deduce is that a boat complement as envisaged above would occupy nearly all the officer's promenade forward and most of the 2nd class promenade aft. 1^{St} class passengers would barely be able to depart from the entrance vestibule on the boat deck but at least they could amble freely on the curtailed central space, mostly between the 2nd and 3rd funnels. The "cluttered" boat deck would have inconvenienced all but the 1st class.

If one decides that collapsible boats at (theoretically) 47 people per boat would suffice rather than the full sized wooden variant, we would need 55 of them. At least they could be compressed somewhat. With their canvas sides retracted, they would only take up a height of about two feet, perhaps even less, meaning that even more could be stacked before one reaches the problems that one would encounter with full-sized boats. But 55 boats means about a total of 4.4 boats per davit, and, though the davits are widely reported to be able to handle 4 boats, there is no reason why they could not accommodate more. The issues of accessibility remain, as no passengers could be placed in the boats from the boat deck due to the clutter. They would have to enter the boats from "A" deck. This is only of trivial concern and such a procedure was done on the night of the disaster; assembling the passengers and crew would be a crowd management problem, but it is difficult to quantify and qualify how effective this would be.

We now have a situation where each davit pair has 3.5 to 4.4 boats. If the passengers could be assembled, and space wastage prevented (that is, no "women and children only" etc.) so that boats were loaded to their gunwales with occupants, we can finally draw some conclusions. Wilding suggested that it would take 20 minutes to ready a boat's falls after one had already left from the same set of davits; this involves retrieving the several hundred feet of rope required and then

247

removing any kinks from the ropes. His estimate seems to be superficially about right. After boat 2 left the *Titanic*, it took this amount of time to ready and lower boat "D" from the same pair of davits. But one needs to examine the practicalities. The next boat aft of No.2, No.4, was lowered from "A" deck, and water was reported to have been only 20 feet below this; boat 2 left a few minutes after this and because the *Titanic*'s nose was in the water, No.2 would have been closer to the water line. When "D" departed, the water was already up to "A" deck, actually spilling on to that deck. If Wilding's "twenty minute" estimate refers to falls designed to lower a boat 60 feet from boat deck to the (normal) waterline, then it is clear that boats 2 and "D" were so close to the water that not all of the hundreds of feet of rope needed to be reeled in, only a length sufficient to get to the water a short distance beneath them. Additionally, when one considers that people wouldn't have been placed in "D" until after the ropes had been attached and the boat hauled over a bulwark, and that some time would have been needed to load the boat, it is obvious that only a fraction of the claimed "20 minutes" between 2 and "D" was spent hauling the falls back up for reattaching to the new boat.

The point of the above discourse is this: consider a boat lowered 60 feet to the waterline. Once set adrift, the davit arms would be cranked back in to accept a new boat and the falls would be retrieved, a process that could take up to twenty minutes. With a new boat being hooked up the davits, it could then be swung out, and the process of loading passengers could begin. Lowering to the water seems to have been about 5 minutes. Therefore 25 minutes would be spent just on collecting the ropes and then lowering. If it takes, say, 10 minutes to fill a boat then we have already used up 35 minutes. 4 boats per davit would therefore consume 110 minutes, or just under two hours. If one assumes that the time of the first boat being deployed from the *Titanic* as 12.45am, it is clear that not enough time is available. Alacrity on the part of the crew could conceivably shave a few vital minutes from this time, and if the boats could be readied closer to (say) 12.20am, a complete evacuation is plausible, though not likely.

The hypothetical scenario becomes more manageable if one considers not the full complement, but the 2200 people who were on the ship that night. We would then need 2.2 boats per davit assuming a full capacity of 65 people. If we round up to 3 boats, then the time required to evacuate these can be reduced to 75 minutes, bringing us up to 2am. There is enough time, but only barely.

Then one must consider how many crew would be required. 2

seamen were needed to feed the falls through the davits, and an officer superintending the lowering process. Obviously no single officer could superintend four boats in any quadrant of boats simultaneously; on the *Titanic*, there were 8 officers and if utilised correctly, two would be deployed at each quadrant of boats, and, ideally, the officer should remain with the boat until it reached the sea which took about 5 minutes. We know from the near flattening of boat 13 by 15 that the watchful eye of a superintendent was not always present. With this proposal, each pair of officers would oversee a pair of boats in each quadrant, and two boats would have to wait about 5 minutes until the officer became free to supervise the next two boats in this "staggered" sequence.

For 16 pairs of davits, we would need 32 seamen. This number is well within the number carried by the *Titanic*. Once the final boats had departed, the seaman manning the falls could effect their own escape by shinning down "life lines" that hung from a wire stretched between the davit arms, and down into the boat once it reached the water.

It is a stark reality. There would possibly not be enough time to evacuate all the personnel from a fully-laden ship, but a partially occupied *Titanic* is just about possible. If the crew had acted in a more expeditious manner, then the evacuation process may have started earlier leaving more time to disembark. But with 20 minutes spare before the ship foundered, there is very little space for error. David Gittins points out that a fair number of the *Titanic*'s lifeboat crews had had to cut the falls, either through unfamiliarity, or malfunction of the release mechanism; with the ropes cut, the falls could not be reused. If this had been enacted of a fully equipped *Titanic*, conceivably banks of lifeboats would be rendered unusable.

This analysis presumes a tidy, organised evacuation. The *Titanic*'s could not be classed as such, and, indeed, inefficiency abounded. But the hypothesis above hints that if there had been enough boats, all 2200 could have survived in the time given. The weary argument that "the *Titanic* crew needed time" or "the *Titanic* needed man power" for the boats is as flimsy as the craft that were lowered that night. There was just about enough time to rescue everyone. Detractors will argue that this author has not discussed the difficulties in assembling passengers at their muster points. This is a valid concern, but one that does not seem amenable to detailed analysis, except to say that a large fraction of passengers had been alerted to get on deck with their lifebelts some 30 minutes after the collision. The problem would then be one of managing the large number of people who would spill onto the deck, and ensuring that said people could actually reach the boats unhindered.

Testing these scenarios is difficult as there seems to be no precedent in maritime history with which we can compare. Consider the criteria; the *Titanic* sank extremely slowly, but help was too far away to save those stranded on the decks. The weather and sea state were calm and in no way affected the evacuation. Meaningful comparisons are impossible to find, but analogies can be drawn with another wreck, and this is laden with irony, for this was the *Britannic*, the *Titanic*'s younger sister, and the last of the *Olympic* class ships. She was launched in February 1914 but never carried a single passenger for the White Star Line. She was immediately requisitioned as a hospital ship during World War One and came to an unfortunate end when she was sunk by a mine in November 1916 near the Greek Island of Kea.

The *Britannic* incorporated the raised bulkheads that had been retro-fitted into the *Olympic*, and the obligatory increase in lifeboats. Additionally, the *Britannic* was fitted with a combination of 12 pairs of Welin davits, and five pairs of huge gantry davit "cranes", which could accommodate 6 boats apiece and were about 37 feet in height. These gantries had motors that could lift the boats and swing them outboard; the falls were designed in such a way to prevent the kinking or fouling that could occur when a boat was lowered, meaning that Edward Wilding's "20 minutes" for the ropes did not apply, and the boats could be lowered as quickly as possible. In total, there were 55 boats, either wooden boats or collapsibles, plus an undetermined number of rafts on deck.

The evacuation of those on board was different from the *Titanic*. The huge initial explosion alerted everyone that something was amiss, and therefore there more of a sense of urgency; on the *Titanic*, the collision with the iceberg was so subtle to most people that the severity of the situation was not appreciated and consequently, the crew was slow to react to loading the boats. The other main difference between the *Britannic* and the *Titanic* was the list of the ship. Both had been ruptured in the starboard bow and the forward portions soon began submerging, but the younger sister's huge list to starboard affected the deployment of boats; on one side, the boats swung too far away from the ship to be accessible, whereas on the other, they collided with the hull during their descent. On the *Titanic*, the ship had listed first to starboard and then to port, but the tilt was never so great as to prevent the boats from being sent safely away.

Probably because everyone on the *Britannic* was aware of the catastrophe, the first boats were launched without orders 18 minutes after the mine's detonation, the official order to abandon ship being given five minutes later. 10 minutes after this, the list was so great that no boats at all could be launched and after a total of 55 minutes, the ship had disappeared beneath the Aegean sea. However, in those few short minutes, 35 boats and their occupants had managed to flee (this author does not know how many boats under davits were eventually lowered). Apart from 30 men who were sliced in the propellers when their boats were launched prematurely, the remaining 1036 people were all saved. Many men were picked up from the warm, balmy water, in contrast to the freezing water of the North Atlantic 3 years earlier which had claimed so many lives.

Other shipwrecks occurred with comparable loss of life, but we must limit our discussion to those whose situations are known. The *Waratah*, as an example, disappeared and no trace has ever been found. We therefore do not the circumstances of her loss. In 1914, *The Empress of Ireland* was holed in a collision, and about 400 were saved, with 1000 perishing. A year later, the *Lusitania* sank after being torpedoed; there were nearly 800 survivors out of nearly 2000 on board. In both these cases, the ships sank extremely rapidly; 14 and 18 minutes respectively. The crew were only able to launch a few of their lifeboats (4 and 6 respectively), and, like the *Britannic*, a large list to starboard prevented their effective use when abandoning ship. Unlike the *Titanic*, these two leviathans sank in close proximity to ships that could rescue those in the lifeboats and water, which were extremely cold. And, unlike the *Titanic*, it was immediately apparent to everyone that there had been an accident.

Paradoxically, the shipping accident that has the highest resonance with the *Titanic* disaster involved a collision that incurred minimal loss of life, and with the vessel herself taking well over a day to sink.

In January 1909, the White Star Line vessel *Republic* collided with an Italian ship, the *Florida* in dense fog having left New York en route to the Mediterranean. Five people perished in the impact. The *Republic*'s Marconi operator tapped out a distress call which was

251

answered by other ships, including another ship of the fleet, the *Baltic*. Leaving a skeleton crew aboard, the people on the *Republic* were transferred to the *Florida* using the former ship's 11 lifeboats, which required twenty trips for each boat. When the *Baltic* arrived, the Florida's and the *Republic*'s passengers and crews were also trans-shipped, a total of several thousand people; in steadily deteriorating seas, this took nearly 8 hours. Even so, the *Republic*, severely listing, stayed afloat and she finally succumbed when she was being towed to shore. She had stayed afloat for over about 39 hours.

Following the sinking of the *Republic*, one of the passengers on the *Baltic* commented in the press that there was room in the boats for a maximum of 57% of her total complement. A general manager of the White Star Line was asked for a reaction and his comments were fascinating: "Our arrangements comply fully with the United States government regulations prescribed by the Board of Supervising Inspectors. They have been frequently inspected and passed by the proper authorities, and, according to the inspectors, are modern, serviceable and efficient. That is all I care to say regarding the equipment on the *Baltic*...It is a well known fact that it is impossible for a steamship in passenger service to carry enough lifeboats to accommodate all hands at once. If this were done so much space would be utilized for lifeboats that there would be no room left for passengers on deck. The necessary number of boats would be carried at the cost of many of the present comforts of our patrons." When asked for an opinion on the criticism that the davits were out of date, difficult to handle and inadequate in the event of emergencies, the White Star representative declined to comment as he was not familiar with them, but did say that, "The United States regulations state that a lifeboat must be fitted with such davits that it can be cleared away in two minutes. Our arrangements comply." One must remember Lightoller of the *Titanic* who sought in evidence to protract the time to ready the boats to ridiculous amounts.

The White Star Line representative concluded with a statement that would no doubt haunt his company in three years time; "The fact that all those passengers were twice transferred without the loss of a single life is proof of the highest efficiency in lifeboat equipment and life saving devices, I believe. I don't know any improvement that could be made. I think the feat of a double transfer in the open ocean is testimony enough of the worth of our lifesaving arrangements." Obviously, in his opinion, lifeboats amounted to little more than "ferries." There is no mention of the boats being considered as possibilities during a full scale evacuation. What if the *Florida*, which was not equipped with wireless and thus did not hear the *Republic*'s C.Q.D. (the first in history, we are told) had not decided to loiter and assist in the rescue? What if the collision had been a great distance from any sources of rescue, or other ships were unable to find the ailing *Republic* in the fog? What if it had taken the *Republic* only a few hours to sink, rather than the astonishing 39 hours during which her bulkheads gallantly held? What if there were no other ships in the area that could quickly take on board the waifs of the *Republic*?

The horrifying scenario became a reality on April 15th,1912. And the fallacy of "boats as mere ferries" was exposed and demolished as the farce it should have been regarded as since 1909.

The sinking of the *Republic* was hailed an example of the miracles of wireless telegraphy; the lack of lifeboats seem to have been eclipsed. It would have been hoped that an extensive inquiry into the sinking would reveal any deficiencies in the ship, its crew and equipment, recommendations made, and revisions implemented, similar to the in-depth, but flawed *Titanic* inquiry held three years later where not only matters directly relating to the ship, but peripheral concerns (the conduct of other ships, the use of wireless etc.) were also probed. But it never happened. The anticipated inquiry never materialised. The official explanation is that the British Board of Trade had no power to compel witnesses from the *Florida*, an Italian vessel to appear in court and that "any public inquiry that might have been held in their absence would necessarily have been of an ex parte character and possibly prejudicial to the interests of the English vessel." Any lessons that could be learned faded from public consciousness. The issue of the boats never become an issue of paramount importance.

It is submitted by this author that had the sinking of the *Republic* been made the subject of an inquiry, the publicity over the lack of boats might have prevented the *Olympic* class ships, or indeed, any ships, from going to sea with their pitiful stock of lifesaving equipment. It would have taken a fine display of legerdemain on the part of the lawyers acting for shipping lines to convince the fare-paying public that it was acceptable to journey to sea knowing that, in the event of a catastrophe, one only had a marginal chance of survival. The caveat to this argument is that before the *Titanic*, very few people had died at sea. In a self-perpetuating argument, ship owners and ship builders could convince themselves that if the design of their creations were sound, their vessels could be thought as of as "lifeboats in themselves," and the need for auxiliary boats negated.

All of this was largely immaterial by midnight on 15th April, 1912. The only thing that truly mattered was the crew's reaction to the impending situation. But there is evidence that very few people knew that the ship would sink, and Smith only confided in one person (Boxhall) of his knowledge of the ship's longevity, and no one else thought to ask the captain, or any of the Harland and Wolff personnel aboard. Perhaps because of this confidence in the *Titanic*'s invincibility, the crew were lackadaisical in uncovering the boats, swinging them out and preparing them to take on their human cargo. These procedures should have taken minutes, and could have been performed with a minimal crew. Instead, the crew wandered around the boat deck, not sure where to go, and failed to stay at their duty stations, sometimes being diverted by officers to other areas. The whole process seems laggard, and it is astonishing that the first half full boat left a full hour after the collision, or a full half hour after original estimates of the ship's lifespan.

Boats that had been prepared at midnight, a task that would have occupied a few minutes, should have been ready to accept passengers as soon as they immediately appeared on the deck. Instead, we hear stories of inexperienced crew fumbling with the equipment, and some boats being readied quite late (being left on the chocks, or "just being swung out") while others were departing, and passengers having to wait while the crew fumbled with the boats. Even if the crew were aware of the approaching calamity, how far should one go to ensure that boats left with as large a contingent as possible? There comes a transition when gentle urgings to enter a boat translates into a panicked order, with the chaos that inevitably ensues with increased insistence. It is difficult to propose a situation that would have ensured a high number of evacuees without brute force, an assured sign that things were awry, if the rockets exploding overhead and the downwards tilt of the bows had not already sparked an inkling that something was quite parlous. Even when the first rocket exploded, the procedure for loading the boats did not seem to have altered markedly.

The evidence gleaned from the inquiries, private accounts and newspaper interviews read like a Chinese Tangram; assemble the pieces in one manner, and one determines one set of conclusions; re-arrange them in a different fashion and one forms new deductions; the conduct on the boat deck was one of supreme stateliness...or else it was undisciplined chaos. The crew were perfunctory, or else they were slow to react. Evasive and dishonest testimony only serve to sully any analysis, which brings us to the conduct of the officers.

As has been oft stated, the captain's leadership was hardly inspiring and he confided in no-one that the ship was doomed, other than Boxhall who had actually asked him; the captain may also have been responsible for the initial incorrect determination of the ship's location in which case, his failings are manifest (as detailed elsewhere). He gave orders that no sane person would have issued, and failed to notice that boats were being lowered half full, practically right under his very nose and tried to call them back minutes after they had left the ship's hull. The fact that the captain had steamed his ship full speed into a region scattered with icebergs and ice fields is tantamount to negligence, and while some researchers cite evidence that Ismay was pressurising him into getting into New York early, we are left with the apothegm: whatever the circumstances, the captain is in ultimate control of the ship and takes full responsibility for her and the people entrusted to him.

Of the other officers, Wilde seems to have upheld the "Women and Children only" mantra, even if this meant sending away boats with empty seats. This is also the credo practised by Lightoller, who claimed that it was his intention to load the boats from the waterline via open gang-ways. On the port side, only two instances of a boat being ordered to open doors was ever heard, and these were within the last half hour or so of the sinking; on the starboard side, orders to stay close to the doors were issued as soon as the boats were lowered, though it is not clear to how many this command was issued. One boat (6) that was sent off fairly early was supposedly told by the 2nd Officer to row to the mystery lights (though he denied issuing such an order), and the only other orders were generic "stay close to the ship" directives; there is hardly anything about staying close to the gang-ways. Lightoller's plan was unilateral; he never told anyone of his intentions until at the inquiries, and the men sent below conveniently disappeared. Had Lightoller simply adopted Murdoch's plan to fill the boats from the water's edge, which some people did hear that night? If so, Lightoller's "plan" could very well have claimed his senior's plan as his own an excuse to detract from any criticism that he had sent off boats with empty spaces. And, if Lowe's comment that "the rich nabobs would take their chances with the good men" is an accurate report of the attitude that night, did some of the officers decide to debar any male passengers from the seats? As stated, many men escaped on the starboard side, but on the port side, only three were ordered in; Peuchen in boat 6, "Racquet

Champion" C. Williams in 14, and a boy with an injured arm in 6. Lightoller's later accomplishments in the inquiries include initially denying that ice warnings had been received from nearby ships (seconds later a telegram from one such vessel was presented to him) and being deceitful about the use of weapons at boat "D". His evasive testimony, obviously designed to deflect criticism from the White Star Line, make his proclamations suspect. Is such a comment commonplace to the remainder of the bridge crew? Possibly, but we can only obtain answers from those who survived, who gave testimony - and whose conduct is open to scrutiny.

1st Officer Murdoch's accomplishments have more merit than his superiors; he allowed men into boats, but was only too keen to lower away where ample space was in abundance, the grossest example being boat 1, which left with less than half its space occupied. Looking for people to fill the empty room would have taken only a few minutes and no effort was made. Soon after, Murdoch was happy to wait while women and children were herded from the port side to boat 9 on the starboard side. Why the hurry at boat 1, but no procrastination at No.9? The rockets were still bursting overhead and the ship's nose was steadily burying itself in the waters of the Atlantic. It is tempting to speculate that Murdoch may have been afforded fresh information on the longevity of the ship and could wait longer, but speculation and conjecture do not amount to proof. Whatever the reason, it is debatable as to how much control Murdoch had over boats 11, 13 and 15, which carried away the most people that night. If he was unable to personally supervise these boats (and it seems a valid question as he on the deck above them and couldn't see how the process of allowing people on board was being effected), then his reputation as the man who would fill the boats to capacity is seriously degraded. If one goes by his actions at boats 1-7, he was more than happy to let the craft go away half full.

4Th Officer Boxhall actions are just as impenetrable as Lightoller's. He was vague about his location when he heard the look-out's bell being rung, then heard an order than no-one else remembered ("Full speed astern"), went below to inspect the damage twice without orders, introduced a significant error into the determination of the ship's distress location and then waited a significant time (about 20 minutes?) before sending up distress rockets after he had seen the mysterious lights off the port bow. If Rowe's recollections are any indication, Boxhall disappeared after the second rocket leaving him and his colleague to send up the rockets and attend to the Morse signal lamp; Boxhall reappeared in time to be ordered into boat 2. Then Boxhall provides evidence that conflicts with others in this boat; that they were to head for the gang-way door, that green flares were to be placed in his boat intentionally, and that there was suction at the stern of the *Titanic*. He even became pugnacious when asked a simple question about the lamps that should have been placed in the emergency boats before sunset.

3Rd Officer Pitman's only failing was after he had left the *Titanic*, when he acceded to the demands of those in his charge not to return to rescue the helpless souls thrashing in the water.

Lowe comes across as a gun-toting hothead, one whose first instinct was to grab his weapon when confronted with an unknown situation. Frequently cited as one of the heroes of the *Titanic* because of his rescue plan, there are indications that he may have acted only after insistence from the ladies in his boat. To be fair, the evidence for this last point is fragmentary and conflicting. Lowe's continued mention that "no officer" went away in a boat before his departure is perplexing; he knew that Pitman had gone away in boat 5. This raises another issue; Lowe departed the *Titanic* without being given orders to do so by a senior officer. This is an obvious dereliction of duty, perhaps even mildly mutinous, but like many other questionable acts enacted that night, it was not pursued at the inquiries.

Only 6th Officer Moody seems to be free of the blemish of criticism; indeed, there are remarkably few sightings of him.

The later antics of Captain Smith, Andrews and Ismay are vague too. Once attention shifted from the forward boats to the aft ones, sightings of this triumvirate ceased, and only recommenced when boat lowerings re-focussed at the forward region of the boat deck. This is a significant gap and one that Ismay never spoke of. What was happening?

Away from the higher echelons, the remaining crew gave no hints of insubordination; they followed their orders - even if they were somewhat dilatory. The general epithet that can be applied is obedience, but there are exceptions. For instance, two stewards who gave evidence that convinced the British Inquiry that steerage passengers were not not restrained in their hurdle to the boats can be shown to be wholly unconvincing; even so, the word "discriminate" seems too strong to apply in all cases where the 3rd class were obstructed. The word "neglect" is more apt.

The Marconi men's efforts undeniably saved many lives. Without them, those in the boats would be left to fend for themselves until chanced upon by a passing steamer. Evidence indicates that it could have been a long time; by 11.20am (when the *Californian* abandoned the search for more survivors and resumed her voyage to Boston), no such "passing steamer" had appeared on the scene despite it being a busy shipping route. Perhaps vessels were avoiding the area because of the ice. Were it not for the Marconi equipment, one shudders to think how long those shivering in the boats would have had to endure the increasingly choppy Atlantic swell.

It is fortunate that the *Titanic*'s wireless equipment had malfunctioned a day earlier. If the set had broken down before or during the disaster it is questionable as to how effective the operators could have been in summoning help. But heroism aside, Junior Operator Bride's stories inspire doubt and provoke questions as to what fully transpired in the wireless room. His ever-changing stories contained many elements accepted as fact by *Titanic* scholars, and this author suggests that it is now time to assess them dispassionately; for instance, the "last chance to send S.O.S." and the mention of the song "Autumn" all generate suspicion that some or all originated from the talented hand of a newspaper copy writer and not the frightened fragmented mind of a young lad who barely escaped the disaster. Then there are the ice warnings, which raises the spectre of accountability, or lack thereof. Most of the warnings were heeded casually or were claimed never to have been seen by the surviving officers. That the warnings were received is beyond doubt and we must conclude that they were (suspiciously) seen by men who could not defend themselves later.

Once free from the doomed hulk of the *Titanic*, the mentality of many of those in the boats changes; ordered to stay close by, many skulk off into the night. "Its our lives now, not theirs," sums up the self preservation instinct well. Passengers or crew, or both, bemoaned suggestions that they should return to help the swimmers. Whether aloof, uncaring or indifferent, it is fair to say that the feeling of those in the boats was correct. To go back into the seething throng would have capsized the boat(s), and anywhere from 12 to 70 people could conceivably be added to the already shocking death toll. It is a scenario that this author hopes that no one will ever have to face; listening to the shrill chorus of the dying only a few hundred yards away, knowing in one's heart that something should be done, but realising that, practically, rescue was an impossible proposition.

258

Life moved on. After recriminations were levelled and inquiries held, claims for recompense filed and the dead mourned, people carried on with their existence. Heroes were praised, charitable funds created, and new ships built. Most of the stewards, scullions and seamen returned to their established life - on the high sea. Disasters at sea were a possibility in their profession and many accepted the risks of being shipwrecked as acceptable. The officers of the *Titanic* never achieved a command of their own, and even the White Star Line foundered too, having been absorbed by Cunard after they had been forced to merge soon after the global economic depression. The shattered hulk of the *Titanic* outlived them all, 2½ miles down, its name being forgotten during the casualty-heavy World Wars. The supposed morals and lessons of the *Titanic* became resurrected in the 1950s and this interest survives to this day, occasionally buoyed when the ship makes headlines (the 1985 discovery of the wreck, the 1997 blockbuster film and so on). The name of the ship is used to highlight any social concern afflicted society - from the Nazi party's film to showcase English decadence, through to the over-used cliche "rearranging the deckchairs on the *Titanic*" used to denote a futile endeavour, and the invocation of the ship's name when the public and media seek to make tiresome comparisons with modern nautical mishaps. The fate of the unsinkable ship has mutated from a simple story of arrogance, conceit, bravery and cowardice into a heroic fable whereby commercial enterprises, such as Hollywood and its ilk, seek to transform a disaster into a lucrative industry. In this respect, we have lost sight of the disaster. Those who seek to perpetuate the romance, heroism and chivalry of the ship evoke the imagery of a grotesque caricature of the *Titanic*. As this author has said in the introduction, the story was not a romantic relic of halcyon days and the mental images we now have are the product of poor research, disinformation and the need from some areas of the *Titanic* communities to foist their own prejudices and pet theories onto the unwary. In this 100th anniversary, this author feels that it is time for history to reclaim the *Titanic*, to jettison the extraneous and inaccurate and to tell the basic story, unsullied by decades of falsehoods and propaganda.

It is to be hoped that this work will go some little way in helping to achieve this goal.

Endnotes

Chapter 1: The Bold Vision

[1] The first mention of a third ship to join this duo was made at the *Olympic*'s arrival in Southampton after her sea trials in 1911. Paul Lee and Mark Chirnside have uncovered information that the third vessel was to be called *Gigantic*, a name which continued the theme of Greek mythology, but whose name has never been conclusively proven to have been considered for the last in the trio. The ship was eventually named *Britannic*. The name *Gigantic* was never officially declared by the White Star Line, and they declared it "a *Gigantic* joke" in the press after the *Titanic* disaster. The name was mentioned quite openly in the press and Harland and Wolff employees, and was referred in documentation made by the manufacturers of the *Titanic's* and *Olympic's* anchors. It is speculated that the name "*Gigantic*" was never officially decided upon because, unlike her sisters, she would not be the largest ship in the world when she entered service (the Hamburg America Line vessel *Imperator* to be launched in May 1912 was over twenty feet longer than the *Olympic* and *Titanic*), and a grandiose moniker implying size was no longer appropriate.

[2] To show how outdated this law was even in 1894, it would not have supplied enough boats for all 4000+ people that could hypothetically be carried on the 18,915 ton *Great Eastern*, launched 36 years earlier! Ironically, the *Great Eastern* suffered damage from a submerged object too (a rock) in an 1862 crossing. Although the length of the resultant damage is not directly comparable to that suffered by the *Titanic* (83 feet for the 692 feet long *Great Eastern*; 250 feet for the 882 feet long *Titanic*), the height of the "hole" (9 feet and 3/4s of an inch respectively) made the *Great Eastern*'s damage far more severe. But, thanks to the ingenious honeycomb of internal bulkheads and compartments the *Great Eastern* prevailed. In this respect, the two ships were very different; the *Great Eastern's* construction meant that, to proceed from one watertight compartment to another, one had to climb over the tops of bulkheads and descend into the desired area. The compartments truly were individual, sealed areas. To make operating life easier, the *Titanic's* compartments had doors.

[3] This figure does not seem to have included the *Huronian*, which disappeared without a trace somewhere in the Atlantic Ocean in 1902. The *Huronian* was a British registered ship, as was *The State of Georgia*, which disappeared on that ocean in 1896. This author has been unable to ascertain definite passenger numbers for these ships. Simple searches on

the internet reveal that many ships form this era disappeared without a trace, and ice is suspected of the cause of some of these disappearances.

[4] The location of two of the collapsibles on the roof of the deckhouses prompts many writers to inform their readers that they were "inaccessible" and that not much care was taken in choosing where to place them. In fact, the collapsibles were provided with portable blocks and tackles that could be lowered with the aid of rings fitted to the first funnel. Whether this was known by the *Titanic*'s 1st Officer Murdoch or 2nd Officer Lightoller is unknown; the former may have been aware of the lowering mechanism during his time on the *Olympic*. Lightoller had not come from the *Titanic*'s sister, but an older ship with older davits. At any rate, the tackle required to lower the boats was stored in the boatswain's store, which, being in the bows of the ship, was already underwater when it came time to prepare these last two boats. Evidently no-one thought to retrieve it during the early stages of the sinking.

[5] Calculations post-disaster showed that, with the 2nd , 4th and 5th compartments flooded to the top, the *Titanic* would not have sunk; these calculations were based on the earliest reported sightings of water entering the hull. These computations also served to demonstrate that if all of the first four compartments were open to the sea, the ship would have stayed afloat, but when the 5th compartment (boiler room No.6) was added, the result was the loss of the ship.

[6] Other vessels of the era were proclaimed to be "unsinkable"; in addition to the *Lusitania* and *Mauretania*, the *Olympic*'s invincibility was also touted in the press. Indeed, after the *Titanic* disaster, the *Olympic* returned to Belfast to be refitted with refinements to her bulkheads, lifeboat provision etc. The press described her that "so far as [is] possible [she is] unsinkable." In 1903, the White Star Line *Cedric* was the subject of rash rumours that she had been involved in a collision and had sunk. Again, the press were told that she was "practically non-sinkable" and that even if she were to be cut into two halves, each segment would float. In 1912 it was said of the *Titanic* that if she were to be cut into three pieces, each portion would remain afloat. In 1909, the public were reminded that the *Republic* had been deemed to be unsinkable after the ship had gone to the bottom.

[7] An example of the tardiness of the work to the *Titanic* may be gleaned from her deck plans. 1st class passengers were given maps of their portion of the ship to help with finding their way around. Some of the deck plans that have survived do not show cabins that were later added; for instance, the Straus's plan, dated December 1911 does not show a pair of cabins added to the "A" deck lobby of the 1st class Grand Staircase, but plans from March 1912 do. This must have been surprising to Francis Browne, who journeyed from Southampton to Queenstown as

he occupied one of these cabins and the plans didn't show his room! He sketched in the location of his state room on his own plan of the ship.

[8] It is not known if the mirror was ever replaced by the clock.

[9] Slocombe's memory, from four decades later, must be slightly awry, as Margaretta Spedding wrote in her diary on April 13th that she had had a session in the Turkish Bath in the morning; she absolutely hated it!

[10] It has been speculated that the railings running along the outside gymnasium wall are such an example of incomplete work, as there seem to be some missing. An alternate hypothesis has been proposed by researchers based on an analysis of the configuration of railings on the *Olympic*; the gaps were possible deliberate to allow the windows to swing open without hitting an obstruction on the wall.

[11] The term "steerage" derives from the location of the 3rd class passengers; down with the "steering" apparatus in the bowels of the ship.

[12] Based on numbers provided by the British Inquiry, the maximum 1st, 2nd, and 3rd class passengers and crew were 905, 564, 1134 and 944 respectively. The actual numbers for the maiden voyage, gleaned from that inquiry, were 325, 285, 706 and 885. There is still some debate as to the accuracy of numbers claimed for the *Titanic* as there are discrepancies between passenger lists. Additionally, certain problems have been voiced about the statistics for other reasons. An example is whether the numbers given include a fireman who jumped ship at Queenstown.

Chapter 2: A Routine Crossing

[1] Indeed, Fred Fleet recalled that the binoculars he used were stamped "Second Officer" and "s.s. "*Titanic*." Hogg's recollection was that they were marked, "Theatre, Marine and field." "Second Officer, S.S. '*Titanic*.'"

[2] Lines was sure that Ismay dined "at the captain's right" at dinner and lunch but Ismay provided a sketch at later inquiries which he claimed showed his favourite table, secluded and off to one side of the main dining saloon; the captain's own table was more centrally located, in a prominent location. Sir Cosmo Duff-Gordon and others stated that, at least on the night of the disaster, Ismay and Smith dined separately.

[3] Hendrickson described the bulkhead as follows: "you could see where the bulkhead had been red hot." It is unclear whether he had seen the steel wall actually glow as he described.

[4] A "growler" is a small, low lying iceberg, the smallest size that is a hazard to shipping.

[5] Mr.Thayer and his son also encountered Ismay, who told them that "two [sic?] more boilers are to be opened up today"; this information comes from John Thayer Jr. In his 1940 memoirs, he writes, "I remember Mr.Ismay showing us a wire regarding the presence of ice and remarking that we would not reach that position until around nine P.M. If Thayer's chronology was correct, this was before they went to dress for dinner at 6.30. Unless Ismay had determined the time when the ice would be encountered, Thayer's description should be met with some scepticism. It seems as if he may have confused Lightoller's timing with his own experiences.

[6] Ismay certainly gained some knowledge of the *Titanic*'s operation, but it is unclear when he gathered this information. On the first day of the U.S. Inquiry, he opened his monologue thus, "We ran from Cherbourg to Queenstown at 70 revolutions. After embarking the mails and passengers, we proceeded at 70 revolutions. I am not absolutely clear what the first day's run was, whether it was 464 miles or 484 miles. The second day the number of revolutions was increased. I think the number of revolutions on the second day was about 72. I think we ran on the second day 519 miles. The third day the revolutions were increased to 75, and I think we ran 546 or 549 miles. I understand it has been stated that the ship was going at full speed. The ship never had been at full speed. The full speed of the ship is 78 revolutions. She works up to 80. So far as I am aware, she never exceeded 75 revolutions. She had not all her boilers on. None of the single-ended boilers [boilers with only 3 furnaces on one end only, as opposed to a regular boiler with 6, 3 on each face] were on." These single ended boilers, in boiler room 1, had previously been used to provide electricity while the ship was in port.

[7] It is not known if this message was prefixed with an M.S.G.

[8] 2nd class passenger Lawrence Beesley's later comments contradict Jewell's: "I should judge there was no wind blowing [on Sunday], for I had noticed about the same force of wind approaching Queenstown, to find that it died away as soon as we stopped, only to rise again as we steamed away from the harbour." In Beesley's opinion, the wind was formed by nothing more than the ship's own motion.

[9] Lightoller's timing of 9.30pm is corroborated by Jewell and Symons in the crow's nest. However, we must mention Hichens, who was running errands between 8 and 10pm. He places the crow's nest instruction closer to 8pm. He said that he had been on the bridge for a few minutes before Moody was ordered to telephone Jewell and Symons. He made no mention of seeing Captain Smith at this time, let alone hearing the conversation between him and Lightoller. Hichens had surely made a mistake in his time. Surely? Hichens also said that the message to the carpenter, which he personally delivered, was just after he came on duty.

263

[10] Boxhall claimed to have seen the captain frequently from 8pm onwards, including a sighting at 9pm, the details of which he could not specify. From 9pm till the time of the collision, Boxhall claimed that he "was talking to him on one or two occasions...Sometimes in the officers' chart room and sometimes at his chart room door ...I was discussing some stellar bearings I had had. I was also standing at his chart room door while he pricked off the 7.30 stellar position of the ship [on the chart]...It would be pretty nearly 10 o'clock, I should think."

[11] Mahala Douglas gave an interesting account at the U.S. Inquiry, "On Saturday ... we saw a seaman taking the temperature of the water. The deck seemed so high above the sea I was interested to know if the tiny pail could reach it. There was quite a breeze, and although the pail was weighted, it did not. This I watched from the open window of the covered deck. Drawing up the pail the seaman filled it with water from the stand pipe, placed the thermometer in it, and went with it to the officer in charge." If Hichens account was to be believed, by Sunday, this deficiency in the ability to measure the temperature of sea water had been corrected as he confirmed that the bucket reached the water.

[12] This would not be the only attempt at aggrandising the *Titanic*'s capabilities. Lloyd's publications reported on April 11th that the *Titanic* was travelling north west to Ireland and was 40 miles west of Lizard at 5.30am and travelling at 23 knots. Between her departure from Ireland until noon on April 12th, the ship's average speed was about 21 knots...and she would increase her speed over time. It would seem strange that the *Titanic*'s started off at a high speed and then actually diminished her velocity!

[13] Interestingly, the *Olympic*'s second voyage to New York was logged as 5 days and 15 hours, much better than her maiden voyage. Suspicions have been levelled that the presence of Harland and Wolff's Lord Pirrie on the ship may have stimulated the need for more speed. However, analysis of the transit times by Samuel Halpern and Mark Chirnside conclude that an error had been made in the determination of the *Olympic*'s first westbound crossing, and that when this is taken into account, the duration of the maiden and 2nd voyages are almost identical.

[14] Seaman Scarrott gave a good description of the iceberg moments after the crash; from his vantage point in the forward well deck, looking aft, the berg looked like the Rock of Gibraltar, with the highest side facing the ship. From Murdoch's points of view, he would have seen a peak ahead of him, and the berg trailing off to starboard; logically, it makes sense to turn to port to avoid the bulk of the ice on the right hand side.

[15] This is a rough summary of the claimed events leading up to the collision. But there are some doubts; Seaman Scarrott was waiting in the

forecastle for a call to attend to duties when he heard the three bells strike. In his estimation 5 or 8 minutes elapsed before the collision. If he is right, this implies a distance from ship to iceberg of 1.8 - 2.9 miles; as we shall see, the distance that experienced ship's captains expected to see an iceberg. Why had it take so long for the ship to perform evasive manoeuvres? Researcher George Behe has assembled an impressive list of statements that hint that, over a 25 minute period, the crow's nest rang the bridge 3 times to warn of ice, but the telephone was never answered. Major Peuchen was in the same lifeboat as Fleet and asked him about the iceberg. Fleet's reply was "that he did not get any reply" when he rang the bell and signalled [telephoned] the bridge. Behe has also uncovered some suggestions that Hichens and Fleet were given financial inducements to keep quiet about what they had seen that night; there are no records of any of the other survivors in the drama being given so-called "hush money."

Titanic Interlude: The Iceberg: Nature Defeats Hubris

[1] The "hard-a-starboard" command derives from the days when ships were operated under tiller command; turning the tiller to starboard turned the the ship's bows to port. The *Titanic*'s wheel was rigged so that turning it to starboard produced a course change to starboard, but the order itself originated from the "tiller" days. "Hard-a-starboard" meant "turn the wheel, and the ship's bows, to port."
[2] Only Boxhall remembered seeing both of the engine room telegraphs being set to "full astern" when he arrived on the bridge after the strike; no survivor who worked in the engineering or boiler rooms recalled the astern order. In 1962, Boxhall remembered that Murdoch told the captain, ""I'm going Full Speed Astern, Sir, on the Port Engine."
[3] When walking to the bridge, Olliver would have had to pass many deck lights, which were mounted on the walls of the forward deck houses on the boat deck, partially dazzling him, which may explain why his sighting of the 'berg (or rather the pointed tip of it), abaft the bridge, and some tens of feet away and already rushing off into the distance, is not of a white chunk of ice, but a "dark blue" colour.
[4] The only timing we have of the retardation of speed of the *Titanic* comes from tests done on the *Olympic* after the disaster. At 18 knots, it took 3 minutes and 15 seconds, and a distance of just over 3000 feet to come to a complete stop. Assuming that the rate of deceleration for a ship moving at 22.5 knots is the same as that of an 18 knot vessel, we find that, in 30 seconds the speed would have been reduced by 2.76 knots, or 33 feet per second. This also assumes that the deceleration is a

constant. It is not known if this test on the *Olympic* was performed with a crew ready to instantaneously act to stop the ship, but it does not seem likely. It is possible that, in the time it took from the bridge crew to react to Fleet's warning to first contact, the *Titanic* would probably not have slowed down to any great degree.

[5] Passenger George Harder described how he saw the iceberg pass by as he looked out of his porthole; he estimated the distance to be 50 to 100 feet away.

[6] One of the few others to describe a haze at any time that night was Alfred Shiers, who came on deck soon after the crash and saw the "iceberg ... in a haze." It is interesting to speculate on just what Shiers did see: he heard the shock while he was reading in his bunk, and walked up 3 flights of steps. He claimed to have "just" seen the "dim" iceberg 4 or 5 minutes after the strike, off the stern, and the *Titanic* was moving very slowly through the water. Without wishing to denigrate his statement, Shiers claimed to have seen a unilluminated shape at least 900 feet away, while his vision was undoubtedly struggling to compensate from going from a lit companionway to a darkened deck.

[7] Author David G.Brown claims that the haze "was starshine reflected onto wisps of fog created when the ice chilled the surrounding atmosphere to below its dew point. A thin layer of fog likely formed just above the surface of the ice." He claims this is called 'ice blink' but this term is actually only used to describe light reflecting off ice onto a low cloud base. That night, there was no cloud base at all, but curiously Ernest Shackleton said later, "On a night such as you have described, if there was a big field of ice, the [ice] blink would most certainly be seen very, very clearly. If there was really what we call big fields, miles and miles of ice, then you would see the edge, what we call the water-sky, that is where the ice-field ends." The captain of a nearby ship, the *Californian*, testified that there was no haze; 47 years afterwards, he claimed that he "observed a brightening along the western horizon...I concluded that it was caused by ice." If he was right, this was from a distance of about a mile.

[8] During the prosecution of the White Star Line in 1915 for negligence, three ships captain's opinions were sought, and they all said that they would not have proceeded at full speed knowing that ice was ahead; they would have slowed down or taken long diversionary courses. One of these experts was Captain Turner, whose ship, the *Lusitania*, was torpedoed and sunk just days afterwards. Whether these captain's opinions were the same in 1912, or were the result of hindsight is impossible to tell.

[9] Edith Rosenbaum also recalled two or three jolts, as did Mrs.Futrelle. Marie Young described "a grinding, wrenching force followed by several

violent bumps."

[10] Woolner's and Shute's comments indicate that the *Titanic* was possibly grounding on the iceberg; given the inaccessibility of the wreck's keel, this seems to be a claim that is impossible to verify. If their accounts are correct, then the *Titanic*'s hull was in contact with the iceberg a lot further aft than is generally accepted.

[11] This is not the first indication of puzzling survivor's accounts. Margaret Brown, in her cabin, claimed that the impact threw her to the floor. Excellent detective work by Daniel Klistorner puts her cabin on "E" deck. Peter Daly was in a nearby cabin, perhaps 45 feet forward of Brown, and his grandson says that he was "startled" by "a thump and a vibration that lasted some seconds," somewhat different from Brown's story. Some 30 feet ahead of Daly, was Norman Chambers, whose impression was of "no great shock" and of "jangling chains." Chambers, of course, was closer to the area of collision. Mr. and Mrs.Beckwith were almost directly above Mrs.Brown, and their account is vastly different: "The bottles on the dressing table in the cabin were not knocked over [by the collision]. So light was the collision that no one realised there was any danger." Next door were the Warrens, and Mrs. Anna Warren said that she was awakened by a "grinding noise and the stoppage of the engines." Then there is Hichens; he was not too far from where Boxhall claimed to be, and he said, "I felt the ship tremble, and I felt rather a grinding nature along the ship's bottom." This is more in line with Boxhall's comments than either Rosenbaum or Robert. Steward Alfred Crawford was in the forward section of "B" deck, and he only said that he "heard" the crash. He mentioned that he was specifically stationed in the area in which Elizabeth Robert's cabin was located, yet he didn't mention being thrown to the ground, like she had.

[12] Walter Lord noted that James McGough, on the next deck down, also had the experience of having ice fall through the window. However, McGough doesn't mention this in his testimony in America, and there seems to be no newspaper record of his cabin mate describing this happening.

[13] This comes from a seaman named Scarrott who related it in a newspaper interview. He did not mention this when questioned at the British Inquiry. One also wonders how this ice could have found its way onto the deck without the iceberg pulverizing boat 1, left swung out at all times for emergencies, or noticed by Boxhall who was walking that very deck (assuming that Boxhall was even there at the time). David G. Brown suggests that the ice may have been formed by being condensed from steam emitted from the exhaust vents on the funnels soon after the impact. But surely ice would be seen around the other funnels too? And why did no-one else mention ice so high up on the decks?

267

Chapter 3: A Precarious Situation

[1] It is speculated that the forward motion of the ship actually increased the force of water flowing into the hull, hastening the ship's doom. Researcher Sam Halpern has performed calculations which indicate that this was not the case. If the front of the ship had been ripped off, the inflowing water would have directly impinged on the bulkheads inside, the resultant pressure being devastating. Since the areas allowing water to enter was roughly perpendicular to the direction of motion, the ship's movement would not have "forced" in any extra water, at a higher pressure into the hull.

[2] Soon after the *Titanic* came to rest in the water, the ship automatically started to vent steam from discharge pipes atop the funnels; this was to prevent a dangerous build-up of pressure. Boxhall was not sure if steam was venting when he went down for his first inspection, but he was sure it was taking place upon his return. Despite the roar of steam being so loud that it hindered normal conversation, it, like the later sound of gunshots, does not seem to have registered in the memory of many survivors. In his book, 2nd class passenger Beesley does not mention it in his first foray to the boat deck before midnight, but does in his second trip perhaps 10 or 15 minutes later, where he likened it to "twenty locomotives blowing off steam in a low key." Lightoller only mentioned the unearthly din when he stepped onto the boat deck after being told that the mail room was awash. The sound did not awaken Lowe at all. However, Colonel Gracie, three decks below, heard the loud issuing of excess steam and a few others deep within the ship mention the volume, but such descriptions are rare and fleeting. Gracie's timing puts it at sometime about 11.45-12.00. How long did the steam discharge go on for? Officer Pitman said that the discharging went on for three quarters of an hour; seaman Jones also mentions it during his attempt to entice Mrs.Straus into boat 8, but it is impossible to know when this happened relative to other events. Lightoller puts the time of finishing at just before boat 4 was launched but this timing, which is derived from his unreliable memoirs, is suspect as he places boat 4 being launched before boat 6; in actuality, boat 4 left the ailing liner a long time after boat 6. In his reminisces many decades later, quartermaster Rowe informed an inquisitor that on the way to the bridge he heard the band playing; he would not have been able to hear them from his route to the bridge if steam was still billowing. Rowe claimed that this was after the first boat(s) had departed, and the first rockets sent aloft if Boxhall's statements are any indication. Passengers Beesley and Gracie

remembered not only seeing but hearing the first rocket fired, something which would have been inaudible above the steam; the first rocket was fired between the loading of boats 5 and 3. All we can say is that the steam discharge has ceased within the first hour.

[3] Saying definitively that the engines has "stopped for good" presents difficulties in this discussion. Olliver's timing can be put at before midnight, before the lifeboats were ordered to be uncovered and swung out. The movements of the engines from the survivors who toiled in the belly of the ship are contradictory: Scott says he recalled "Stop", then 10 or 15 minutes later "slow ahead", ten minutes later then "stop", then 4 or 5 minutes elapsed before "slow astern" and then 5 minutes after this, "stop"; Dillon's version is that the telegraph from the bridge rang about 2 seconds before the crash, then a minute and a half later, the engines stopped; anther half minute and the command was "slow astern" which lasted for two minutes, then stop, then ahead for 2 minutes, then stop for good. Dillon's memory may be suspect; he recalled the watertight doors closing three minutes after the impact which is nonsense. And save for two people, one of whom was Boxhall and another who admitted that the disaster had affected his memory - no-one recalled the engines being run astern during the initial attempt to evade the iceberg. The confusing commands to run the engines backwards and forwards may have been an attempt, suggests researcher David Gittins, to ascertain any damage to the propellers

When was the final command to the engines issued?

Some evidence comes from 2nd class passenger Lawrence Beesley who was on deck minutes after the impact and had gathered a few scraps of information from passengers in the 2nd class smoking room, some of whom had seen the iceberg through the windows. With the reassurance that things did not seem amiss, Beesley headed back to his room, but he saw two things of interest: first of all, an officer starting to pull off the tarpaulin on lifeboat 16, and also that the *Titanic* had resumed her motion, evidenced by a "little white line of foam" snaking off the bow. The officer may be Moody, where Pitman was to find him a few minutes later, but the timing puts Beesley's observations at about midnight which is when the crew were heading on deck to unlace the boats. Beesley then went down to his room and the faint vibration could still be felt, as he placated three nervous ladies who were alarmed at the cessation of motion; Beesley directed them to placing their hands on a nearby bath where the vibrations of the engines, almost directly below, could be more clearly felt. When Beesley returned to the boat deck moments later with his life jacket, the *Titanic*'s journey had ended for good. Because of the steam venting (see above), it is debatable as to whether the *Titanic* even had any steam to allow her movement to continue.

[4] If other evidence is to be believed, Lightoller and Pitman had already exchanged words about the collision, apparently when they went on deck. Lightoller had already surmised that the ship had struck something and arrived at the conclusion that it was ice due to their proximity to the Grand Banks of Newfoundland. Pitman recalled asking his superior if they had hit something and the 2nd Officer replied, "Yes, evidently."

[5] Lowe later said that Boxhall had told him that the ship had hit an iceberg, but Lowe had no memory of this, saying that he must have been informed while he was asleep: "You must remember that we do not have any too much sleep and therefore when we sleep we die." Did "die" in this context mean that he was "dead to the world"?

[6] The *Titanic* had two tanks, one fore and one aft, to aid "trimming" of the vessel. If the bow or stern of the ship was seated too deep in the water, these tanks could be flooded to bring level equilibrium to the ship.

[7] As already noted, the bridge was evidently getting impatient for a report from the carpenter: quartermaster Olliver, 4th Officer Boxhall and Evans were all ordered to find the carpenter, the first two of these being direct orders from the captain. Who was the officer that Evans had met and who issued the instructions to seek the carpenter? The 5th Officer was still in bed, and as for the other officers who are unaccounted for, 6th Officer Moody seems the only likely candidate. Evans had considerable experience in the Royal and Merchant Navy and it is hard to believe he could mistake the braids etc. of the 5th/6th Officer for the Chief Officer who, by Hemming's evidence had been in the very area to assess the damage to the prow of the ship. Evans would later call Murdoch the "chief officer" in his testimony at the inquiries, and he also makes reference to Lowe and Lightoller so he at least recognised the 2nd and 5th officers. But would Moody have the authority to order a sounding of the ship on his own volition? It is likely that he was ordered by the captain. Also, if we remember that Haines and Hemming saw the chief officer, it is obvious that the captain was sending whatever men he had to elicit information, with him being on the command post of the ship; but why did he not awaken Lightoller, Pitman or Lowe? Boxhall, of course, had performed an inspection without orders.

[8] Presumably, the carpenter had gone up to the bridge, where he encountered firstly Boxhall heading down to look for him, and then to Captain Smith; this would be very approximately at about 11.50pm

[9] His testimony seems to indicate "F" deck but he didn't seem sure; it is more likely he meant "G" deck.

[10] Johnson testified that the water was on "F" deck, but Wheat's sighting, after Johnson's, confirms that the water was on "G" deck.

[11] Stewardess Annie Robinson also claimed to have seen the water. She claimed that she saw "the mail man" pass along the crew's corridor

and then return with Captain Smith and one other (her testimony is confusing as to whether it was Purser McElroy or Thomas Andrews she had seen; if it was Andrews he had gone to the mail room twice, the first occasion on his own, being seen by Johnson, and then with the captain.) After the captain and his companion had gone, Robinson went to inspect the damage herself. She saw water "within 6 steps of coming on "E" deck." This description is hard to reconcile with those of Johnson, Wheat or Chambers who saw water after Robinson, but at a lower level. Robinson seems to have made comments in public that were not probed at the British Inquiry. Shan Bullock writes, "Overhearing him say to Captain Smith on the Upper deck ["E" deck], "Well, three have gone already, captain," an unnamed 'stewardess' ran to the lower stairway and to her surprise found water within six steps of her feet." This is undoubtedly Robinson. The rest of Robinson's comments in Bullock's book includes material not covered at the Inquiry. Did she deliberately omit them, or were they the product of someone's imagination? It is impossible to say. Neither Robinson, nor the only other stewardess called to the inquiry (Elizabeth Leather) were interrogated very vigorously, unlike their male counterparts. A solution to the difference of observed water levels is that Smith headed down below decks twice; the first time as seen by Johnson, and the second as seen by Robinson when the water level in the mail area had risen above that seen by Chambers and others.. If this is so, this second excursion may have been the one seen by Helen Bishop et al, and when the "don lifebelts" order was issued. One further problem arises with Robinson's story, if Bullock's story is true. Smith and Andrews' inspection had to have taken place after midnight; there are too many witnesses who place Smith on the bridge before 12am, and it is impossible for him to have headed below and back up in time without someone noting his absence. But he have evidence from Hemming that before midnight, Andrews knew that the ship was doomed, and he undoubtedly knew more than three compartments had been breached for this to be true. Why did Andrews tell Captain Smith after midnight that "three have gone already" if he must have known already that more compartments were open to the sea?

[12] Barrett later told the occupants of "his" lifeboat (No.13) that at the time of the impact, he was warming a pan of soup of a convenient piece of equipment. "I could do with that hot soup now," he muttered to his makeshift crew as he trembled in his thin clothing which was no protection against the freezing night air.

[13] The dampers were valves above the furnaces to control the draught flow and hence combustion of the coals.

[14] Beauchamp remarked that the watertight doors dropped "5 minutes" after the order to stop, which is clearly wrong. He also does not

seem to have been in a position to see the water pouring in through the side of the ship. Using the dimensions of the boiler room, and the estimate of the height of the iceberg damage as averaging ¾s of an inch in height as calculated by Harland and Wolff Naval Architect Edward Wilding, crude calculations show that it is probable that about 3 tonnes of water per second was entering the boiler room with water jetting in at about 40 feet per second. It would have taken just over two minutes for water to have reached such a depth to start to obscure the hole, and, as we shall see, there is evidence of lights going out in other boiler rooms. Beauchamp probably did not see the rent in the side of the hull. He is also probably mistaken about taking 15 minutes to draw the fires too, if Barrett's and Hendrickon's stories are any indication, discussed elsewhere. As an aside, we can presume that some of the fires in boiler room number 2 were not drawn, as the steam from these boilers were used to power the emergency dynamos.

[15] Were they trying to pump water out of boiler room 6 or any water in the bilges? Incidentally,there was no way to pump water out of the coal bunker that had been injured.

[16] As we shall soon see, firemen Hendrickson and Cavell also recounted being sent to the engine room for lamps. Unless the boiler room lights went out quite a few times, this helps to pin this part of the story down and Hendrickon's and Olliver's recollections tells us that this must have happened well within the first 15 minutes of the collision.

[17] This is slower than in boiler room 6, but much depends on human estimates of timings. How well were those fires drawn in boiler room 6? 2nd Officer Lightoller was blown clear of the ship by a blast of hot air from below as the bridge dipped under hours after this. Could this have come from an uncleared boiler? It is hard to reconcile how hot air could originate from a closed, but admittedly, not watertight boiler, to migrate upwards to Lightoller's position, which was on top of the officer's quarters, in front of, and slightly to the side of the first funnel.

[18] George Kemish wrote to Walter Lord that he saw "an engineer" fall and break his leg; although declining to name him, how did Kemish know? Only Barrett, Harvey and Shepherd were in the room at this point.

[19] The only other instance of someone sustaining injuries, other than Charlotte Collyer's account of a stoker with missing fingers, comes from a newspaper interview with steward Percy Keen. His account is hearsay: "One of the engineers got horribly mangled when the doors in the bulkheads were closed. His injuries were terrible, and, as there was no chance of releasing him, he implored that he might be shot to put him out of his misery. This, I have been told, was done." This account does not seem likely for two reasons: first of all, the doors could be re-opened, and this was indeed done, and secondly, the bulkhead doors

272

required 25 to 30 second to close, which was done gradually. It is only in the last 18 to 24 inches that the doors sliced down like a guillotine. Is it possible that someone was so unobservant that he did not notice a door closing above him?

[20] The accounts of the "flooding" of boiler room 5 by some authors are pure fiction. It is likely that it was the coal bunker door and not the bulkhead that gave way, the door not being watertight. Barrett never saw Harvey or Shepherd swamped or overcome by the water as recounted in some works.

How much water was being admitted by the hole in the coal bunker? Estimates are highly subjective. It was calculated that the average height of the iceberg damage was ¾s of an inch. Barrett said the hole extended two feet past the bulkhead. We can estimate a theoretical maximum amount of water entering the hull: about 5 cubic feet per second, or 0.1 tonnes per second. This is over 250 pints of water in one second. This seems excessively high. A modern fire reel delivers a minimum of 1/3 litre of water per second, about the same as a garden hose. If we use this, and accept Barrett's estimate of 1 hour and 30 minutes before he vacated boiler room 5, we can work out how much water would have to be contained in the bunker. This works out to be 1600 litres or 56 cubic feet. The floor of the coal bunkers are 2 feet below the floor of the boiler room, and have a surface area of approximately 300 square feet. 0.33 litres of water in this space would give a depth of just 2 inches. This allows us to place boundaries on the estimate of water admitted. The space enclosed by the empty forward starboard coal bunker in boiler room 5 was, to the height of the watertight door, is about 2300 cubic feet. If this bunker was catastrophically flooded and then opened, it would empty its contents and the water would, after the initial torrent, level out across the whole compartment, which has a surface area of 5200 square feet. If all the water was released, the total depth above the floor plates would be about 1/3 foot and the boiler room would only seemingly be temporarily awash. This amount of water would have a mass of some 47 tonnes. The pumps in the boiler room couple cope with 250 tonnes per hour, plus a possible additional 125-150 tonnes per hour. Many spectators suggest that following the "rush of water," the boiler room was doomed. Was it?

Interestingly, it was reported in the press that "Leading stoker [Thomas] Threlfall states that ... the watertight doors were closed, but they were opened to bring through an engineer with a broken leg, and were closed after him again." However, some elements of his story in that newspaper are provably wrong (viz. the parts about him taking refuge on a raft with other fireman and Chief Engineer Bell swimming up and declining a place on the boat). Although, as we shall see, the watertight doors leading up to this compromised boiler room were opened, there are no survivor's accounts stating that the door leading into the injured compartment was ever re-opened; in fact, this door was explicitly mentioned as being left closed in testimony. And with good reason too; if it was flooding, it would also have allowed water into the undamaged room(s) aft.

[21] Presumably, the watertight door between boiler room 3 and 4 closed automatically when water raised the floatation device used to detect water in the room. Also, were the pumps activated in boiler room 4? That amount of water was sufficiently small to be tackled successfully by the bilge pumps.

[22] When were the watertight doors to the turbine room and the stokeholds opened? Dillon and Scott indicate that 30 minutes had passed, but this seems too long. Quartermaster Olliver, during his sojourn to the engine room, noticed that the door to the stokehold was open. When he returned to the bridge, after waiting "2 or 3 minutes" for a reply from Bell, Olliver was sent on an errand to tell the boatswain to uncover the boats. We know this occurred at about midnight, so the doors must have been heaved up within the first 20 minutes. There is more data to support an "early" re-opening of the watertight doors, and how long it took to heave them up. Dillon was in boiler room 2 making his way forward by hoisting up the doors when he heard the order to draw the fires from the boilers. He had already passed through two sets of doors, and had two more to open. This order to pull the fires was certainly made a short amount of time after the collision according to inferences we can make from Barrett's and Hendrickson's recollections of the lights going out and being forced to fetch lamps from the engine room. Did the engineers receive an order from the captain to re-open the doors, or did they work on their own cognisance?

Titanic Interlude: The Boats: Inefficiency And Panic

[1] The ordering of the boats is taken from the work of Bill Wormstedt, George Behe and Tad Fitch.

[2] Mrs. Ryerson told the U.S. Inquiry that it was "an officer" at the window who barred her son; but a few years later during litigation testimony, she said that it was Dodd. Interestingly, an oft repeated story, regarded as apocryphal, states that John Jacob Astor, who had just put his pregnant wife aboard boat 4, placed a hat on a young boy (Mr.and Mrs.Carter's son is the sometimes quoted person) to disguise his appearance with the comment that "he" was now a girl and could go in the boat.

[3] A mathematical formula calculated that the 40 people would be

allowed in the cutters.

[4] During the filming of James Cameron's '*Titanic*', davits built to the original specifications, and constructed by the original manufacturers were installed on the near full-size set; although these davits were constructed from modern materials and were slightly smaller than their 1912 counterparts, it surprised the crew to see the arms of the davits flex so much when lowering the boats.

[5] If the captain did exclaim upon the half-filled condition of the boats, he must have been myopic. He was, at the very least, practically alongside boat 6; indeed, he even placed an "Italian" boy aboard to help with the rowing. Mrs.Brown noted that when boat 6 reached the water, she looked up and saw Captain Smith peering down on them "like a solicitous father" and directed them to row to the lights of a mysterious ship in the distance. Smith must have been able to see how many were in the boat, from a height of some 60 feet! On the other hand, Major Peuchen was sure that a whistle was heard, and Mrs.Candee claims that the helmsman of the boat was keen on turning back. One can only guess who is right in this confusing mess.

[6] Boat 15's numbers do not include those of steward Rule because of his admitted memory problems.

[7] Alfred Peacock, a Ship surveyor for the Board of Trade testified that collapsible boats of the type carried on the *Titanic* had been tested successfully with the equivalent weight of 47 people.

[8] Beauchamp was also in boat 13 and recalled some loading of the boat took place on the boat deck.

[9] Steward Percy Keen claimed in a newspaper interview that he was in boat 5, but the details he provided (the *Titanic* having a list to port, his boat being the last on the starboard side to leave (he probably wouldn't have known of boat "C", all the way forward), a fireman being in charge of the boat and there being no officer in his craft) points to him being in boat 15; the "5" must have been a transcription error by the journalist. If so, his account is interesting: he says that his fellow stewards formed themselves into "a police force. They ranged themselves opposite each boat and saw to it that the sea rule, 'women and children first', was strictly observed. Others of the bedroom stewards went below and brought up the women and children." Keen also remarked upon some of his group who "let out with their fists at one or two men who attempted to get into the boats." Since we know boats 11, 13 and 15 were loaded at the same time, and from the same location, it would seem very odd if his cordon was in effect only around boat 15. More than likely, men were held back from these boats. Moody was nearby on deck "A" when this was happening, but Murdoch almost certainly was not aware of what has happening on the deck below.

[10] I have omitted steward Hart and his rescue of the 3rd class in boat 15 from this discussion because of doubts about his story, which will be described elsewhere.

[11] Even when there is evidence to place people in a boat, debate still ensues. For instance, Lillian Asplund, just 5 at the time, recalled vividly how her mother and young brother Felix entered the boat through a window. The boat abruptly began to descend, leaving Mr.Asplund just enough time to drop Lillian into the boat. The sight of her father and 3 young brothers, ranging in ages from 5 to 13, peering down at them stayed with her till she died. None of them were saved. But which boat was it? It could apply to boats 4, 11, 13 or 15. Indeed, boat 11 was lowered so abruptly that 2nd class passenger Ruth Becker was left behind, with her mother yelling at her to get in the next boat (13), which she did. Researcher's attempts to form a cogent and definitive lifeboat list are sometimes hampered by disinformation from descendants; for instance, the family of Frank Goldsmith, Jr persist in their campaign to tell us that he and his mother were saved in boat "D". They won't listen or debate Frank's story that his lifeboat has Chinese/Phillipino stowaways, or that they had to push the boat away from the *Titanic*'s hull due to the huge list. Both of these point to boat "C", not "D".

[12] The maximum length of a thwart of an ordinary lifeboat was 9 feet; with 6 people huddled on this, it would be uncomfortably tight.

[13] Of interest is that the fact that these four boats - 5, 9, 11 and 13, still had their masts, sails and rigging in the boat, thereby reducing the available space even more!

[14] It is incredible that Lawrence Beesley managed to jump 10 feet from the boat deck into boat 13 without causing any upset to the boat or occupants. Even more incredible is that he managed to find a seat when dozens must have been standing!

[15] Seaman McGough was helping to lower boat 14; he then departed the sinking liner in boat 9, the first of the aft starboard boats to leave. We therefore speculate that the first four boats at the forward end of the starboard boat deck were lowered, followed by 14 (and by inference, 12 and 16 which left at the same time), then followed by boat 9, and then 11, 13 and 15. If the 50 gap exists because of the interdiction of the lowering of boats 12, 14 and 16 between boats 7,1 and then 9, it can be reduced by a few minutes as Numbers 14 and 16 seemed to have departed simultaneously. The analysis claims a 5 minute gap between each boat being lowered.

[16] Scanning the *Titanic*'s crew roster, we can ascertain that there were 29 Able (Bodied) Seamen (A.B.), on board, plus six quartermasters, and 6 lookouts (2 of the lookouts, Symons and Evans actually helped to lower the boats), so there were a total of 41 people who definitely could help

to ready a boat.

[17] Seaman George Moore testified in America thus: "There were 6 quartermasters, 6 lookout men, 13 in the port watch, 12 in the starboard watch, and 7 day hands." This was the sum total of all the seamen on the ship. Interestingly, this number (44) tallies with Seaman Osman's number, but he did not include quartermasters in this number. In his tally, he listed the following as seamen: "25 altogether in both watches, 13 in one watch and 12 in the other; then there was 2 deckmen, the cook of the forecastle, 2 window cleaners, 6 lookout men, and 2 masters-at-arms counted with the seamen."

[18] It should be noted that seaman Lucas claimed that boat "D" did not have a lamp; two witnesses in the boat contradict this, but did state that there was not enough oil to make the lamp work.

[19] Why was there a building momentum of panic at the aft portside and not the starboard side? Two possibilities present themselves; Lawrence Beesley reported that men on the starboard side were told they would be taken off on the port side; anyone with a modicum of survival instinct would necessarily want to stay close to the best chance of salvation. The other possibility lies in the fact that the after most starboard boats were lowered to, and loaded from "A" deck. For anyone chancing upon the boat deck at this location, all they would see were empty davits; the boats would have looked as if they had already gone, even though they were only about 5 or 6 feet below the level of the boat deck.

Titanic Interlude: Left To Die?

[1] The inclusion of only one Bostwick gate in the trio of stairs leading up the communal open space for steerage on "D" deck is interesting. Why this one gate? If there were others in this area, they would not seem to have been locked immediately after the collision as steerage passengers collected on the forward well deck to see the ice that had been deposited there in the collision, and then were able to descend back to their quarters. Some researchers have speculated that gates were so commonplace on the ship that it would perhaps have been superfluous to mark them on a ship's plan...but why mark only two in that case? Unless more detailed plans are unveiled we can say that the infamous, over-used, cliched Bostwick gates were hardly in abundance.

[2] Interestingly, Chief Baker Charles Joughin mentions that he saw some steerage pass through the kitchen - either an allusion to an open

277

gate, or the use of the crew's service stairs that went from deck "E" to the boat deck.

[3] Other researchers may provide slightly different casualty figures; the numbers here are illustrative only.

[4] It is widely assumed that Buckley was describing a scene on the forward well deck, where seaman Poigndestre saw an accumulation of steerage men about 40 minutes after the collision. But reading Buckley's evidence gives a different conclusion: before the scuffle at the gate, he went back to his cabin for his lifejacket but was thwarted by the water in his quarters. He said "all the boys and girls were coming up against me. They were all going for the deck." It sounds as if he had come from an area where both sexes were congregating; the aft well deck. Also, no women were seen in the forward well deck, unlike the area that Buckley describes. If Buckley's incident did take place at the stern, it led up to 2nd class, not 1st class space as he stated, but would he really have known where the stairs led? Such gates only had a notice warning 3rd class not to enter. There is no mention of where it would have led, either 1st class at the bow from the forward well deck, or 2nd class at the stern from the aft well deck.

[5] Margaret Murphy was berthed in the same cabin as Katie Gilnagh, as was Katie Mullen. Mullen's descendants confirm that the party were blocked when they tried to go up on deck, and that Farrell used an axe to smash down the barrier, before tussling with the crew member who had tried to bar their progress.

[6] In 1958, Edwina Corrigan (nee Troutt) was interviewed, and notes made at the time are of interest: "Without I am sure meaning to be callous Mrs.Corrigan described how a horde of foreigners tried to break out from the bowels of the ship, all carrying their possessions on their heads. "Horrible people," she said, "they must have been fourth class passengers." When asked what happened to them she explained that thanks to the vigilance of the crew and the officers with their revolvers, they were kept back behind the barriers and prevented from swamping the lifeboats." Miss Troutt was a second class passenger, incidentally.

[7] "Italian" seems to be a general term for those deemed to be undesirable steerage personnel, or to have exhibited reprehensible behaviour. 5Th Officer Lowe's use of the term at the U.S. Inquiry forced him to provide a written apology after a complaint from the Italian ambassador.

[8] What happened to these steerage men? Did they ascend to the boats, only three decks above? Unlikely, as no 3rd class were noticed that high up at this point in the *Titanic* chronology. If they did ascend the stairs from the well deck to "B" deck, they would have had to go through a 1st class door directly in front of them and, then by trial and error, head

aft to the Grand Staircase - the only stair nearby - and then up to the boat deck, a fairly simple journey. Or they could have used the same "crew only" stairs used by Poingdestre to emerge at the very front of the boat deck. Did these 3rd class men return below, and then head aft with their fellow passengers? A possibility. Or were they trapped on the forward well deck by rising water below them? The route that Poingdestre took down to his quarters, and the route the steerage would have taken up were different, so we cannot say where the water was at this point in the 3rd class territory. We know that it was sufficiently far forward for water to crash through a wooden bulkhead from 3rd class areas into Poingdestre's sleeping area, forcing him back up on deck.

[9] Vera Dick may provide contrary data; she remarked seeing "a number of immigrants rushing up the stairs, yelling and screaming and fighting to get to the boats. Officers drew guns and told them if they moved toward the boats they would be shot dead." Dick left in boat 3, the third one on the starboard side, and none of her fellow cast-offs recalled such an event. Dick's story may have been exaggerated by a journalist; it includes the incorrect information that after the impact, "There were terrified screams from all parts of the boat. Women came rushing upon deck with hardly any clothes upon them." True, women did appear on deck, but not instantly as the article implies, and people's perception of events was not one of panic but one of bemusement. If there is a nugget of truth, Dick may have referred to the stokers who were seen on deck when the first boats were being prepared, but this is admittedly not a satisfying explanation as she would certainly have been able to differentiate between steerage men and partially clothed, soot encrusted stokers. Incidentally, Mrs. Futrelle claimed to have seen "the black faced" group of men after they had burst into "the saloon" and where they huddled in one corner.

[10] This 25 included people from other sections that Hart was not responsible for.

[11] From the Grand Staircase opening to boat 15, the main source of illumination was provided by windows from the 1st class lounge, reading and writing room, and smoking room whose windows extended slightly to the boat deck above. After that, the only source of illumination would be occasional bulkhead mounted lamps on the deck houses surrounding the last two funnels, and behind these, the 2nd class entrance. There is little data to indicate whether these 1st class rooms were open, with the exception of the smoking room; Gracie saw an entourage in there before the boats were launched, and found no-one to be seen in any of the other rooms as he headed from aft forwards; there is also a controversial sighting of Thomas Andrews in this room just before the ship sank. John Thayer Jr claimed to have seen the band in the lounge at about

12.15am, or soon before Gracie's search, but Thayer's account dates from 1940, and he does not mention this in this 1912 versions: he describes a "milling crowd" in the lounge that paid little attention to the band playing lively tunes. Mrs. Futrelle mentions being in "the saloon" at at this time, when some stokers burst in on then, but gives little information as to where this was. One theory is that, with the desire to get everyone on deck and to the boats, the rooms would be locked after their closing time (the lounge was due to close at 11.30, the reading and writing room at 11.30pm, and the smoking room's lights extinguished by midnight). Perhaps the smoking room's closure was overlooked, but then again, the 2nd class smoking room was closed at midnight. The thrust of this analysis is that any light spilling out on to the boat deck from these rooms would be scant.

[12] No relation to the boatswain, who perished.

[13] At least, according to Ranger; Scott saw a lot of firemen, but is not sure whether there were any passengers nearby. These firemen were probably those who left the bowels of the ship with him a little while earlier.

[14] There are a few other instances where the "everyone to the starboard side" order was heard. Gracie heard it shortly before Hemming's mention of it; indeed, it provided the impetus to head to the other side where he found two ladies that he was sure had already been placed in a boat, and he marched them to the last boat under davits, "D". The straightening order did not completely restore the equilibrium, if, indeed, it had any affect at all; a steward by the name of Hardy recalled that the ship still had a list to port when "D" departed. The time difference between Hemming and Gracie would be mere minutes, but in those minutes, the extra tonnage of water entering the ship could conceivably have altered the *Titanic*'s dynamics. Another possibility is that the order heard by Gracie was not taken up with relish by many people; the boats on the starboard side had to all intents and purposes rowed off into the night, and to the layman, unaware that there were two boats on the roof, the only one left was "D". To leave the prospect of a place in a boat and head away, with the water only 10 or 15 feet below would be tantamount to suicide. Regarding other similar orders to migrate passengers, Lightoller heard the "straighten her up" order, but this directive was uttered by Wilde, and he repeated it. This was when he was dealing with boat 6 when he first noticed a list to port, or some considerable time before the stories of Thayer, Gracie, Hemming et al. described above. It is unclear where boat 6 falls into a chronology of lifeboats, and whether Lightoller means that the boat was being loaded with people, or whether the boat itself was simply being readied. There is conflicting evidence of a list to port or starboard: Hichens describes a list

280

to starboard when he was on deck and when boat 6 was lowered - indeed the occupants had to push the boat away from the *Titanic*'s hull during the descent; boat 8's crewman Crawford says a list to port. Lightoller's evidence of an "early" list to port is troublesome (as is some of his other testimony, some cynics say!): in order of boat departing, we have the evidence of Norman Chambers (a starboard list before getting in boat 5), the recollection of Mrs.Dodge (a slight list when boat 5 went down), Pitman (no list at all before disembarking in No.5), George Symons (a slight list to starboard when No. 1 was lowered) and Sir Cosmo Duff-Gordon, also in boat 1, who did not notice, but was told of a slight list to starboard. It is difficult to synchronise boats on the opposite sides of the ship, but we know from steward Crawford's evidence that boat No.5 left before No.8, and this was approximately the time of boat 6's departure. The most important thing is that, ordering passengers to starboard to correct a list on that side could exacerbate the slope. Maybe Lightoller got confused about when the straightening order was given?

[15] The Master At Arms, Henry Bailey, took command of boat 16. He was not called to testify.

[16] The only other source for this boat at the enquiries was a steward named Rule; sadly I have had to discount his testimony as he admitted suffering from memory problems after the disaster.

[17] Some of the firemen tried - and succeeded - in gaining access to boats 5, 3 and 1 on the other side of the ship to where Peuchen saw them ordered away. This author suspects that this attempt to drive firemen from the boats could have resulted in gaps in the stokers' chronologies after leaving their posts below. Ironically, the stokers were described as being unwilling to participate in boat drills; now they were among the first on deck and looking for escape!

[18] Although Senior incorrectly mentions seeing Ismay in a barely loaded lifeboat the majority of the story does conform to our knowledge of events on the *Titanic*.

[19] Some, like Gracie, have claimed that Mauge was referring to one of the forward-most boats, but he agreed with his interrogator that he was referring to "the last four". Furthermore, the boat was stopped between decks, and that someone on the *Titanic* grabbed the back of his coat to pull him back on board after he had jumped. This last point refers to the aft portion of boats, as the "A" deck windows were closed for the forward 4 boats and no-one would be able to reach into a boat. The information about being stopped between decks points directly to boats 11, 13 and 15.

Chapter 4: Impending Catastrophe

[1] If Lowe had already armed himself when he came on deck, we can say that the "officer" was undoubtedly Murdoch. If he felt so aggrieved about the stokers in the boat why did he not order them out, and off the deck like Wilde had done (as described elsewhere in this work)? And why did Murdoch allow 5 stokers in the next boat to go, accounting for nearly 50% of the boat's total occupancy? It seems more likely that he was perturbed at people entering the boat without his permission.

[2] Can we draw any inference from the situation on the deck when the pistols were dispensed? Probably not; we know that Murdoch was seen with his gun when boat 9 was loaded; by this time, the aft port side boats had been the location of a struggle where many male passengers sought to enter them without permission. The use of weapons to quell unseemly behaviour at this point makes sense. Retrieving weapons when boat 6 was being prepared does not, as there are no indications of any situation occurring that would have prompted them being obtained, unless one includes Stengel's and Harper's comments at boats 3 and 5. Lightoller's 1912 implied timing of getting his gun just before easing the boats off the roof is roughly in line with other evidence (he had his gun when "D" was launched, moments before), and the desire to protect oneself from a barrage of desperate passengers; again, consistent with an "later" rather than an "early" desire to arm oneself.

[3] The boatswain must have reacted instinctively to some extent. He apparently ordered that the doors be closed, but could not have known what had happened so soon after the strike. Seaman Frank Evans recalled being sent below to find the carpenter, and the boatswain inquired who he was looking for. Upon being told that he had "gone up" and then asking what had happened, Evans informed him that he thought the ship had struck an iceberg, and the boatswain "went up" (to the bridge?). Also, it is prudent to mention Boxhall, when he inspected the areas on "F" deck; the watertight doors forward were not closed then. It should also be noted that this refers to the manually operated doors, and not the electrically powered ones in the boiler rooms.

[4] Interestingly Gracie wrote in some accounts that the only people he saw in the smoking room included Mr.Ryerson, but there is ample evidence that he stayed with his wife until she departed in boat 4, a short space of time before the sinking. The others that Gracie saw were single men.

[5] The design of the ship may help to explain the listing of the *Titanic* at various points that night; soon after the collision, the ship was registering a list of 5° to starboard. This seems to have gradually diminished during the sinking, before become a huge list to port. By the time that the later boats were departing, those on the starboard side

282

were rubbing down the ship's hull; those on the port side had such a gap that people had to jump across the chasm. Researcher Sam Halpern has calculated that, by the time boat 10 had departed, perhaps within the last 30 to 45 minutes, the list was now 10°;. In the early stages of the sinking, the damage to the 3rd and 4th compartments was confined to the starboard side by the fireman's passage that ran through it, causing a list by virtue of the weight of water confined there. When the water reached the top of the tunnel, the water could pass over to the port side of the ship. Then there is the matter of the water rising in the mail rooms which opened to starboard. However, when the water inside boiler rooms 5 and 6 reached the level of the escape doors, it could then pass onto the port side, the weight of water on that side pulling the ship down.

[6] Woolner's statement in America that he saw the captain "between the two lifeboats that were farthest astern on the port side, giving orders" is clearly in error; the captain never ventured that far aft, and deck "A", although being "glassed in" with retractable screens forward, was open at this point in the ship's superstructure, making Woolner's added comments nonsensical.

[7] Two things stand out from Beesley's account; firstly, he does not mention people loaded into boat 9 from the boat deck, which we know is the case, and which must have happened in sight of him. The other is the identity of the officer who issued this order. "He had apparently been off duty when the ship struck, and was lightly dressed, with a white muffler twisted hastily round his neck." This could allude to Chief Officer Wilde, 2nd Officer Lightoller, 3rd Officer Pitman, or 5th Officer Lowe. Lightoller spent all his time on the port side, and Pitman and Lowe were occupied with the forward most boats on this side of the ship; indeed, it is possible that Pitman had already left the ship. This implies, if Beesley's "off duty" observation is correct, that this was Wilde; the only problem with this is that he spent the majority of his time on the port side, with Lightoller and the captain.

[8] After boat 8 had departed, the order was for anyone nearby to head aft, exacerbating the crowd problem where hundreds had gathered. It does seem odd that there is no mention of any 2nd or 3rd class passengers at the forward most boats prior to this.

[9] Another one of Mrs. Futrelle's writings alters the wording of this order slightly to "Women remain here [on "A" deck.] Men back to "B" deck." This makes little sense; no one else mentions being held so far below, and although Mrs.Futrelle clearly knows the distinction between the boat deck, "A" and "B" deck, it is possible that she had mistaken and confabulated the decks. To give an example, she mentions finding her husband lighting fellow passenger Colonel Astor's cigarette while they "stood strung along the rail smoking," her story implying that this

283

occurred on "B" deck, but the word "rail" indicates either "A" deck or the boat deck. Futrelle's account is a confusing mesh of details; despite the men being ordered to "B" deck, she sees Colonel Astor on the boat deck helping his pregnant wife into boat 4 ... which we know went from "A" deck. How did Colonel Astor manage to evade the "men down to "B" deck" blockade? Mrs.Futrelle confronts this dilemma by saying that Astor's wife had fainted when she learned that they were to be separated, and he had obtained permission to help their nurse carry her. But we know from other accounts that men were seen on "A" deck and the boat deck at this time and afterwards. If Mrs.Futrelle's story is to be believed, after depositing his wife in the boat, the Colonel then went below, to "B" deck, where she found him with her husband and the men "strung along the rail". Mr.Futrelle then took her to another boat, but there is no indication that she was taken "up" to the boat deck from a lower deck. The only conclusion that can be reached is that Mrs.Futrelle's memory had become confused. How much of her account can be trusted?

[10] Lookout George Hogg gave evidence that he was ordered to fetch a Jacob's ("rope") Ladder from the forecastle. As soon as he arrived on deck with it, the boatswain ordered him to throw it down (presumably, abandon it on the deck); a pity that the mechanism used to lower boats "A" and "B" from the roof of the officer's quarters wasn't obtained at the same time, as this was stored under the forecastle too.

[11] Hichens comment is contradicted by a seaman by the name of Jones; he testified that upon arriving on the boat deck, he "got the collapsible boat on the port side ready." This boat was inboard of the permanently swung-out emergency boat 2, and therefore hooking it up to the davits was not possible until No.2 had gone. All one could do is unlace the cover of the boat, and Jones's comments make it clear that this happened soon after he got on deck. And yet Hichens says this boat was still laced up 20 minutes later.

[12] Lookout Lee, who had vacated the crow's nest at the same time as Fleet, gave evidence that he saw men who were due to go on the 12 till 4am duty shift come up, carrying their bags from their flooding quarters. The men were "standing by; they did not know whether they would have to go below or not." Lee heard the boatswain call "the other watch" to get the boats ready; after the "other watch" had turned out, those who had just gone below went off to the boats.

[13] Snyder left in the very first boat, so even if one allows 5 or 10 minutes for a boat to be "filled", his observation may not apply to the other boats which left after his, which of course he would be unable to see.

[14] Buley's timing might be off. He said he saw the lights of a nearby

steamer "ten minutes after we struck" and this was "When we started turning the boats out." But the boats were being turned out at least 20 minutes after the collision.

[15] A fact should be remembered for those boats that were adjacent and shared a set of davits; because of the way the davits were engineered, only one boat out of two could be swung out at once. The mechanism was then "reset" and the other boat could then be moved out. For example, boats 10, 12, 14 and 16 were located such that (say) boats 10 and 14 could be swung out, and once this was done, 12 and 16 could be attended to. This may have provided a little latency in the preparation process.

[16] The contentious issue of the *Californian* will be omitted from this narrative; suffice it to say that many people believe that it was the ship that was seen by the *Titanic* ... and vice versa. Contrary opinions exist but the debates often degenerate into acrimony.

[17] The first rocket was undoubtedly sent up between the loading and lowering of boats 5 and 3; the British Inquiry puts this time as being between 12.55 and 1.00am, in line with the sighting on the *Californian* which would be 12.47-12.52am.

[18] Rockets were evidently stored on the forward as well as the aft bridge; a sensible procedure as the regulations specified that rocket firing locations should be located at opposite sides of the ship. On the *Titanic*, this was on the forward starboard side, the other would therefore be aft aft, and to port. It is to be speculated that Boxhall ordered more detonators (which came in boxes of 12) to be brought forward in case he ran out.

Titanic Interlude: Timings and Tribulations

[1] In fairness, the diary has events that could not have been determined contemporaneously: her mention that "...[the men in the boat] rowed on after a light on the horizon which afterwards proved to belong to the *Californian*" - at detail that she could not have not known about for at least a few hours. Strangely, her diary gets the time of collision correct, but a letter written by Mrs.Spedden on April 18th puts the time at 11.55.

[2] Ray's exact wording was, "I went along "E" deck and forward, and the forward part of "E" deck was under water. I could just manage to get through the doorway into the main stairway. I looked to see where the water was and it was corresponding on that side of the ship to the port side."

[3] Barrett did note at the inquiries that as a rule, a stoker never carries

a watch when on duty. We must also wonder how many other crewmen, stokers or not, also did not wear a timepiece.

[4] There was a clock in the reciprocating engine room, but not in the turbine room; Dillon did not take any particular notice what time it was, and thought the clock was put back about 20 minutes. One wonders in vain how long he "knocked about" for. If he was on duty then he should have reported back to his duty station promptly.

[5] Another worker in the engine room, Scott, also says he too was ordered out of the engine room at 1.20am. He noticed no water in the alleyway, but the door through which he would have emerged would not have allowed him to see if any water was coming up the corridor from forward; Scott then went aft. While below, he helped free a co-worker who had been trapped by a closing watertight door, and then assisted to open the doors to allow easy travel between the various compartments aft of the boiler room. It was a quarter to one when he was told to hoist up these doors. Unfortunately Scott is not clear whether the watertight doors forward were open, but at one point he did say, "No, I never noticed [the doors] because I could not see them open." If Olliver is right, they had already been open for nearly an hour. Stoker Thomas Threlfall also says that he was ordered up at 1.20am. He, and his colleagues were ordered below by the second Engineer, Mr.Hesketh, to draw the fires from the boilers soon after the "all hands on deck" order was given, which was nearly midnight. Hesketh eventually told Threlfall and his men, "We've done all we can me. Get out now." It seems doubtful that he and his men would take well over an hour to rake the coals from the furnaces.

[6] Cavell does not seem very clear about the timing or whether he left the boiler room once or twice; he says that he first saw the passengers about an hour and a half after the collision, but sees them "wet" 2 hours after the strike.

[7] If the timing of boat 7 is indeed correct as being 12.45am, boat 5 at 12.55am, boat 3 at 1am, and boat 1 at 1.10am as claimed by the British Inquiry, deductions can be made about the state of the *Titanic* and how it related to Cavell's sighting of the steerage passengers. Olliver in boat 5 said that the *Titanic* was 15-20 feet down at the bows, and Symons in No.1 described that the ports under the ship's forward name plate was awash. Even as early as 12.55am, the majority of 3rd class berths in the bow would be flooded, and yet it is claimed that passengers were seen loitering in the alleyway an hour to an hour and a half after the collision. They must have seen the water coming creeping up the alleyway toward them.

[8] Hendrickson was ordered to get lamps for boiler rooms 5 and 6; if Olliver's testimony is correct, this is before the watertight doors were

opened from the engine rooms forward, and hence before midnight. It seems unlikely that boiler rooms 4, 5 and 6 suffered from separate lighting failures.

[9] Wheat referred to seeing five or six male passengers (steerage evidently) dragging their boxes and bags from forward, heading aft, down the alleyway.

[10] Both Barrett and Cavell eventually wound up on the boat deck at practically the same time; Cavell got to the boat deck in time to see boat 13 being lowered and got into boat 15; Barrett got to boat 13 to find it "pretty well filled." Boats 15 and 13 left at virtually the same time.

[11] The exception seems to be Colonel Gracie, who said in his book that he was aroused by a "sudden shock" and glanced at his watch "which [he] had changed to agree with the ship's time on the day before and which now registered twelve o'clock. Correct ship's time would be about 11.45." The fifteen minute discrepancy is not reminiscent of the time changes that would have happened on 13th/14th April, and it is possible that Gracie was awoken by something else, perhaps the sound of steam being discharged, which he does admit to hearing at this time.

[12] On the other hand, Lookout Hogg later said that he was awakened at 11.40 by the collision; his fellow look-out (Evans) remarked to him five minutes later that they should get dressed to go on duty. If Evans had seen a clock, he may have assumed that it was adjusted time (or 12.08 in April 14th time) and that they were indeed due on duty in 15 minutes. In reality, they had another 38 minutes to go before their watch commenced.

[13] Postal worker J.S.March's body was later retrieved from the North Atlantic and was found to have a watch that had stopped at 1.27am; adding 47 minutes on gives 2.14am. It seems that March had adjusted his watch by the full 47 minutes too. Likewise, 3rd class passenger Malkolm Johnson's own watch had its hands frozen at 1.37am, or 2.24am. One puzzle though is Robert Norman's watch: it read 3.07. Norman had probably forgotten to reset his watch, and it was still running on April 13th time. When we compensate for this, it becomes about 2.20am. The other suggestion, which should not be taken too seriously, is that Norman had adjusted his watch the wrong way.

[14] Strangely, Gracie's watch, which he claimed was still set to the time of the previous day, also stopped at 2.22am. Coincidentally, or otherwise, his own deduction of the claimed time of the impact was 11.45- the same time as Thayer's. Based on a study of his location when he went into the water, Thayer probably went into the water just moments before Gracie.

[15] The majority of the time of the sinking are obtained from passenger's and crew's own watches. No one seemed to have cared to

look at the on-board clocks, with one exception. Irene Harris wrote that she "passed the bridge at 2.20am as someone mentioned the time, and the ship went down exactly at 2.30 according to one of the men in the collapsible." In one incarnation of this story, she saw the clock on the bridge herself. She left the ship in the last lifeboat to be lowered, and the 10 minute difference does not allow enough time for her to get into the boat and reach a distance of 50 to 150 yards (according to others in the same boat) if we assume that the timings are accurate and consistent with each other: "the man" in the boat may have had a watch that was a few minutes off. But, the "2.20am" itself raises difficulties. The bridge would have been under water at this point. And if the ship had retarded its clocks by 23 or the whole 47 minutes, the time by Thayer's - and other's watch for the sinking would be in the region of 2.43am or 3.07am which is not what happened. To be charitable, Mrs.Harris's statements seem unreliable.

Titanic Interlude: Andrews And Ismay: The Good And The Bad?

[1] The only other sources of the ship's expected lifespan comes from Boxhall, who was told by the captain that, after the boats had been ordered to be prepared for lowering, the *Titanic* had only an hour to an hour and a half left; and Jack Thayer Jnr. who wrote in 1940 that "shortly after midnight" Mr.Andrews told him that he did not give the ship "much over an hour to live." In 1932, Thayer wrote that, "shortly" after the impact, "My father joined me in a few minutes. Walking all around the ship on "A" deck, nothing could be seen in the way of any ice or other obstructions and it was some minutes before anyone was able to advise us what the trouble was. We were joined shortly by J. Bruce Ismay, managing director of the White Star Line and some engineers who had designed and constructed the ship. They immediately went on a tour of the ship, taking some 25 minutes. I visited the swimming pool and post office [sic] department. Water was coming in very rapidly. We were then ordered to go back to our cabins and dress fully and put on life preservers. Dressed, we went on deck, my mother, my father and myself, and stood around talking with other passengers for some time. Mr. Ismay and the engineers from Harlan & Wolf [sic], the firm which built the ship, advised us they didn't give the ship more than an hour." Thayer does not seem to have mentioned his encounters with Ismay, Andrews or anyone else in his other versions as far as this author can ascertain. Were they later inventions?
[2] Steward Mackay also saw Smith come down the working staircase on

to "E" deck and, presumably, to the chief engineer's office further aft, where Chef's Secretary Mauge saw him. Mackay said that, 10 minutes later, Smith returned and went back up the staircase. Neither Mackay nor Mauge mention seeing Andrews. Mackay's timings seem odd; he claimed to have seen Smith 35 minutes after the collision, and soon after the captain had ascended the stairs, Mackay heard another order from 2nd Steward Dodd, for all stewards to get out of their quarters, rouse their passengers, assist with the lifebelts and proceed to the boat deck. Mackay had no passengers under his charge, so he went direct to the boat deck, where passengers had already congregated. If Ostby's account is any indication, then Smith must have ordered passengers to put on belts twice; once before he headed down the Grand Staircase, and then soon after he left "E" deck, where Mackay saw him.

[3] The timing seems to be awry: "When [Johnson] heard [Andrews reassuring the ladies, it] was just a quarter of an hour after she struck, not much more," or about 11.55pm. As stated, Andrews accompanied the captain, and we know that Smith was on the bridge until about midnight, when Boxhall reported the water in the mail room; if Johnson was one of those who had retarded their watch by 23 minutes, it would give Smith and Andrews time to get down to "D" deck and be seen near the dining room, confer with the engineer(s) and then inspect the flooding mail rooms.

[4] Coincidentally (?), just after seeing Andrews, Sloper said that "someone else appeared at this moment and said that the water was rushing in through the squash court wall." Warren left a few minutes after Sloper, in the next boat (No.5). Had they been privy to the same information? Had they seen Andrews, with the "look of terror" at the same time?

[5] Gracie's watch read midnight when he awoke, and he claims that this represented 11.45 in actual time as he had neglected to adjust his watch for westward progress across the Atlantic. He does not mention seeing the crew working on the boats, which happened after midnight. Gracie's mention of a "day suit" is interesting as it does not relate to other evidence. At the U.S. Inquiry, Gracie places this sighting of Ismay after he had retired to his cabin to pack his luggage and was returning on deck: "As I went up on deck the next time I saw Mr. Ismay with one of the officers. He looked very self contained, as though he was not fearful of anything, and that gave encouragement to my thought that perhaps the disaster was not anything particularly serious."

[6] If this was before midnight, then how did Smith know the ship was badly damaged? Boxhall had returned with a report of there being no damage in the areas he had inspected. Andrews pre-midnight report of "half an hour to live" may have filtered to the captain, as perhaps had

289

Chief Officer Wilde's report of the damage reported under the forecastle. Wilde may have known that water was rushing into the cargo holds, as others in the bow had seen it; he certainly knew that the forepeak tank had been punctured.

[7] The second occasion when Ismay went up to the deck was seen by a steward named Crawford who saw the White Star Chairman leave his room with another steward by the name of Clark; Crawford says that this happened after the order to put on lifejackets was issued. Ismay's testimony is confusing on this point; at the U.S. Inquiry, he says that he met Bell and heard the boat order some 30 to 40 minutes after the collision; in Britain, he says that he heard the boat order just 20 minutes afterwards. This is somewhat important; if Ismay had heard the order to get the boats out, and had met Bell just moments before this, Ismay's testimony is slightly suspicious, as quartermaster Olliver had only just returned from delivering a message to the Engineer in the engine room mere moments before.

[8] Lightoller saw Ismay standing alone on the uppermost deck as the boats were being cleared away; the 2nd Officer bade him "good evening". The 2nd Officer does not recall a reply. This is a minor quibble with Ismay's evidence; Lightoller was exclusively working on the port side that night.

[9] Did Lowe's remonstration with Ismay cause him to stop lowering the boat, causing one side to pitch up?

[10] This raises two important questions; many of Ismay's answers to questions put to him at the inquiries reek of evasion. In many instances, he states that he did not know, had no recollection, or could not even estimate the simplest of matters. He was hardly the "vital" eyewitness that the 'officer' thought he might be. The other is a valid point raised by researcher Paul Lee: "Ismay was the first witness to be called at the inquiries; if he did decide at an early point to lie, then this was a dangerous gambit. He couldn't have known who would be called, and any number of people might have contradicted him at later stages of the inquiries. On the other hand, if he did decide to lie, then he must have known that he would be very foolish to alter his story later, with so much bile directed at him from the press and public."

Chapter 5: Acceptance of Fate

[1] The traditional belief that boat 8 rowed continuously all night to the mystery ship is contradicted by Mrs White, who claimed that after rowing for 30 to 45 minutes it became obvious that the other ship was unreachable, and they turned around and headed back towards the

Titanic.

[2] It is not known how fast the lifeboats were rowed that night but it seems unlikely that they could have reached the other ship in time. Dissent comes from the testimony of steward Johnson who gave the incredible and scarcely believable claim that his boat (2), with two oars rowing and two "dipping" managed to pull 1½ to 2 miles in half an hour!

[3] This boy's entry to the boat seems to have been unobserved by many, for there are a few tales of this boy as being a "stowaway," "an Italian" and hiding somewhere in the bowels of the boat until they had rowed out a safe distance.

[4] The plug was a stopper in the bottom of the lifeboat; during a voyage, it wasn't fitted to allow excess accumulated rain and sea water to drain from the boat (even though most of the boats had canvas covers). Obviously, in the water, it was essential that the plug be in place.

[5] This anecdote comes from Peuchen. Helen Candee gives a different version. She says that Hichens thought he heard the order to come alongside and was for turning back until he was reminded by the passengers that the captain's final orders were to keep the boats together and row away from the ship. Candee heard this order given, and it seems to be a variation of the order heard by Mrs. Margaret "Molly" [sic] Brown when they reached the water, and when the captain gave them instructions to row to the light in the distance - all boats keeping together. Hichens claimed that no orders were given when the boat was in the water.

[6] Interestingly, Hichens was hailing other boats and asking them what officer was on duty at the time of the sighting. He claimed there was only one on the bridge when the collision occurred, which is correct, as the other officer was in the wheelhouse, where he was located.

[7] Although 40 was the determination of the boat's capacity using a mathematical formula, the lifeboat identification plaque puts the number of people at 33.

[8] Minor variations of this exist, such as "Yes I wish you would", "Oh certainly, do; I shall be very pleased" and "Very glad if you would."

[9] This might be a description of Major Archibald Butt, the military advisor to the President of the United States.

[10] Symons knew Lowe personally, and claimed that he never saw him at all that night. Symons had helped with boats 3 and 5 and it is surprising that Lowe's altercation with Ismay did not stay in his memory. Seaman Horswell also did not see Lowe at boat No.1, and Taylor was dubious having seen him. Sir Duff Gordon thinks that Lowe may have been there but was not sure as it was dark.

[11] It is possible that he may not have been heard due to the

impossibly loud noise of the steam venting from the funnels.

[12] Boat 1's navigation is confusing; Stengel claimed that they rowed towards the ship's light on the horizon, but after Boxhall's green flares were seen in boat 2, he suggested that they turn around to find the source of this new illumination. Symons confirmed that they initially headed for the mystery ship's light and that they, acting under his command, did return to the area of the wreck after the cries had finished their dreaded chorus, but saw no-one, and eventually found and accompanied another boat. In his estimation it had taken 25 to 45 minutes to return to the wreck. Horswell also mentioned heading towards the light after pulling a little way from the ship and stopping for about a quarter of an hour. They were still rowing when the *Titanic* went down, which contradicts those who say they had stopped at this time. Collins also said that the boat turned around as soon as they thought they had escaped the suction. In his estimation, it took an hour to return. Pusey's story is that they sat for 20 minutes when the ship sank, and then rowed towards the light, coming into contact with two other boats. He does not think boat 1 rowed back. Sheath says they pulled back to the other boats. Taylor stated that, after hearing the two passengers agreeing with the lady about the danger (see later), Symons ordered them to row away but he did not know in which direction; he did not known whether they went back to where the ship had foundered. Sir Duff Gordon did not hear Symon's order to pull back to the other boats; in fact, he claimed to have heard no instructions regarding the actions of the boat at all.

[13] Mrs Thayer says this about boat 4: "As the boat was being lowered, when it was still about 12 feet above the water, we heard the order given above to 'Let her go', and only our shouting and protestations to those above prevented the letting go of the tackles while we were yet that distance above the water." One wonders how accurate this is: no-one else mentioned this, and doubts about Mrs.Thayer are nurtured when she recalled that she passed an overturned lifeboat soon after reaching the water, which is incorrect. She also says that "at least two men from steerage slid down the davit ropes into the boat" but these were actually crewmen who had been ordered in at the last minute to bolster the undermanned boat's complement. Mrs.Ryerson also mentions that the ropes seemed to stick and that a knife was called for but not used until they got to the water.

[14] Imanita Shelley in boat 10 also alleges that the tackle refused to work and it took considerable time (5-15 minutes) to reach the water, and that when they arrived, the casting off mechanism failed to work and the ropes had to be cut. But Seaman Evans, also in the boat, disputes this: he stated that the women were packed so tightly that it was impossible to reach the release mechanism, and they manually had to lift

the lifeboat off the hooks attached to the falls.

[15] On the other hand, 3rd class passenger Charles Dahl's account does point to "an" officer being at boat 15, as he was given permission to lower himself, hand over hand into it as it descended. 6Th Officer Moody has been placed tentatively as being on "A" deck when some of the last boats at the aft end were departing, so this could have been him.

[16] Surprisingly, there are a few cases where, upon safely reaching the water, the oars were still found to be lashed together. Only the provision of convenient knives by passengers and crew managed to release them. The lack of knives is a surprise; Passenger Gracie passed his own up to the roof of the officer's quarters when the attempt was made to release boat "B" of its moorings. Steward Sidney Daniels also recalled passing his knife up but it is impossible to say if this was to cut "B" or "A" free.

[17] Lowe was in the vicinity of boat 5 when it was lowered and he must have seen 3rd Officer Pitman placed in command; why then did Lowe say that he had seen 5 boats go away without an officer in charge? Speculation on some *Titanic* forums is that, for some reason, there was a degree of animosity between the two men, and Lowe did not regard him as an "officer." In an affidavit given to the New York consulate, Lowe added a little to his comments at the British Inquiry: "I stated to Moody that I had seen five boats go away without a responsible person in them, meaning by this an officer." There is no evidence to support or counter the "animosity" argument, but it is a curious mistake from Lowe. His testimony in America indicates that he heard Murdoch order Pitman into boat 5.

[18] The White Star Line had provided Webley revolvers for the crew, but Lowe had his own gun, a Browning Automatic, capable of discharging eight shells. A few passengers had their own weapons; Norman Chambers; "Baron Von Draschtedt" who unloaded his gun in his lifeboat prompting Pitman to tell him to save his bullets; and, most poignant of all, Michel Navratil, who was kidnapping his two young children from a failing marriage. He placed his sons in a boat but did not join them. When his body was recovered, a loaded gun was found. A *Carpathia* passenger claimed that before he boarded his boat, Sir Cosmo Duff-Gordon put a gun in his pocket.

[19] There are isolated stories of passengers being shot and some of these are discussed elsewhere in this work. Ellen Shine, for instance, gave an interview in which she stated that four men from steerage who refused to obey an officer's order to vacate a boat were shot dead, their bodies being thrown into the sea. Granted, other variants of this interview omit the shooting portion, which leaves us to wonder how accurate this anecdote is. It is not likely that a consensus will ever be reached on these veracity of these stories and many researchers dismiss

them.

[20] Regarding boat 2, seaman Osman declared that a box was placed in his craft, only for him and his superior, Boxhall, to discover that it was actually a tin of green flares rather than the intended biscuits. Boxhall himself claimed that he ordered the flares to be put in the boat.

[21] The only way for water to have reached his cabin was via the working alleyway, but Joughin insisted that he only saw it in his room. He also said that he returned to the boat deck via a crew's access stairway that went from forward of his cabin to the boat deck. If the alleyway was flooded, he would have had extreme difficulty reaching the stairway. Indeed, he said that he didn't see any water at all in the alleyway, which is hard to believe given other evidence and does not assist Joughin's credibility. At the British Inquiry, he offered his opinion that the ship "had shipped some water forward, or a quantity of ice that had melted and had run down; but I did not give it a second thought, because it was not serious." This seems laughable, but another solution he proposed makes more sense: "If [the water] had been higher I should have thought something about it, but under the circumstances I thought it might have been a pipe burst, because there was a pipe burst on the *Olympic* from the engineers' quarters and we got the same water. It might have been the same thing."

[22] It is commonly cited that alcohol would exacerbate one's susceptibility to the cold, hastening one's demise. If Joughin's tale is true, it is one instance where this long accepted fact is incorrect. But then again, metabolism varies from individual to individual.

[23] One wonders what "the other boat" was. Perhaps boat 4, the next one aft? Since everyone who got into that boat entered it from the next deck down, Boxhall probably saw the people as his boat was lowered to the water.

[24] Gracie claims not to have heard Lightoller's pistol being discharged and one wonders why this is. But, when looking through the various stories of survivors, it is striking how many people did not hear Lowe's gunshots, or even the sound of the band playing. Proximity seems to have played no part in this; Beesley was mere yards away from Lowe's antics with his gun, and he did not mention the sound of shots. Some people in the lifeboats did remember the sounds of gunfire, or perhaps the sound of the wires supporting the funnels as they broke. Many, unless they were in the immediate vicinity, heard nothing at all.

[25] It has been claimed that the instances of suction were only noted with the rapidly submerging bow, but not the stern. In this author's opinion, with so few being saved from the water, it is impossible to tell. Baker Joughin spoke of there being no suction when the stern sank but his account has dubious details. It may be that people were sucked to

the stern but did not live to recount their experiences. The majority of those who clambered onto "A" and "B" boats were to be found on the starboard side of the boat deck, predominantly near the bridge.

[26] Sunderland's story is contradicted by Lightoller, who says that when he first got to "B" there was no one else on it.

[27] Lightoller later claimed that the opening of the forward expansion joint had caused the funnel to give way. The joints were gaps in the superstructure that were covered with a rubber sheath that allowed them to flex freely in the sea, reducing the strain on the hull. The aft wires supporting the funnel ran across the joint and snapped, the starboard one almost immediately after the port one. This pulled the funnel over to that side of the ship near where Lightoller was located. This picturesque description was gleaned from Lightoller and entered into his autobiography. He did not go into such graphic details in his 1912 testimony, and it is debatable as to what he could have seen, from a vantage close to the waterline. Marine Architect Edward Wilding provided an alternate explanation in 1912; "The funnels are carried from the casings in the way of the comparatively light upper decks - that is, the boat deck and a deck. When these decks became submerged and the water got inside the house, the water would rise outside much faster than inside, and the excessive pressure on the comparatively light casings which are not made to take a pressure of that kind would cause the casing to collapse [which] would take the seating from under the funnel and bring the funnel down."

[28] In his autobiography, Lightoller claimed that when he finally clambered onto boat "B", the lights were still burning. Cook John Collins confirmed Lightoller's 1912 account; Collins was washed off the deck and ended up on "B" with 15 or 16 others; by inference, this was after the funnel had collapsed since he does not mention it. When he came to the surface after being sucked down, he looked at the *Titanic* and the lights were on, but these had been extinguished when he got onto the boat.

[29] The bow of the ship sank fairly slowly, allowing water in gradually so that when it finally slipped under, the water pressure had equalised. The stern, on the other hand, sank so rapidly that its flooding would have been catastrophic. Any air pockets would have imploded due to the increasing water pressure as the ship plunged deeper.

[30] The most plentiful quantity of debris were pieces of cork. A passenger on the rescue ship *Carpathia* described the cork as resembling the blocks placed in lifejackets for buoyancy, but other evidence suggests that they actually originated from the cold storage spaces near the stern; cork was used to insulate these areas. Steward Fred Ray also said that cork was used to insulate the "deepest" 1st class cabins from the heat originating from the engine and boiler rooms.

295

[31] Gracie came to the surface, and found added buoyancy from a floating plank and then a wooden crate. As he surfaced, he heard a "slight ... gulp" behind him, and when he looked the *Titanic* had gone. It is subjective to estimate how long Gracie was underwater, but he told one newspaper that, "The 2nd Officer and J.B.Thayer, Jr. who were swimming near, told me that just before my head appeared above the water, one of the *Titanic*'s funnels separated and fell apart near me, scattering bodies in the water." This is obviously a reference to the 1st funnel. This indicates that the time span between the funnel falling, Gracie resurfacing and the ship having disappeared could be measured in seconds. However, with waterlogged eyes and lungs screaming for air, Gracie was obviously more concerned with his own survival than absorbing the details of the *Titanic*'s finale.

[32] Common sense decrees that the stern falling back to the sea would cause a huge splash of water, but there is no evidence for this. Either everyone who witnessed the splash perished, or the stern didn't catastrophically fall back down again, but was subject to a "restraining force" that prevented it from falling down freely with great force. If this is true, it may be that there still some connection between the bow and stern sections before these too became severed.

Titanic Interlude: C.Q.D. ... S.O.S. ... M.G.Y.

[1] Although the *Mount Temple*'s wireless log had 41 46 N, 50 14 W written for the entry at 10.25pm, Captain Moore testified in his evidence that 41 44 N, 50 24W was the first set of coordinates received. Moore also said he turned his ship around after receiving the corrected position of 41 46 N, 50 14 W.

[2] We must make mention of a ship called the *Asian* which heard "51 46" due to "weak signals."

[3] To save time when transmitting, wireless operators of the Marconi and rival companies employed the use of short-hand "cipher codes". For instance, C.Q., which phonetically is "seek you," means "all stations listen" with the D appended for "distress"; D.D.D. means "shut up"; "O.M." means "Old Man," a polite form of address; "T.U." means "Thank you" and so on. "S.O.S." was the new signal used to signal distress and was used because it is recognisable as three dots, three dashes and three dots.

[4] Already discussed, this is the "inconsequential" position calculated by Lowe to be entered in the order book for the ship's night time watch officers. Researcher Samuel Halpern has duplicated the "20" miles discrepancy using evidence given by Lowe, and confirms that the *Titanic*

would have been this distance ahead of the Lowe position at 7.30pm.

[5] An explanation for Bride's inability to remember the names of the answering ships may come from the timing and the situation on the *Titanic*. The *Asian* established contact with the *Titanic* at practically the same time as the *Carpathia*. Bride stated that he went outside to report to the captain, and in the meantime, contact with the *Asian* may have been established. It may have understandably slipped Phillips's mind to tell his junior about this new communication. The next ship to get in contact was the *Olympic*, according to Bride, and this was 27 minutes after the *Carpathia* acknowledged that she was coming to their assistance at 10.35pm New York Time. The *Carpathia* may have been the very first ship that they heard from that had replied with the positive news that they were coming to help, explaining why Bride was sent outside to inform the captain of this welcome information. The *Ypiranga* and the *Mount Temple* heard the emergency call but due to the noise of steam from the *Titanic*'s funnels, Phillips may not have known who he was in contact with; the same could be said about the *Frankfurt*'s calls at this time. Indeed, Bride mentions the steam in his Marconi report; "the noise of escaping steam directly over our cabin [was causing] a deal of trouble to Mr. Phillips in reading the replies to our distress call, and this I also reported to Capt. Smith, who by some means managed to get it abated." The *Carpathia* and the *Ypiranga* both mention that the *Titanic* could hear nothing for the sound of steam, messages sent at precisely the same time (10.35pm). In his evidence in America, the *Carpathia*'s wireless man, Cottam, noted that he informed the *Titanic* that the *Olympic* had called; at the time, the *Olympic* could not be heard because of the steam discharge. The first indication of the *Olympic* hearing anything of the *Titanic*'s plight is noted at 10.50pm New York Time. It is perhaps indicative of the relative strength of these ship's wireless installations, plus proximity and atmospheric effects that some vessels were heard above the noise of steam, but others weren't. As for other ship mentioned at this time (*La Provence*), there is no record of her being an active participant in the flurry of messages. She is only mentioned once in the wireless logs, and this is to denote that she had received the call for assistance.

[6] In America, Boxhall was asked to elaborate about the time of the first distress call. He stated that it went out about "35 minutes" after the collision, or 12.15am, which fits in with neither the 1:33 or 2:02 claims. Does Boxhall's "35 minutes" refer to "his" position or the earlier one, claimed to have been sent out by Smith? If the former, the signals for help were already being sent out 10 minutes before "35 minutes" had elapsed, putting their dispatch at 12.05am on the *Titanic* which is close to the claimed 1 hour and 33 minute time difference with New York.

[7] A possible explanation for the 10 minute wait presents itself if one discounts Boxhall's testimony that he had already sent up rocket(s) when Rowe and Bright were summoned to the bridge with detonators; Rowe would, in the 1960s estimate that the time to get to the bridge from the poop was about ten minutes. This would include the time required to clamber up crew access ladders with cumbersome and heavy boxes. Boxhall would necessarily have to wait this time for the rocket firing equipment to arrive.

[8] Bride had gone out to tell Smith that they had just been in touch with the *Carpathia* - the very ship that Boxhall claimed to have been told about when he delivered his new position.

[9] Due to the lack of energetic particles from the sun interacting with the atmosphere after sunset, the range of wireless transmissions has been known to increase dramatically at night. Bride himself said, "...we came around Belfast, when we exchanged the last message with Teneriffe and Port Said." These stations are some 2000-3000 miles distant. This was after the *Titanic* had left Belfast at 8pm on April 2nd, 1912, following the issuing of her seaworthiness certificate after her sea trials earlier that day.

[10] Bride seems to be unfairly maligning the *Frankfurt*, which, incidentally, was using a wireless system that was a rival to the Marconi installation. Bride testified that the *Frankfurt* was the first ship to respond; she was actually the 8th station to get the C.Q.D. and the 4th to reply that she was coming, and this was after the *Carpathia* and others, only some of which Bride mentioned in evidence. It should be noted that the first pre-C.Q.D. contact between the *Titanic* and the *Frankfurt* was at about 10.25pm, when the former ship asked his counterpart on the *Frankfurt* to "get his position." This was done, and 15 minutes later (a reasonable time considering that the bridge crew would have to compute the location), the *Titanic* replied with her own position and asked the *Frankfurt* to come to her assistance. There is nothing in the wireless log of the *Frankfurt* to indicate any urgency in the 10.25pm message; if the operator has missed the actual C.Q.D. calls, he may have thought the request to get his position was a routine call. Phillips may have thought that the *Frankfurt* had heard the distress calls; if this hypothesis is right, the *Frankfurt* would indeed be one of the very first to respond, corroborating Bride.

Other comments can be made about Bride's statements on the *Frankfurt*. He stated that after they had transmitted their location to the *Frankfurt*, Phillips was told to "stand by", and that they never got the *Frankfurt*'s own position. "Considerably over twenty minutes later" according to evidence at the U.S. Inquiry, the Frankfurt asked out of the blue what was the matter, and Phillips, incensed that the sense of urgency had not

298

been appreciated, rattled off the rebuke informing his counterpart on the other ship that he was a fool, and to "stand by." This is not what the wireless logs of the Frankfurt or the other ships record: after the initial message about the position at 10.25pm, contact was re-established at 10.40pm New York Time, and within eight minutes, the *Frankfurt* had acknowledged the distress call and said that she was on her way. Between 11.15 and 11.26, further confirmation of the rescue effort was relayed, with the *Titanic* replying "tks" (thanks); this message was overheard by the *Ypiranga*. The final set of communications were between 11.49 and 11.55 but the exchange is not recorded. Far from being a "twenty minute" gap between the first and last Frankfurt exchange, the timing is closer to 1 and a quarter hours. It is possible that a temporary loss of communication between the *Titanic* and the *Frankfurt* prompted the latter ship to politely enquire what was wrong, only to be met with Phillips' stern brush-off. And Bride, so adamantly sure that they never obtained the *Frankfurt*'s position was wrong about this too: the location was sent out at about 10.46 and was overheard and noted in other logs. Further retransmission of the position occurred at 11.00am and possibly at midnight. Of course Bride may not have known of the reply if he was, as he said, passing progress reports to the captain outside or if Phillips had neglected to inform him of any reply. Another explanation for Phillips' rebuke could be found in further questioning of Bride: "Of course I could not read what Mr. Phillips was receiving, but I could read what he was sending, and I judged that the *Carpathia* and the Frankfurt had both called up together, and the Frankfurt had persisted in calling and was interfering with Mr. Phillips in reading the *Carpathia*'s message." This was about the time that the captain had instructed the wireless operators to abandon their efforts. Wireless Operator Durrant of the *Olympic* and Cottam of the *Carpathia* raise interesting points. Their evidence confirms that the *Titanic* gave her position and asked "Are you coming to our assistance?" and after twenty minutes, a reply was transmitted asking "What is the matter with you?" Phillips then tapped back that they had struck an iceberg and were sinking and asked his counterpart on the *Frankfurt* to tell his captain to come. "OK Will tell the bridge right away." It is suggested that, in the latency of 20 minutes, the operator on the *Frankfurt* had already rushed off to tell the bridge, but had neglected to ask what was actually amiss with the *Titanic*. This happened fairly early on in the exchange of messages and not, as Bride would claim, right towards the end when they had already been discharged by the captain.

[11] This message was obviously used to convey desperation as the boilers were not in the engine room; all the captain had told them was that "the engine rooms were taking water and that the dynamos might

not last much longer." The wireless men must have garbled the message slightly.

[12] In fairness, we must repeat vital points made elsewhere. From Quartermaster Rowe's evidence, the well deck was underwater when his boat put off. But when did his boat ("C") leave? Astute readers will know that debate exists about the timing of this departure. Rowe himself puts the time at 1.25 when he left the bridge to get into the boat, and it took 5 minutes to reach the water. Rowe's estimate of how long it took before the ship sunk was 20 minutes. Steward Pearcey, also in "C", puts the time of departure at 1.40am. If Rowe was right and we consider the evidence that the ship foundered a little while after "C" left, this would put the well deck being awash as being 1.30 (according to Rowe), 1.40 (according to Pearcey) or 2.00 (2.20 less 20 minutes as deduced from Rowe's evidence). There are strong hints that the times reported by Rowe and Pearcey may have been 20 minutes behind due to the purported clock change that night.

[13] Bride testified in London that when Phillips came back from his excursion outside, there was a heavy list to port. The timing of lifeboat launchings is not concrete, but it would seem that, at the time of the first 4 boats on the starboard side being lowered, there was a slight list to starboard; the list to port only became evident during the latter stages of the sinking, giving more corroboration to the contention that the *Baltic* communication occurred late in the sinking, at the time of the forward well deck being awash.

Chapter 6: Salvation

[1] Although many of those in the boats described separate voices originating from different quarters when the ship slipped under the water which then merged into one chant, at least one person said that, as the *Titanic* vanished, "an almighty shriek" went up. The reality, knowing what we know now about the human body's reaction to thermal shock, was likely different. Upon being immediately submerged, an involuntary gasp results in an intake of water, which may partially or completely fill the lungs. Subsequent gasps suppress the body's natural desire to cry out. If the person survives this initial reaction, once (temporary) adaptation to the coldness is achieved, a person may be able to cry out. Also, of course, if a person is submerged relatively slowly, from the lower extremities upwards (say), a person's ability to acclimatise to the coldness is better.

[2] Karl Behr's story was slightly different. Rather than Pitman issuing, and then countermanding the order to row back, Behr said, "the officer

300

in charge of our boat, seeing the men swimming in the water, refused to go back, and I guess he was right, for he claimed we surely would have been swamped by the hundreds in the water."

[3] Martha Stephenson and Elizabeth Eustis' account mentions that the crew in boat 4 were implored to pull away from the ship but they refused; it was now that they picked up Scott, Ranger and Hemming who were swimming towards them (interestingly, Ranger claimed that he never went into the water). One man was drunk and had a bottle of whisky in his pocket. Perkis, the quartermaster in charge of the boat, threw the bottle overboard, and the drunk was put in the bottom of boat with a blanket thrown over him. After getting in these three men, the crew said how fast the ship was going, and the women again implored them to pull for their lives. This time their protests were successful. Mrs. Thayer partially corroborates this as she says that two of the men were drunk "and gave us much trouble all the time." The identity of the "drunk" is interesting; Frank Prentice had stopped on the *Titanic* till the last second and admitted to having a bottle of brandy which was the offending article that was thrown overboard. Perkis was apparently afraid that the brandy, if drunk, would have a detrimental effect on the boat's occupants. There is no evidence that Prentice was drunk. There is a possibility that the human body's reaction to hypothermia, including inability to co-ordinate muscles, confusion, terminal burrowing and slow and laboured movement may be mistaken for intoxication.

[4] Colonel Gracie collated a list of people in the lifeboats for his book, and the incidents associated with each boat. He lists 7 people as having been taken from the sea (this does not include Ranger who did not actually enter the water). Gracie's tally indicates that 2 of the 7 who died in the boat after rescue.

[5] One account of Dillon's escape, which I have been unable to verify, is that he got his "share" of alcohol before leaving the *Titanic* after word had reached him that drinks were "on the house"; another story is that he toppled overboard. Dillon may be the "fireman" referred to by Prentice: "...we picked up two firemen who had been in the water a long time [Dillon claims twenty minutes], and one afterwards died in the boat as a result of exposure. The other fireman went crazy, and kept trying to clamber out of the boat, but I managed to keep him down."

[6] Hoyt was a somewhat large individual and it took a large amount of effort to hoist him aboard boat 14; he was bleeding at the nose and mouth and despite loosening his collar to help him breathe, and rubbing his limbs to aid the circulation he "was too far gone."

[7] Collyer's account said that Lowe initially dismissed a rescue attempt of this man because he did not answer their hails, and saying "Whats the use? He's dead likely, and if he isn't there's other better worth saving

that a Jap!" Lowe changed his mind and headed back to collect the man, whom, after a little coercion with his seized-up joints, rapidly came to, pulling vigorously at an oar. Lowe was astounded, "By Jove! I'm ashamed of what I said about the little blighter. I'd save the likes of him six times over if I got the chance."

[8] May Futrelle is seemingly describing being in boat "D" but in other interviews she gives conflicting information as to whether she was in the same boat as Mrs.Harris or not (who was in "D"). It is likely that Futrelle was in boat 9, which did not pick up anyone from the water.

[9] Steward Burke claimed that his boat, No.10, was cut adrift from the other three in order to go up to a collapsible boat that was in distress. "When they cut our boat adrift I found an officer in another boat had come to the aid of this collapsible boat ["A"?], so we remained there for some hours, drifting about. At daybreak, we made fast to another officer's boat, and we arrived alongside of the *Carpathia* with these two boats tied together." If Burke in No.10 was near "A" no-one else saw him. The mention of the "other officer" is tantalising, as Boxhall didn't speak of being lashed to another boat at this point. Certainly, Lightoller's entourage were rescued by two other craft. Pitman's boat (5) was lashed to another (7) and of course Lowe in 14 temporarily tied up with four others, one of which was 10, but Burke's comments are a mystery.

[10] Seaman Scarrott's story told to the UK investigation is that Lowe ordered all the boats to head back to the ship's location after she had foundered; his evidence is very clear on this point. This first attempt to save the swimmers was unsuccessful as no one could be found; it was only after this that 4 of the boats were tied together, and Scarrott went with Lowe in another attempt. This time, hundreds of bodies were located. There is only one other account of a boat in this tiny collection of vessels (namely, No.12) going back (see above). Scarrott also says that Lowe only waited a couple of minutes after the sinking before embarking on their first mission. This conflicts with other evidence that a large period of time, over an hour or more, was spent waiting for the cries to diminish.

[11] Only 337 bodies were recovered from more than 1500 lost, the remainder having been carried on by the confluence of the Labrador Current and the North Atlantic Drift, which were present in the area; some bodies would have sunk to the bottom a considerable time after the disaster and some distance away. Hypothermia was not the only killer at play that night. The sinking of *The Empress of Ireland* two years later suggests a deficiency in the design of the lifejackets which similar to the ones worn on the *Titanic*. The jackets were secured around the waist with cord, and if someone were to hit the water wearing it, it would have ridden up the body and struck the chin, potentially breaking a

person's neck. Also, it has been suggested that if the water was sufficiently cold, rapid exposure to it could conceivably stop a person's heart.

[12] Poingdestre also spoke of another boat joining them after boat 14 had gone to search for survivors.

[13] Only Mrs.Spedden in No.3 states that "we tied up to a boat filled with women once, but the rope broke and we got pretty well separated from all the other boats." Strangely, she does not mention this in her diary, written at the time the *Titanic* sank, and when her memories would be less tainted.

[14] In further questioning in America, Hogg adds another detail, namely that he wanted to assist in picking up people, but he had an order from 'the boat'; "We have done our best; go on to the *Carpathia*; we have picked up all we can find;" and I said "Very good." If one neglects the mention of the *Carpathia*'s name (it is doubtful that anyone at that time would know the identity of the new arrival on the scene at that time), Hogg's statement implies that this exchange was made when the *Carpathia* was in sight, or well after 4am by which time the cries from the water would have long since ceased and everyone would be dead.

[15] Boxhall claimed that he felt suction as he rounded the stern forcing him to pull away; Osman stated that there was no suction, but that they could not get round the starboard side due to the ship's list, which makes little sense. In other pronouncements, Boxhall said he felt "a little suction" or "quite a lot of suction" and one wonders which, if any, is correct. At the time of his boat's sojourn, the *Titanic* had a list of about 10° to port which would have been no impediment in circumnavigating around the stern of the ship.

[16] Lady Duff Gordon's astonishing claim is that she heard terrible cries before the *Titanic* sank but nothing afterwards which conflicts with every other witness to the catastrophe.

[17] Collins denied that anybody had ever said anything about rowing away from the suction. Sir Duff Gordon said that Mr.Stengel called out two or three times "let us go that way" and "Boat ahoy!" but he doubts that any one paid much attention to him. Duff Gordon asked him to be quiet.

[18] Assistant cook Collins mentioned seeing a green light a few miles off the stern just before he was swept in the water. His timing may be off (he said it was about half an hour before the *Titanic* sank), but the location would be right for where Boxhall's boat was to be found. Interestingly, quartermaster Rowe mentioned in later life that he saw a white light off the *Titanic*'s stern, which Captain Smith told him was a planet. But any planets would be high in the sky, and would not be mistaken for the stern light of a boat receding in the distance, which is

what Rowe claimed to have seen. Captain Rostron of the rescue ship *Carpathia* reported seeing that he and his crew had observed the mast lights and a red light of a ship close to the wreck site as they steamed to the *Titanic*; this ship has never been identified. Combining these observations (and including Collins' sighting which may have been Boxhall's boat), they point to a ship somewhere to the rear of the wreck site.

[19] Although many in the boats saw the *Carpathia*'s rockets, there is only one instance of them being heard. Stoker Fred Barrett had temporarily taken leave from his command of boat 13 and was snoozing under a blanket. A sound like guns far off awoke him and jolted upright, saying "That was a cannon!" No one remembers seeing the blue Cunard identification lights that night.

[20] A photograph exists of collapsible "D" approaching the *Carpathia*, and it shows women aboard, contrary to Seaman Lucas's statement that all the ladies had been moved from "D" to 12. Still, it was dark when the ladies were transferred.

[21] Also in boat 14, seaman Evans also observed the scene, but says that Lowe did fire his gun four times, into the air when 150 yards from boat "A". Evans said that Lowe "told people in this boat it was to warn them not to rush our boat when we got alongside." There is no mention - perhaps understandably - of the threatening language used by the 5th Officer. Seaman Scarrott's testimony is different: "After we came back from the wreckage where we had taken one of those rafts in tow, Mr. Lowe emptied his pistol into the water; as regards the number of rounds left in it I cannot say, but I think he emptied five rounds out of it." Lowe was emphatic that he never used his gun again after using it to ward off the unruly crowd as boat 14 dropped from the decks. One wonders who was right, but this is an observation endemic to the whole *Titanic* story.

[22] Harris's account does have at least one element that is incorrect; she says that, after the bedraggled occupants had been plucked from their watery craft, "the other boat sank. With it went two stark figures. They were men who had died while drifting." In actual fact, boat "A" was later found drifting a month later by another White Star Line vessel, the *Oceanic*, and was taken to New York to join the 13 other boats that had been salvaged by the *Carpathia*. The bodies of three men were found on board; Thomas Beattie and an unidentified sailor and a fireman. All were buried at sea.

[23] It is claimed that the people from boat "A" went into boat 14; if so, this would boost the number on board from the 7 to 9 initial members of the search party, with 3 rescued and one body, to approximately 25. A poor quality photograph of 14 approaching the *Carpathia* exists, and, while it is impossible to determine occupancy, it is far from full. Lowe

claimed that No. 14 had 45 people on board after his various rescues were completed. Previously, Lowe had also over exaggerated the number in boat 1 from a pitiful 12 to something more honourable.

[24] This was the only body that was seen by the *Carpathia*; the *Californian* did not see any. James Bisset, a crewman on the *Carpathia* suggested that, at a distance, the white lifejackets would be unmistakeable from the ice that was scattered in the water. A crewman on the *Californian* could not shake the conviction that the "seals" he saw on the distant ice floes were actually human; and a report many days later reported that bodies had been seen perched on a ledge on an iceberg close to the scene of the wreck. It is thought that the bodies had been carried further on by the currents in the area, but it seems odd that the bodies and debris had become "uncoupled" from each other, moving in different directions. Only about 25% of those lost were recovered by passing ships or vessels chartered by the White Star Line. Where had the rest gone? It is commonly cited that the pairs of shoes lying side by side on the ocean floor near the *Titanic* wreck are the final indicators of human remains. The bodies and clothing were consumed by marine life, but the shoes were impervious. However, the detailed photographic study of the wreck site in 1985 and 1986 revealed only two or three pairs of shoes lying together.

Titanic Interlude: The Fate of Heroes

[1] The two ladies who were said to have helped McCormack were Margaret and Kate Murphy. This author has been unable to locate any stories in which they confirm his story. Margaret does provide an interesting tale of her own: "Just as the davits were being swung outward, a Chinaman pushed a woman out of boat and took her place. Sailors grabbed him and handed him back to the deck. Then someone shot him and his body tumbled into the water." There are no other details proffered to suggest when or where this was claimed to have happened.

[2] Despite having counsel to represent 3rd class interests, not one steerage passenger was called at the British Inquiry, which found not an ounce of proof that there had been discrimination against the lowest class.

[3] The *Californian* had been in wireless contact with the *Titanic* before the collision, but her operator was asleep when the C.Q.D. and S.O.S. calls were transmitted. Interestingly, it was Bride, and not Phillips, who "spoke" to the *Californian*.

[4] Whiteley's claims regarding the "last dinner" on the *Titanic* are interesting too. This meal was to be the finest ever served on a ship, he

claimed. In attendance were Ismay, who sat alone, 1st class passengers Mr. and Mrs. Astor who dined with Dr. O'Loughin and the captain, along with some others. Passengers starting strolling in after 6.30pm, and the conversation became very animated, with the captain joking with Mr.Astor, and occasional words from Ismay. Whiteley did not see the captain drink anything, although wine was present. The main topic of conversation was the new ship, and some bets were made on the speed of the *Titanic* prompting O'Loughlin, seated with his assistant and the Astors, to raise a glass of champagne saying, "Let us drink to the mighty *Titanic*." The others cried out in approval and joined him in drinking a toast to the new vessel. According to Whiteley, a big banquet was being planned after arrival in New York in anticipation of the transatlantic speed record being broken. This story seems unlikely on the face of it, although we do know that Ismay and O'Loughin did dine together in the restaurant that night, during the dinner party in honour of Captain Smith. It is unclear whether the Astors, the most prominent people aboard, were in the restaurant. However, 1st class passengers sir and Lady Duff Gordon were present. Their testimony at the British Inquiry does not mention any of the so called "gaiety" in the restaurant, but Lady Duff Gordon's autobiography in 1932 describes an interesting scene: "...at neighbouring tables people were making bets on the probable time of this record-breaking run. Bruce Ismay, Chairman of the White Star Line, was dining with the ship's doctor next to our table, and I remember that several men appealed to him as to how much longer we should be at sea. Mr. Ismay was most confident and said that undoubtedly the ship would establish a record."

[5] On the other hand, it has been noted that some survivors, such as Archibald Gracie, Peter Daly and Richard Williams - who were on deck till the last, mention only "light, cheerful music." It is interesting to ponder just how much attention these men would have given to the band at the very end; certainly, these gentlemen's location (on the other side of the *Titanic* to the band) makes them questionable eye/ear-witnesses. Gracie was adamant that "Nearer My God To Thee" was not played as he claimed that only two (!) survivors had been quoted in the newspapers as having heard it, no-one he questioned recalled it played, and that, despite claiming not to be able to recognise any of the tunes played, he would have noticed if this "tactless warning of immediate death" had been struck up by the band. Gracie's final pronouncement on the matter, mere weeks before his death was that if the band had dared to play the tune "panic would have ensued" and they would have been restrained. Gracie did not seem to realise that at the end, with "chaos" imminent, and little hope of salvation, it wouldn't have mattered then what was played anyway.

[6] Indeed, some survivors, such as Gershon "Gus" Cohen and the Countess of Rothes contend that the band didn't play at all that night (to be fair Cohen's statements did vary between hearing no music at all and then being specific in not hearing "Nearer My God To Thee.")

[7] Mrs.Gold's accounts are interesting for its description of where the band were at this point; in one story, she just says that they were on "A" deck. Another version put them in the saloon, which we assume is one of the public rooms on "A" deck, below the boat deck where the musical ensemble are customarily located. But Gold's story is confusing in another respect; she talks about being in No.11 boat and that two German stowaways were in the boat, one of them concealing himself underneath her skirts for warmth. But then she talks about people in her boat, including Mrs.Ryerson and her two daughters, Mrs.Carter and "American" Mrs.Douglas; the Ryersons were in boat 4; Mrs.Carter, whom Gold described as "the wife of the U.S. Minister at Bucharest [sic]" did not survive although another lady of the same name did escape in boat 4; "American" Mahala Douglas was in boat 2. It is doubtful that any male stowaways could have entered boat 4 without 2nd Officer Lightoller noticing and being expelled; indeed, Lightoller was certainly hostile to stewardesses, like Gold, entering boats. And boat 2 was not launched from "A" deck. This author suspects Gold may somehow have become confused. This leaves researchers with a problem; do we dismiss her stories because of these conflicts in her evidence? But if the band did play on deck "A" and Gold was in boat 4, they did not play there for long. A very short space of time later, Hugh Woolner looked down it's length and saw no-one; however, the band may have been in a recessed alcove near the Grand Staircase foyer and thus invisible to Woolner but this seems ridiculous as they would have had no audience. Or the band could have headed back to the upper deck. This would have been a few short minutes before Bride heard the music of the band coming from somewhere aft. Bride does not place the band on "A" deck or the boat deck; indeed he never saw them at all. There is one other point to consider: if the band was indeed somewhere near boat 11, they would have had to have had their lifebelts with them before this boat was launched. Assuming that Gracie is correct in saying that the band put down their instruments half an hour before the ship foundered, they could not have done so to retrieve their lifebelts, since boat 11 departed a lot longer than 30 minutes before the sinking. And by that time, they already had their lifebelts. If this author was to be pressed to give an opinion, it would be that Gold escaped in boat 11, and that her identification of the passengers had become confused.

[8] Wormstedt and Fitch include Richard N.Williams in their list of "primary accounts" but this seems to be a mistake as he reports only

hearing the sound of gunfire, but not of seeing casualties. Many of the sources listed by Wormstedt and Fitch as being "secondary" also seem to include first-hand accounts of shooting, but with varying degrees of veracity. This narrative will focus on the primary sources only.

[9] How would Jansson know it was the "Chief Officer"? Had the two been acquainted? Quite a few survivors referred to Murdoch as the "Chief Officer" that night, and it speculated that he was still wearing his officer's jacket with "Chief's" stripes and braids on it. A photograph exists of Lightoller on board the *Titanic* whilst at Queenstown harbour on April 11th, and he was still wearing "1st Officer's stripes". This was a few days after he was relegated to 2nd Officer upon the arrival of Wilde to take over the post as Chief. It is speculation that Murdoch was still wearing the wrong coat on April 14th/15th though.

[10] If the shooting did not take place at boat "A" the only other candidate is boat "C" but Murdoch and Moody are reported to have been working at "A" which was prepared after "C." We know from Woolner and others that there was gunfire at "C".

[11] One curious aspect of the Rheims/suicide claim is what he did after the shooting. He wrote, "We were about 1,500 people left on board without any means of escape. It was death for us all. I can not convey how calm everyone was. We said goodbye to all our friends and everyone prepared himself to die properly. Joe [Rheim's uncle's brother in law, Joseph Loring] took both my hands and said, "George if you survive look after my babies. If I live you will not have to worry about Mary." I then left him for one minute to go back to my cabin and find our photograph, then went up to join Joe on the deck." From a point near the gymnasium, Rheims leapt into the sea. The traditional time for the shooting/suicide is when the boat deck was underwater, with water washing around people's knees. Rheims cabin was almost directly underneath where the suicide was said to occur, and yet Rheims was able to go to his cabin to collect his photographs. His room would have been underwater and inaccessible.

[12] Customarily placed on the starboard side, one dissenter to the location of the purported suicide was Mrs Widener in boat 4, who claimed to have seen the captain dive into the sea from the bridge, moments after an officer committed suicide. However, according to Hemming who swam for the craft, boat 4 was 200 yards off "on the port quarter" just after he left the bridge area and moments before the end. Therefore, this puts the boat some distance at the left rear of the *Titanic*. The suicide, if it happened, is generally thought to have happened on the front right of the ship. Mrs.Widener must have been possessed of exceptionally good eyesight, and our assumptions wrong if a nugget of truth exists in her account. Her story is probably an exaggeration or fabrication of the

press. Interestingly, Bride did put the captain's dive into the sea from the port side of the bridge.

Bibliography

Selected reading:

Ballard, Robert, "The Discovery of the *Titanic*", Hodder and Stoughton, 1987

Barratt, Nick, "Lost Voices From the *Titanic*", Preface, 2009

Beveridge, Bruce et al., "*Titanic* - The Ship Magnificent (Vols 1 and 2)", The History Press, 2008

Behe, George M., "*Titanic*: Safety, Speed and Sacrifice", Transportation Trails, 1997

Behe, George M., "On Board RMS *Titanic*", Lulu, 2010

Brown, David G., "Last Log of the *Titanic*", McGraw Hill, 2000

Byceson, David, "The *Titanic* Disaster", Patrick Stephens, 1997

Davie, Michael, "The *Titanic* - The Full Story of a Tragedy", Grafton, 1987

Eaton, John P. & Haas, Charles, "*Titanic* - Triumph and Tragedy", Patrick Stephens, 1995

Gittins, David, "*Titanic*: Monument and Warning", electronic book, c.2005

Hyslop, Donald et al., "*Titanic* Voices", Southampton City Council, 1994

Klistorner, Daniel et al., "*Titanic* in Photographs", The History Press, 2011

Lord, Walter, "A Night To Remember", Penguin, 1987

Lord, Walter, "The Night Lives On", Viking, 1986

Lynch, Don et al, "Ghosts of the Abyss", Da Capo, 2003

Lynch, Don et al, "*Titanic* - An Illustrated History", Hodder and Stoughton, 1992

McCarty, Jennifer Hooper et al., "What Really Sank The *Titanic*", Citadel, 2008

Molony, Senan, "The Irish Aboard *Titanic*", Wolfhound, 2000

O'Donnell, E.E., "Father Browne's *Titanic* Album", Wolfhound, 1997

Winocur, Jack (Editor), "The story of the *Titanic* as told by its survivors", Dover Publications, 1960

"Report on the loss of the S.S. *Titanic*", Alan Sutton, 1990

Periodicals consulted:

The *Titanic* Historical Society journal, the *Commutator*

Titanic International Society journal, *Voyage*

Various newspapers, including the London and New York "Times" and others as available on Google News

Websites

www.titanicinquiry.org
www.encyclopedia-titanica.org
www.titanic-model.com
www.titanic-titanic.com
www.titanichistoricalsociety.net
www.wormstedt.com
www.titanicebook.com
www.titanicology.com
www.paullee.com
www.marconigraph.com
www.markchirnside.co.uk

Index

(NB: The name *Titanic* has been omitted from this index)

312

315

317

319

Printed in Great Britain
by Amazon